Quicken® 2003

THE OFFICIAL GUIDE

Maria LANGER

McGraw-Hill Osborne

New York Chicago San Francisco
Lisbon London Madrid Mexico City Milan
New Delhi San Juan Seoul Singapore Sydney Toronto

McGraw-Hill/Osborne
2600 Tenth Street
Berkeley, California 94710
U.S.A.

To arrange bulk purchase discounts for sales promotions, premiums, or fund-raisers, please contact **McGraw-Hill**/Osborne at the above address.

Quicken® 2003: The Official Guide

234567890 FGR FGR 019876543

ISBN 0-07-222618-8

Publisher	**Copy Editor**
Brandon A. Nordin	Lunaea Weatherstone
Vice President & Associate Publisher	**Proofreader**
Scott Rogers	Mike McGee
Acquisitions Editor	**Indexer**
Megg Morin	Irv Hershman
Project Editor	**Computer Designers**
Jody McKenzie	George Toma Charbak, Melinda Moore Lytle
Acquisitions Coordinator	**Illustrators**
Tana Allen	Michael Mueller, Lyssa Wald
Technical Editor	**Series Design**
Mike Barden	Peter F. Hancik

This book was composed with Corel VENTURA™ Publisher.

To the Quicken 2003 Beta Support/Technical Support Team
in Tucson, AZ: Thanks for all your help!

Contents at a Glance

Contents

Part III   The Investing Center

Part VI   The Tax Center

Part VII   Appendixes

Acknowledgments

This book, like any other, is the end product of a lot of imagination and hard work by many people. I'd like to take a moment to thank the people who were involved with the creation of this book.

First, thanks to Megg Morin, Acquisitions Editor at McGraw-Hill/Osborne. Megg and I worked together to fine-tune the outline for this book so it more closely matched the revised Quicken 2003 interface. She also helped me brainstorm for ideas that would add more value for readers to this book. With her help, I was able to make this edition of our Quicken book the best yet.

Many thanks go out to the folks at Intuit, including Mike Barden, Caroline Hu, Linda Pan, and Todd Santos. Another thanks goes out to the Quicken 2003 development team, for fine-tuning an already great program to make it even better. And a huge thanks goes out to the Quicken 2003 beta support team down in Tucson, for helping me to better understand the inner workings of Quicken.

More thanks go out to the production and editorial folks at McGraw-Hill/ Osborne, including Jody McKenzie, Lunaea Weatherstone, Tana Allen, Peter Hancik, Lyssa Wald, Michael Mueller, Tara Davis, and John Patrus.

A huge thanks to Jeremy Judson at McGraw-Hill/Osborne for suggesting me for the Quicken Press books. Five years and still going strong!

The last thanks goes to Mike for his continued patience and support.

Introduction

Choosing Quicken to organize your finances was a great decision. Quicken has all the tools you need to manage your personal finances. Its well-designed, intuitive interface makes it easy to use. And its online and automation features make entering transactions and paying bills a snap. But if that isn't enough, Quicken also offers features that can help you learn more about financial opportunities that can save you time and money—two things there never seems to be enough of.

Choosing this book to learn Quicken was also a good decision. As the Official Guide, it has Intuit's "seal of approval"—which means that Intuit, the developer of Quicken, was involved throughout the book's planning, writing, and production stages. The book was even reviewed for accuracy by the folks at Intuit's Technical Support Department.

This introduction tells you a little about the book and a little about me—so you know what to expect in the chapters to come.

About this Book

Throughout this book, I tell you how to get the most out of Quicken. I start by explaining the basics—the common, everyday tasks that you need to know just to use the program. Then I go beyond the basics to show you how to use Quicken to save time, save money, and make smart financial decisions. Along the way, I show you all of Quicken's features, including many that you probably didn't even know existed. You'll find yourself using Quicken far more than you ever dreamed you would.

Every book is based on certain assumptions, presents information in a certain order, and uses certain conventions to communicate information. This book is no different. Knowing the book's assumptions, organization, and conventions can help you understand how to use this book as a learning tool.

Assumptions

In writing this book, I had to make a few assumptions about your knowledge of your computer, Windows, Quicken, and financial management. These assumptions give me a starting point, making it possible for me to skip over the things that I assume you already know.

What You Should Know About Your Computer and Windows

To use this book (or Quicken 2003, for that matter), you should have a general understanding of how to use your computer and Windows. You don't need to be an expert. As you'll see, Quicken uses many standard and intuitive interface elements, making it easy to use—even if you're a complete computer novice.

At a bare minimum, you should know how to turn your computer on and off and how to use your mouse. You should also know how to perform basic Windows tasks, such as starting and exiting programs, using menus and dialogs, and entering and editing text.

If you're not sure how to do these things, check the manual that came with your computer or try working through the Windows Tour. These two resources can provide all the information you need to get started.

What You Should Know About Quicken and Financial Management

You don't need to know much about either Quicken or financial management to get the most out of this book: I assume that both are new to you.

This doesn't mean that this book is just for raw beginners. I provide plenty of useful information for seasoned Quicken users—especially those of you who have used previous versions of Quicken—and for people who have been managing their finances with other tools, such as other software (welcome to Quicken!) or pencil and paper (welcome to the new millennium!).

Because I assume that all this is new to you, I make a special effort to explain Quicken procedures, as well as the financial concepts and terms on which they depend. New concepts and terms first appear in italic type. By understanding these things, not only can you better understand how to use Quicken, you can communicate more effectively with finance professionals such as bankers, stock brokers, and financial advisors.

Organization

This book is logically organized into seven parts, each with at least two chapters. Each part either covers general Quicken setup information or one of Quicken's five financial centers. Within each part, the chapters start with the most basic concepts and procedures, most of which involve specific Quicken tasks, and then work their way up to more advanced topics, many of which are based on finance-related concepts that Quicken makes easy to master.

I want to stress one point here: it is not necessary to read this book from beginning to end. Skip around as desired. Although the book is organized for cover-to-cover reading, not all of its information may apply to you. For example, if you're not the least bit interested in investing, skip the chapters in the Investing Center part. It's as simple as that. When you're ready for the information that you skipped, it'll be waiting for you.

Now here's a brief summary of the book's organization and contents.

Part One: Quicken Setup and Basics

This part of the book introduces Quicken's interface and features and helps you set up Quicken for managing your finances. It also provides the information you need to set up and test Quicken's online features. If you're brand-new to Quicken, I highly recommend reading at least the first three chapters in this part of the book.

Part One has four chapters:

- **Chapter 1:** Getting to Know Quicken
- **Chapter 2:** Using Quicken Guided Setup
- **Chapter 3:** Setting Up Accounts, Categories, and Classes
- **Chapter 4:** Going Online with Quicken and Quicken.com

Part Two: The Cash Flow Center

This part of the book explains how to use Quicken to record financial transactions in bank and credit card accounts. One chapter concentrates on the basics, while another goes beyond the basics to discuss online features available within Quicken and on Quicken.com. This part of the book also explains how to automate many transaction entry tasks, reconcile accounts, and use Quicken's extensive reporting feature.

There are five chapters in Part Two:

- **Chapter 5:** Recording Bank and Credit Card Transactions
- **Chapter 6:** Using Online Banking Features
- **Chapter 7:** Automating Transactions and Tasks
- **Chapter 8:** Reconciling Your Accounts
- **Chapter 9:** Examining Your Cash Flow

Part Three: The Investing Center

This part of the book explains how you can use Quicken and Quicken.com to keep track of your investment portfolio and get information to help you make smart investment decisions. The first chapter covers the basics of Quicken's investment tracking features, while the other two chapters provide information about online investment tracking and research tools and the features within Quicken.com that help you evaluate your investment position.

There are three chapters in Part Three:

- **Chapter 10:** Entering Your Investment Transactions
- **Chapter 11:** Using Transaction Download and Research Tools
- **Chapter 12:** Evaluating Your Position

Part Four: The Property & Debt Center

This part of the book concentrates on assets and liabilities, including your home and car and related loans. It explains how you can track these items in Quicken, and provides tips for minimizing related expenses.

There are three chapters in Part Four:

- **Chapter 13:** Monitoring Assets and Loans
- **Chapter 14:** Managing Household Records
- **Chapter 15:** Keeping Tabs on Your Property & Debt

Part Five: The Planning Center

This part of the book tells you how you can take advantage of Quicken's extensive, built-in planning tools to plan for your retirement and other major events in your life. As you'll learn in this part of the book, whether you want financial security in your retirement years or to save up for the down payment on a house or college education for your children, Quicken can help you. It covers Quicken's Planners, as well as its financial calculators. It also provides a wealth of tips for saving money and reducing debt.

There are three chapters in Part Five:

- **Chapter 16:** Planning for the Future
- **Chapter 17:** Using Financial Calculators
- **Chapter 18:** Reducing Debt and Saving Money

Part Six: The Tax Center

This part of the book explains how you can use Quicken's Tax Center features to simplify tax preparation, plan for tax time, and reduce your tax liability.

Part Six has two chapters:

- **Chapter 19:** Simplifying Tax Preparation
- **Chapter 20:** Planning for Tax Time

Part Seven: Appendixes

If 20 chapters of information aren't enough for you, there are two appendixes with additional information you might find useful when working with Quicken:

- **Appendix A:** Managing Quicken Files
- **Appendix B:** Customizing Quicken

Conventions

All how-to books—especially computer books—have certain conventions for communicating information. Here's a brief summary of the conventions I use throughout this book.

Menu Commands

Quicken, like most other Windows programs, makes commands accessible on the menu bar at the top of the application window. Throughout this book, I tell you which menu commands to choose to open a window or dialog or to complete a task. I use the following format to indicate menu commands: Menu | Submenu (if applicable) | Command.

So, for example, if I wanted you to choose the One Step Update command under the Online menu, I'd tell you to choose Online | One Step Update. If I wanted you to choose the Find command from the Find & Replace submenu under the Edit menu, I'd tell you to choose Edit | Find & Replace | Find.

Keystrokes

Keystrokes are the keys you must press to complete a task. There are two kinds of keystrokes:

Keyboard Shortcuts   Keyboard shortcuts are combinations of keys you press to complete a task more quickly. For example, the shortcut for "clicking" a Cancel button may be to press the Esc key. When instructing you to press a key, I provide the name of the key in small caps, like this: ESC. If you must press two or more keys simultaneously, I separate them with a hyphen, like this: CTRL-P.

Literal Text   Literal text is text that you must type in exactly as it appears in the book. Although this book doesn't contain many instances of literal text, there are a few. I display literal text in bold type, like this: **Checking Acct.** If literal text includes a variable—text you must substitute when you type—I include the variable in bold italic type, like this: ***Payee Name.***

Icons

I use icons to flag two specific types of information:

New in Quicken 2003   In addition to interface changes, the folks at Intuit made changes to Quicken's feature set. The New in Quicken 2003 icon identifies many new features.

Quicken Premier Only   This book covers Quicken Deluxe and Quicken Premier. The Quicken Premier Only icon identifies those features available in the Premier version of Quicken only.

Other Features

This book includes two other features that make it more than just a book about Quicken:

Sidebars

Not everyone is well-versed in the world of finance. If you're new to personal financial management, be sure to check out the sidebars, which are full of useful financial information that's not Quicken-specific. They'll help you understand your finances and some of the options available to you as you take control of your finances.

Quicken Quick Tips

I've been using Quicken for years and have learned all kinds of ways to get the most out of Quicken to manage my finances. I share my tips for using Quicken in the Quicken Quick Tips you'll find throughout this book.

About the Author

Finally, let me tell you a little bit about me.

I graduated from Hofstra University with a BBA in Accounting in—well, you don't really need to know *when*. I worked as an accountant, auditor, and financial analyst over the next eight years. Then I realized that I really didn't like what I was doing every day and took the necessary steps to change careers. I've written more than 40 computer books since the change, many of which are about business and productivity software such as Word, Excel, and FileMaker Pro. In 1998, I wrote *Quicken 99: The Official Guide,* and I'm very pleased to be updating and revising it for each update of Quicken.

I use Quicken. I've been using it for years. I use it to manage five bank accounts and four credit card accounts, to track three mortgages and a home equity loan, and to pay all my bills (online, of course). I also use its investment features to track my portfolio and research the companies in which I invest. While I don't use all Quicken features regularly, I've used most of them at least once to keep track of my finances and plot my financial future.

Frankly, I can't imagine not using Quicken. And I'm glad to have the opportunity to show you why you should agree.

Quicken Setup and Basics

This part of the book introduces Quicken's interface and features. It begins by explaining how to install Quicken and showing you the elements of its user interface. It offers an entire chapter with instructions for setting up Quicken for the first time using the new Quicken Guided Setup feature. It tells you all about Quicken's accounts, categories, and classes, and explains how you can modify the default setup to add your own. Finally, it explains why you should be interested in online access and how you can set up Quicken to access the Internet and Quicken.com. The chapters are:

Getting to Know Quicken

In this Chapter:

- *An overview of Quicken*

- *Installing Quicken*

- *Starting Quicken*

- *The Quicken interface*

- *Onscreen Help*

Chapter 1

If you're brand new to Quicken, get your relationship with Quicken off to a good start by properly installing it and learning a little more about how you can interact with it.

In this chapter, I provide a brief overview of Quicken, explain how to install and start it, take you on a tour of its interface, and show you how to use its extensive Onscreen Help features. Although the information I provide in this chapter is especially useful to new Quicken users, some of it also applies to users who are upgrading.

What Is Quicken?

On the surface, Quicken is a computerized checkbook. It enables you to balance your accounts, and organize, manage, and generate reports for your finances. But as you explore Quicken, you'll learn that it's much more. It's a complete personal finance software package—a tool for taking control of your finances. Quicken makes it easy to know what you have, how you are doing financially, and what you should do to strengthen your financial situation.

What Quicken Can Help You Do

At the very least, Quicken can help you manage your bank and credit card accounts. You can enter transactions and have Quicken generate reports and graphs that show where your money went and how much is left.

Quicken can help you manage investment accounts. You can enter transactions and have Quicken tell you the market value of your investments. Quicken can also help you organize other data, such as the purchase price and current worth of your possessions, the outstanding balances on your loans, and vital information you may need in the event of an emergency.

With all financial information stored in Quicken's data file, you can generate net worth reports to see where you stand today. You can also use a variety of financial planners to make financial decisions for the future. And Quicken's tax features, including export into TurboTax and the Deduction Finder, can make tax time easier on you and your bank accounts.

Quicken's online features can automate much of your data entry. Online banking enables you to keep track of bank account transactions and balances and to pay bills without writing checks or sticking on stamps. Online investing enables you to download investment transactions and, with the new Quicken Brokerage powered by Siebert feature, initiate trades right from within Quicken. You can also read news and information about investment opportunities and advice offered by financial experts.

Now tell me, can the paper check register that came with your checks do all that?

Quicken Basic, Deluxe, Premier, and Premier Home & Business

Intuit offers several versions of Quicken for managing personal finances: Basic, Deluxe, Premier, and Premier Home and Business.

Quicken Basic is an entry-level product designed for people who are new to personal finance software. As its name suggests, it includes basic features to track bank accounts, credit cards, investments, budgets, and loans. It also enables you to use online account access and payment, shop for insurance and mortgages, and download investment information for a brokerage account.

Quicken Deluxe is more robust. Designed for people who want to take a more active role in financial management, investments, and planning, it includes all the features in Quicken Basic plus the financial alerts feature, money-saving features for taPx time and debt reduction, free access to investment information, and the Emergency Records Organizer and Home Inventory features.

Quicken Premier, which is a new Quicken product, has all the features of Quicken Deluxe, plus additional features for investing and tax planning and preparation.

This book covers Quicken Premier. Although much of its information also applies to Quicken Basic and Deluxe, this book covers many features that are not included in the Basic version and a handful of features that are not include in the Deluxe version. (I use the Quicken Premier Only icon to identify those features that are only in Quicken Premier.) If you're a Quicken Basic or Deluxe user, consider upgrading to Quicken Premier so you can take advantage of the powerful features it has to offer.

One more thing—Intuit also offers a special version of Quicken for small business owners: Quicken Premier Home & Business. This one program can handle all of your personal and basic business financial needs. If you're juggling the financial records for your personal life and a small business, be sure to check out Quicken Premier Home & Business—it can make the task a lot easier.

Getting Started

Ready to get started? In this section, I explain how to install, start, and register Quicken.

Quicken Premier Components

Quicken Premier comes with a number of components that are installed as part of a standard installation:

- **Quicken Program** is the Quicken program.

- **Deduction Finder** is a Quicken feature to help you minimize your taxes by maximizing your deductions. The Deduction Finder is covered in Chapter 20.
- **Quicken Home Inventory** is a program that helps you track the value of your possessions, organized by each room in your home. Quicken Home Inventory is covered in Chapter 14.
- **Emergency Records Organizer** (or ERO) is a Quicken feature that enables you to store important information that may be useful in the event of an emergency. The ERO is covered in Chapter 14.
- **Debt Reduction** is a Quicken feature to help you analyze your debt so you can reduce it quickly and cost effectively. The Debt Reduction Planner is covered in Chapter 18.

Normally, an Express installation of Quicken (as discussed in the next section) installs all of these components.

Installing Quicken

Quicken uses a standard Windows setup program that should be familiar to you if you've installed other Windows programs.

First-Time Installation

Insert the Quicken 2003 CD into your CD-ROM drive. A dialog should appear, offering to install Quicken 2003 on your hard disk. Click the Install Quicken button to start the Quicken installer.

If this dialog does not automatically appear, you can start the installer by following these steps:

1. Click the Start button on the Windows task bar.
2. Click Settings.
3. Click Control Panel.
4. Double-click Add/Remove Programs.
5. Click Install.
6. Click Next.
7. Click Finish.

The installer displays a series of dialogs with information and options for installing Quicken. Read the information in the Welcome dialog and click Next to continue. When asked to agree to a software license agreement, click Yes (if you don't agree, the installation process will cancel). In the Type Of Installation dialog, which is shown next, select one of two types of installations:

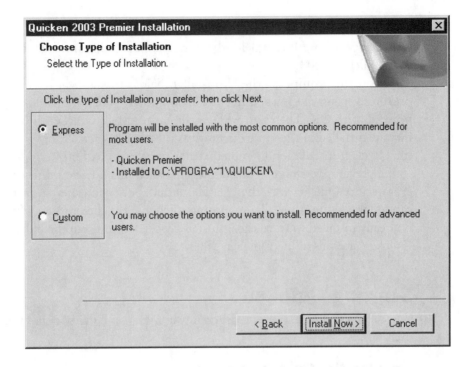

- **Express** installs all Quicken Premier options and features. (This book illustrates Quicken Premier as installed by an Express installation on Windows ME.)
- **Custom** enables you to pick and choose among the Quicken components discussed earlier in the section titled "Quicken Premier Components" and to choose the location on your hard disk in which you want to install Quicken. This option is for "power users" who want to customize their Quicken installation.

If you're not sure what to select, go with Express. (It really has everything you need.) Then click Install Now.

Wait while Quicken copies files to your hard disk. (Quicken's files are installed in C:\Program Files\QUICKEN\.) After a few moments, the installer will display a Quicken Installation Complete dialog. Eject the CD and click Finish. (Your computer may restart automatically.) You're now ready to use Quicken 2003.

Upgrading from a Previous Version

To upgrade from a previous version of Quicken, begin following the instructions in the previous section, "First-Time Installation." When you click the Install Now button, a dialog may appear, telling you that you are attempting to install Quicken in the same directory as another installation and offering to uninstall the existing version. Click Yes. You will then be prompted to confirm that you want to remove the previous version of Quicken. Click Yes again. Only the Quicken program files are deleted; your data files remain intact and can be used with Quicken 2003.

Follow the prompts in the Uninstaller dialogs that appear to remove the previous version of Quicken from your computer. When the Uninstaller is finished, click OK. Then wait while the installer installs Quicken 2003. Quicken's files are installed in the same directory as the previous version of Quicken. When the Quicken Installation Complete dialog appears, click Finish.

If a previous version of Quicken was installed in a different directory—for example, C:\Quickenw\—the Quicken installer may not offer to uninstall it. You can use the Custom installation option to choose the directory in which Quicken is already installed to force the uninstall process or uninstall the older version of Quicken after installing Quicken 2003.

Starting Quicken

You can start Quicken several different ways. Here are the two most common methods.

Opening the Quicken Shortcut

An Express installation of Quicken places a Quicken Premier 2003 shortcut icon on your Windows desktop. Double-clicking this shortcut opens Quicken Premier.

Opening Quicken from the Task Bar

You can also use the Windows task bar's Start button to start Quicken and other Quicken components. Choose Start | Programs | Quicken | Quicken 2003 Premier to start Quicken.

Preparing a Data File

Quicken stores all of your financial information in a Quicken data file. Before you can use Quicken, you must either create a data file with Quicken Guided Setup or convert an existing data file for use with Quicken 2003.

New User Startup

If you're a brand-new Quicken user, a Welcome To Quicken 2003 dialog like the one shown next appears. You have two options.

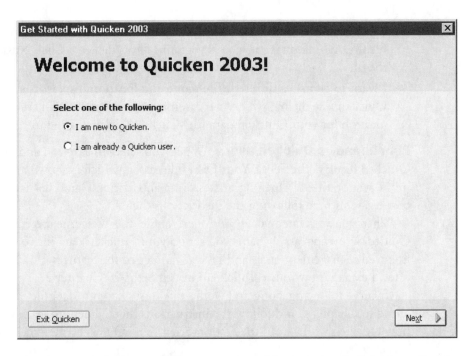

I am new to Quicken.   When you select this option and click Next, Quicken displays a dialog like the one shown next. You have two options:

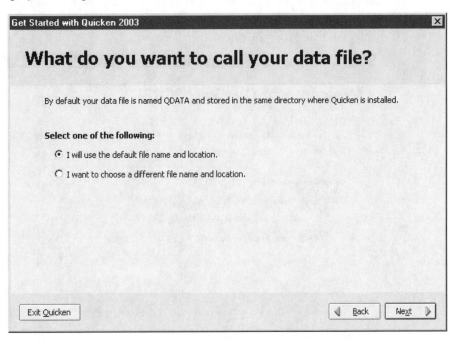

- **I will use the default file name and location** tells Quicken to name your data file QDATA and save it in C:\Program Files\Quicken\. Click Next to create the file.

- **I want to choose a different file name and location** displays the Create Quicken File dialog, which you can use to enter a name and select a disk location for your Quicken data file. Click OK in the dialog to create the file.

I am already a Quicken user.   When you select this option and click Next, Quicken displays the Select Your Data File dialog, which is shown and discussed in the section titled "Opening or Restoring an Existing Data File" later in this chapter. Continue following the instructions there.

When you've created your Quicken data file, the Welcome screen of Quicken Guided Setup appears. It helps you set up your Quicken data file to meet your financial management goals and take advantage of the features Quicken has to offer. I explain how to use Quicken Guided Setup in Chapter 2.

If you're following along and would like to set up your data file now, skip ahead to Chapter 2 and follow the instructions there. Then, to learn more about how Quicken works, read the section titled "The Quicken Interface" later in this chapter.

Opening or Restoring an Existing Data File

If you upgraded from a previous version of Quicken, when you first start Quicken, it searches for existing data files on your hard disk. If it finds one, it displays a dialog like the one shown next:

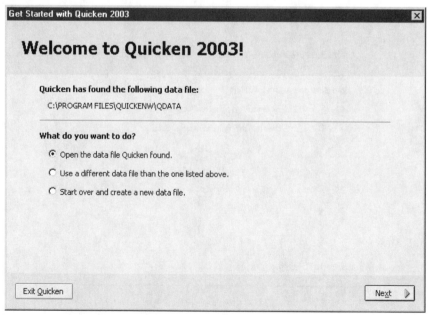

You have three options:

Open the data file Quicken found.   This option opens the data file indicated near the top of the dialog. Continue following the instructions in the section titled "Converting an Existing Data File."

Use a different data file than the one listed above.   This option enables you to select a different data file on your hard disk to use with Quicken. When you select this option and click Next, Quicken displays the Select Your Data File dialog (shown next), which offers three options:

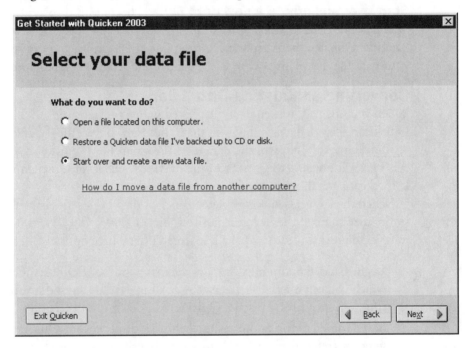

- **Open a file located on this computer** displays the Open Quicken File dialog, which you can use to select a file on your hard disk. After selecting and opening a file, continue following the instructions in the section titled "Converting an Existing Data File."
- **Restore a Quicken Data file I've backed up to CD or disk** enables you to open a backup file for use with Quicken 2003. (This option only works with files you created using Quicken's Backup command, which is discussed in Appendix A.) When you select this option and click Next, Quicken displays the Restore dialog, which you can use to select the drive designation of the disk containing the backup. You can then use the Restore Quicken File dialog to locate and open the file you want to restore. When restoration is complete, Quicken instructs you to open the data file from the File menu.

Choose File | Open and use the Open Quicken File dialog to locate and open the data file. If a dialog appears, telling you that you have to convert the data file, continue following the instructions in the section titled "Converting an Existing Data File."

- **Start over and create a new data file** displays the Create Quicken File dialog, which you can use to enter a name for your new Quicken data file. Quicken then displays Quicken Guided Setup so you can set up your data file. I explain how to use Quicken Guided Setup in Chapter 2.

Start over and create a new data file.   This option displays the Create Quicken File dialog, which you can use to enter a name for your new Quicken data file. Quicken then displays Quicken Guided Setup so you can set up your data file. I explain how to use Quicken Guided Setup in Chapter 2.

Converting an Existing Data File

When you open a Quicken data file created with a previous version of Quicken, Quicken displays a dialog telling you that it needs to convert the data file. Click OK.

Quicken saves a copy of the data in C:\Program Files\Quicken\Q02FILES\; this makes it possible to go back to the previous version of Quicken if necessary. It then converts the data file for use with Quicken 2003.

When the conversion is complete, Quicken displays a series of dialogs that summarize some of the new features in Quicken 2003. Click Next in each screen to read about these features. The last screen offers three options:

- **Begin Guided Setup now** displays the first window of Quicken Guided Setup, which you can use to fine-tune your existing data file to take advantage of all of Quicken's features. I discuss Quicken Guided setup in Chapter 2.
- **Skip Guided Setup and use Quicken now** displays your Quicken Home window (refer to Figure 1-1), which I discuss later in this chapter.
- **Watch Video** displays a video that tells you more about what Quicken can do for you. When the video is complete, you'll return to this window so you can either begin or skip Quicken Guided Setup.

Registering Quicken

Sooner or later, when you launch Quicken after setting up a Quicken data file, the Product Registration dialog shown next appears. It tells you about the benefits of registering Quicken and offers buttons for getting more information or beginning the registration process.

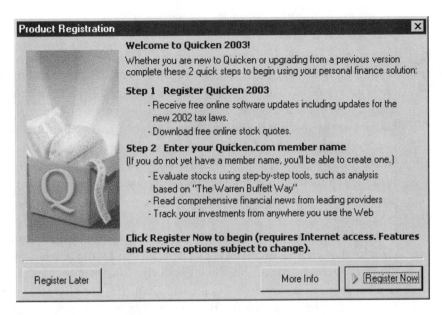

The registration process has two parts. The first part is the basic product registration, which enables you to receive online software updates and download online stock quotes for free. The second part enables you to enter your Quicken.com member name, so you can customize certain features of Quicken.com to show your data. (If you don't have a member name, you'll be prompted to create one.) As you'll learn in Chapter 4 and throughout this book, Quicken.com is full of great features to help you manage your finances from any computer with an Internet connection, anywhere in the world. You'll need an Internet connection to complete the registration process and to access features on Quicken.com.

To start the registration process, click the Register Now button. Then follow the instructions that appear on the screen to enter information about yourself and your Quicken.com member name and password. When the registration process is complete, you can continue working with Quicken.

The Quicken Interface

Quicken's interface is designed to be intuitive and easy to use. It puts the information and tools you need to manage your finances right within mouse pointer reach. You never have to dig through multiple dialogs and menus to get to the commands you need most.

In this section, I tell you about the components of the Quicken interface and explain how you can use them to make your work with Quicken easy.

Account Bar

The account bar, which is brand new in Quicken 2003, lists each of your Quicken accounts, organized by Center, on the left side of all Center and register windows (refer to Figures 1-1 and 1-3 later in this chapter). If you can't see all of the accounts in the account bar, you can click the triangle button at the top or bottom of the account bar to scroll the bar's contents. You can also click the triangle button beside a Center heading to hide or display the list of accounts beneath it. By default, account balances appear in the bar; you can click the Hide Amounts button at the bottom of the bar to hide them from view. (This also makes the account bar narrower so more information appears in the window beside it.)

The Center name headings in the account bar are actually buttons you can click to view each Center window. The Quicken Home button, which appears above the account bar, displays the Quicken Home window (refer to Figure 1-1). The account names are links; click an account name to view its register (refer to Figure 1-3). You can customize the account bar to move accounts from one Center to another or hide an account from the account bar; I explain how in Chapter 3.

Windows

Quicken displays information in windows. It has different types of windows for the different types of information it displays.

Centers

Centers, such as the Cash Flow Center, provide information about your financial status. They also offer clickable links to access related Quicken and Quicken.com features. Quicken's Centers got a complete overhaul for Quicken 2003 so they contain more useful information and links to details and reports.

There is a Center for each major area of Quicken:

- **Quicken Home** (see Figure 1-1) provides an overview of your finances, including alerts, current bills and scheduled transactions, and Online Update status. You can create new views to show the things that interest you most; I tell you how in Appendix B.
- **Cash Flow Center** provides information about your cash, bank, and credit card accounts, as well as income and expenses. I discuss the Cash Flow Center and its options in detail in Part Two of this book.
- **Investing Center** provides information about your investment accounts and individual investments. I cover investing and the Investing Center in Part Three.

Figure 1-1 • The Quicken Home window displays a variety of information about your finances.

- **Property & Debt Center** provides information about asset and liability accounts, including your home, car, related loans, and auto expenses. I discuss the Property & Debt Center and related features in Part Four.
- **Planning Center** gives you access to Quicken's financial planners, as well as the assumptions you need to set up to use the planners effectively. I discuss Quicken's financial planners and the Planning Center in Part Five.
- **Tax Center** provides information related to your taxes, including projected taxes, a tax calendar, and your year-to-date income and tax-related expenses. I cover Quicken's tax features and the Tax Center in Part Six.

List Windows

A list window (see Figure 1-2) shows a list of information about related things, such as accounts, categories, classes, or scheduled transactions. You can use a list window to perform tasks with items in the list.

Figure 1-2 • The Category List window displays a list of categories and transfer accounts.

Register Windows

You use a register window (see Figure 1-3) to enter and edit transactions for a specific account. Each account has its own register. Page tabs at the top of the window enable you to switch from the register entries to account information. A Bills and Scheduled Transactions list may appear at the bottom of some registers; you can hide this list if you like. I tell you more about using registers throughout this book.

Report Windows

Quicken 2003 introduces a new style of report window (see Figure 1-4) that enables you to quickly create and access subreports based on a main report.

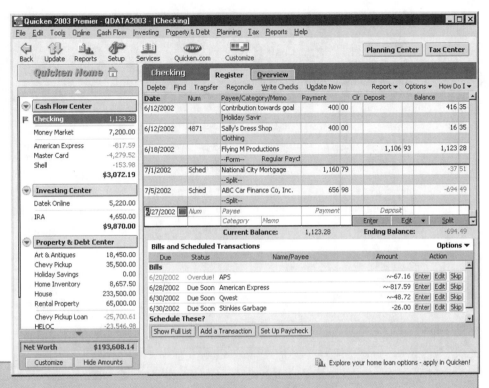

Figure 1-3 • Here's a register window for a checking account.

A list of all reports appears in the left column of the window. Click a report link to view the report in the main window. To create a subreport, double-click a report line item. You can also use options and buttons at the top of the window to work with, customize, and save reports.

Internet Window

Quicken features a built-in Web browser, which enables you to view information on Quicken.com from right within Quicken in an Internet window (see Figure 1-5). I tell you more about Quicken's built-in browser and Quicken.com in Chapter 4.

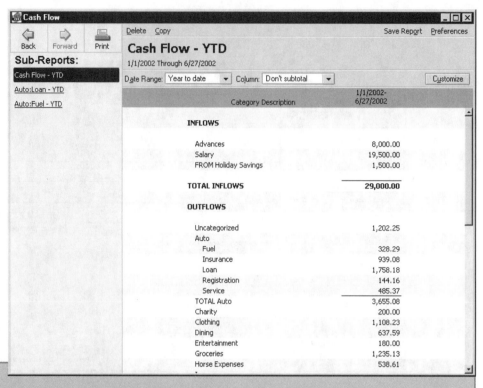

Figure 1-4 • In Quicken 2003, the report window has been overhauled to make it easier to work with reports.

Features and Commands

Quicken offers a number of ways to access its features and commands, including standard Microsoft Windows elements such as menus and dialogs, and Quicken elements such as the toolbar, button bar, and links and buttons in Center windows.

Menus

Like all other Windows programs, Quicken displays a number of menus in a menu bar at the top of the screen. You can choose commands from the menus in three ways:

- Click the menu name to display the menu. If necessary, click the name of the submenu you want (shown next), and then click the name of the command you want.

- Press ALT to activate the menu bar and press the keyboard key for the underlined letter in the menu that you want to open. If necessary, press the key for the underlined letter in the submenu that you want to open and then press the key for the underlined letter in the command that you want.

- Press the shortcut key combination for the menu command that you want. A command's shortcut key, if it has one, is displayed to the right of the command name on the menu, as shown next.

Figure 1-5 • Quicken.com content, such as the main page of the Investing channel, appears in an Internet window like this.

Shortcut Menus

Shortcut menus (which are sometimes referred to as *contextual* or *context-sensitive* menus) can be displayed throughout Quicken. Point to the item for which you want to display a shortcut menu and click the right mouse button. The menu, which includes only those commands applicable to the item, appears at the mouse pointer:

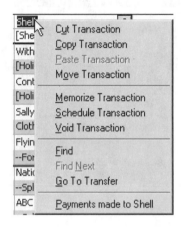

Dialogs

Like other Windows applications, Quicken uses dialogs to communicate with you. Some dialogs display a simple message, while others include text boxes, option buttons, check boxes, and drop-down lists you can use to enter information. Many dialogs also include a Help button that you can use to get additional information about dialog options.

Toolbar

The *toolbar* is a row of buttons along the top of the application window, right beneath the menu bar (see Figures 1-1 and 1-3), that gives you access to other navigation techniques and features. The toolbar is customizable; I explain how to customize it in Appendix B. Here's a quick look at the buttons that appear by default.

- **Back** displays the previously open window.
- **Update** opens the One Step Update dialog so you can connect to the Internet and update all your online information at once. I discuss One Step Update in Chapter 7.

- **Reports** displays the main Reports and Graphs window, which you can use to create reports and graphs based on Quicken data. I cover Quicken's reporting feature in detail in Chapter 9.
- **Setup** displays the Quicken Guided Setup window, which you can use to customize your Quicken data file. Quicken Guided Setup is covered in detail in Chapter 2.
- **Services** displays the Quicken Services window, which provides information about additional Quicken services.
- **Quicken.com** displays the Quicken.com home page in an Internet window. I introduce Quicken.com in Chapter 4.
- **Customize** opens the Customize Tool Bar dialog so you can customize the toolbar. I explain how to customize the toolbar in Appendix B.

Button Bar

The *button bar* is a row of textual buttons and menus that appears just above the contents of many Quicken windows (refer to Figures 1-2, 1-3, and 1-4). Most items on the button bar, which vary from window to window, are buttons; simply click one to access its option. The items with triangles beside their names are menus that work just like the menu bar menus.

Keep in mind that Quicken's onscreen Help may refer to the button bar as the toolbar. I refer to it as the button bar throughout this book to differentiate between it and the graphical toolbar at the top of the window.

Links and Buttons in Center Windows

Center windows, such as the Quicken Home window shown in Figure 1-1, include underlined links and buttons you can click to get more information about using Quicken or access its features. Although this book tends to concentrate on menu commands for accessing features, most of Quicken's features can also be accessed through various Center windows.

Onscreen Help

In addition to the How Do I menu in the button bar of many Quicken windows, and the Help button in dialogs, Quicken includes an extensive Onscreen Help system to provide more information about using Quicken while you work. You can access most Help options from the Help menu:

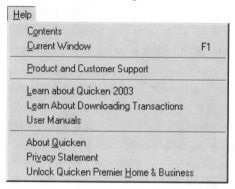

Here's a brief summary of some of the components of Quicken's Onscreen Help system.

Quicken Help

Quicken's Onscreen Help uses the same Help engine as most Windows programs. You can use it to browse or search Help topics or display Help information about a specific window.

Browsing or Searching Help

Start by choosing Help | Contents. A Quicken Help window like the one shown next appears. The left side of the window has three tabs for browsing Help topics:

- **Contents** lists Help topics organized in "books." Clicking a link displays information in the right side of the window:

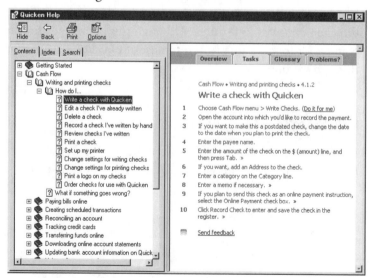

Quicken Quick Tip
Quicken's built-in Help system is a great source of information about using Quicken features. In addition to providing step-by-step instructions for using Quicken, it also offers advice on how to utilize some of Quicken's lesser-known features. Think of Quicken Help as a supplement to this book; between these two resources, all of your Quicken questions should be answered.

- **Index** lists Help topics alphabetically. You can enter a keyword at the top of the index list to narrow down the topics. Double-click a topic to display information about it in the right side of the window.

- **Search** enables you to search for information about a topic. Enter a search word in the top of the tab, then click the List Topics button. Double-click the title of a topic in the search results list to display information about it in the right side of the window.

As shown in the previous illustration, Quicken 2003's onscreen Help now offers four tabs on the right side of the Quicken Help window. Clicking a book topic displays the Overview tab for the topic. Clicking a Help document topic displays the Tasks tab for the topic, as shown previously. You can also click the Glossary tab to display a clickable list of terms used throughout Quicken or the Problems? tab to explore troubleshooting information.

Getting Context-Sensitive Help
Quicken's Help menu offers two commands to get Help for the window with which you are working:

- **Current Window** displays the Quicken Help window with information about the active window. This is probably the quickest and easiest way to get information about a specific topic or task with which you are working. You can also access this command by pressing F1.

- **Troubleshooting this Window** displays the Quicken Help window with troubleshooting information for the active window. This command, which is not available for all windows, offers a quick way to get solutions for problems you might be having.

Product and Customer Support
The Product And Customer Support command on the Help menu opens the Product And Customer Support window (see Figure 1-6), which offers links you can click to explore support options available on the Intuit Web site. Clicking a link displays related information in the window.

Figure 1-6 • Use this window to access product and customer support options on the Web.

Videos

Quicken's Help menu includes two commands for watching narrated videos about Quicken:

- **Learn about Quicken 2003** displays a window like the one in Figure 1-7, which you can use to access videos about Quicken in general, new Quicken 2003 features, and several specific Quicken 2003 features.
- **Learn About Downloading Transactions** displays a window you can use to access a video with an overview of Quicken's online account services or individual online features.

User Manuals

In addition to the brief printed manuals that come with the Quicken 2003 Deluxe or Premier CD-ROM, an electronic copy of the Getting Started with

Figure 1-7 • Click links in this window to learn more about Quicken 2003 and its features.

Quicken manual is automatically installed on your hard disk when you install Quicken. Choose Help | User Manuals, then click the link labeled "electronic copy of Getting Started with Quicken" in the window that appears. Quicken uses your default Web browser to open an Adobe Acrobat PDF file containing the information in the 88-page Getting Started manual.

Exiting Quicken

When you're finished using Quicken, choose File | Exit. This saves your data file and closes the Quicken application.

Sometimes when you exit Quicken, you'll be asked if you want to back up your Quicken data file. I tell you how to back up data files in Appendix A.

Using Quicken Guided Setup

In this Chapter:

- *Overview of data files and accounts*

- *Quicken user goals*

- *Adding accounts*

- *Adding paychecks*

- *Scheduling bills*

- *Next steps*

Chapter 2

To use Quicken, you must set up your Quicken data file for your financial situation. This means creating accounts and entering starting balance information.

Quicken 2003's new Guided Setup makes setting up a Quicken data file easy by prompting you for information about yourself, your financial goals, and your accounts. You can you use it when you first start using Quicken and any time you need to change how you use Quicken to manage your finances.

In this chapter, I explain how to use Quicken Guided Setup to create or modify a Quicken data file to meet your financial management needs. I also review how you can use information in your Quicken Home window to fine-tune your data file to take advantage of all of Quicken's features.

Before You Begin

Before you start the setup process, it's a good idea to have an understanding of how data files and accounts work. You should also gather together a few documents to help you properly set up your accounts.

Data Files

All of the transactions you record with Quicken are stored in a *data file* on your hard disk. This file includes all the information that makes up your Quicken accounting system.

Although it's possible to have more than one Quicken data file, it isn't usually necessary. One file can hold all of your transactions. In fact, it's difficult (if not downright impossible) to use more than one Quicken file to track a single account, like a checking or credit card account. And splitting your financial records among multiple data files makes it impossible to generate reports that consolidate all of the information.

When would you want more than one data file? Well, you could use two data files if you wanted to use Quicken to organize your personal finances and the finances of your business, which has entirely separate bank, credit, and asset accounts, or if you're using Quicken to track the separate finances of multiple individuals.

Appendix A covers a number of data file management tasks, including creating additional data files and backing up your data files.

Accounts

An *account* is a record of what you either own or owe. For example, your checking account is a record of cash on deposit in the bank that is available for writing checks. A credit card account is a record of money you owe to the credit card company or bank for the use of your credit card. All transactions either increase or decrease the balance in one or more accounts.

Quicken Guided Setup helps you create accounts within Quicken so you can track the activity and balances in your bank, credit card, investment, and other accounts.

What You Need

To properly set up accounts, you should have balance information for the accounts that you want to monitor with Quicken. You can get this information from your most recent bank, investment, and credit card statements. It's a good idea to gather these documents before you start the setup process so they're on hand when you need them.

If you plan to use Quicken to replace an existing accounting system—whether it's paper-based or prepared with a different computer program—you may also find it helpful to have a *chart of accounts* (a list of account names) or recent financial statements. This way, when you set up Quicken accounts, you can use familiar names.

Quicken Guided Setup

Quicken Guided Setup offers an easy-to-use interface for setting up a Quicken data file. It walks you through the setup process, step by step, making it difficult to forget any aspect of your finances.

In this part of the chapter, I explain how to use Quicken Guided Setup to set up or modify your Quicken data file.

Getting Started

As discussed in Chapter 1, Quicken Guided Setup appears automatically when you start using Quicken as a new user. If you're an upgrading user, Quicken gives you an opportunity to use Quicken Guided Setup after it converts your existing Quicken data file. But you can also display Quicken Guided Setup at any time by clicking the Setup button in the toolbar or by choosing Tools | Quicken Guided Setup.

The first thing that appears when you start Quicken Guided Setup is its Welcome window, which is shown in Figure 2-1. It tells you a little about Guided Setup and what it helps you do. You can click the Watch Video button in the Welcome window to display a menu of narrated video topics. Click a topic

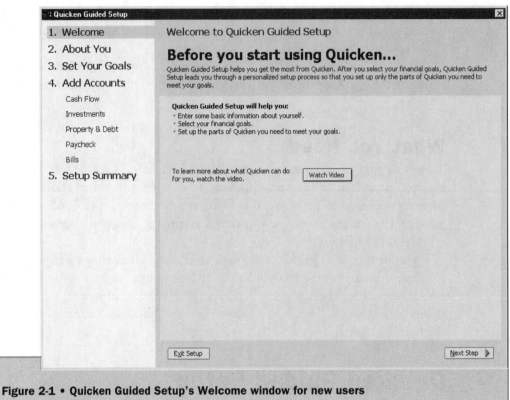

Figure 2-1 • Quicken Guided Setup's Welcome window for new users

to display its video. The Watch Video button appears in all Quicken Guided Setup windows, so you can access it at any time.

If you already have a Quicken data file, the Welcome window offers two options:

- **Help me change my goals or set up additional accounts, bills, and paychecks** displays the Set Your Goals window of Quicken Guided Setup, where you can indicate additional goals for using Quicken. I discuss this window later in this chapter.

- **Show me a complete summary of all the items I have set up in Quicken** displays the Setup Summary window of Quicken Guided Setup, where you can review and modify all of the accounts, paychecks, and bills you have set up in Quicken.

Although you can click any of the items in the navigation bar on the left side of the Quicken Guided Setup window to skip around through the setup process, the best way to go through Guided Setup is to click the Next Step button at the bottom of the screen. This takes you through each applicable window, in a logical, easy-to-follow order.

Entering Information About You

The About You window of Quicken Guided Setup (see Figure 2-2) prompts you to enter information about yourself, your spouse, and some of your property. It also asks whether you want to track a business with Quicken. This information is used by Quicken Guided Setup for Quicken's planning features and to determine what categories you'll need to record your transactions. I tell you about Quicken's Planners in Part Five of this book and about Quicken categories in Chapter 3 and throughout this book.

When you are finished entering information in this window, click Next Step.

Figure 2-2 • The About You window of Quicken Guided Setup

Setting Your Goals

The Set Your Goals window of Quicken Guided Setup appears next (see Figure 2-3). It offers check boxes you can toggle to tell Quicken what you want to use it for. Read each item and the explanation beneath it, then toggle check boxes as desired. As you turn on check boxes, a green "Goal" box appears to the right of items in the Add Accounts area, as you can see in Figure 2-3.

The options you select here determine what information Quicken will prompt you for throughout the remaining Guided Setup steps. Just turn on the check boxes for the goals you have now; you can always return to Quicken Guided Setup to change your goals. These instructions assume you have turned on all the check boxes, so the remainder of my discussion may include topics that don't appear for you now. Just skip the instructions you don't need. You can always come back to them later when you need them.

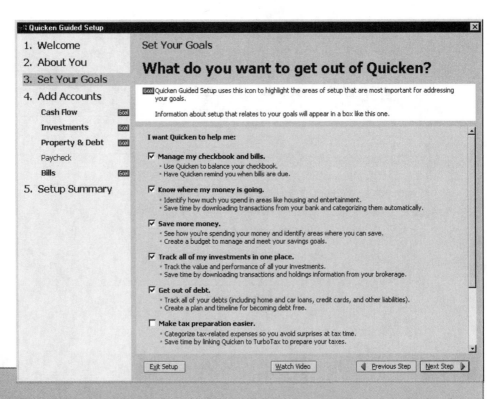

Figure 2-3 • The Set Your Goals window of Quicken Guided Setup, with a few goals already checked off

Adding Accounts

Quicken Guided Setup displays a window to add accounts to each Center used
to track account balances and transactions: Cash Flow, Investing, and Property
& Debt. The windows that appear vary depending on the goals you indicated in
the Set Your Goals window (refer to Figure 2-3). This is where those bank, credit
card, and investment statements you gathered before starting the setup process
will come in handy—you'll enter the ending balance dates and amounts from
each statement when you create each account.

Cash Flow Accounts

The Cash Flow window (see Figure 2-4) enables you to add accounts that you'll
track using Quicken's Cash Flow Center features. The window displays buttons
for four different types of accounts: Checking, Savings, Credit Card, and Cash.
Although these account types are pretty self-explanatory, you can consult the
description beside them just in case you're not sure what they're for.

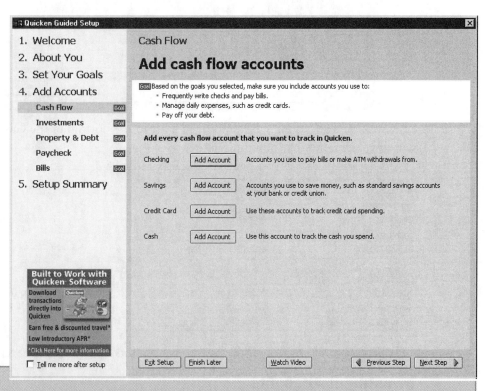

Figure 2-4 • The Cash Flow window of Quicken Guided Setup

To add an account, click the Add Account button beside the type of account you want to create. The first screen of an Account Setup dialog, like the one shown next for a checking account, appears. Enter the appropriate information in each box and click the Next button. Quicken walks you through the process of setting up the account and its starting balance. I provide details for creating cash flow accounts in Chapter 5; consult that chapter for more information about setting up these accounts.

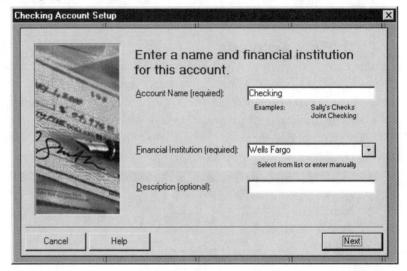

As you create accounts, they appear in a list in the bottom of the Cash Flow window. It might look something like this:

Spending & Savings Accounts			
Account	Financial Institution		Ending Balance
Spending			
Checking	Wells Fargo		2,693.55 Edit Delete
Savings			
Money Market	Western Financial Bank		24,282.97 Edit Delete

Credit Card Accounts					
Account	Financial Institution	Credit Limit	Available	Balance	
American Express	American Express	Not Set	?	-2,136.72 Edit Delete
Wells Fargo MasterCard	Wells Fargo	11,000.00	10,916.97	-83.03 Edit Delete

When you are finished adding cash flow accounts, click the Next Step button.

Investment Accounts

The Investments window (see Figure 2-5) enables you to add accounts that you'll track using features in Quicken's Investing Center. The window displays buttons

Figure 2-5 • The Investments window of Quicken Guided Setup

for four types of accounts: Brokerage, IRA or Keogh, 401(k) or 403(b), and Single Mutual Fund. A brief description beside each account explains what it is for.

To add an account, click the Add Account button beside the type of account you want to create and use the series of dialogs that appear to enter information about the account. Although you'll enter information about the account name and financial institution, you will not enter account balances during setup— that comes later. I provide details for creating investment accounts and entering starting balance information in Chapter 10; turn to that chapter for assistance.

As you set up investment accounts, they appear in a list at the bottom of the window, as shown next. When you are finished adding accounts, click the Next Step button.

Investment & Retirement Accounts			
Account	Financial Institution		
Investment			
Datek Online	Datek Online	Edit	Delete
Retirement			
Profit Sharing Keogh	Janus	Edit	Delete

Property & Debt Accounts

The Property & Debt window (see Figure 2-6) enables you to add accounts for tracking assets and liabilities, such as your home, car, and related loans. The window displays buttons for four types of accounts: House, Vehicle, Asset, and Liability. Although these account types are pretty self-explanatory, descriptions appear beside them so there's no question about what they're for.

To add an account, click the Add Account button beside the type of account you want to create. Then use the Account Setup dialogs that appear to enter information about the account and its balance. When you create a house, vehicle, or asset account, Quicken prompts you to enter information about any related loans and creates the loan accounts automatically. It even sets up loan amortization and payment information, if necessary. I explain how to create property and debt accounts and set up related loans in Chapter 13; consult that chapter for detailed instructions.

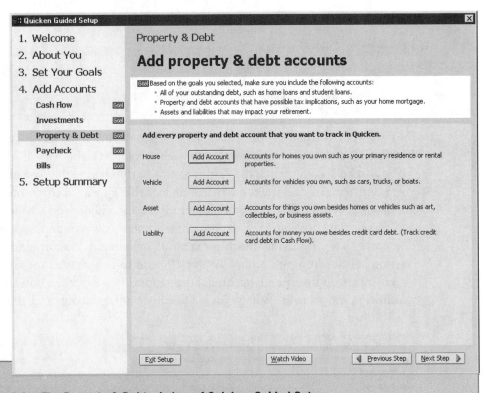

Figure 2-6 • The Property & Debt window of Quicken Guided Setup

The property and debt accounts you create appear in the bottom half of the Property & Debt window, as shown next. When you are finished adding accounts, click the Next Step button.

Property & Debt Accounts	
Account	Ending Balance
Property (Assets)	
Chevy Pickup	35,000.00 Edit Delete
Horses & Tack	3,500.00 Edit Delete
House	230,000.00 Edit Delete
Jeep	15,000.00 Edit Delete
Debt (Liabilities)	
Chevy Pickup Loan	-24,568.94 Edit Delete
House Loan	-103,165.71 Edit Delete

Setting Up Your Paycheck

The Paycheck window of Quicken Guided Setup (see Figure 2-7) allows you to enter information about the paychecks you (and your spouse) receive into Quicken. This enables Quicken to automatically enter your take-home pay while

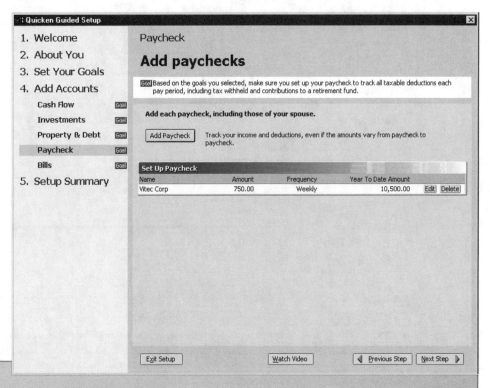

Figure 2-7 • The Paycheck window of Quicken Guided Setup, with one paycheck already set up

it keeps track of all payroll deductions. If you get a regular paycheck, setting up this feature can save data entry time while making your Quicken data file more complete.

To set up a paycheck, click the Add Paycheck button. The Paycheck Setup dialog appears. Follow its steps to enter information from a recent pay stub. I explain how to set up a paycheck in Chapter 7, so you can consult that chapter for detailed instructions. Each paycheck you set up appears in the Paycheck window, as shown in Figure 2-7. When you are finished entering paychecks, click the Next Step button.

Scheduling Bills

The Bills window of Quicken Guided Setup (see Figure 2-8) enables you to schedule regular bill payments, whether the amounts are the same or different

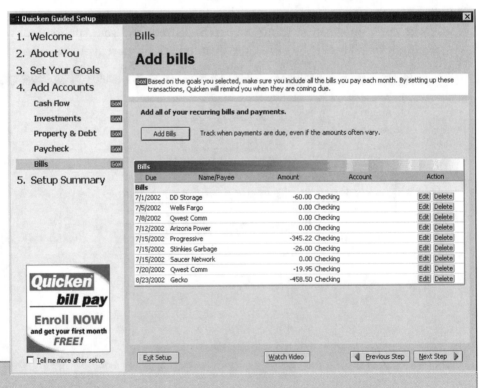

Figure 2-8 • The Bills window of Quicken Guided Setup, with a handful of bills set up

each time they're paid. This feature makes it virtually impossible for you to forget a scheduled payment, while automating most of the bill payment entry task.

To get started, click the Add Bills button. Quicken displays a dialog like the one shown next. Turn on check boxes beside each type of payment you make regularly and enter the number of regular payments you make. For example, if you pay rent for your apartment each month, turn on the Rent check box and make sure 1 is entered in the box beside it. If you set up a mortgage or loan payment as a scheduled payment in the Property & Debt window, you can omit it from this dialog since it will already be set up. Here's what it might look like when you're done:

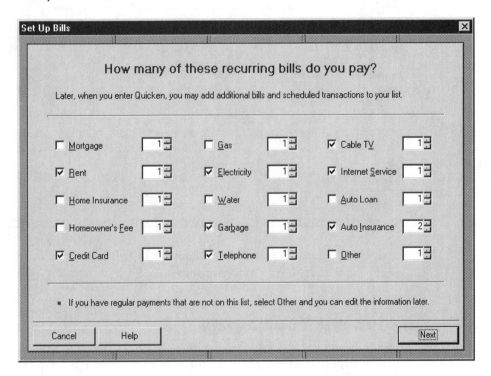

When you click the Next button, Quicken displays a dialog you can use to enter the bill information, including the payee, account from which the bill will be paid, category to charge the payment to, payment amount, payment frequency, and the next date the bill is due. Click on a field's contents to change it. I tell you more about categories in Chapters 3 and 5; you can consult those chapters if you need help setting the category, or just accept the default settings, which are likely to be correct. If a payment's amount varies from month to month, leave the Amount field set to 0.00 for that payment. When you're finished, the dialog might look like this:

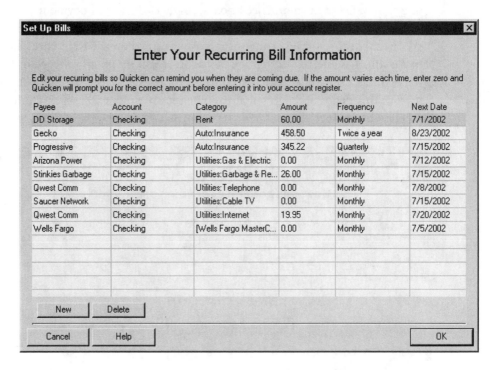

Click Done. The bills you scheduled appear in the Bills window, as shown was in Figure 2-8. Click Next Step to continue.

Reviewing Your Setup

The Setup Summary window (see Figure 2-9) summarizes all of the information you have set up in your Quicken data file. Scroll through the information to see if it's complete. You can always add an account, paycheck, or bill by clicking the Add Account, Add Paycheck, or Add Bills button in the appropriate area. You can also modify an item's settings by clicking its Edit button, or delete an account by clicking its Delete button. Or, if you prefer, you can click one of the links on the left side of the window to return to a specific setup area.

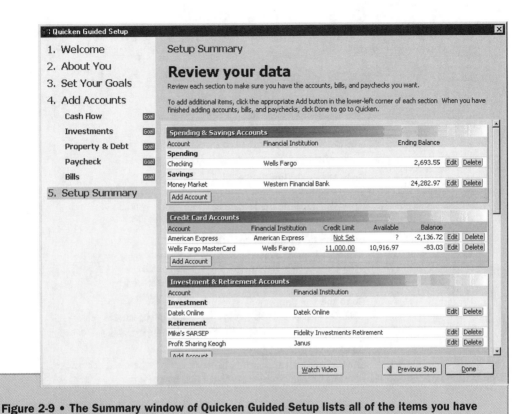

Figure 2-9 • The Summary window of Quicken Guided Setup lists all of the items you have set up in Quicken.

When you're satisfied with the setup, click Done. The Quicken Guided Setup window disappears and you can continue working with Quicken.

Next Steps

Each time you launch Quicken, the first thing it displays is the Quicken Home window, a customizable Center window that contains "snapshots" of your financial information. (I explain how to customize this window in Appendix B.) Among the default snapshots is Next Steps To Meet Your Financial Goals, which includes suggestions for exploring Quicken features to get the most out of the software.

Here's what it looks like right after setting up a Quicken data file with the settings shown in Figure 2-9:

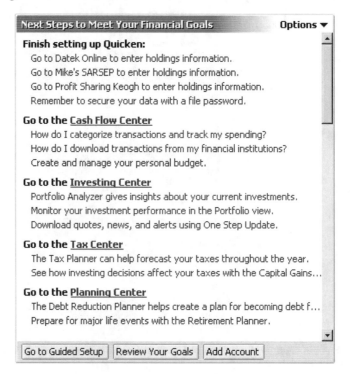

Using the Next Steps Snapshot

Buttons at the bottom of the Next Step snapshot and menu commands in the snapshot's Options pop-up menu enable you to perform specific tasks:

- **Go to Guided Setup** (button) or **Quicken Guided Setup** (menu command) displays the Welcome window of Quicken Guided Setup, which you can use to change or review your Quicken setup.

- **Review Your Goals** (button and menu command) displays the Set Your Goals window of Quicken Guided Setup (refer to Figure 2-3), so you can review or change your goals for using Quicken.

- **Add Account** (button) displays the Add New Account dialog, which you can use to add any type of Quicken account to your data file. I tell you more about adding accounts throughout this book.

- **Hide All Tasks** (menu command) collapses the Next Step snapshot's lists so only the headings appear.

- **Show All Tasks** (menu command) expands the Next Step snapshot's lists so you can see both the headings and the list items.

Finishing Quicken Setup

The first list within the Next Steps snapshot includes suggestions for completing your Quicken setup, as well as learning more about Quicken features that can save you time and protect your data. Clicking a list item in this area displays a dialog to help you complete a task or get more information.

If you have set up investment accounts, Quicken suggests that you enter holding information into the accounts. That's a good idea—until you enter this information, your Quicken data file will not be accurate and up to date. I explain how to enter holdings into investment accounts in Chapter 10.

Quicken may also suggest that you set up Bill Pay. You can use this feature, or the online payment feature with your bank, to pay your bills online. This saves time and can even save money. I explain how to set up online payments and Bill Pay in Chapter 6.

Exploring Other Next Steps

The Next Steps snapshot also contains links you can click to explore other Quicken features. Click a link to learn more about a feature or use it. Links beginning with the phrase "Go to" enable you to jump to a specific window or feature. Links beginning with the phrase "How do I" display Help topics. Explore these links on your own; the features they access are covered throughout this book.

Setting Up Accounts, Categories, and Classes

In this Chapter:

- *Overview of setting up accounts*

- *Working with the Account List*

- *Setting up categories and subcategories*

- *Working with the Category List*

- *Setting up classes*

- *Working with the Class List*

When you first set up your Quicken data file, it includes a number of default categories based on questions you answered in the Quicken Guided Setup process. Don't think you're stuck with just those categories. You can add and remove categories at any time. The same goes for accounts—you can add them as you see fit. Modifying the accounts and categories in your Quicken data file is a great way to customize Quicken to meet your needs.

In this chapter, I explain how to modify and work with the Quicken accounts and categories you'll use to organize your finances. I also explain how to set up an optional categorization feature: classes.

Accounts

You must have at least one account to track your finances with Quicken. While many of your expenditures may come from your checking account, you probably have more than one account that Quicken can track for you. By setting up all of your accounts in Quicken, you can keep track of balances and activity to get a complete picture of your financial situation.

If you used Quicken Guided Setup to set up your Quicken data file, as discussed in Chapter 2, you should already have most—if not all—of your Quicken accounts set up and ready to use. If you didn't set up all of your accounts, you can use Quicken Guided Setup now to do so—click the Setup button in the toolbar to start Guided Setup and consult Chapter 2 to learn more about it.

This part of the chapter tells you a little more about Quicken's accounts and how you can use the Account List window to create and modify your accounts.

Types of Accounts

As discussed in Chapter 2, an *account* is a record of what you either own or owe. Quicken offers different kinds of accounts for different purposes. In Quicken 2003, Intuit has reorganized and simplified the accounts available to Quicken users. Table 3-1 summarizes the accounts and how they are organized within Quicken.

What You Own

In accounting jargon, what you own are *assets*. In Quicken, an asset is one type of account, but there are several others:

Spending   Spending accounts, which are displayed in the Cash Flow Center, are used primarily for expenditures. Quicken distinguishes between two different types of spending accounts: Checking and Cash.

Account Type	Center	Center Group	Asset or Liability
Checking	Cash Flow	Spending	Asset
Savings	Cash Flow	Savings	Asset
Credit Card	Cash Flow	Credit	Liability
Cash	Cash Flow	Spending	Asset
Brokerage	Investing	Investment	Asset
IRA, SEP, Keogh	Investing	Retirement	Asset
401(k), 403(b)	Investing	Retirement	Asset
Single Mutual Fund	Investing	Investment	Asset
House	Property & Debt	Asset	Asset
Vehicle	Property & Debt	Asset	Asset
Asset	Property & Debt	Asset	Asset
Liability	Property & Debt	Liability	Liability

Table 3-1 • Overview of Quicken Account Types and How They Are Distributed Among Quicken's Centers

Savings   Savings accounts, which are displayed in the Cash Flow Center, are used to record the transactions in savings accounts.

Investment   Investment accounts, which are displayed in the Investing Center, are for tracking the stocks, bonds, and mutual funds in your portfolio that are not in retirement accounts. Quicken distinguishes between two types of investment accounts: Brokerage and Single Mutual Fund.

Retirement   Retirement accounts, which are also displayed in the Investing Center, are for tracking investments in retirement accounts. Quicken distinguishes between two types of retirement accounts:

- IRA, SEP, Keogh
- 401(k), 403(b)

All retirement accounts should fall into either of these two broad categories.

Asset   Asset accounts, which are displayed in the Property & Debt Center, are for tracking items that you own. Quicken distinguishes between three different types of asset accounts: House, Vehicle, and Asset.

What You Owe

The accounting term for what you owe is *liabilities*. Quicken offers two kinds of accounts for amounts you owe:

Credit   Credit, which is displayed in the Cash Flow Center, is for tracking credit card transactions and balances.

Liability   Liability, which is displayed in the Property & Loans Center, is for tracking loans and other liabilities.

Setting Up Accounts

You create new accounts with the Account Setup dialog. No matter what type of account you create, Quicken steps you through the process, prompting you to enter information about the account, such as its name and balance. In this section, I explain how to use the Account Setup dialog to set up new accounts and tell you what kind of information you'll have to enter for each account type.

Getting Started

Begin by opening the Account Setup dialog for the type of account you want to create. There are several ways to do this; here are three of them:

- Click the Add Account button in a Quicken Guided Setup window, as discussed in Chapter 2.
- Choose Cash Flow | Cash Flow Accounts | Add Account, Investing | Investing Accounts | Add Account, or Property & Debt | Property & Debt Accounts | Add Account. Then select the type of account you want to create in the dialog that appears and click Next.
- Choose Tools | Account List (or press CTRL-A) to display the Account List window (see Figure 3-1 later in this chapter). Click the Add Account button in its button bar to display the Add New Account dialog shown next. Then select the type of account you want to create and click Next.

The exact title and appearance of the Account Setup dialog will vary depending on the type of account you are creating. In the following illustration, I've begun creating a credit card account.

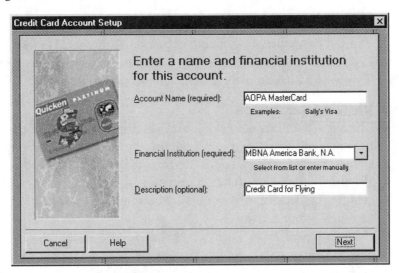

Entering Account Information

The Account Setup dialogs all work very much the same, no matter what they are titled or what options they include. Use the Next button to walk through the account creation process. You can click Back at any time to go back and change information. You know you're finished when the Next button is replaced with a Done button; click it to save the account information.

Account information includes the account name, financial institution, an optional description, the account balance, and the date of the account balance. Almost every type of Quicken account requires this information. If you don't know the balance of an account, you may set it to $0.00 and make adjustments later, either when you get a statement or when you reconcile the account.

I provide details for creating specific types of accounts throughout this book:

- Cash Flow Center accounts are covered in Chapter 5.
- Investing Center accounts are covered in Chapter 10.
- Property & Debt Center accounts are covered in Chapter 13.

Finishing Up

When you've finished entering information for a new account, click the Done button. You may be prompted to enter more information about the account, depending on the type of account and the financial institution you selected for it.

The detailed instructions in Chapters 5, 10, and 13 for creating specific account types review all of the additional information you may have to enter.

Working with the Account List

You can view a list of all of your accounts at any time. Choose Tools | Account List or press CTRL-A. The Account List window, which has two tabs, appears. This window has been completely redesigned for Quicken 2003.

Viewing Accounts

The View Accounts tab (see Figure 3-1) displays a list of all accounts organized by center and group. For each account, the account's name, online services status, number of transactions, description, and balances appear. The window also provides subtotals for each group of accounts, as well as totals for each center. The Balance total at the very bottom of the window is the net of all accounts—your net worth.

Account	Online Services	Status	Trans	Description	Current Balance	Ending Balance
Cash Flow						
Spending						
Checking	Activated		1	Maria's Checking	2,693.55	2,693.55
Cash Account			1		85.00	85.00
				Subtotal	2,778.55	2,778.55
Savings						
Money Market			1	Maria's Money Market	24,282.97	24,282.97
Credit						
American Express	Activated		1		-2,136.72	-2,136.72
AOPA MasterCard			1	Credit Card for Flying	0.00	0.00
Wells Fargo MasterCard	Activated		1		-83.03	-83.03
				Subtotal	-2,219.75	-2,219.75
				Total	24,841.77	24,841.77
Investing						
Investment						
Datek Online	Activated		0		0.00	0.00
Retirement						
Mike's SARSEP			0		0.00	0.00
Profit Sharing Keogh			0		0.00	0.00
				Balance Total:	180,607.12	180,607.12

Figure 3-1 • The View Accounts tab of the Account List window lists all of your accounts and their balances.

Managing Accounts

The Manage Accounts tab (see Figure 3-2) enables you to work with the accounts you have set up in Quicken. You can use this tab to customize the display of accounts in lists, including the account bar.

Hiding an Account   To hide an account from view, turn on the check box in the Hide In Quicken column for the account. This disables the other two check boxes and removes the account from view in any list in which it would appear. In fact, it even disappears from the View Accounts tab of the Account List window (refer to Figure 3-1) unless you choose View Hidden Accounts from the window's Option menu. You may want to use this feature to remove accounts you no longer use or need to see—without removing the transactions they contain. Keep in mind that you cannot use a hidden account in a transaction; to do so, you must first unhide the account.

Excluding an Account's Balance in Totals   To exclude an account's balances in subtotal and total calculations, turn on the check box in the Don't

Figure 3-2 • **The Manage Accounts tab of the Account List window enables you to customize the display of accounts.**

Include In Totals column for the account. This displays the balances for the account in gray in the View Accounts tab and omits the balances from any totals calculated in Quicken.

Removing an Account from the Account Bar   To remove an account from the account bar, turn on the check box in the Remove From Bar column for the account. Although the account remains in the View Accounts tab of the Account List window and other lists and menus where it would normally appear, it no longer appears in the account bar. You may want to use this feature to keep the account bar short by excluding accounts you seldom access.

Changing the Order of Accounts   To change the order in which accounts appear in the Account List window and account bar, select an account and click the Move Up or Move Down button to move it. You can move an account to any position within its group.

Changing an Account's Group   To change the group in which an account appears, select the account and click the Change Group button. A Change Group dialog like the one shown next appears. The options it offers depend on the type of account. Select a new group for the account and click the OK button. The account moves to that group in the Account List window and the account bar. If you assign a group in a different center, the account even moves to menus of accounts for that center—for example, choosing the Asset option in the following dialog moves the Checking account to the Property & Debt Accounts submenu under the Property & Debts menu.

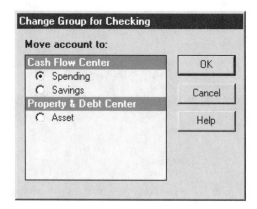

Other Account Management Tasks

You can use the button bar for either tab of the Account List window to perform a number of other account management tasks. Select the account you want to work with and click a button:

- **Go To** opens the register for the selected account. I explain how to use the various types of account registers throughout this book. (You can also open an account by double-clicking its name in the Account List window or clicking it in the account bar.)

- **Edit** displays the General Information tab of the Account Details dialog for the selected account. As shown next, this dialog includes basic information about the account that you can view or edit. The Online Services tab, when available, tells you whether online services are available for the account and whether they are activated. It also lets you deactivate online services. (I tell you more about online account services in Chapters 6 and 11.)

- **Delete** enables you to delete the selected account. It displays a dialog you can use to confirm that you want to delete the account. You must type **yes** into the dialog and click OK to delete the account. Remember, when you delete an account, you permanently remove all of its transactions from your Quicken data file. To get the account out of sight without actually deleting it and its data, consider hiding it instead. I explain how earlier in this chapter in the section titled "Working with the Account List."

- **Set Up Online Services**, when available, displays the Online Account Activation dialog, which you can use to enable online account access features for the account. This option is only available for certain types of accounts and certain financial institutions. I explain how to use this dialog in Chapters 6 and 11.

- **Add Account** displays the Create New Account dialog, shown earlier in this chapter, so you can create a new account.

- **Print** prints an account list.
- **Options** offers commands for changing the view of the Account List window.
- **How Do I** offers commands that display Help windows for a variety of common Account List window tasks.

Categories

When you create a data file, Quicken automatically creates dozens of commonly used categories based on options you set. Although these categories might completely meet your needs, there may be times when you'll want to add, remove, or modify a category to fine-tune Quicken for your use.

Types of Categories

There are basically two types of categories: income and expense:

Income   Income is incoming money. It includes things such as your salary, commissions, interest income, dividend income, child support, gifts received, and tips.

Expense   An expense is outgoing money. It includes things such as insurance, groceries, rent, interest expense, bank fees, finance charges, charitable donations, and clothing.

Subcategories

A *subcategory* is a subset or part of a category. It must be the same type of category as its primary category. For example, the Auto category may be used to track expenses to operate your car. Within that category, however, you may want subcategories to record specific expenses, such as auto insurance, fuel, and repairs. Subcategories make it easy to keep income and expenses organized into manageable categories, while providing the transaction detail you might want or need.

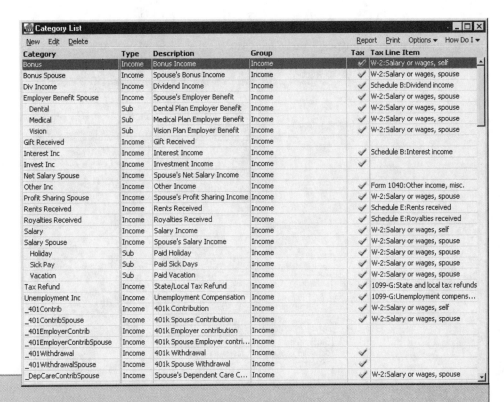

Figure 3-3 • The Category List, with categories automatically created by Quicken

Displaying the Category List

You can view a list of all of your categories at any time. Choose Tools | Category List. The Category List appears (see Figure 3-3). For each category, it displays the category name, type, description, group, and tax information. You can use the Category List to create, edit, and delete categories.

Creating a New Category

To create a new category, start by displaying the Category List window (see Figure 3-3). Then click the New button on the button bar. The Set Up Category dialog appears. Enter information about the category—the following illustration shows an example—and click OK.

Here's a quick summary of the kind of information you should provide for each category:

Category information The basic category information includes the category name, which is required, and the description and group, which are optional. Groups are used primarily for budgeting, so I discuss them in Chapter 18. For now, you can either leave the Group box empty or choose an existing group from the drop-down list.

Type Use options in the Type area to select the type of category: Income, Expense, or Subcategory. In addition to properly classifying income and expense items, the type of category you specify will determine where the category appears in reports and graphs. For example, income categories always appear before expense categories, and subcategories appear immediately below their parent categories. If you select Subcategory, you must choose a category from the drop-down list beside it. If you do not have complete control over spending for an expense category, you can turn on the Spending Is Not Discretionary check box. This option, which is also used primarily for budgeting, applies to required fixed expenditures such as rent, car insurance, and child care.

Tax   You can use the tax area options to specify whether a category is tax related and, if so, what tax form it appears on. This can be a real timesaver at tax time by enabling you to organize your income and expenditures as they are on tax forms. I tell you more about using Quicken at tax time in Chapter 19. You are not required to enter anything in this area.

When you've finished entering information in the Set Up Category dialog, click OK. The category is added to the list.

Adding Multiple Categories at Once

Quicken makes it easy to add multiple related categories all at once. For example, suppose you just got married (congratulations!) and want to add categories for married people to your Quicken data file. Choose Add Categories from the Options menu on the Category List window's button bar to display the Add Categories dialog, which is shown next. Choose a category group from the Available Categories drop-down list, then click to select each category you want to add. When you click Add, the selected categories appear in the Categories To Add list. Click OK to add the categories and dismiss the dialog.

Editing and Deleting Categories

You can also use the Category List window (see Figure 3-3) to edit or delete a category. Select the name of the category you want to edit or delete, and then click the Edit or Delete button on the button bar.

Edit   The Edit button displays the Edit Category dialog, which looks and works just like the Set Up Category dialog, for the selected category. You can use this to make just about any change to a category. You can even "promote" a subcategory to a category by changing its type.

Delete   Clicking the Delete button displays different dialogs depending on the category that is selected:

- If you selected a category with no subcategories, the Delete Category dialog, which is shown next, appears. You can use this dialog to delete the selected category or replace it with another throughout your data file. Remember, when you delete a category without replacing it with another category you permanently remove the category from all of the transactions that referenced it, resulting in uncategorized transactions.

- If you selected a category with subcategories, a dialog tells you that you can't delete a category with subcategories.
- If you selected a subcategory, a dialog offers to merge the subcategory with its parent category. Click Yes to merge the category and subcategory; click No to delete the subcategory without merging it. Keep in mind that when you delete a subcategory without merging it with its parent category, you permanently remove the subcategory from all of the transactions that referenced it, resulting in uncategorized transactions.

Other Category List Options

Buttons and menus on the right end of the Category List window's button bar (see Figure 3-3) enable you to perform other tasks with list contents.

- **Report** creates a report of the transactions for the selected category. I tell you more about creating reports in Chapter 9.
- **Print** prints a category list.
- **Options** is a menu with additional options for working with the Category List window, including the Add Categories command discussed earlier in this chapter in the section titled "Adding Multiple Categories at Once."
- **How Do I** is a menu that includes commands for displaying Help windows for a variety of common Category List window tasks.

Classes

A *class* is an optional identifier for specifying what a transaction applies to. For example, if you have two vehicles for which you track expenses, you can create a class for each vehicle, such as "Jeep" and "Chevy Truck." Then, when you record a transaction for one of the vehicles, you can include the appropriate class with the category for the transaction.

I want to stress here that using classes is completely optional. It's not necessary to set them up or use them at all. In fact, many Quicken users—including a few I know at Intuit—don't take advantage of this feature. It's your decision.

Displaying the Class List Window

Quicken maintains a list of all the classes you create. You can display the Class List by choosing Tools | Class List, or by pressing CTRL-L. Here's an example with some classes I created:

Quicken Quick Tip

I use classes in my Quicken data file to track income and expenses by project, so I can clearly see how much each project costs and earns. Because Quicken can produce reports based on categories, classes, or both, classes offer an additional dimension for tracking and reporting information.

Creating a New Class

Click the New button on the button bar in the Class List window. The Set Up Class dialog, which is shown next, appears. Use it to enter information about the class.

Only one piece of information is really necessary: the class name. You may want to make it short so it's easy to remember and enter. The description can be used to provide additional information on what the class is used for. The copy number enables you to associate different classes with different but similar activities. For example, if you have two separate businesses for which you report activity on two Schedule Cs, you can assign Copy 1 to one business's classes and Copy 2 to the other business's classes.

When you click OK, the class is added to the list. You can create as many classes as you like.

Working with the Class List Window

You can use buttons in the button bar near the top of the Class List window to work with the class list or a selected class:

- **New** enables you to create a new class as discussed earlier.
- **Edit** enables you to modify the currently selected class name or other information.
- **Delete** enables you to delete the currently selected class. When you delete a class, the class name is removed from all transactions in which it appeared. (The transaction remains properly categorized.)
- **Report** prints a transaction report by class. I tell you more about Quicken's reporting features in Chapter 9.
- **Print** prints the class list.
- **How Do I** is a menu of Help topics related to the Class List window.

Going Online with Quicken and Quicken.com

In this Chapter:

- *Benefits of going online with Quicken*

- *Getting connected to the Internet*

- *Setting up Quicken for an Internet connection*

- *Testing and troubleshooting your connection*

- *An introduction to Web surfing*

- *Accessing Quicken.com*

- *Quicken financial partners*

Many of Quicken's features work seamlessly with the Internet. If you have access to the Internet, either through a connection to an Internet service provider (ISP) or through a connection to an online service such as America Online, you can take advantage of these online features to get up-to-date information, automate data entry, pay bills, and obtain Quicken maintenance updates automatically.

In this chapter, I tell you why you might want to take advantage of Quicken's online features. Then I explain how to set up Quicken to go online. Finally, I tell you a little about surfing the Web and introduce you to Quicken.com, Intuit's excellent financial information Web site.

Going Online

If you're already using your computer to access the features of the Internet or online services such as America Online, you probably already know a lot about it. In this part of the chapter, I fill in any gaps in your knowledge by telling you about the benefits of going online with Quicken and addressing any security concerns you might have. Finally, for the folks who aren't already online, I explain what you need to connect to the Internet to use Quicken's online features.

Why Go Online?

Before I go any further, I want to remind you that you don't *have* to go online to use Quicken. Quicken is a good financial management software package, even without its online features. But Quicken's online features make it a *great* financial management software package. As you'll see in this section and throughout this book, Quicken uses the Internet to help you make better financial decisions. How? By providing you with information and resources that are relevant to your personal financial situation.

The best way to explain the benefits of going online is to list a few of the features online users can take advantage of.

If You Have a Bank Account, You Can Benefit

Throughout the month, you write checks and mail them to individuals and organizations. You enter these transactions in your checking account register. At month's end, you reconcile the account. You can do all this without going online. I tell you how in Chapters 5 and 8.

But if you register for transaction download with your bank, you can download all bank account activity on a regular basis so you know exactly when the transactions hit your account—even the ATM and debit card transactions you always forget to enter. If you register for online payment, you can pay your bills without licking another envelope or pasting on another stamp. I explain how all this works in Chapter 6.

If You Have Credit Cards, You Can Benefit

Do you have credit cards? Then you can take advantage of Quicken's credit card tracking features, which I cover in Chapter 5, to keep track of your charges, payments, and balances. You don't need to go online.

But if you sign up for transaction download, all your credit card charges can be downloaded directly into Quicken, eliminating the need for time-consuming data entry, while giving you an up-to-date summary of your debt and how you spent your money. I tell you more about this in Chapter 6.

If You Invest, You Can Benefit

Quicken can keep track of your investments, whether they are 401(k) accounts, mutual funds, or stocks. You can enter share, price, and transaction information into Quicken, and it will summarize portfolio value, gains, and losses. It'll even keep track of securities by lot. You don't need to go online to track your investments. I explain how in Chapter 10.

But with online investment tracking, Quicken can automatically obtain quotes on all the securities in your portfolio and update your portfolio's market value. Depending on your brokerage firm, you may also be able to download transactions, account balances, and holdings. Quicken can also alert you about news stories that affect your investments and automatically download the headlines so you can learn more with just a click. You can also get valuable up-to-date research information about securities that interest you, so you can make informed investment decisions. And if you sign up for the new Quicken Brokerage powered by Siebert service, you can even initiate trades from within Quicken! I tell you about all this in Chapter 11.

If You Want to Save Money, You Can Benefit

Mortgages. Car loans. Bank accounts. Insurance. All of these have one thing in common: their rates vary from one provider to another. Shopping for the best deal can be time-consuming work—wading through newspaper and magazine ads, making calls, visiting banks. Quicken can help you understand the basics of loans, banking, and insurance. Its planners can help you evaluate the deals you learn about, and all without going online.

But with the help of Quicken's built-in Internet links, you can shop for the best deal online, without leaving the comfort of your desk, getting newspaper ink all over your hands, or spending an afternoon listening to music while on hold. Up-to-date rates are only a mouse click away with an Internet connection and Quicken to guide you.

Enough Already!

If all this doesn't convince you that going online with Quicken can help you save time, save money, and get smarter, stop reading and skip ahead to Chapter 5. You'll probably never be convinced. I will say one more thing, however: after using Quicken's online features for more than six years now, I can't imagine using Quicken any other way.

Security Features

Perhaps you're already convinced that the online features can benefit you. Maybe you're worried about security, concerned that a stranger will be able to access your accounts or steal your credit card numbers.

You can stop worrying. The folks at Intuit and the participating banks, credit card companies, and brokerage firms have done all the worrying for you. They've come up with a secure system that protects your information and accounts.

PINs

A *PIN,* or *personal identification number,* is a secret password you must use to access your accounts online. If you have an ATM card or cash advance capabilities through your credit card, you probably already have at least one PIN, so the idea shouldn't be new to you. It simply prevents anyone from accessing the account for any reason without first entering the correct PIN.

An account's PIN is initially assigned by the bank, credit card company, or brokerage firm. Some companies, like American Express, require that your PIN consist of a mixture of letters and numbers for additional security. You can change your PINs to make them easier to remember—just don't use something obvious like your birthday or telephone number. And don't write it on a sticky note and attach it to your monitor!

If you think someone might have guessed your PIN, you can change it. In fact, it's a good idea to regularly change all your PINs and passwords—not just the ones you use in Quicken.

Encryption

Once you've correctly entered your PIN, the instructions that flow from your computer to the bank, credit card company, or brokerage firm are encrypted.

This means they are encoded in such a way that anyone able to "tap in" to the transactions would "hear" only gibberish. Quicken does the encryption using, at a minimum, the 56-bit single Data Encryption Standard (DES). Quicken is also capable of encrypting data with stronger methods, including the 128-bit RC4 or 168-bit triple DES. Once the encrypted information reaches the computer at the bank, credit card company, or brokerage firm, it is unencrypted and then validated and processed.

Encryption makes it virtually impossible for any unauthorized party to "listen in" to your transaction. It also makes it impossible for someone to alter a transaction between the moment it leaves your computer and the moment it arrives at your bank, credit card company, or brokerage firm for processing.

Other Security Methods

Quicken also takes advantage of other security methods for online communications, including Secure Sockets Layer (SSL) encryption, digital signatures, and digital certificates. Together, all of these security methods make online financial transactions secure—even more secure than telephone banking, which you may already use!

Quicken Quick Tip

If you're really concerned about security, and my discussion here hasn't explained things well enough for you, be sure to read the Security In Quicken topic in the Appendixes of Quicken's built-in Help system. It provides details about Quicken's security features, as well as tips for keeping your data safe and secure.

Getting Connected

To take advantage of Quicken's online features, you need a connection to the Internet. You get that through an ISP. An *ISP* is an organization that provides access to the Internet, usually for a monthly fee. These days, literally thousands of ISPs can provide the access you need for Quicken's online features.

If you don't already have an account with an ISP, you must set one up before you can configure Quicken to use its online features. Check your local phone book or newspaper to find an ISP near you. Your ISP can explain everything you need to get connected and help you set up your computer to go online.

Setting Up and Testing an Internet Connection

To use Quicken's online features, you may need to set up Quicken for your Internet connection. This part of the chapter explains how to set up, test, and troubleshoot a Quicken Internet connection.

If you went through the Quicken Guided Setup process as discussed in Chapter 2 and created accounts that utilize Quicken's online features, chances are that Quicken is already set up to utilize your Internet connection. If that is the case, you can skip this section, unless you need to modify or troubleshoot your connection.

Internet Connection Setup

Choose Edit | Preferences | Internet Connection Setup. The Internet Connection Setup dialog, which has been completely revised and simplified for Quicken 2003, appears:

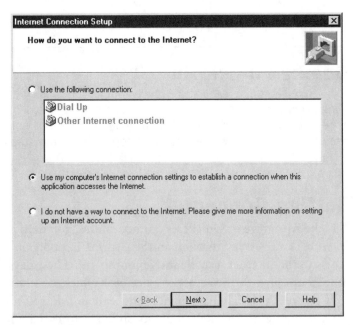

This dialog offers three options:

- **Use the following connection** enables you to select from an existing list of Internet connections. This list is maintained by Windows based on Internet connection profiles you create with the Internet Connection Wizard. If you have only one connection profile (like I do), the only item in this list will be Other Internet Connection. If you select this option, when you click Next, the dialog explains what to do when you need to connect to the Internet.

- **Use my computer's Internet connection settings to establish a connection when this application accesses the Internet.** This option tells Quicken to use your active Internet connection profile to connect to the Internet from within Quicken. If you select this option, when you click Next, the dialog tells you a little about your connection. Quicken will automatically connect to the Internet using these settings any time it needs to.

- **I do not have a way to connect to the Internet. Please give me more information on setting up an Internet account.** Select this option only if you do not already have an Internet connection set up within Windows. When you click Next, Quicken provides additional instructions for getting an ISP and using the Internet Connection Wizard to set up your connection.

Make your selections in the dialog and click Next or Done to get more information or complete the setup process. If you need help setting up an Internet connection, consult Windows Help.

You can change the options for an Internet connection profile at any time. Just follow these instructions again.

Testing Your Connection

Once you've set up Quicken for an Internet connection, you're ready to test it. Here are two simple tasks to get you started.

Visiting Quicken.com

A good connection test is a visit to Quicken.com, Intuit's feature-packed financial Web site for Quicken users and other visitors. I tell you more about Quicken.com later in this chapter and throughout this book. For now, let's just connect to it to make sure your Internet connection works.

Choose Online | Quicken On The Web | Quicken.com. Quicken attempts to connect to the Internet using the settings in the Internet Connection Setup dialog.

What you see during the connection process will vary depending on your ISP. If you use an online service such as America Online, the service's access software may start automatically to make the connection. You may be prompted to enter a username or password. Other dialogs may appear. It may be necessary to switch from connection software back to Quicken by clicking the Quicken button on the Windows task bar.

When the connection is complete, Quicken requests the Quicken.com home page. It appears in a Web browser window (see Figure 4-1).

If you were already connected to the Internet when you accessed one of Quicken's online features, or if you have a direct connection to the Internet, you won't see the connection happening. Instead, the Quicken.com page will simply appear in a Web browser window (see Figure 4-1).

Disconnecting from the Internet

To manually disconnect from the Internet when you have finished using Quicken's online features, choose File | Disconnect. One of two things will happen:

- If you are connected via an online service such as America Online, Quicken may tell you that it cannot disconnect from the Internet. Switch to the online service's access software by clicking its name in the task bar, and then use that software to disconnect from the Internet.

- If you are connected via another ISP, Quicken may display a dialog offering to disconnect from the Internet. Click Yes to disconnect.

Figure 4-1 • The Quicken.com home page, which changes throughout the day, every day

Quicken also reminds you to disconnect from the Internet each time you exit the program. The dialog that appears even offers to disconnect for you.

Troubleshooting Connection Problems

If you follow the instructions I provided throughout this chapter, you shouldn't have any trouble connecting to the Internet with Quicken. But things aren't always as easy as they should be. Sometimes even the tiniest problems can prevent you from successfully connecting and exchanging data.

In this section, I provide some troubleshooting advice to help you with connection problems you may experience. Check this section before you start pulling out your hair and cursing the day computers were invented.

Setup Problems

To determine whether the problem is a Quicken setup problem or a general Internet setup problem, exit Quicken and try connecting to the Internet from another program, such as your regular Web browser or e-mail program.

- If you can connect to the Internet from another program but not from Quicken, the problem may be with Quicken's Internet connection setup. Go back to the section titled "Internet Connection Setup," earlier in this chapter, and repeat the setup process. You'll probably want to select the second option in the Internet Connection Setup dialog.

- If you can't connect to the Internet from any other program or with dial-up networking (for dial-up connections), the problem is with your Internet setup for Windows, your modem (for dial-up connections), or your network (for direct connections). You must fix any problem you find before you can successfully set up and connect with Quicken. Consult Windows Help for assistance.

Modem Problems

Problems with a dial-up connection may be related to your modem. Try each of the following, attempting a connection after each one:

- Check all cables between your computer and your modem (if you have an external modem), and between your modem and the telephone outlet.

- Check the telephone line to make sure it has a dial tone and that it is not being used by someone else or another program.

- Turn off your modem and then turn it back on. Or, if you have an internal modem, restart your computer. This resets the modem and may resolve the problem.

If you can connect but have trouble staying connected, try the following:

- Make sure no one is picking up an extension of the phone line while you are online.
- Make sure call-waiting is disabled by entering the appropriate codes for the dial-up connection.
- Have the phone company check the line for noise. If noise is detected, ask the phone company to fix the problem. (It shouldn't cost you anything if the line noise is the result of a problem outside your premises.)

Network Problems

Problems with a direct connection may be related to your network. Try these things, attempting a connection after each one:

- Check all cables between your computer and the network hub or router.
- Check to make sure the correct proxy server information was entered into Windows Internet Connection Wizard.
- Restart your computer. Sometimes resetting your computer's system software can clear network problems.
- Ask your system administrator to check your network setup.

Exploring Quicken.com

The World Wide Web has had a greater impact on the distribution of information than any innovation since the invention of movable type hundreds of years ago. The Web makes it possible to publish information almost instantly, as it becomes available. Accessible by anyone with a computer, an Internet connection, and Web browsing software, it gives individuals and organizations the power to reach millions of people worldwide without the delays and costs of traditional print and broadcast media.

While this power to publish has flooded the Internet with plenty of useless and trivial information, it has also given birth to exceptional Web sites, full of useful, timely, and accurate information that can make a difference in your life. Quicken.com, Intuit's site, is one of the best financial information sites around.

In this part of the chapter, I'll lead you on a short tour of Quicken.com and other Quicken features on the Web. My goal is to introduce you to what's out there so you can explore the areas that interest you most.

Quicken Quick Tip

Keep one thing in mind as you read through this chapter: Quicken.com is an incredibly dynamic Web site that changes frequently. The screen illustrations and features I tell you about will probably appear differently when you connect. In addition, brand-new features might be added after the publication of this book. That's why I won't go into too much detail. The best way to learn about all the online features of Quicken and Quicken.com is to check them out for yourself.

An Introduction to Web Surfing

Before I start my overview of Quicken on the Web, let me take a moment to explain exactly what you're doing when you connect to Quicken.com and the other Quicken features on the Web. If you're brand new to *Web surfing*—that is, exploring Web sites—be sure to read this section. But if you're a seasoned surfer, you probably already know all this stuff and can skip it.

One more thing: this section is not designed to explain everything you'll ever need to know about browsing the World Wide Web. It just provides the basic information you need to use the Web to get the information you need.

Going Online

When you access Quicken's online features, you do so by connecting to the Internet through your ISP. It doesn't matter whether you connect via a modem or a network, or whether your ISP is America Online or Joe's Dial-up Internet Service. The main thing is having a connection or a conduit for information.

Think of an Internet connection as some PVC piping running from your computer to your ISP's, with a valve to control the flow of information. Once the valve is open (you're connected), any information can flow through the pipe in either direction. You can even exchange information through that pipe in both directions at the same time. This makes it possible to download (or retrieve) a Web page with your Web browser while you upload (or send) e-mail with your e-mail program.

Quicken's online features use the pipe (or connection) in two ways:

- The integrated Web browser enables you to request and receive the information you want. It's live and interactive—click a link, and a moment later your information starts to appear. Quicken can display Web pages in its built-in Internet window (see Figure 4-1) or your default browser's window (see Figure 4-2).

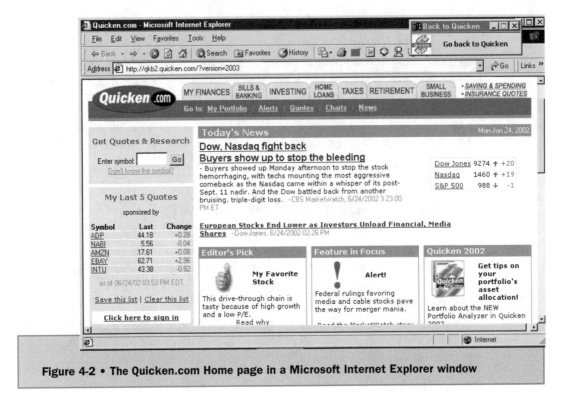

Figure 4-2 • The Quicken.com Home page in a Microsoft Internet Explorer window

- The transaction download, online payment, and several other features work in the background to communicate with financial institutions with which you have accounts. Quicken sends information you prepared in advance and retrieves the information the financial institution has waiting for you.

This chapter concentrates on Web browsing with Quicken—using Quicken's integrated Web browser to access interactive features on Quicken.com. But it also provides some information to help you find financial institutions that work with Quicken for the transaction download and online payment features.

Navigating

The main thing to remember about the Web is that it's interactive. Every time a Web page appears on your screen, it'll offer a number of options for viewing other information. This is known as navigating the Web.

Hyperlinks and Forms You can move from page to page on the Web in two ways, both of which are illustrated in Figures 4-1 and 4-2:

- **Hyperlinks** (or links) are text or graphics that, when clicked, display another page. Hypertext links are usually underlined, colored text. Graphic links sometimes have a colored border around them. You can always identify a link by pointing to it—your mouse pointer will turn into a hand with a pointing finger.
- **Forms** offer options for going to another page or searching for information. Options can appear in pop-up menus, text boxes that you fill in, check boxes that you turn on, or option buttons that you select. There often are multiple options. You enter or select the options you want and click a button to send your request to the Web site. The information you requested appears a moment later.

Other Navigation Techniques   Several of the buttons on the Quicken browser's toolbar (refer to Figure 4-1) are navigation buttons:

- **Back** displays the previously viewed page.
- **Next** displays the page you viewed after the current page. This button is only available after you have used the Back button.
- **Stop** stops the loading of the current page. This may result in incomplete pages or error messages on the page. You might use this button if you click a link and then realize that you don't really want to view the information you requested.
- **Refresh** loads a new copy of the Web page from the Web site's server. This button is handy for updating stock quotes or news that appears on a page.
- **Quicken.com** takes you to the Quicken Home page (refer to Figure 4-1).

In addition, the button bar for Quicken's built-in browser window includes a Full Browser button. Clicking this button starts and switches to your default Web browser. Quicken continues to run in the background. You can switch back to it at any time by clicking its icon on the Windows task bar or by clicking the Go Back To Quicken button in the window that appears over the Browser window (refer to Figure 4-2).

Working Offline

When you've finished working with online features and if you have a dial-up connection, you may want to disconnect. This frees up your telephone line for incoming calls. You can continue working offline with features that don't require Internet access.

To work offline, choose File | Disconnect. Quicken displays a dialog offering to disconnect you from the Internet. Click Yes.

If you're connected via a direct network connection, the Disconnect command will not be available because you can't disconnect.

Accessing Quicken on the Web

You can access Quicken's online features using commands on its Online menu. One of these commands, Quicken On The Web, is really a submenu with several options for Quicken Web features.

Quicken.com

Quicken.com is Intuit's financial Web site. Although designed to be of most use to Quicken users, most of its features are accessible to anyone. Tell your friends about it.

Quicken.com is divided into different *channels*, or areas of information. You can go to a channel by clicking its tab or link near the top of the Quicken.com home page (refer to Figures 4-1 and 4-2). As this book went to press, the channels included My Finances, Bills & Banking, Investing, Home Loans, Taxes, Retirement, Small Business, Saving & Spending, and Insurance Quotes. You can explore each of these channels on your own to learn more about them.

Quicken Support

The Quicken Support command takes you to the Quicken Support Home page. This is where you can find answers to frequently asked questions, information about solving problems with Quicken, and program updates. Use this command when you can't find the information you need in this book or with Quicken's Onscreen Help feature.

Quicken Products

The Quicken Products command takes you to the Shop Intuit Home page, where you can learn more about and purchase other Intuit products, including checks and supplies and TurboTax, a tax preparation software product that works with Quicken. Stop by once in a while to check out special offers and new products.

Participating Financial Institutions

If you're interested in keeping track of your finances with the least amount of data entry, you should be considering Quicken's online features for transaction download and online payment. I explain the benefits of these features near the beginning of this chapter. Chapters 6 and 11 tell you how to use them. But you can't use them until you've set up an account with a participating financial institution and applied for the online account services you want to use.

When you create a bank, credit card, or investment account as discussed in Chapters 2 and 3, Quicken prompts you to enter the name of your financial institution. Quicken can determine whether your financial institution is one of the participating financial institutions and prompt you to set up transaction download and online payment features, if they are available. If you've already set up your accounts for Online Services, you can skip this section. But you may find it useful if you're shopping around for another financial institution and want one that works with Quicken.

Finding a Participating Institution

Finding a Quicken financial partner is easy. Choose Online | Participating Financial Institutions. The Apply For Online Financial Services window appears (see Figure 4-3). This page, which is updated each time a new partner comes on board, offers links with information about each of the partner institutions. To get information about a specific institution, click a link in the Online Financial Services area to narrow down the list of institutions. Then click a link in the Financial Institution Directory area. Information about the financial institution appears in the main part of the window.

Note that if you have not set up Quicken for your Internet connection or registered the Quicken software, a dialog may appear telling you that you need to do one or both of these things to continue. Follow the prompts within the dialog as necessary. Eventually, the Apply For Online Financial Services window (see Figure 4-3) will appear.

Participating financial institutions offer four types of online financial services:

- **Banking Account Access** enables you to download bank account transactions directly into your Quicken data file.
- **Credit/Charge Card Access** enables you to download credit or charge card transactions directly into your Quicken data file.
- **Investment Account Access** enables you to download brokerage and other investment account transactions directly into your Quicken data file.
- **Payments** enables you to send payment instructions from within Quicken. This makes it possible to pay bills and send payments to anyone without writing a check.

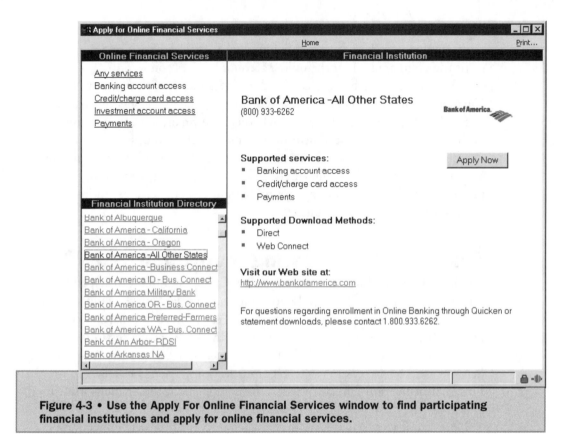

Figure 4-3 • Use the Apply For Online Financial Services window to find participating financial institutions and apply for online financial services.

Within the Quicken program, the first three services are referred to as *transaction download* and the last one is referred to as *online payments*.

If your bank, credit card company, or brokerage firm is not on the list, you have three options:

Change financial institutions. I know it sounds harsh, but if your bank or credit card company doesn't support online banking services with Quicken and you really want to use this feature, you can find a financial institution that does support it and open an account there.

Wait until your financial institution appears on the list. The list of participating institutions is updated quite often. If your bank or credit card company doesn't appear there today, it may appear next month—or next year. You can hurry things along by asking your financial institution to become a participating institution. They might add this feature if enough customers ask for it.

Use Quicken Bill Pay and Quicken Credit Card.   If all you're interested in is the online payments feature, you can use Quicken Bill Pay. This enables you to process online payments from your existing bank accounts. There's no need to change banks or wait until your bank signs on as a participating financial institution. If you'd like to download credit card transactions into Quicken, sign up for the Quicken Credit Card. You can learn more about Quicken Bill Pay and Quicken Credit Card in the Quicken Services window; choose Tools | Quicken Services to display it.

Applying for Online Financial Services

The information pane of the window for the financial institution you selected (see Figure 4-3) provides information about how you can apply for online banking. In most cases, you'll either click the Apply Now button to apply or learn more, or call the toll-free number that appears onscreen and speak to a company representative. This gets the wheels turning to put you online. It may take a few days to get the necessary access information, so apply as soon as you're sure you want to take advantage of the online financial services features.

The Cash Flow Center

This part of the book explains how to use Quicken to keep track of the bank and credit card accounts in the Cash Flow Center. It starts by explaining the basics of manually recording bank and credit card transactions, then tells you how you can take advantage of online transaction entry and payment processing features such as Online Account Services and Bill Pay. It explains how you can tap into the power of Quicken to automate many entry tasks, thus saving you time. It also explains how to reconcile accounts and how to use Quicken's extensive reporting feature to learn more about what you have and how you're doing financially. This part has five chapters:

Chapter 5: *Recording Bank and Credit Card Transactions*

Chapter 6: *Using Online Banking Features*

Chapter 7: *Automating Transactions and Tasks*

Chapter 8: *Reconciling Your Accounts*

Chapter 9: *Examining Your Cash Flow*

Part Two

Recording Bank and Credit Card Transactions

Chapter 5

In this Chapter:

- *Creating cash flow accounts*

- *Entering payments and other transactions*

- *Writing and printing checks*

- *Entering credit card transactions*

- *Transferring money*

- *Working with existing transactions*

- *Using splits and classes*

At Quicken's core is its capability to manage your bank accounts. This is probably Quicken's most used feature. You enter the transactions, and Quicken keeps track of account balances and the source and destination of the money you spend. You can even have Quicken print checks for you.

Using similar transaction entry techniques, Quicken can also keep track of credit card accounts. You enter transactions as you make them or at month's end when you receive your statement and pay your bill. Quicken keeps track of balances and offers you an easy way to monitor what you used your credit card to buy. It also enables you to keep an eye on how much your credit cards cost you in terms of finance charges and other fees.

Getting Started

Before you can use Quicken to track bank and credit card transactions, you should prepare by creating the necessary accounts and having a good idea of how recording transactions works. In this section, I provide an overview of the account types, along with examples of transactions you might make. I also provide detailed step-by-step instructions for creating cash flow accounts.

Overview of Accounts and Transactions

Most of the transactions you track with Quicken will involve one or more of its banking and cash accounts. Here's a closer look at each account type, along with some transaction examples. As you read about these accounts, imagine how they might apply to your financial situation.

Bank Accounts

Quicken offers two types of accounts that you can use to track the money you have in a bank:

- **Checking** accounts include check writing privileges. These accounts usually have a lot of activity, with deposits to increase the account balance and checks that decrease the account balance.

- **Savings** accounts are for your savings. These accounts usually don't have as much activity as checking accounts. You can use a savings account to track the balance in a certificate of deposit (CD), holiday savings club, or similar savings account.

Generally speaking, bank account transactions can be broken down into three broad categories: payments, deposits, and transfers.

Payments   Payments are cash outflows. Here are some examples:

- You write a check to pay your electric bill.
- You withdraw money from your savings account to buy a gift for your mother.
- You use your ATM card to withdraw spending money from a bank account.
- You use your debit card to buy groceries.
- You pay a monthly checking account fee.

Deposits   Deposits are cash inflows. Here are some examples:

- You deposit your paycheck in your checking account.
- You sell your old computer and deposit the proceeds in your savings account.
- Your paycheck or Social Security check is deposited into your bank account as a direct deposit.
- You earn interest on your savings account.

Transfers   A transfer is a movement of funds from one account to another. Here are some examples:

- You transfer money from an interest-bearing savings account to your checking account when you're ready to pay your bills.
- You transfer money from a money market account to your home equity line of credit account to reduce its balance.

Credit Card Accounts

Credit card accounts track money you owe, not money you own. Some credit cards, such as MasterCard, Visa, American Express, and Discover, can be used in most stores that accept credit cards. Other credit cards, such as Macy's, Dillards, and Texaco, can only be used in certain stores. But they all have one thing in common: if there's a balance, it's usually because you owe the credit card company money.

Credit card account transactions can also be broken down into two categories: charges and payments.

Charges   Charges result when you use your credit card to buy something or the credit card company charges a fee for services. Here are some examples:

- You use your Visa card to buy a new computer.
- You use your Discover card to pay for a hotel stay.
- You use your Texaco card to fill the gas tank on your boat at the marina.

- A finance charge based on your account balance is added to your Macy's bill at month's end.
- A late fee is added to your MasterCard bill because you didn't pay the previous month's bill on time.
- A fee is added to your American Express bill for annual membership dues.

The opposite of a charge is a *credit*. Think of it as a negative charge; don't confuse it with a payment. Here are two examples:

- You return the sweater you bought with your American Express card to the store you bought it from.
- In reviewing your MasterCard bill, you discover that a merchant charged you in error, and you arrange to have the incorrect charge removed.

Payments   Payments are amounts you send to a credit card company to reduce your balance. Here are three examples:

- You pay the minimum amount due on your Visa card.
- You pay $150 toward the balance on your Macy's card.
- You pay the balance on your American Express card.

Cash Accounts

Quicken also offers cash accounts for tracking cash expenditures. For example, you might create an account called My Wallet or Spending Money and use it to keep track of the cash you have on hand. Cash accounts are like bank accounts, but there's no bank. The money is in your wallet, your pocket, or the old coffee can on the windowsill.

Cash accounts have two types of transactions: receive and spend.

Receive   When you receive cash, you increase the amount of cash you have on hand. Here are some examples:

- You withdraw cash from the bank for weekly spending money.
- You sell your *National Geographic* magazine collection for cash at a garage sale.
- You get a twenty-dollar bill in a birthday card from your grandmother.

Spend   When you spend cash, you reduce your cash balance. Here are some examples:

- You buy coffee and a newspaper and pay a bridge toll on your way to work.
- You give your son his allowance.
- You put a twenty-dollar bill in the birthday card you send to your granddaughter.

Creating Cash Flow Accounts

In Chapter 3, I briefly discuss how to use the Account Setup dialog to create new Quicken accounts. Here are the details for creating each type of Cash Flow Center account.

Creating Checking or Savings Accounts

The steps for creating a checking or savings account are virtually the same, so I'll just go through the process for one type of account—a checking account.

Begin by displaying the Account Setup dialog as discussed in Chapter 2 or 3. The first screen should look like this:

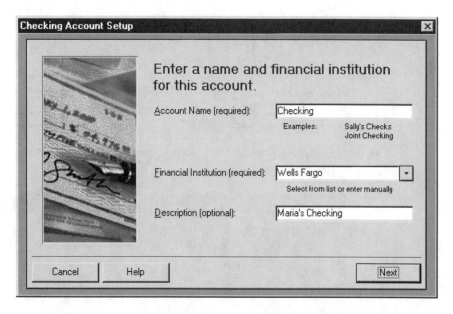

Enter a name for the account in the Account Name box. Then enter your bank's name in the Financial Institution box. You can use the drop-down list to select a name or you can enter a name by typing it in. As you type, Quicken attempts to fill in a name from its list. Make sure the bank name is correct, especially if the account is enabled for online account services. You can also enter a description for the account in the Description box. When you're finished, click Next.

If you entered the name of a bank that wasn't in the Financial Institution drop-down list, Quicken displays a dialog like the one shown next. It lists bank names that are similar to what you typed. (For this example, I typed in "Well Fargo" rather than "Wells Fargo.") If your bank is in the list, select the top option button and click the bank name. If it isn't, select the bottom option button and make sure the correct name is entered in the box beneath it. Then click Next.

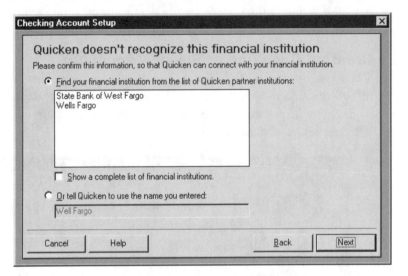

As shown next, Quicken prompts you to enter your bank account ending statement date and balance. You have three options:

- Enter the ending statement date and balance from your most recent bank statement. This is the quickest, accurate way to create an account. The statement date becomes your account's start date and you will only enter transactions that were made after that date or that did not clear that bank statement.

- Enter the ending statement date and balance from an earlier bank statement. This is also an accurate way to create the account, but it will require that you play "catch up" to enter more transactions into Quicken. (If you use online account services, however, you may be able to have several months' worth of data entered automatically for you; I explain how in Chapter 6.)

- Enter today's date and **0** in the dialog. This is fast, but it certainly isn't accurate. You'll eventually have to either adjust the beginning balance for the account or use the reconciliation feature to create an adjusting entry after your first reconciliation.

When you click the Done button in the dialog, one of two things will happen:

- If the bank you entered in the first screen does not offer online account services, the Account Setup dialog disappears and the account register for the account appears (refer to Figure 5-1 later in this chapter).

- If the bank you entered in the first screen offers online account services, one of the following dialogs appears. Use the dialog to set up for online account services; I explain how in Chapter 6. When you are finished, the account register for the account appears (refer to Figure 5-1 later in this chapter).

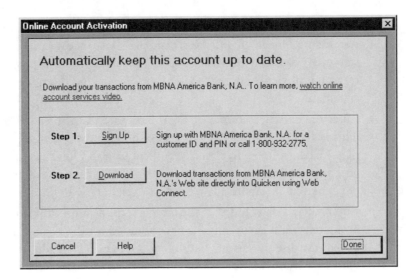

Tips for Cash Flow Accounts

Here are a few additional things to keep in mind when creating accounts for the Cash Flow Center:

- Give each account a name that clearly identifies it. For example, if you have two checking accounts, don't name them "Checking 1" and "Checking 2." Instead, include the bank name (such as "USA Bank Checking") or account purpose (such as "Joint Checking") in the account name. This prevents you from accidentally entering a transaction in the wrong account register.

- If you create a bank or credit card account with a balance date and amount from a bank statement—the recommended way—be careful not to enter transactions that already appear on that statement or in previous statements.

- Entering your credit limit for a credit card account enables Quicken to alert you when you get close to (or exceed) your limit.

- Using a cash account to track every penny you spend, from the cup of coffee you buy at work in the morning to the quart of milk you pick up on your way home that evening, isn't for everyone. You may prefer to track only large cash inflows or outflows and record the rest as miscellaneous expenses.

Creating a Credit Card Account

Creating a credit card account is very similar to creating a checking or savings account, so you can follow the instructions in the previous section to get the job done. Along the way, Quicken will prompt you to enter your credit limit. If the account has one—most do—enter it. When you click Done in the last screen, Quicken will either display the new account's register or prompt you to set up online account services. I explain how to set up online account service features in Chapter 6.

Creating a Cash Account

Creating a cash account is also similar to creating a checking or savings account, but Quicken doesn't prompt you to enter your financial institution. Unless you plan to enter transactions you made before you created the account, you'll probably use today's date and the contents of your wallet or pocket as the starting balance information.

Entering Transactions

To make the most of Quicken, you must enter transactions for the accounts you want to track. You can do this manually, as discussed in this chapter, or, if the account can be enabled for online account services, automatically via download, as discussed in Chapter 6. Either way, you'll need to know how to enter transactions for Cash Flow accounts.

There are different ways to enter transactions, based on the type of transaction you want to enter:

- Use *registers* to record virtually any type of transaction, including manual checks, bank account payments and deposits, credit card charges and payments, and cash receipts and spending.
- Use the *Write Checks window* to record checks to be printed by Quicken.
- Enter *transfers* to transfer money from one account to another.

Using Account Registers

Quicken's account registers offer a standard way to enter all kinds of transactions. As the name suggests, these electronic account registers are very similar to the paper checking account register that comes with your checks.

To open a register, click its name in the account bar or choose its name from the Cash Flow Accounts submenu under the Cash Flow menu. The account window appears. If necessary, click the Register tab to display the account register window (see Figure 5-1). Use it to enter and record transactions.

Checking	Register	Overview							

Delete Find Transfer Reconcile Write Checks Set Up Online   Report ▾ Options ▾ How Do I ▾

Date	Num	Payee/Category/Memo	Payment		Clr	Deposit		Balance	
6/15/2002	ATM	Withdrawal	50	00				2,643	55
		[Pocket Money]							
6/15/2002	2016	Double D Western World	125	62				2,517	93
		Horse Expenses Feed							
6/18/2002	2017	APS	97	25				2,420	68
		Utilities:Gas & Elect							
6/20/2002	DEP	Advisor Publications				350	00	2,770	68
		Writing Income May Article							
6/21/2002	TXFR	Transfer	500	00				2,270	68
		[Money Market]							
6/25/2002	2018	Deuce Hardware	87	96				2,182	72
		Home Repair Roof Repair Stuff							
6/28/2002 ▦	Num	Payee	Payment			Deposit			
		Category Memo			Enter	Edit ▾		Split	▾

Ending Balance: 2,182.72

Bills and Scheduled Transactions				Options ▾
Due	Status	Name/Payee	Amount	Action
Schedule These?				
7/18/2002		APS	-97.25	Yes No

Show Full List   Add a Transaction   Set Up Paycheck

Download transactions from Wells Fargo!

Figure 5-1 • The account register window for a checking account

Overview of the Account Register

Before I begin my discussion of entry techniques, let's take a closer look at the account register window in Figure 5-1.

Scheduled Transactions   If the account has scheduled transactions, a list of those transactions may appear in the bottom half of the window, as shown in Figure 5-1. You can hide the list by choosing Close from the Options pop-up menu at the top of the Bills And Scheduled Transactions area. You can show the list by choosing View Scheduled Transactions from the Options menu in the Register window's button bar. I tell you more about scheduled transactions in Chapter 7.

Downloaded Transactions   If the account is enabled for transaction download, an online account service feature, and you have downloaded transactions, a list of those transactions may appear in the bottom half of the register window. I explain how to work with this split window in Chapter 6.

The Button Bar   This window's button bar includes a number of buttons and menus for working with transactions and changing the window's view:

- **Delete** deletes the selected transaction. When you click this button, a dialog appears to confirm that you really do want to delete the transaction.
- **Find** enables you to search for transactions based on a variety of criteria.
- **Transfer** enables you to create a transfer transaction.
- **Reconcile** enables you to reconcile the account.
- **Write Checks** displays the Write Checks window, which you can use to write checks to be printed from Quicken.
- **Set Up Online** displays the Online Account Activation dialog (shown earlier) so you can enable online account services, if they are available for the account.
- **Report** displays a menu of reports that are available for the selected transaction. Use commands to generate reports right from within the account register window. I tell you more about Quicken's reporting features in Chapter 9.
- **Options** displays a menu with options for changing the window's view and sorting transactions. The One-Line Display command collapses register entries so they show only one line per transaction. The View commands determine what information appears in the register window. The Register Options command opens the Register Options dialog, which you can use to customize the way account registers look and work; I tell you more about customizing Quicken in Appendix B.
- **How Do I** displays a menu of Help topics related to the account register window.

Basic Entry Techniques

To enter a transaction, begin by clicking in the first empty line at the end of the account register window (refer to Figure 5-1). This activates a new, blank transaction. You can then enter transaction information into each field and press ENTER to complete the transaction.

Although the entry process is pretty straightforward, here are a few things to keep in mind when entering transactions.

Advancing from Field to Field   To move from one text box or *field* to another when entering transactions, you can either click in the next field's text box or press the TAB key. Pressing TAB is usually quicker.

Using Buttons   Buttons appear when certain fields are active:

- When the Date field is active, a calendar icon appears. You can click it to display a calendar and then click calendar buttons to view and enter a date.
- When the Payment or Deposit field is active, a calculator icon appears. You can click it to use a calculator and enter calculated results.

Using the Num Field   The Num field is where you enter a transaction number or type. You can enter any number you like or use the drop-down list (shown next) to display a list of standard entries; click an option to enter it for the transaction. You can also press the + or − key on the keyboard to increment or decrement the check number while the Num field is active.

- **Next Check Num** automatically increments the most recently entered check number and enters the resulting number in the Num field.
- **ATM** is for ATM transactions. You may also want to use it for debit or check card transactions.
- **Deposit** is for deposits.
- **Print Check** is for transactions for which you want Quicken to print a check. Quicken automatically enters the check number when the check is printed.
- **Send Online Payment** is for online payments. This option only appears when online payment is enabled for the account. I tell you about paying bills online in Chapter 6.
- **Online Transfer** is for online transfers of funds from one account to another. This option only appears when online payment is enabled for the account. I tell you about online banking in Chapter 6.

- **Transfer** is for a transfer of funds from one account to another.
- **EFT**, which stands for Electronic Funds Transfer, is for direct deposits and similar transactions.

QuickFill As you start to enter the name of a payee or payer that is already in your Quicken data file, Quicken may fill in the entire name and most recent transaction for you. This is Quicken's QuickFill feature, which I tell you more about in Chapter 7.

Automatic Categorization After entering a payee for the first time, Quicken may fill in the category for you. This is Quicken's automatic categorization feature, which enters categories based on thousands of payee names programmed into it. You'll find that in most cases, Quicken assigns an appropriate category. But you can change the category if you like and, from that point on, Quicken's QuickFill feature will use the category you assign for future transactions to that payee. Chapter 7 provides more information about QuickFill.

Entering New Categories If you enter a category that does not exist in the Category List, Quicken displays the New Category dialog, shown next, which offers to create the category for you. Click Yes to use the Set Up Category dialog to create a new category or click No to return to the register and enter a different category. If you turn off the Prompt Before Creating New Categories check box in the New Category dialog, Quicken will automatically display the Set Up Category dialog every time you enter a category that does not exist in the Category List. I explain how to create categories in Chapter 3.

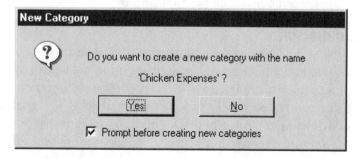

Entering Multiple Categories To enter more than one category for a transaction, click the Split button. I explain how to enter transactions with splits a little later in this chapter.

Entering Subcategories   When you choose a subcategory from the Category field's drop-down list, Quicken automatically enters the subcategory's parent category name, followed by a colon character (:) and the subcategory name. To type in a subcategory, use the same notation. Here's what it might look like in a register entry:

6/28/2002	2008	Agnew Automotive	425	97			1,601	87
		Auto:Service						

Entering Memos   You can enter a brief memo about the transaction in the field to the right of the Category field. This memo can help you remember what a transaction is for.

Using Transaction Buttons   As shown in Figure 5-1, two buttons and a menu appear on the second line for the active transaction. You can use these buttons to work with the transaction:

- **Enter** enters the transaction into the account register. If Quicken's sound option is turned on, you should hear a cash register *ch-ching* sound when you click it. (You can turn Quicken sounds on or off in the General Options dialog, which I discuss in Appendix B.)
- **Edit** displays a menu of editing options for the transactions. I discuss some of the Edit menu's commands later in this chapter.
- **Split** opens the Split Transaction Window for the transaction. I explain how to enter a transaction with splits next.

Using Splits

A *split* is a transaction with more than one category. For example, suppose you pay one utility bill for two categories of utilities—electricity and water. If you want to track each of these two expenses separately, you can use a split to record each category's portion of the payment you make. This enables you to keep good records without writing multiple checks to the same payee.

To record a transaction with a split, click the Split button in the account register or Write Checks window when entering the transaction. The Split Transaction window, which is shown next, appears. Click in the first blank line and select a category. If desired, enter a memo for the category in the Memo field. Then enter the amount for that category in the Amount field. Repeat this process for each category you want to include in the transaction. Here's what the Split Transaction window might look like with two categories entered:

	Category	Memo	Amount
1.	Utilities:Gas & Electric	Electricity	97 42
2.	Utilities:Water	Water	24 97
3.			
4.			
5.			
6.			
7.			
8.			
9.			
10.			
11.			
12.			
13.			
14.			
15.			
16.			

If you entered a transaction amount before clicking the Split button, you can monitor the Remainder and Transaction Total values in the Split Transaction window to make sure you've accounted for the entire transaction amount. If you entered an incorrect amount, you can click the Adjust button to adjust the transaction amount to match the Split Total.

When you're finished entering transaction categories, click OK or press ENTER. If you left the transaction amount empty before clicking the Split button, a dialog appears, asking if you want to record the transaction as a payment or deposit. Select the appropriate option and click OK.

As shown next, the word *Split* appears in the Category field for the transaction in the account register window:

Two buttons appear beside the category field when you activate a transaction with a split:

- The green check mark displays the Split Transaction window so you can review and edit the transaction.
- The red X clears all lines from the split. Use this option with care—it permanently removes all category information from the transaction.

Using Classes

As discussed in Chapter 3, a class is an optional identifier for specifying what a transaction applies to. To include a class in a transaction, enter a slash (/) followed by the class name after the category. Here's an example in the register window:

6/28/2002	2009	Dan The Man Home Repairs	158 97			1,442 90
		Home Repair/House				

If you enter a class name that is not on the Class List, Quicken displays the Set Up Class window so you can create the class on the fly. I explain how to create classes in Chapter 3.

Tracking Credit Cards with Quicken

Tracking bank account transactions and balances is just one part of using Quicken. It's also a great tool for tracking credit cards. Knowing how much you owe on your credit cards helps you maintain a clear picture of your financial situation.

How you use Quicken to track your credit cards depends on how accurate you want your financial records to be and how much effort you're willing to spend keeping Quicken up to date.

Credit Card Tracking Techniques

You can use either of two techniques for paying credit card bills and monitoring credit card balances with Quicken:

- Use your checking account register or the Write Checks window to record amounts paid to each credit card company. Although this does track the amounts you pay, it doesn't track how much you owe or the individual charges.
- Use a credit card account register to record credit card expenditures and payments. This takes a bit more effort on your part, but it tracks how much you owe and what you bought.

In my opinion, it's worth the extra effort to track your credit card expenditures and balances in individual credit card accounts. And if you utilize Quicken's transaction download feature for your credit card accounts, as I discuss in Chapter 6, it won't take much time or effort to get the job done.

Recording Transactions

You can use two strategies for recording transactions in credit card accounts. Choosing the strategy that's right for you makes the job easier to handle.

Enter as You Spend

One strategy is to enter transactions as you spend. To do this, you must collect your credit card receipts—which might be something you already do. Don't forget to jot down the totals for any telephone and online shopping you do. Then, every day or every few days, sit down with Quicken and enter the transactions.

While this strategy requires you to stay on top of things, it offers two main benefits:

- Your Quicken credit card registers always indicate what you owe to credit card companies. This prevents unpleasant surprises at month-end or at the checkout counter when you're told you've reached your limit. It also enables you to use the alerts feature to track credit card balances; I tell you about that in Chapter 9.
- At month-end, you don't have to spend a lot of time entering big batches of transactions. All (or at least most) of them should already be entered.

I'll be the first to admit that I've never been able to use this strategy. I just don't like holding on to all those pieces of paper. (Of course, since signing up for transaction download, all this information is entered automatically for me.)

Enter When You Pay

The other strategy, which you may find better for you, is to enter transactions when you get your monthly statement. With this strategy, when you open your credit card statement, you'll spend some time sitting in front of your computer with Quicken to enter each transaction. If there aren't many, this isn't a big deal. But it could take some time if there are many transactions.

Of course, the main benefit of this strategy is that you don't have to collect credit card receipts and spend time throughout the month entering your transactions. But you still have to enter them! This is the method I use for the one credit card I have that I cannot access online yet.

Entering Credit Card Transactions

Entering credit card transactions isn't very different from entering checking account or savings account transactions. Here are a few examples, all of which are illustrated in Figure 5-2.

Entering Individual Charges   Open the account register for the credit card account. Then enter the charge transaction, using the name of the merchant that accepted the charge as the payee name. You can leave the Ref box empty.

Credit : AOPA MasterCard		Register	Overview						

Delete   Find   Transfer   Reconcile   Set Up Online   Report ▾   Options ▾   How Do I ▾

Date	Ref	Payee/Category/Memo		Charge		Clr	Payment	Balance	
5/20/2002		Opening Balance		415	22	R		415	22
		[AOPA MasterCard]							
6/12/2002		Wickenburg Municipal Airport		32	50			447	72
		Recreation	Fuel for 39L						
6/18/2002		Guidance Helicopters		66	20			513	92
		Education	Books						
6/20/2002		MBNA		6	84			520	76
		Interest Exp							
6/22/2002		Guidance Helicopters					21 50	499	26
		Education	Returned Book						
6/28/2002		MBNA America					200 00	299	26
		[Checking]							
5/28/2002	Ref	Payee		Charge			Payment		
		Category	Memo				Enter Edit ▾ Split		

	Credit Remaining:	14,700.74	Ending Balance:	299.26

Figure 5-2 • Typical credit card account transactions

Entering Credits   Enter the transaction just as if it were a charge, but put the amount of the credit in the Payment box. This subtracts it from your account balance.

Entering Finance Charges   In the credit card account register, enter the name of the credit card company as the payee and the amount of the finance charge as a charge. You can use the Interest Exp category for the transaction.

Entering Payments   In the account register for your checking account or in the Write Checks window, enter a payment transaction with the credit card company name in the Payee box. Enter the credit card account name in the Category text box; you should find it as a transfer account at the bottom of the Category drop-down list that appears when you activate the field. The checking account register transaction should look like the one shown next. Figure 5-2 shows what this transaction looks like in the credit card account register.

6/28/2002	2010	MBNA America	200 00		1,242 90
		[AOPA MasterCard]			

Entering Cash Transactions

Although Quicken enables you to keep track of cash transactions through the use of a cash account, not everyone does. The reason: most people make many small

Quicken Quick Tip

Personally, I don't track all cash transactions. I only track expenditures that are large or tax deductible. You may want to do the same. If so, you still need to set up a cash account, but you don't need to record every transaction. That's what I do; Figure 5-3 shows an example.

cash transactions every day. Is it worth tracking every penny you spend? That's something you need to decide.

Cash Receipts   Cash receipts may come from using your ATM card, cashing a check, or getting cash from some other source. If the cash comes from one of your other accounts through an ATM or check transaction, when you record that transaction, use your cash account as the transfer in the Category field. That increases your cash balance. Here's what the transaction might look like in your checking account:

6/5/2002	ATM	Withdrawal		50	00			2,123	77
		[Pocket Money]							

Important Cash Expenditures   In your cash account, record large, tax-deductible, or other important cash expenditures like any other transaction. Be sure to assign the correct category.

Other Cash Expenditures   Throughout the week, you may spend fifty cents for a newspaper, a dollar for a cup of coffee, and about twelve dollars for lunch at

Cash : Pocket Money   Register   Overview

Delete   Find   Transfer   Update Balance   Report ▾   Options ▾   How Do I ▾

Date	Ref	Payee/Category/Memo		Spend		Clr	Receive	Balance	
6/1/2002		Opening Balance					55 00	55	00
		[Pocket Money]							
6/5/2002		Withdrawal					50 00	105	00
		[Checking]							
6/12/2002		Anita's Cocina		23	54			81	46
		Dining	Lunch with Patty						
6/15/2002		Radio House		28	52			52	94
		Computer	CD-R discs						
6/25/2002		Miscellaneous Cash Expenditures		12	94			40	00
		Misc							
3/25/2002 ▦	Ref	Payee		Spend			Receive		
		Category	Memo				Enter Edit ▾ Split		

Figure 5-3 • Typical cash account transactions

your favorite hamburger joint. Recording transactions like these can be tedious, so don't bother if you don't want to. Instead, at the end of the week, compare your cash on hand to the balance in your cash account register. Then enter a transaction to record the difference as an expenditure. You can use the Misc category and put anything you like in the Payee field.

Writing Checks

Quicken's Write Checks window uses a basic check-like interface to record checks. You enter the same information that you would write on an actual check. You then tell Quicken to print the check based on the information you entered. (I explain how to print checks later in this chapter.)

To open the Write Checks window, choose Banking | Write Checks or press CTRL-W. The Write Checks window, which is shown in Figure 5-4, appears. If necessary, choose the name of the account for which you want to write checks from the pop-up menu in the document window's title bar. Then enter the necessary information for a check and record the transaction.

Overview of the Write Checks Window

The Write Checks window (refer to Figure 5-4) is a busy place, with a lot of information and options. Before I explain how to use it to enter transactions, let's take a look at its options.

The Button Bar   The Write Checks window's button bar includes a number of buttons and menus for working with transactions and changing the window's view:

- **Delete** deletes the selected transaction. When you click this button, a dialog appears to confirm that you really do want to delete the transaction.
- **Find** enables you to search for transactions based on a variety of criteria.
- **Edit** is a menu full of commands for creating, editing, and working with transactions. I discuss many of these commands later in this chapter.
- **Order Checks** enables you to order check stock that is compatible with Quicken.
- **Payments** displays the Scheduled Transactions List, which I discuss in Chapter 7.
- **Payees** displays the Online Payee List, which I cover in Chapter 6.
- **Report** displays a menu of reports that are available for the selected transaction. Use commands to generate reports right from within the Write Checks window. I tell you more about Quicken's reporting features in Chapter 9.

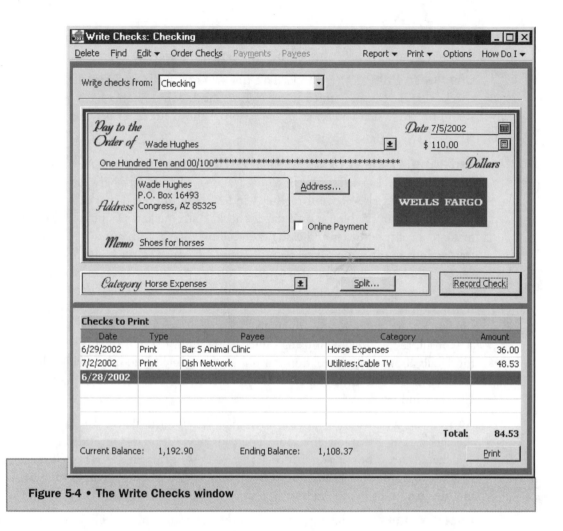

Figure 5-4 • The Write Checks window

- **Print** enables you to print checks.
- **Options** displays the Check Options dialog, which you can use to customize the way the Write Checks window looks and works; I tell you more about customizing Quicken in Appendix B.
- **How Do I** displays a menu of Help topics related to the Write Checks window.

Account List   The Write Checks From drop-down list near the top of the window displays a list of accounts from which you can write checks. Be sure to choose the correct account from the list before entering check information.

Check Form   The middle of the window displays a form that looks and works a lot like a paper check. This is where you enter transaction information.

Checks To Print   The Checks To Print area of the window lists all of the checks that have been entered in the Write Checks window that have not yet been printed. When you enter a transaction in the Write Checks window, it is added to this list.

Entering Transactions in the Write Checks Window

The Write Checks window (refer to Figure 5-4) is like a cross between a paper check and Quicken's account register window. You fill in the check form like you would fill in the blanks on a paper check. But Quicken's QuickFill feature makes data entry quicker and easier by recalling entry information from similar transactions to the same payee, and its Auto-Categorize feature can automatically "guess" the category for many new transactions. In addition, you must enter a valid Quicken category in the Category field, just like you would when entering a transaction in the account register. Clicking the Record Check button completes the transaction and adds it to the Checks To Print list.

Consult the section about using Quicken's account registers to enter transactions for details about the information that should be entered into most fields. Here are a few additional things to consider when entering transactions in the Write Checks window:

Addresses on Checks   If you enter an address on the check, you can mail the check using a window envelope. The address is automatically added to the Quicken Address Book. You can click the Address button in the Write Checks window to display the Edit Address Book Record dialog, which you can use to modify an address in the Address Book.

Check Memos   If you enter a note on the memo line of a check, it might be visible if you mail the check in a window envelope.

Online Payments   An Online Payment check box appears in the Write Check window if online payment is enabled for the account for which you are writing a check. I tell you about online payments in Chapter 6.

Transferring Money

You can also record the transfer of funds from one account to another. You might find this feature especially useful for recording telephone or ATM transfers.

Using the Transfer Dialog

One way to record a transfer is with the Transfer dialog. Open the account register window for one of the accounts involved in the transfer transaction and click the Transfer button on the button bar. The Transfer dialog, which is illustrated next, appears. Choose the source and destination accounts from the drop-down lists, enter a transaction date and amount, and click OK.

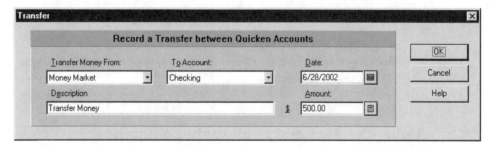

Recording a Transfer in the Account Register Window

The Transfer dialog isn't the only way to record a transfer. You can also record a transfer in the account register window of either the source or destination account. When you choose Transfer (TXFR) from the Num drop-down list, the Category drop-down list displays only transfer accounts. Choose the other transfer account from the list and complete the transaction.

The following illustrations show a transfer from a money market account to a checking account. Here's what the money market account transaction looks like:

6/28/2002	TXFR	Transfer Money	500	00				3,782	97
		[Checking]							

And here's what the corresponding checking account transaction looks like:

6/28/2002	TXFR	Transfer Money			500	00		2,623	77
		[Money Market]							

Working with Existing Transactions

So far, this chapter has concentrated on entering transactions. What do you do when you need to modify a transaction you already recorded? That's what this section is all about.

Searching for Transactions

Quicken includes four commands to help you locate and work with transactions:

- **Find** enables you to search for transactions in the active account based on any field.
- **Find Again** searches for transactions matching the previously entered Find criteria.
- **Find/Replace** enables you to find transactions based on any field and replace any field of the found transactions.
- **Recategorize** enables you to find transactions for a specific category and replace the category.

The following sections take a closer look at each of these commands.

Using the Find and Find Again Commands

To use the Find command, begin by opening the account register or Write Checks window for the account that you want to search. Then choose Edit | Find & Replace | Find, click the Find button on the window's button bar, or press CTRL-F. The Quicken Find dialog, which is illustrated next, appears.

Start by choosing an option from the Search drop-down list, which includes all register fields for a transaction. Then choose a Match If option to indicate how the search criteria should be matched. Enter the search criteria in the Find box. If you enter a space in the Find box, Quicken searches for entries for which

Quicken Quick Tip

You might find it helpful to use the Sort options (on the Options menu in the account register window's button bar) to change the sort order of transactions. For example, sorting by check number groups the transactions by the Num field, making it easy to find transactions by number or type. You can quickly move to a specific date or transaction number by dragging the scroll box. The QuickScroll feature displays the date and number of the transaction that will appear when you release the scroll box.

the Search field is blank; this is a great way to find uncategorized transactions. To search backwards (relative to the currently selected transaction), turn on the Search Backwards check box.

After setting up the search, if you click the Find button, Quicken selects the first match found in the window. You can then click the Find button again to find the next match. If you click the Find All button, Quicken displays the Quicken Find window, which lists all the matches it found. You can double-click a match to view it in the account register window.

The Find Again command uses the criteria set up in the Quicken Find dialog, which Quicken remembers throughout your Quicken session. Later, to conduct the same search, you can choose Edit | Find & Replace | Find Next, or press SHIFT-CTRL-F.

Using the Find/Replace Command

The Find/Replace command works throughout Quicken, not just with the active account register or Write Checks window. To use it, choose Edit | Find & Replace | Find/Replace. The Find and Replace dialog appears. The top part of the dialog looks and works very much like the Quicken Find dialog. You can turn on the Show Matches In Split check box if you want Quicken to find all matches, including those that appear in splits.

Once you set up the search and click the Find All button, a list of matches appears in the bottom half of the dialog, as shown next. Set options in the Replace and With boxes. Then click beside each found item you want to change to place a green check mark beside it. Click Replace to replace all checked items with the replacement options you specified. A dialog confirms that the replacement has been made.

Using the Recategorize Command

The Recategorize command works like the Find/Replace command, but it finds and replaces only categories. For example, suppose you were using the Misc category a little more often than you should, and you know that some transactions could be recategorized. You can use the Recategorize command to find transactions with the Misc category and then change some or all of them to a more appropriate category.

Choose Edit | Find & Replace | Recategorize to display the Recategorize dialog. Start by using the Find menu on the dialog's button bar to choose the type of transaction you want to find: Transactions (entered transactions), Memorized Transactions, or Scheduled Transactions. Then choose a category from the Search Category drop-down list and click Find All. A list of matches appears in the Recategorize dialog, as shown next. Select the transactions for which you want to change the category, choose a new category, and replace the categories for selected transactions all at once.

Changing Transactions

Quicken enables you to change a transaction at any time—even after it has been cleared. This makes it possible to correct errors in any transaction you have entered.

If all you want to do is change one of the fields in the transaction—such as the category, date, or number—simply find the transaction in the appropriate account register, make changes as desired, and click the Enter button to record them.

The Edit drop-down menu (shown next) that appears in the account register window for the currently selected transaction offers other options for working with a selected transaction:

- **Restore Transaction** enables you to change a transaction back to the way it was before you started changing it. This option is only available if you have made changes to the selected transaction.
- **New Transaction** enables you to create a new transaction for the account. This does not affect the currently selected transaction.
- **Insert Transaction** enables you to insert a transaction before the selected transaction in the account register. This does not affect the currently selected transaction.
- **Delete Transaction** deletes the selected transaction. This is the same as clicking the Delete button in the button bar. Remember, deleting a transaction removes the transaction from the Quicken data file, thus changing the account balance and category activity.
- **Memorize Transaction** tells Quicken to add the selected transaction to its list of memorized transactions. Memorized transactions are used for the QuickFill feature, which I discuss in Chapter 7.

- **Schedule Transaction** enables you to schedule the transaction for a future date or to set up the transaction as a recurring transaction. I tell you more about scheduling transactions in Chapter 7.
- **Void Transaction** marks the selected transaction as void. This reverses the effect of the transaction on the account balance and category activity without actually deleting the transaction.
- **Copy Transaction** copies the selected transaction.
- **Paste Transaction** pastes the last-copied transaction into the current account register. This option is only available after a transaction has been copied. You might want to copy a transaction to paste it into another register if you realize that you entered it in the wrong register. You can then go back and delete the original transaction.
- **Go To Transfer** displays the selected transaction in the account register for the other part of a transfer. For example, if the selected transaction involves the checking and savings accounts and you are viewing it in the checking account register, choosing the Go To Transfer command displays the same transaction in the savings account register. This command is only available if the selected transaction includes a transfer.
- **Go To A Specific Date** enables you to move to a different date within the register. This does not affect the currently selected transaction.

Printing Checks

Quicken's capability to print checks enables you to create accurate, legible, professional-looking checks without picking up a pen (or a typewriter). In this section, I explain how to print the checks you enter in the Write Checks window, discussed earlier in this chapter.

Getting the Right Checks

Before you can print checks from Quicken, you must obtain compatible check stock. Quicken supports checks in a number of different styles:

- **Voucher checks** pair each check with a similarly sized voucher form. When you print on a voucher check, the transaction category information, including splits and classes, can be printed on the voucher part.

- **Wallet checks** pair each check with a stub. When you print on a wallet check, the transaction information is printed on the stub.
- **Standard checks** print just checks. There's no voucher or stub.

In addition to these styles, you can get the checks in two different formats for your printer:

- **Sheet-fed** or **page-oriented checks** are for laser and inkjet printers.
- **Continuous checks** are for pin-feed printers.

A catalog and order form for checks may have come with your copy of Quicken. You can use it to order checks. If you have an Internet connection, you can order checks online from within Quicken by choosing Cash Flow | Quicken Services | Order Checks & Supplies, or by clicking the Order Checks button in the button bar of the Write Checks window (see Figure 5-4).

Setting Up

Quicken must also be set up to print the kind of checks you purchased. You do this once, and Quicken remembers the settings.

Choose File | Printer Setup | For Printing Checks to display the Check Printer Setup dialog shown here. Use the drop-down lists and option buttons to specify settings for your printer and check stock. Here are a few things to keep in mind when making settings in this dialog.

Partial Page Printing Options

If you select the Page-Oriented option and either Standard or Wallet checks in the Check Printer Setup dialog, you can also set options for Partial Page Printing Style. This enables you to set up the printer for situations when you're not printing an entire page of checks.

- **Edge** is for inserting the page against one side of the feeder. The left or right edge of the checks enters the feeder first.
- **Centered** is for centering the page in the feeder. The left or right edge of the checks enters the feeder first.
- **Portrait** is also for centering the page in the feeder, but in this case, the top edge of each check enters the feeder first.

If your printer supports multiple feed trays, you can also set the source tray for partial and full pages by choosing options from the Partial Page Source and Full Page Source drop-down lists.

Continuous Printing Options

If you select the Continuous option and either Standard or Wallet checks in the Check Printer Setup dialog, the dialog changes to offer two Continuous options:

- **Bypass The Driver** should be turned on for a continuous printer that skips checks or prints nothing.
- **Use Low Starting Position** should be turned on for a continuous printer that cuts the date or logo off your checks.

Checking the Settings for Page-Oriented Checks

If you're using page-oriented checks, you can check your settings by printing a sample page on plain paper. Here's how:

1. Click the Align button in the Check Printer Setup dialog.
2. In the Align Checks dialog that appears, click the Full Page Of Checks button.
3. In the Fine Alignment dialog, click the Print Sample button.
4. When the sample emerges from your printer, hold it up to the light with a sheet of check stock behind it. The sample should line up with the check.
5. If the sample does not line up properly with the check stock, set Vertical and/or Horizontal adjustment values in the Fine Alignment dialog. Then repeat steps 3 through 5 until the alignment is correct.
6. Click OK in each dialog to accept your settings and close it.

Printing

Once setup is complete, you're ready to print checks. Insert the check stock in your printer. Then choose File | Print Checks, or click the Print button in the Write Checks window. The Select Checks To Print dialog, which is shown next, appears. Enter the number of the first check that will be printed in the First Check Number box. Then set other options as desired. If you select the Selected Checks option, you can click the Choose button to display a list of checks and check off the ones you want to print. Click Done in that window to return to the Select Checks To Print dialog.

When you click Print First or OK, Quicken sends the print job to your printer. It then displays a dialog asking if the checks printed correctly. You have two options:

- If all checks printed fine, just click OK.
- If there was a problem printing the checks, enter the number of the first check that was misprinted and then click OK. You can then go back to the Select Checks To Print dialog and try again.

Using Online Banking Features

Chapter 6

In this Chapter:

- *Benefits and costs of online banking*

- *Setting up Online Account Services*

- *Downloading and comparing transactions*

- *Setting up payees*

- *Processing online payments and transfers*

- *Entering transactions on the Web*

- *Updating your Quicken accounts on Quicken.com*

Life can be pretty hectic sometimes—too hectic to keep track of your bank accounts, pay bills before they're overdue, and buy stamps to mail your bills. Quicken's Online Account Services enable you to do most (if not all) of your banking from the comfort of your own home so banking can be a lot less of a chore. There are several features that can be used separately or together:

- **Transaction Download** enables you to download bank and credit card account activity and transfer money online between accounts.
- **Online Payment** enables you to pay bills online, without manually writing or mailing a check. (Quicken Bill Pay offers the features of Online Payment, even if your bank does not support it.)

In addition, two banking-related features work in conjunction with Quicken.com:

- **WebEntry** enables you to enter Quicken transactions on the Web. This makes it possible to record Quicken transactions from anywhere in the world.
- **Bank Account Update** enables you to upload your account balances to Quicken.com so you can view them from any computer with Internet access.

In this chapter, I explain how these features work and how you can use them to save time while keeping track of your finances.

The instructions in this chapter assume that you have already configured Quicken for an Internet connection. If you have not done so, do it now. Chapter 4 provides the instructions you need to set up and test an Internet connection. This chapter also assumes that you understand the topics and procedures discussed in Chapters 3 and 5. This chapter builds on many of the basic concepts discussed in those chapters.

Online Account Services: The Details

Here's a closer look at Quicken's Online Account Services, including what the services are, how they work, and how you can expect to benefit from them.

Transaction Download

Quicken's Transaction Download feature can perform several tasks, depending on your financial institution. Here's the scoop.

How It Works

Generally speaking, financial institutions can support Transaction Download several ways:

Direct Connect   Many financial institutions support direct communication between Quicken and the financial institution's server. This so-called *Direct Connect* method is the most powerful way to use the Transaction Download feature. To download transactions, you simply click a button in Quicken's Online Center window, provide brief instructions and a PIN, and wait while Quicken gets the information you want. Quicken does all the work.

Web Connect   Many financial institutions that don't support Direct Connect enable you to download specially formatted *Web Connect* files. To do this, you must log into your financial institution's Web site, using the information your financial institution supplies, navigate to a download page, and indicate what data you want to download. Once the Web Connect file has been downloaded, Quicken reads it and knows exactly which Quicken account it applies to. This is the next best thing to Direct Connect.

QIF Download   Just about any financial institution that has a Web site supports Quicken's QIF format for downloading transactions. Although this is a functional way to download data from a financial institution into a Quicken data file, it requires a lot more effort. I explain how to import QIF document files into Quicken in Appendix A.

Downloaded Transactions

Bank account transaction downloads include all deposits, checks, interest payments, bank fees, transfers, ATM transactions, and debit card transactions. Credit card transaction downloads include all charges, credits (for returns), payments, fees, and finance charges. Quicken displays all of the transactions, including the ones you have not yet entered in your account register, as well as the current balance of the account. A few clicks and keystrokes is all it takes to enter the transactions you missed. This feature makes it virtually impossible to omit entries, while telling you exactly how much money is available in a bank account or how much money you owe on your credit card account. No more surprises in that monthly statement.

Additional Features of Direct Connect

If your financial institution supports Direct Connect, you may also be able to take advantage of the following two features:

Transfer money between accounts.   If you have more than one bank account at the same financial institution, you can use Online Account Access to transfer money between accounts. Although many banks offer this feature by phone, it usually requires dialing a phone number and entering an account number and PIN while navigating through voice prompts. Even if you get a real person on the phone, you still have to provide the same litany of information every time you call. With Direct Connect, you merely enter a transfer transaction and let Quicken do the rest.

Send e-mail messages to your financial institution. Ever call the customer service center at your bank or credit card company to ask a question? If you're lucky, real people are waiting to answer the phone. But if you're like most people, your financial institution uses a call routing system that requires you to listen to voice prompts and press telephone keypad keys to communicate with a machine. Either way, when a real person gets on the line, you have to provide all kinds of information about yourself just to prove that you are who you say you are. *Then* you can ask your question. The e-mail feature that's part of Direct Connect enables you to exchange e-mail messages with your bank or credit card company's customer service department. You normally get a response within one business day.

Online Payment and Quicken Bill Pay

Online Payment enables you to send a check to anyone without physically writing, printing, or mailing a check. You enter and store information about the payee within Quicken. You then create a transaction for the payee that includes the payment date and amount. You can enter the transaction weeks or months in advance if desired—the payee receives payment on the date you specify.

Online Payment is one of the least understood Quicken features. Many folks think it can only be used to pay big companies like the phone company or credit card companies. That just isn't true. You can use Online Payment to pay any bill, fund your IRA, donate money to a charity, or send your brother a birthday gift.

How It Works

Suppose you use Quicken to send Online Payment instructions to pay your monthly bill at Joe's Hardware Store. You've already set up Joe as a payee by entering the name, address, and phone number of his store, as well as your account number there. Quicken sends your payment instructions to your bank, which stores it in its computer with a bunch of other Online Payment instructions. When the payment date nears, the bank's computer looks through its big database of payees that it can pay by wire transfer. It sees phone companies and credit card companies and other banks. But because Joe's store is small, it's probably not one of the wire transfer payees. So the bank's computer prepares a check using all the information you provided. It mails the check along with thousands of others due to be paid that day.

Joe's wife, who does the accounting for the store (with Quicken Premier Home & Business, in case you're wondering), gets the check a few days later. Although it looks different than a handwritten check, when she deposits it with the other checks she gets that day, it clears just like any other check. The amount of the check is deducted from your bank account and your account balance at Joe's. If you use Transaction Download, the check appears as a transaction. It also appears on your bank statement. If your bank returns canceled checks to you, you'll get the check along with all your others.

When the Money Leaves Your Account

The date the money is actually withdrawn from your account to cover the payment varies depending on your bank. There are four possibilities:

- One to four days before the payment is processed for delivery
- The day the payment is processed for delivery
- The day the payment is delivered
- The day the paper check or electronic funds transfer clears your bank

To find out when funds are withdrawn from your account for online payments, ask your bank.

The Benefits of Online Payment

Online Payment can benefit you in several ways. You can pay your bills as they arrive, without paying them early—the payee never receives payment before the payment date you specify. You don't have to buy stamps, and the bank never forgets to mail the checks.

Quicken Bill Pay

If your bank does not support Online Payment, you can still take advantage of this feature by signing up for Quicken Bill Pay. This service works with your checking account like Online Payment does.

Costs

The cost of Quicken's online account services varies from bank to bank. Check with your bank to see what the exact fees are. Here's what you can expect:

- Transaction Download is often free to all customers or to customers who maintain a certain minimum account balance. Otherwise, you could pay up to $5 for this service.

- Online Payment is sometimes free, but more often it costs from $5 to $10 per month for 20 to 25 payments per month. Each additional payment usually costs 40¢ to 60¢. Again, some banks waive this fee if you maintain a certain minimum balance.
- Quicken Bill Pay is $9.95 for up to 20 payments and $2.49 for each set of five payments after that. (These costs are subject to change.)

If you think this sounds expensive, do the math. Here's an example. I get 20 payments per month for $5. If I had to mail 20 checks, it would cost me $7.40. So I'd actually save $2.40 per month if I made 20 online payments. Even if I don't make 20 payments a month, I also don't have to stuff envelopes, apply return address labels, or stick on stamps. My bills get paid right on time, I earn more interest income, and I haven't bounced a check in over five years.

Does it sound like I'm sold on this feature? You bet I am!

Security

If you're worried about security, you must have skipped over the security information in Chapter 4. Go back and read that now. It explains how Quicken and financial institution security works to make Online Account Services safe.

Setting Up Online Account Services

To use the online account services supported by Quicken, you must configure the appropriate Quicken accounts. This requires that you enter information about your financial institution and the account with which you want to use these features.

Applying for Online Account Services

Before you can use one of the online account services, you must apply for it. I tell you how at the end of Chapter 4. Normally, all it takes is a phone call, although some banks and credit card companies do allow you to apply online. Another way to apply or get application information is to click the Sign Up Now button that appears in the Online Account Activation dialog shown later in this chapter.

To learn more about and apply for Quicken Bill Pay, choose Cash Flow | Quicken Services | Pay Bills Online. After reading the information in the Quicken Services window that appears, click the Enroll Now button to connect to the Internet and fill out the Quicken Bill Pay Application form. You'll have to print and mail the application, along with a voided check, to the address supplied on the form to get things started.

The application process for these services usually takes a week but may take less. You'll know that you're ready to go online when you get a letter with setup information. The setup information usually consists of the following:

PIN (Personal Identification Number)   You'll have to enter this code into Quicken when you access your account online. This is a security feature, so don't write down your PIN on a sticky note and attach it to your computer screen. There is a chance that your financial institution may send this information separately for additional security.

Customer ID Number   This is often your Social Security number or taxpayer identification number.

Bank Routing Number   Although your bank might send routing number information, Quicken doesn't need it. It knows what financial institution you're using based on the information you provide when you create the account. That's why it's so important to choose the correct financial institution when you create an account.

Account Number for Each Online-Access-Enabled Account   This tells your financial institution which account you want to work with. In many instances, Quicken doesn't need this information either.

Setting Up Online Account Services

With customer ID and PIN in hand, you're ready to set up your account (or accounts) for Online Account Services. There are a number of ways to set up; rather than cover them all, I'll cover the most straightforward method. If you've been using Quicken for a while, you'll see that the setup process is now quicker and easier in Quicken 2003.

Setting Up for Direct Connect and Quicken Bill Pay

At the end of the account creation process, if your financial institution supports Online Account Services via Direct Connect, an Online Account Activation dialog will appear.

If the account has already been set up, but has not been activated for Online Account Services, you can display the Online Account Activation dialog by switching to the account register for the account and clicking the Set Up Now button that appears in the bottom of the window:

Enter your Customer ID and PIN in the appropriate boxes and click Next. (Or, if you prefer, simply enter this information in the boxes at the bottom of the account register window, shown previously, and click Set Up Now.) Quicken connects to the Internet and downloads information about your accounts from your financial institution. If it prompts you to change your PIN, use the dialog that appears to do so.

Quicken displays a dialog like the one shown next, listing all of the accounts at the financial institution which have Online Account Services enabled. Use this dialog to match your online-enabled accounts with Quicken accounts. Select an account in the scrolling list, then select one of the options beneath the list:

- **Match to this Quicken account** enables you to select an existing Quicken account from the drop-down list.

- **Add new account to Quicken** enables you to enter a name for a new Quicken account.
- **Do not use this online account in Quicken** ignores the online account and does not match or create a Quicken account for it.

After selecting an account and an option, click the Accept button to assign the online account to the Quicken account. You can repeat this process for all accounts that appear in the dialog. This makes it possible to set up a bunch of accounts at once, thus speeding up the setup process. When you're finished matching accounts, click Next. A summary dialog like the one shown next summarizes the accounts that have been activated and the services they have been activated for.

The dialog may include a check box labeled Help Me Download Now. (This check box does not appear if you have just created the account using Quicken Guided Setup.) For now, turn this check box off. Click Done. A little Service Agreement Information dialog may appear next. It tells you that online financial services are provided by your financial institution and not Intuit. (I think the lawyers at Intuit whipped this one up.) Read the contents of the dialog and click OK.

Setting Up for Web Connect

At the end of the account creation process, if your financial institution supports Online Account Services via Web Connect, an Online Account Activation dialog will appear. Click the Download button.

If the account has already been set up, but has not been activated for Online Account Services, open the account register for the account and click the Download From Web Site button that appears in the bottom of the window:

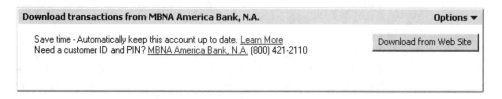

Quicken launches its internal Web browser and connects to the Log In page for your Financial Institution. At the same time, it may open Quicken Help and display the Web Connect Help screen. You can use Help to get more information or click its Close button to get it out of the way.

Log in to your account on your financial institution's Web site. Then navigate to the page where you can download your account statement and download it. If several formats are offered, it's vital that you choose Web Connect.

When the download is complete, switch back to Quicken. A dialog like the one shown next should appear.

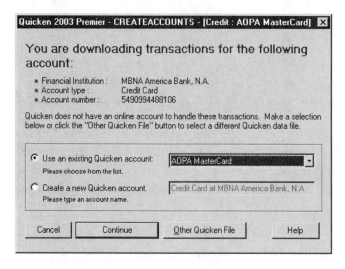

You have two options:

- **Use an existing Quicken account** enables you to choose an existing Quicken account from the drop-down list. Make sure you choose the correct account!
- **Create a new Quicken account** enables you to enter a name for a new Quicken account.

Click Continue. Quicken imports the data into the account register and displays the Online Update Summary window, which I discuss later in this chapter. Click Done.

Quicken may display the account register for the account next. If so, you'll see the imported transactions at the bottom of the window. I explain how to review and accept downloaded transactions later in this chapter.

Checking Online Account Service Status

You can confirm that an account has been set up for Online Account Services. Open the account's register and click the Overview tab. The Account Attributes area should indicate whether services are available or activated. Here's an example:

Account Attributes	Options ▼
Account Name	Checking
Description	
Financial Institution	Wells Fargo
Account Number	1012788
Routing Number	1221052
Customer ID	1496065
Transaction Download	Activated
Online Payment through ...	Activated
View on Quicken.com	Available
Edit Account Details	Change Online Services

Clicking the Change Online Services button in the Attributes area displays the Online Services tab of the Account Details dialog. You can use this dialog to activate or, in this case, deactivate online account services.

The Online Center

When you enable Online Account Services, you can use the Online Center to work with Quicken's online features. This window gives you access to all the lists and commands you need to download transactions, create payments, transfer money, and exchange e-mail with your financial institution.

Using the Online Center Window

To open the Online Center window, choose Online | Online Center. Figure 6-1 shows what the Transactions tab of this window looks like with one of my financial institutions selected.

Figure 6-1 • The Online Center window gives you access to all online features for your bank accounts.

A number of button bar buttons and menus enable you to work with the window's contents:

- **Delete** removes the selected transaction.
- **Payees** displays the Online Payee List window, which I discuss later in this chapter.
- **Repeating** displays the Repeating tab of the Scheduled Transaction List window, along with the Create Repeating Online Payment dialog. I tell you more about both of these features later in this chapter.
- **Contact Info** displays the Contact Information dialog for the currently selected financial institution. You can use the information in the dialog to contact the bank or credit card company by phone, Web site, or e-mail.
- **PIN Vault** gives you access to Quicken's PIN Vault feature, which I discuss in Chapter 7. (This option may only appear if you have online banking features enabled for accounts at more than one financial institution.)
- **Print** prints the transactions that appear in the window.

- **Options** displays a menu of commands for working with the current account or window.
- **How Do I** provides additional instructions for working with the Online Center window.

Downloading and Reviewing Transactions

One of the main features of Online Account Services is the capability to download transactions from your financial institution into Quicken. You do this with the Transactions tab of the Online Center window (refer to Figure 6-1). Here's how you can take advantage of this feature.

Connecting to the Financial Institution with Direct Connect

If your financial institution supports Direct Connect, you can download all transactions from right within Quicken.

In the Online Center window, choose the name of your bank or credit card company from the Financial Institution drop-down list. If necessary, click the Transactions tab. Then click the Update/Send button. The Online Update For This Account dialog, which is shown next, appears. Click to toggle the check marks beside the instructions you want to send, enter your PIN, and click Send.

Wait while Quicken connects to your bank. A status dialog appears while it works. When Quicken has finished exchanging information, the status dialog disappears and the Online Update Summary window (see Figure 6-2) takes its place. Continue following the instructions in the section titled "Viewing Downloaded Transactions."

Downloading a Web Connect File

If your financial institution supports Web Connect, you'll have to log into your financial institution's Web site and manually download the statement information just as you did when you first set up the account for Online Account Services.

In the Online Center window, choose the name of your bank or credit card company from the Financial Institution drop-down list. If necessary, click the Transactions tab. Then click the Update/Send button. Quicken connects to the Internet and displays your financial institution's Log In page. Log in, navigate to the page where you can download statements, and download the statement or transactions you want. If necessary, switch back to Quicken. It should automatically import the transactions you downloaded into the correct account and display an Online Update Summary window like the one in Figure 6-2. Continue following the instructions in the section titled "Viewing Downloaded Transactions."

Downloading and Importing a QIF File

If the only way your financial institution supports Online Account Services is via a QIF file, use your Web browser to log into your financial institution's Web site and download a QIF file of transactions. Then follow the instructions in Appendix A to import the file into the correct Quicken account. You can then view imported transactions as instructed next.

Viewing Downloaded Transactions

After transactions have been imported into Quicken via Direct Connect or Web Connect, the Online Update Summary window appears. As shown in Figure 6-2, it summarizes the activity that took place while you waited and provides information about other online-enabled accounts that were not updated. This window has been revised in Quicken 2003 to show more information in an easier to read format.

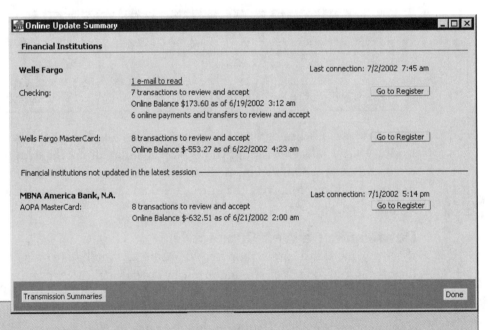

Figure 6-2 • **The Online Update Summary summarizes the activity of online sessions.**

There are three ways to proceed:

- Click the Done button in the Online Update Summary window to dismiss it. Then, in the Account bar, click the name of an account with downloaded transactions. As shown next, an orange flag appears beside the name of each account with downloaded transactions.

- Click the Done button in the Online Update Summary window. If necessary, choose Online | Online Center to display the Online Center window again. The downloaded transactions appear in the Transactions tab of the window when the financial institution and account are selected (see Figure 6-3). You can then click the Compare To Register button in that window to view the account register with the downloaded transactions in the bottom half of the window (see Figure 6-4).
- Click the Go To Register button in the Online Update Summary window for an account for which you want to review transactions. The account register window appears with the downloaded transactions in the bottom half of the window (see Figure 6-4).

If you have imported a QIF file into Quicken, you can review imported transactions by opening the account register for the account you imported transactions into. The transactions should appear in the bottom half of the register window, as shown in Figure 6-4.

If downloaded transactions do not appear in the bottom half of the account register, choose View Compare To Register from the Options pop-up menu on the register window's button bar.

Keep in mind that the first time you connect via Direct Connect, the bank sends all transactions from the past 60–90 days. After that, only new transactions will be downloaded. For Web Connect and QIF file downloads, you can often determine the transaction period when you set up the download.

Figure 6-3 • The Online Center window lists the downloaded transactions that have not yet been reviewed and accepted.

Comparing Downloaded Transactions to Register Transactions

Your job is to compare the downloaded transactions to the transactions already entered in your account register. This enables you to identify transactions that you neglected to enter or that you entered incorrectly. In addition, because Quicken will automatically enter a date, transaction number, and amount—and in the case of some transactions, the payee and category (based on previously memorized transactions)—using this method to enter a transaction can be much faster than entering it manually in the account register window.

The Status column in the bottom half of the account register window (refer to Figure 6-4) identifies three types of transactions:

- **Match** identifies transactions that match those in the register. This will happen if the transaction has already been entered in the Quicken register.
- **New** identifies transactions that do not appear to be in the register.
- **Accepted** identifies matched transactions that you have accepted.

Credit : Wells Fargo MasterCard	**Register**	Overview						

Delete Find Transfer Reconcile Update Now   Report ▾ Options ▾ How Do I ▾

Date	Ref	Payee/Category/Memo		Charge		Clr	Payment	Balance	
5/16/2002		Sizzling Wok		20	87	c		20	87
		Dining							
5/19/2002		Fry'S Electronic				c	29 00	8	13
		Computer	CD-Rs						
5/19/2002		Woodys Store		13	09	c		4	96
		Auto:Fuel	Jeep						
5/23/2002		WF MasterCard					176 08	171	12
		[Checking]							
5/23/2002	Ref	House Berlin		35	00	c	*Payment*		
		Dining					Enter	Edit ▾	Split

Ending Balance: 171.12

Accept Transactions into Register: 1 of 8 completed

WELLS FARGO	Data From: Financial Institution			Online Balance: As of:	$553.27 6/22/2002

Status	Date	Num	Payee	Charge	Payment	
Match	5/23/2002		Payment		176.08	Accept All
Accepted	5/19/2002		Return		29.00	Done
New	5/23/2002		House Berlin	35.00		
				Accept	Edit ▾	
New	6/4/2002		Payment		5.40	
New	6/14/2002		Takara Sake	74.91		
New	6/19/2002		Petco 1108	37.19		Help
New	6/19/2002		Shell No.5029361	23.27		

Figure 6-4 • Downloaded transactions appear in the bottom half of the register window for an account with downloaded transactions.

When you select a transaction in the bottom half of the window, the transactions below it shift down to make room for a blank line with a button and a menu. You can use these to work with the selected transaction.

Accepting a Matched Transaction   If a transaction matches one in the register, you can accept it by selecting it in the list at the bottom of the window and clicking the Accept button. (When accepting downloaded transactions, a small **c** appears in the Clr column of the register to indicate that the item has cleared the bank, but has not yet been reconciled.)

Entering and Accepting a New Transaction   To enter and accept a new transaction, select the transaction in the bottom half of the window. Quicken begins preparing a register transaction entry for it, as you can see in Figure 6-4. Fill in the missing details, including the payee, category, and memo. Then click Enter in the top half of the window or Accept in the bottom half. Quicken enters and accepts the transaction.

Unmatching a Matched Transaction   If a matched transaction really shouldn't be matched, select it in the bottom half of the window and choose Unmatch or Make New from the Edit pop-up menu beneath it. There's a subtle difference between these two commands:

- **Unmatch** tells Quicken that it got the match wrong, but this command lets Quicken attempt to match it to another transaction. As a result, it may come up with another match. It's your job to determine whether the new match is correct. If it can't find a match, the status changes to New.
- **Make New** tells Quicken that the transaction shouldn't match any existing transaction. The status changes to New and can then treat it as a new transaction.

Manually Matching a Transaction   If a downloaded transaction identified as New should match one in the register, or if a single transaction corresponds to multiple transactions in your account register, you can manually match them up. In the bottom half of the window, select the transaction that you want to manually match, and choose Match Manually from the Edit pop-up menu beneath it. The Manually Match Transactions dialog, which is shown next, appears. Turn on the check boxes for each transaction you want to include in the match. The Difference noted near the bottom of the dialog should equal zero; if it does not, Quicken includes the difference in the transaction but does not categorize it. When you click Accept, Quicken creates an entry for the transaction that includes each of the register transactions (and any differences) on a separate split line. You can click the Split button for the transaction to edit it as desired.

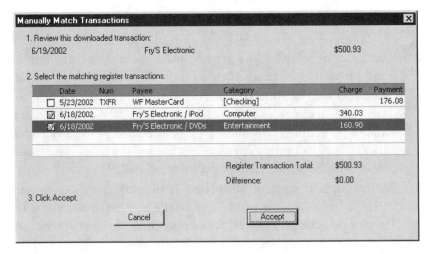

Deleting a New Transaction To delete a new transaction, select the transaction in the bottom half of the window and choose Delete from the Edit pop-up menu beneath it. A confirmation dialog appears; click Yes to remove the transaction from the list. This option is especially useful the first time you download transactions from your financial institution. You may download transactions that have already been reconciled or predate your Quicken account. Unmatch transactions as necessary, then Delete them from the transaction list.

Comparing Transactions from Different Sources If an account has downloaded transactions from different sources, a Data From drop-down list of sources, like the one shown next, appears at the top of the downloaded transactions list in the account register window. Choose a source from the list and review and accept the payments that appear as instructed here. Some financial institutions may require that you accept certain types of transactions before you review others. When there is only one source of transactions, the drop-down list does not appear.

Accept Transactions into Register: 0 of 6 completed

| WELLS FARGO | Data From: |
| | Payments & Transfers ▾ |

Finishing Up When you've finished comparing transactions to register transactions, click the Done button. If you failed to accept all of the transactions, Quicken displays a dialog offering to finish now or later. If you click the Finish Later button, the unaccepted transactions are saved for the next time you compare transactions. Keep in mind that downloaded transactions that have not been accepted may not be entered in your account register. Thus, your register balance may be misstated until you accept all downloaded transactions.

Paying Your Credit Card Bill

If payment on your credit card bill is due, you're notified in the Online Update Summary window when you successfully download transactions via Direct Connect. When you've finished reviewing, comparing, and accepting downloaded transactions, you can use Quicken to review your bill and enter a payment transaction.

If necessary, choose Online | Online Center to display the Online Center window. Click the Payment Information button in the Transactions tab. A dialog like the one shown next appears, providing information about the statement date, minimum payment due, and account balance:

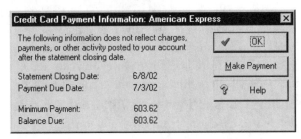

If you click the Make Payment button, the Make Credit Card Payment dialog appears. Begin by selecting an Amount To Pay option. If you select Other Amount, enter the amount in the text box. Then select a payment method option and choose a payment account.

The option you select in the Payment Will Be area determines what happens when you click OK:

- **Printed Check** displays the Write Checks window, with the payment transaction already filled in. Edit the transaction as necessary and click the Record Check button to complete it. The check can be printed the next time you use the Print Checks command. I explain how to use the Write Checks window in Chapter 5.

- **Hand-Written Check** displays the account register window, with the payment transaction already filled in. Edit the transaction as necessary and click the Enter button to complete it. You must then write the check by hand. I explain how to use an account register window to enter transactions in Chapter 5.

- **Online Payment** displays the Payments tab of the Online Center window with the payment transaction already filled in. Edit the transaction as necessary and click the Enter button to complete it. The payment instruction will be sent to your bank the next time you click the Update/Send button. To use the Online Payment option, one of your bank accounts must be set up for Online Payment through your bank or Quicken Bill Pay. In addition, the credit card company must be set up as an online payee. I tell you more about making online payments in the next section.

Making Online Payments

The Payments tab of the Online Center window enables you to enter payment instructions for accounts for which you have enabled the Online Payment feature. Figure 6-5 shows what it looks like.

Figure 6-5 • Use the Payments tab of the Online Center window to make online payments.

In the rest of this section, I explain how to set up online payees, enter payment information for one-time and repeating payments, and work with payment instructions.

Entering Online Payee Information

To send payments from your account, your bank must know who and where each payee is. To ensure that your account with the payee is properly credited, you must also provide account information. You do this by setting up online payees.

Click the Payees button in the Online Center window or choose Online | Online Payee List. The Online Payee List window shown in Figure 6-6 lists all the individuals and organizations you pay using the financial institution indicated in the drop-down list with Quicken's Online Payment feature.

You can use options on the button bar to work with selected items in the window:

- **New** enables you to create a new online payee.
- **Edit** enables you to modify the information for the selected online payee.
- **Delete** removes the selected online payee. Deleting a payee simply deletes the payee's information from the Online Payee List. It does not change any transactions for a payee. You cannot delete a payee for which unsent payment instructions exist in the Online Center window.

- **Use** switches you back to the Payments tab of the Online Center window (see Figure 6-5) and inserts the selected payee into the payment form.
- **Report** displays a report of all payments made to the selected online payee.
- **Print** prints a list of online payees.
- **How Do I** provides instructions for performing specific tasks with the Online Payee List window.

To create a new online payee, click New to display the Set Up Online Payee dialog, shown next. Fill in the boxes by entering the payee name and address, your account number on the payee's records, and the payee's phone number.

Figure 6-6 • The Online Payee List window lists all of the online payees set up with your financial institution.

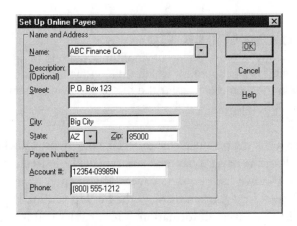

When you click OK, a dialog containing the information you just entered appears. Check the information in this box carefully. If there is an error, your payment might not reach the payee, or it might not be properly credited to your account. Remember, your bank will not be sending a billing stub with the payment—just the payment. When you're satisfied that the information is correct, click OK. The payee is added to the list with a default lead time of four days. I explain what lead time is all about later in this chapter.

Entering Payment Instructions

If necessary, switch back to the Payments tab of the Online Center window (see Figure 6-5). Then fill in the fields in the middle of the window with the payment information:

- **Processing Date** is filled in automatically by Quicken based on the delivery date and lead time. You can't change it.
- **Delivery Date** is the date you want the payee to receive payment. This is the date the bank will either write on the check or make the electronic funds transfer. The check may be received before that date, depending on the mail. The date you enter, however, must be at least the same number of business days in advance as the lead time for the payee—usually four days. That means if you want to pay a bill on Wednesday, June 27, you must enter and send its instructions to your bank on or before Friday, June 22. (Whenever possible, I give the bank an extra two days. So, in the previous example, if the bill is due on June 27, I'd instruct the bank to pay on June 25. This isn't because I don't have confidence in Quicken or my bank. It's because I have less confidence in the postal service.) To process payment as soon as possible, just enter today's date and Quicken will adjust the date for you.

Quicken Quick Tip

Another way to enter online payment instructions is right in the account register window for the account for which Online Payments is enabled. Simply enter **SEND** in the Num field, enter the remaining transaction information as usual, and click Enter.

- **Payee** is the online payee to receive payment. Quicken's QuickFill feature fills in the payee's name as you type it. If desired, you can choose it from the drop-down list of online payees. If you enter a payee that is not in the Online Payee List, Quicken displays the Set Up Online Payee dialog so you can add the new payee's information. This enables you to create online payees as you enter payment instructions.
- **$** is the amount of the payment.
- **Category** is the category to which the payment should be associated. You can either enter a category, choose one from the drop-down list, or click the Split button to enter multiple categories.
- **Memo**, which is optional, is for entering a note about the transaction.

When you've finished entering information for the transaction, click Enter. The transaction appears in the list in the bottom half of the window. You can repeat this process for as many payments as you want to make.

Scheduling Repeating Online Payments

Some payments are exactly the same every month, such as your rent, a car loan, or your monthly cable television bill. You can set these payments up as repeating online payments.

Here's how it works. You schedule the online payment once, indicating the payee, amount, and frequency. Quicken sends the instructions to your bank. Thirty days before the payment is due, your bank creates a new postdated payment based on your instructions. It notifies you that it has created the payment. Quicken automatically enters the payment information in your account register with the appropriate payment date. The payment is delivered on the payment date. This happens regularly, at the interval you specify, until you tell it to stop.

(Using this feature to pay an amortized loan such as a mortgage works a little differently. I tell you about it later in this chapter.)

In the Online Center window's button bar, click the Repeating button. A Scheduled Transaction Type dialog appears. (If it does not appear, choose Online Payment from the Create New menu in the button bar of the Scheduled Transaction List window that does appear.) Select the Repeating Online Payments option and click OK.

The Create Repeating Online Payment dialog, which is shown next, appears. Fill in the form to indicate the first payment date, account (if more than one is enabled for online payment), payee, category, and amount. Then set schedule and register entry options in the bottom of the dialog and click Authorize. I tell you more about setting options for scheduled payments in Chapter 7.

The payment you created appears in the Repeating Online tab of the Scheduled Transaction List window, shown next.

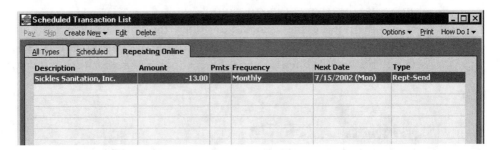

You can use button bar options to work with items listed in this window:

- **Pay** processes the transaction immediately. This button is grayed out for repeating online payments because it does not apply.
- **Skip** skips the currently due payment for the transaction. This button is also grayed out for repeating online payments because it does not apply.
- **Create New** enables you to create a new repeating online payment or other type of scheduled transaction. I tell you more about this menu in Chapter 7.

- **Edit** enables you to modify the selected repeating online payment.
- **Delete** removes the repeating online payment from the list, thus canceling future payments.
- **Options** offers commands for changing the sort order of payments in the list.
- **Print** prints a list of repeating online payments.
- **How Do I** provides instructions for completing tasks with the Scheduled Transaction List.

Linking a Repeating Online Payment to an Amortized Loan

Repeating online payments are perfect for paying off loans. After all, loan payments are the same every month and must be paid by a certain date. You can set up a repeating online payment instruction, send it to your financial institution, and let Quicken and your bank make the payments automatically every month for you.

Set up the repeating online payment instruction for the loan payment as instructed in the earlier section "Scheduling Repeating Online Payments." Don't worry about all the categories that are part of a loan payment transaction. Just choose the loan account as the category. You don't even have to get the date or amount right. When you link the transaction to the loan, Quicken will make the necessary adjustments. Be sure to click Authorize to save the payment instruction.

Choose Property & Debt | Loans or press CTRL-H to display the Loans window. If necessary, choose the loan account's name from the Choose Loan menu in the button bar to display the information for the loan for which you want to use the payment instruction.

Click the Edit Payment button to display the Edit Loan Payment dialog. Then click the Payment Method button. In the Select Payment Method dialog, select Repeating Online Payment. Then choose the repeating online payment

Quicken Quick Tip

The best part of the Repeating Online Payment feature is that once a payment instruction is sent, you don't have to do a thing to continue paying regularly. The more payments you make with this feature, the more time you save.

instruction you created from the Repeating Payment drop-down list. It might look something like this:

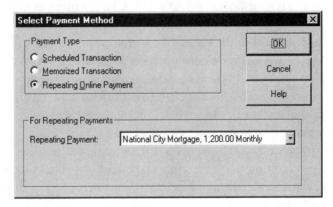

Click OK in each dialog to dismiss it. Quicken links the loan payment to the repeating online payment instruction. It makes changes to the payment instruction, if necessary, to match the payment categories and split information. The next time you connect to your financial institution, the instruction will be sent, and payments will begin.

Sending Payment Instructions

Remember the bills I told you about? The ones waiting on a table by the door to be mailed? Payment instructions that have not yet been sent to the bank are just like those stamped envelopes. They're ready to go, but they won't get where they're going without your help.

Once your payment instructions have been completed, you must connect to your bank to send the instructions. In the Online Center window, click the Update/Send button. Quicken displays the Online Update window, which lists all of the payment instructions, including any repeating payment instructions. Enter your PIN and click the Update Now button.

Wait while Quicken establishes an Internet connection with your bank and sends your payment (or payment cancellation) instructions. When it has finished, it displays the Online Update Summary window. Click Done.

In the Payments tab of the Online Center window, the word Sent appears in the Status column beside the payment instructions that have been sent to your bank.

Canceling a Payment

Occasionally, you may change your mind about making a payment. Perhaps you found out that your spouse already sent a check. Or that you set up the payment for the wrong amount. For whatever reason, you can cancel an online payment that you have sent to your bank—as long as there's enough time to cancel it.

Here's how it works. When you send a payment instruction to your bank, it waits in the bank's computer. When the processing date (determined by the number of days in the payee's lead time and the payment date) arrives, the bank makes the payment. Before the processing date, however, the payment instructions can be canceled. If you send a cancel payment instruction to the bank before the processing date, the bank removes the instruction from its computer without sending payment to the payee. Quicken won't let you cancel a payment if the processing date has already passed. If you wait too long, the only way to cancel the payment is to call the bank directly and stop the check.

Keep in mind that canceling a payment instruction isn't the same as stopping a check. If you send the cancel payment instruction in time, the bank should not charge a fee for stopping the payment.

Canceling a Regular Online Payment   In the Online Center window, select the payment that you want to cancel and click the Cancel Payment button. Click Yes in the confirmation dialog that appears. The word Cancel appears in the Status column beside the payment. Use the Update/Send button to send the cancel payment instruction.

Stopping a Single Repeating Online Payment   In the Online Center window, select the payment you want to stop, and click the Cancel Payment button. Click Yes in the confirmation dialog that appears. The word Cancel appears in the Status column beside the payment. Use the Update/Send button to send the cancel payment instruction. Note that the payment may not appear in the Online Center window unless you have reviewed and approved all downloaded payment transactions, as instructed earlier in this chapter.

Stopping All Future Payments for a Repeating Online Payment   In the Scheduled Transaction List window, select the payment you want to stop and click Delete. Click Yes in the confirmation dialog that appears. The transaction is removed from the list. Then use the Update/Send button in the Online Center window to send the cancel payment instruction.

Transferring Money Between Accounts

If you have more than one account enabled for Online Account Services via Direct Connect at the same financial institution, you can use the Transfers tab of the Online Center window, shown in Figure 6-7, to transfer money from one account to another.

Figure 6-7 • Use the Transfers tab of the Online Center window to transfer funds from one account to another at the same financial institution.

Enter the transfer information—source account, destination account, and amount—in the fields in the middle of the window. When you click Enter, the information is added to the list of transfers at the bottom of the window.

Like payment instructions, you must send transfer instructions to your bank in order for the transaction to take place. Click the Update/Send button, enter your PIN, and click the Update Now button. Then wait while Quicken sends the instructions.

When Quicken has finished, it displays the Online Update Summary window. Review the information in this window and click Done. The word Sent appears in the Status column of the Online Center window's Transfers tab beside the transfer instructions that have been sent to your bank.

Exchanging E-mail with Your Financial Institution

You can use the E-mail tab of the Online Financial Services Center window (see Figure 6-8) to exchange e-mail messages with financial institutions for which you

Figure 6-8 • The E-mail tab of the Online Center window is where you can exchange e-mail with your financial institution.

have enabled Online Account Services via Direct Connect. Keep in mind that not all financial institutions support this feature.

Creating an E-mail Message

In the Online Center window, click Create. If a Create dialog like the one shown next appears, use it to set general options for your e-mail message. If your message is about an online payment, choose the account from the Account drop-down list and select the payment from the Payments scrolling list.

When you click OK, a Message window appears. Use it to compose your e-mail message. When you click OK, the message is saved. It appears in the bottom half of the E-mail tab of the Online Center window (see Figure 6-8), ready to be sent to your financial institution.

Exchanging E-mail Messages

Using e-mail is a lot like having a box at the post office. When you write a letter, you have to get it to the post office to send it to the recipient. When you receive a letter, you have to go to the post office and check your box to retrieve it. E-mail works the same way. Connecting is a lot like going to the post office to send and retrieve messages.

In the Online Center window, click the Update/Send button. Quicken displays the Online Update window, which includes any e-mail messages you may have created that need to be sent. Enter your PIN and click the Update Now button. Then wait while Quicken establishes an Internet connection with your bank and exchanges e-mail.

When Quicken has finished, it displays the Online Update Summary window. Review the information in this window and click OK. The word *Sent* appears in the Status column beside the e-mail messages that have been sent to your bank.

Reading an E-mail Message

When your bank sends you an e-mail message, it appears in the E-mail tab of the Online Center window (see Figure 6-8). To read the message, select it and click Read. The message appears in a message window. If desired, you can click the Print button to print the message for future reference.

WebEntry

Quicken's WebEntry feature enables you to enter transactions for your Quicken accounts via the Web. You use a Web browser to navigate to a specific Web page on the Quicken.com site, enter your user ID and password if prompted, and enter transactions. Then, when you're back at your desk with Quicken running, you can use the One Step Update command to download transactions stored on the Web into your Quicken data file.

Quicken Quick Tip

WebEntry is especially useful if you're away for an extended period of time. By entering transactions periodically via the Web, you won't have to enter them all at once when you return.

You must register Quicken before you use this feature. Registering Quicken sets up a Quicken.com account for you to store your transaction information.

Entering and Reviewing Transactions

Use a Web browser to navigate to the Quicken.com home page at http://www.quicken.com/. Scroll down and click the Quicken WebEntry link— you'll find it at the bottom of the page. The WebEntry page appears. Figure 6-9 shows an example of what it looks like with a transaction ready to be entered.

If the WebEntry window includes a link prompting you to log in to Quicken.com, click the link to log in to your Quicken.com account. You must do this before you can enter transactions with WebEntry.

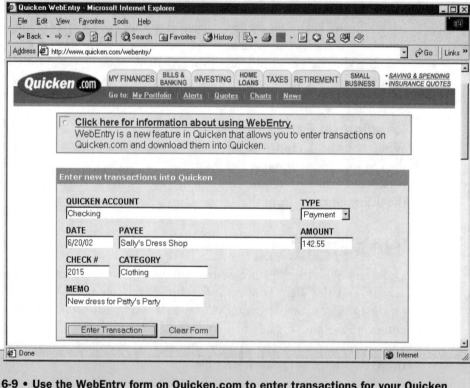

Figure 6-9 • Use the WebEntry form on Quicken.com to enter transactions for your Quicken data file.

Enter transaction information into the form and click Enter Transaction to enter the transaction into the Web database. Repeat this process for as many transactions as you like. Don't worry if you don't know the exact name of an account or category; you can correct any errors when you download the transactions into Quicken.

You can review the transactions you enter by scrolling down in the window after entering any transaction. The Review WebEntry Transactions area lists each transaction stored in the database on Quicken.com, as shown here:

Review WebEntry transactions				
07/02/02	**Money Market**	**Quicken Press**		**$2000.00**
		Royalties	Advance for Quicken Book	Deposit
STATUS: Not Downloaded	Delete	Edit		
6/25/02	**Checking**	**Withdrawal**		**$50.00**
	ATM	Misc	Spending Money	Payment
STATUS: Not Downloaded	Delete	Edit		
6/20/02	**Checking**	**Sally's Dress Shop**		**$142.55**
	2015	clothing	Dress for Patty's Party	Payment
STATUS: Not Downloaded	Delete	Edit		

Downloading Transactions into Quicken

When you're ready to download WebEntry transactions into Quicken, click the Update button on Quicken's toolbar. The One Step Update dialog, which I tell you more about in Chapter 7 and elsewhere throughout this book, appears. Make sure the check mark beside Download WebEntry Transactions From Quicken.com is turned on. Then click Update Now. If a Quicken.com Login dialog appears, enter your username and password in the appropriate boxes and click OK.

Quicken establishes a connection to the Internet and displays a status dialog while it updates information. When it's finished, it displays the Online Update Summary window, which informs you that your Web transactions were downloaded. Click Done.

Accepting Transactions

You're not done yet. The downloaded transactions must be accepted into the Quicken accounts. Open the account register for an account for which you have downloaded a WebEntry transaction. The window appears with a split with the downloaded transactions in the bottom half, like this:

If you have downloaded transactions from other sources such as Online Account Services, you may need to choose WebEntry from the Data From drop-down list in the bottom half of the window to view WebEntry transactions. This menu only appears if you have downloaded data from multiple sources.

Does this transaction list look familiar? It should! It's almost identical to the one in Figure 6-4. It works the same, too. You can learn more in the section titled "Comparing Downloaded Transactions to Register Transactions" earlier in this chapter.

Using WebEntry Again

The next time you use WebEntry, you should notice two things:

- Drop-down lists appear for the Quicken Account and Category fields. These drop-down lists are updated each time you download WebEntry transactions. This makes it easier to accurately enter transactions in the future.
- The transactions you entered on the Web and then imported into Quicken have the status Sent To Quicken. These transactions will not be sent again.

Updating Your Bank Accounts on Quicken.com

Quicken enables you to upload your account balances to Quicken.com, where you can view them from any computer in the world.

Why would you want to do that? Well, suppose you're traveling for business and one of the local shops has an incredible, hand-woven Navajo rug that you really want to buy. You're not sure how much money is in your checking account, and you don't want to write a check for the purchase unless you know for sure that you can cover it. So while you're at work checking your portfolio on Quicken.com (as discussed in Chapter 11), you take a peek at your account balance, which your spouse has been updating with Quicken while you're away. Fortunately, you have enough, and you can make the purchase. You can even use WebEntry to enter that big check in your account (as discussed in the previous section).

Think this might be helpful? Here's how you set it up and make it happen.

Enabling Account Update

Choose Edit | Preferences | Customize Online Updates to display the Customize Online Updates dialog. Click the Accounts tab to display a list of the Quicken accounts than can be displayed on the Web, as shown next. Click to place a check mark beside each account you want to view on the Web. Then click OK to save your settings.

Updating Account Information

Click the Update button on Quicken's toolbar to display the One Step Update dialog shown earlier in this chapter. An Update My Banking Accounts On Quicken.com option should appear in the dialog; click to put a check mark beside it. Then click Update Now. Wait while Quicken connects to the Internet and sends your data. (You may have to log in to Quicken.com; if so, a dialog will appear.) Click Done in the Online Update Summary dialog that appears. You're done.

Checking Account Balances on Quicken.com

You can view your account balances on Quicken.com by using a Web browser to visit http://www.quicken.com/myfinances/ (the home page for the My Finances channel on Quicken.com). Figure 6-10 shows what this page might look like; as you can see, it includes not only your bank accounts, but Portfolio Export information as well. (I tell you more about Portfolio Export in Chapter 11.) To see account balances, click the Show Balances link at the top of the account list.

Keep in mind that you must be logged in to Quicken.com for your account information to appear. If you are not logged in, Quicken will prompt you to log in.

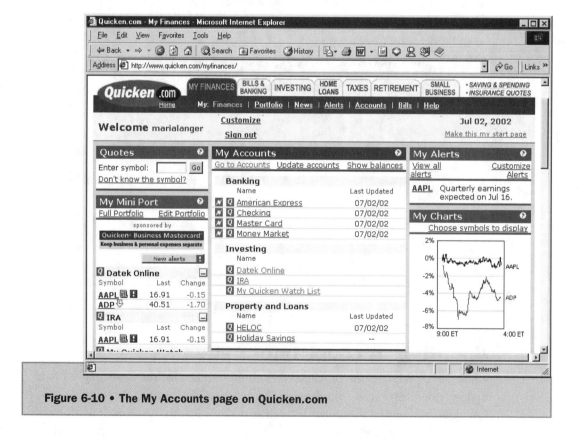

Figure 6-10 • The My Accounts page on Quicken.com

Automating Transactions and Tasks

In this Chapter:

- *QuickFill and memorized transactions*

- *Scheduled transactions*

- *Calendar*

- *Paycheck setup*

- *Address book*

- *One Step Update and the PIN Vault*

- *Scheduling updates*

Quicken includes a number of features to automate the entry of transactions. You got a glimpse of one of them, QuickFill, in Chapter 5. In this chapter, I tell you about QuickFill and the other features you can use to automate transaction entries or remind yourself when a transaction is due. I also explain how you can use Quicken's One Step Update feature to handle all of your online tasks at once. I'm sure you'll agree that these features can make data entry and other Quicken tasks quicker and easier.

Before you read this chapter, make sure you have a good understanding of the data entry techniques covered in Chapter 5. This chapter builds upon many of the basic concepts discussed there.

QuickFill and Memorized Transactions

As you enter transactions, Quicken is quietly working in the background, memorizing information about each transaction. It creates a database of memorized transactions, organized by payee name. It then uses the memorized transactions for its QuickFill feature.

How It Works

QuickFill works in two ways:

- When you enter the first few characters of a payee name in the Write Checks or account register window, Quicken immediately fills in the rest of the name. When you advance to the next text box or field of the entry form, Quicken fills in the rest of the transaction information based on the last transaction for that payee.
- You can select a memorized transaction from the drop-down list in the payee field of the Write Checks or account register window. Quicken then fills in the rest of the transaction information based on the last transaction for that payee.

QuickFill entries include amounts, categories, and memos. They can also include splits and classes. For example, you might pay the cable or satellite company for television service every month. The bill is usually the same amount each month. The second time you create an entry with the company's name, the rest of the transaction is filled in automatically. You can make adjustments to the amount or other information as desired and save the transaction. It may have taken a minute or so to enter the transaction the first time, but it'll take only seconds to enter it every time after that.

By default, the QuickFill feature is set up to work as discussed here. If it does not, check the QuickFill options to make sure they are properly set. I tell you how in Appendix B.

Working with the Memorized Transaction List

If desired, you can view a list of memorized transactions, as shown in Figure 7-1. Just choose Cash Flow | Memorized Transaction List, or press CTRL-T.

Button Bar Buttons

You can use buttons on the button bar to add, modify, delete, or use memorized transactions:

- **New** displays the Create Memorized Transaction dialog, which you can use to create brand-new transactions without actually entering them into any register of your Quicken data file. Just use the dialog's form to enter transaction information and click OK. The new transaction appears in the Memorized Transaction List window.

Description	Amount	Type	Memo	Category	Lock	Show on Calendar
AZ Dept Of Trans	-144.16	Pmt		Auto:Registration		
Dangerway Supermarket	-219.44	Pmt		Groceries		
Gecko	-423.22	Pmt		Auto:Insurance		
House Hamburg Restaurant	-140.00	Pmt		Dining		
March Of Dimes	-100.00	Pmt		Charity		
Maria Langer	-20.00	Onln		Bonus		
Osborne/McGraw Hill	4,000.00	Dep		Advances		
Quicken Press	2,000.00	Dep	Advance for Quicken Book	Advances		
Quickie Oil	-34.10	Pmt		Auto:Service		
Sally's Dress Shop	-142.55	Pmt	Dress for Patty's Party	Clothing		
Shell	-25.66	Pmt		Auto:Fuel		
The Chevy Dealer	-415.66	Pmt		Auto:Service		
The Mecca Restaurant	-35.40	Pmt		Dining		
Transfer Money	-2,000.00	Pmt		[Checking]		
Triple D Western World	-65.88	Pmt	Feed	Horse Expenses		
United Way	-100.00	Pmt		Charity		
Webb Center	-112.00	Pmt	Show	Entertainment		
Withdrawal	-50.00	Pmt	Spending Money	Misc		
World Champion Diamondbacks	-68.00	Pmt	Baseball Game	Entertainment		

Figure 7-1 • Each line in the Memorized Transaction List represents the last transaction recorded for a payee.

- **Edit** displays the Edit Memorized Transaction dialog for the currently selected transaction. This dialog looks and works like the Create Memorized Transaction dialog.

- **Delete** displays a dialog asking you to confirm that you really do want to delete the selected memorized transaction. If you delete the transaction, it is removed from the Memorized Transaction List only—not from any register in the Quicken data file.

- **Use** displays the appropriate register for entering the transaction and fills in the transaction's information for you. You must click the Enter button to accept the entry.

- **Report** displays a Payee Report for the currently selected transaction's payee.

- **Options** offers commands for changing the sort order and other view options for the Memorized Transaction List.

- **Print** prints a list of memorized transactions.

- **How Do I** provides additional information for completing tasks with the Memorized Transaction List window.

Quicken Quick Tip

Quicken can remember the first 2,000 transactions you enter—that's 2,000 payees! After that, it stops memorizing transactions. You can use the Delete button to delete old transactions to make room for new ones. You can also use options in the General tab of the General Options dialog to have Quicken automatically delete unused memorized transactions after the number of months you specify. I tell you how in Appendix B.

Other Options

You can also use two buttons at the bottom of the window to change settings for a selected transaction:

- Click the Lock button to toggle the locked setting for the selected transaction. When locked, none of the information in the transaction can be changed when the transaction is used.

- Click the Calendar button to toggle the Financial Calendar setting for the selected transaction. When enabled, the transaction will appear on the Financial Calendar's transaction list (refer to Figure 7-2).

Bills and Scheduled Transactions

One of my favorite Quicken features is the ability to tell Quicken about the bills and other transactions that need to be made in the future—especially the ones that happen on a regular basis. This scheduled transactions feature, when fully utilized, can not only prevent you from forgetting to pay bills, but it can completely automate the transaction entry process.

In this part of the chapter, I tell you more about scheduled transactions, including how to set up and use them.

Overview of Scheduled Transactions

Generally speaking, there are two types of scheduled transactions:

- **One-time transactions** are future transactions that you expect to record only once. For example, suppose you are arranging to purchase some furniture. You have already paid a deposit for the furniture and you know that the balance will be due at month-end, when the furniture is delivered. That month-end payment can be scheduled in advance.
- **Recurring transactions** are transactions that occur periodically, on a regular basis. Many of your monthly bills are good examples: rent or mortgage payments, car payments, utility bills—unfortunately, there are too many to list!

Scheduled transactions aren't only for payments. You could schedule transactions for incoming funds, too, such as an expected bonus or a monthly child support check you receive. You can even schedule your paycheck—but I recommend using Quicken's Paycheck Setup feature, which I discuss later in this chapter, to do that.

Making the Most of Scheduled Transactions

Quicken's scheduled transactions feature is one of the best time-saving features Quicken offers. By taking full advantage of this feature, you can minimize the time you spend entering transactions into Quicken. That's a good thing, right? After all, you have better things to do with your time than punch numbers into a computer.

Here are a few suggestions from a seasoned Quicken user (yours truly) about how you can make the most of the scheduled transactions feature. See how many you can use—and how much time they can save you.

Set up all recurring transactions as scheduled transactions.
Recurring payments are things like monthly and quarterly bills for rent, mortgage, insurance, utilities, and other regular bills. Recurring deposits are things like your paycheck, commissions, and other regular income. Set them all up, even if the amounts vary from one payment or deposit to the next. The quickest way to set these up is with Quicken Guided Setup, as discussed in Chapter 2, but the Create Scheduled Transaction dialog covered in this chapter offers more flexibility. Not only does having these transactions set up in advance make them quick and easy to enter, but it enables you to take advantage of Quicken's budgeting and forecasting features, which I cover in Chapter 18.

Use paycheck setup to track gross pay and deductions.   Paycheck setup may take a bit of time to set up, but it can save you a lot of time and effort while keeping close track of your gross pay and all deductions. This enables you to utilize Quicken's tax planning and reporting features without spending a lot of time to enter data. Be sure to set up all paychecks for the people included in your Quicken data file—normally you and, if you're married, your spouse.

Let Quicken automatically enter transactions whenever possible.   If Quicken automatically enters transactions for you, entering recurring transactions is a real no-brainer. Quicken does all the entry work; all you do is make the payment or deposit. The only unfortunate thing about this option is that it works best with transactions that have the same amount each time they are made. Still, I'm sure you'll find enough transactions to take advantage of this.

Use online payment or check printing feature.   Scheduled transactions seem to work best when coupled with either Quicken's online payment feature, which is covered in Chapter 6, or its check printing feature, which is covered in Chapter 5. (Of the two, I prefer online payments, for reasons I expound in Chapter 6.) Once the transaction is entered, Quicken can either automatically send payment instructions when you connect to your financial institution or automatically print checks for payments when you print all checks. So not only is Quicken entering the transaction details for you, but it's making the payments, too!

Record transactions several days in advance.   You don't have to wait until you make a payment or deposit to record the associated transaction. You can enter transactions in advance so your account register reflects both the current and future balance. Just be sure to enter the transaction due dates rather than entry dates when entering them into Quicken. I especially like doing this for payments, because Quicken can clearly show me that even if I have a nice fat balance today, transactions due over the next few days may leave considerably less to work with. I use this, in effect, as a very short-term forecasting tool. (Quicken's cash flow forecasting feature, which I cover in Chapter 18, does a better job of predicting the future.)

Set up reminders based on how often you use Quicken.   When you schedule a transaction and indicate that Quicken should prompt you to enter it, you can specify the number of days in advance that you should be reminded. Set this value based on how often you use Quicken. For example, if you use Quicken only once a week, set this value to 10. If you use Quicken every other day, set it to 4. This way, you're sure to be reminded in time to enter a scheduled transaction and make the payment or deposit associated with it.

Creating a Scheduled Transaction

Quicken offers several ways to schedule transactions. I cover two of them in this chapter.

Using Quicken Guided Setup

One of the great improvements to Quicken's setup process is the ability to schedule bills and other transactions from within Quicken Guided Setup. It makes the process quick and easy by enabling you to set up multiple recurring bills at once. I explain how this works in Chapter 2; if you haven't already explored this feature, you may want to check it out now. Click the Setup button in the toolbar, then click Bills in the Quicken Guided Setup window that appears to get started.

Using the Create Scheduled Transaction Dialog

Another way to create a scheduled transaction is with commands in the Scheduled Transaction List window. Choose Cash Flow | Scheduled Transaction List, or press CTRL-J. The Scheduled Transaction List window, which is shown in Figure 7-2, appears. I tell you more about this window a little later in this chapter. For now, let's concentrate on the Create New menu in the window's button bar.

The Create New menu offers five options:

- **Online Payment** enables you to schedule an online payment. This is the same as using the Payments tab of the Online Center window, but offers additional scheduling options. I discuss online payments and the Online Center window in Chapter 6.

Description	Amount	Pmts	Frequency	Next Date	Type
DD Storage	-60.00		Monthly	7/1/2002 (Mon)	Payment
ABC Auto Finance Co.	-656.98	44	Monthly	7/3/2002 (Wed)	Payment
National State Mortgage	-1,330.17	111	Monthly	7/5/2002 (Fri)	Payment
Vitec Corp	563.16		Weekly	7/5/2002 (Fri)	Payment
Wells Fargo	0.00		Monthly	7/5/2002 (Fri)	Payment
Qwest Comm	0.00		Monthly	7/8/2002 (Mon)	Payment
Arizona Power	0.00		Monthly	7/12/2002 (Fri)	Payment
Progressive	-345.22		Quarterly	7/15/2002 (Mon)	Payment
Saucer Network	0.00		Monthly	7/15/2002 (Mon)	Payment
Stinkies Garbage	-26.00		Monthly	7/15/2002 (Mon)	Payment
Qwest Comm	-19.95		Monthly	7/20/2002 (Sat)	Payment
Joe's Furniture	-650.00	1	Only Once	7/31/2002 (Wed)	Payment
Gecko	-458.50		Twice a year	8/23/2002 (Fri)	Payment

Figure 7-2 • The Scheduled Transaction List window lists all recurring and one-time scheduled transactions.

- **Payment** enables you to schedule a payment that does not utilize Quicken's online payment or check printing features. This is the same as using the account register window, but offers additional scheduling options. I discuss using account registers to enter payments in Chapter 5.

- **Print Check** enables you to schedule a payment that will utilize Quicken's check printing feature. This is the same as using the Write Check window, but offers additional scheduling options. I discuss using the Write Check window to enter payments in Chapter 5.

- **Deposit** enables you to schedule a deposit. This is the same as using the account register window, but offers additional scheduling options. I discuss using account registers to enter payments in Chapter 5.

- **Paycheck** enables you to set up a paycheck. I explain how to use this feature in the section titled "Using Paycheck Setup" later in this chapter.

No matter which one of the first four options you choose, if you have at least one Quicken account set up for the Online Payment feature (covered in Chapter 6), the Scheduled Transaction Type dialog appears. This dialog, which is new in Quicken 2003, offers two options:

- **Single Or Multiple Scheduled Payments** enables you to create a one-time or recurring payment or deposit.
- **Repeating Online Payments** enables you to create a repeating online payment. I explain how to do this in Chapter 6, so I won't repeat the instructions here.

Select Single Or Multiple Scheduled Payments and click OK. The Create Scheduled Transaction dialog appears, as shown next. This dialog got a new name and a new look in Quicken 2003. Use it to enter information about the transaction, including the account, payee, category or transfer account, memo, and scheduling information. You can click the Split button to enter more than one category for the transaction. When you're finished setting up the transaction, click OK to save it.

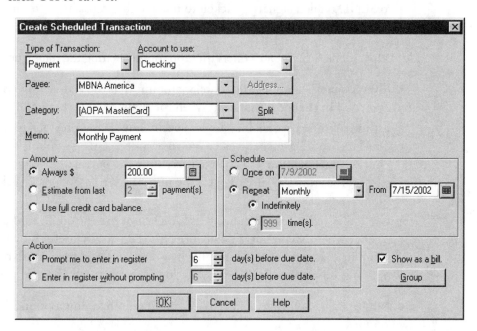

The Create Scheduled Transaction dialog has quite a few options that don't appear elsewhere in Quicken. Here's a closer look at each of them.

Type Of Transaction   The type of transaction you choose determines how the transaction will appear in your account register when it is entered, and may trigger other Quicken features. There are four options:

- **Payment** records the transaction as a payment, which decreases the balance in a cash flow account. The Num field in the account register for the transaction remains blank; you can always fill it in later if desired. Use this option for handwritten checks or cash payments.

- **Deposit** records the transaction as a deposit, which increases the balance in a cash flow account. The Num field in the account register is set to DEP. Use this option for deposits.
- **Print Check** records the transaction as a payment using a check to be printed. This decreases the balance in a cash flow account. The Num field in the account register is set to PRINT, which signals Quicken to include the transaction among checks to be printed. Use this option for scheduling transactions using Quicken's check printing feature.
- **Online** records the transaction as an online payment, which decreases the balance in a cash flow account. The Num field in the account register is set to SEND, which signals Quicken to include the transaction among payment instructions to send.

Amount   The Amount area offers three options for setting the transaction amount:

- **Always** enables you to enter a dollar amount that the transaction will always use. You can change the amount when the transaction is entered, if necessary.
- **Estimate From Last** enables you to specify how many previous transactions Quicken should average to calculate an amount. This is a rolling average; Quicken's calculation will change every time the payment is made. If you select this option, be sure to enter the number of transactions Quicken should include.
- **Use Full Credit Card Balance** tells Quicken to use the credit card account's balance when calculating a payment. This is especially useful for credit card accounts that must be paid in full when due, such as American Express. This option is only available if the transaction is to make a credit card payment.

Schedule   The Schedule area enables you to set scheduling options. You have two options:

- **Once On** enables you to specify a transaction date for a one-time transaction.
- **Repeat** enables you to set options for a recurring transaction. Choose a frequency option from the first drop-down list. Your options are Only Once (the default option), Weekly, Every Two Weeks, Twice A Month, Every Four Weeks, Monthly, Every Two Months, Quarterly, Twice A Year, and Yearly. Enter a starting date in the box beside it. Then choose one of the two

options beneath it to determine how many payments should be made. Choose Indefinitely to schedule transactions until you tell Quicken to stop by deleting the scheduled transaction. You can probably use this option for most of your bills. The option *N* Times schedules transactions for a specific number of periods. You can use this option for loan payments—although they may seem to go on forever, they do eventually end. For example, if you are scheduling a transaction for monthly payments on a four-year car loan and four payments have already been made, you'd choose Monthly in the drop-down list and enter 44 in the text box.

Action   The Action area offers two options for how Quicken should handle the transaction when it's due to be recorded:

- **Prompt Me To Enter In Register** tells Quicken to include the transaction in the Bills And Scheduled Transactions lists, to remind you to enter it. Enter a value in the text box to determine how far in advance Quicken should start reminding you.

- **Enter In Register Without Prompting** tells Quicken to automatically enter the transaction without bothering you about it. This is an extremely powerful option that can save you time and effort if used properly. Enter a value in the text box to determine how far in advance Quicken should enter the transaction.

Quicken Quick Tip

It's important to remember that scheduling a transaction is not the same as recording it. You must record a transaction in order to have it appear in the appropriate register, print a check for it, or send an online payment instruction for it. Scheduling the transaction is only part of the job—the big part. You still have to make sure those transactions are entered in a timely manner.

Viewing Scheduled Transactions

Quicken displays scheduled transactions in three places: the Scheduled Transaction List window, the Bills And Scheduled Transactions lists that appear in various places throughout Quicken, and the Calendar. Here's a quick look at each.

The Scheduled Transaction List

The Scheduled Transaction List window (refer back to Figure 7-2) displays a list of all future transactions. To view and work with the list, choose Cash Flow | Scheduled Transaction List, or press CTRL-J.

Button Bar Options   You can use button bar options to create, modify, delete, or enter scheduled transactions:

- **Pay** immediately enters the selected transaction into the appropriate register.
- **Skip** enables you to skip the payment (or next payment) of that transaction.
- **Create New** enables you to create a new scheduled transaction. I explain how to use this menu and the dialogs it displays earlier in this chapter.
- **Edit** displays the Edit Scheduled Transaction dialog, which I discuss a little later, so you can modify the selected transaction.
- **Delete** removes the scheduled transaction. It does not remove any transactions that have already been entered in a register.
- **Options** offers commands for changing the way the Scheduled Transaction List window is sorted.
- **Print** prints a list of scheduled transactions.

- **How Do I** provides instructions for completing tasks with the Scheduled Transaction List window.

Window Tabs   The Scheduled Transaction List window has three tabs that organize the transactions:

- **All Types** displays all scheduled transactions.
- **Scheduled** displays all scheduled transactions that are not repeating online payments.
- **Repeating Online** displays only repeating online payments. I discuss repeating online payments in Chapter 6.

Bills and Scheduled Transactions Lists

Bills And Scheduled Transactions lists appear in a number of places throughout Quicken. For example:

- The Quicken Home window includes a Current Bills And Scheduled Transactions list, shown next. It lists overdue and upcoming bills and displays a small calendar that indicates days on which transactions are due.

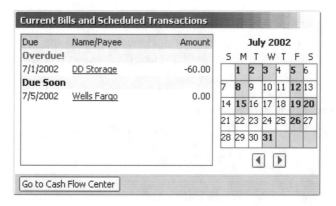

- The My Data tab of the Cash Flow Center window displays a complete list of Bills And Scheduled Transactions, shown next. You can click a button beside each transaction to enter, edit, or skip it.

Due	Status	Name/Payee	Amount	Action
Bills				
7/1/2002	Overdue!	DD Storage	-60.00	Enter Edit Skip
7/5/2002	Due Soon	Wells Fargo	0.00	Enter Edit Skip
7/8/2002		Qwest Comm	0.00	Enter Edit Skip
7/12/2002		Arizona Power	0.00	Enter Edit Skip
7/15/2002		Progressive	-345.22	Enter Edit Skip
7/15/2002		Stinkies Garb...	-26.00	Enter Edit Skip
7/15/2002		Saucer Network	0.00	Enter Edit Skip
7/15/2002		MBNA America	-200.00	Enter Edit Skip
7/20/2002		Qwest Comm	-19.95	Enter Edit Skip
7/31/2002		Joe's Furniture	-650.00	Enter Edit Skip
8/23/2002		Gecko	-458.50	Enter Edit Skip
Deposits and Other Scheduled Transactions				
7/3/2002		ABC Auto Fin...	-656.98	Enter Edit Skip
7/5/2002		National Stat...	-1,330.17	Enter Edit Skip
7/5/2002		Vitec Corp	563.16	Enter Edit Skip
Schedule These?				
7/28/2002		Humongous ...	-122.39	Yes No
8/2/2002		Dish Network	-48.53	Yes No

Show Full List | Add a Transaction | Set Up Paycheck

- Each account register window can include a Bills And Scheduled Transaction list like the one shown next. The list only includes the transactions scheduled for that account. You can click a button beside each transaction to enter, edit, or skip it. If this list does not appear in the bottom of a register window, choose View Scheduled Transactions from the Options menu in the register's button bar to display it.

Bills and Scheduled Transactions				Options ▼
Due	Status	Name/Payee	Amount	Action
Bills				
7/1/2002	Overdue!	DD Storage	-60.00	Enter Edit Skip
7/5/2002	Due Soon	Wells Fargo	0.00	Enter Edit Skip
Schedule These?				
7/28/2002		Humongous Utility Co, Inc.	-122.39	Yes No
8/2/2002		Dish Network	-48.53	Yes No
Show Full List	Add a Transaction	Set Up Paycheck		

Buttons and Menu Commands   The Bills And Scheduled Transactions lists usually include several buttons at the bottom of the list and an Options menu at the top of the list. You can use these buttons and menu commands to get more information about transactions, display the Scheduled Transactions List window, add scheduled transactions, or set up a paycheck. The options that appear vary depending on where the list appears within Quicken.

Schedule These?   The Schedule These? list in a Bills And Scheduled Transactions list displays transactions that Quicken "thinks" you might want to schedule for the future. It builds this list based on categories used in the transactions or transactions you have entered more than once. Here are a few things you can do to work with this list:

- To instruct Quicken to look for more items for the list, choose Scan For Recurring Transactions from the Options pop-up menu at the top of the Bills And Scheduled Transactions list. If Quicken finds any more candidates for the list, it adds them.

- To schedule a transaction in the list, click the Yes button beside it. Quicken displays the Edit All Future Transactions dialog, which I discuss a little later in this chapter, so you can turn the transaction into a scheduled transaction.

- To remove a transaction from the list, click the No button beside it.

- To remove all transactions from the list, choose Reject All Candidate Transactions from the Options pop-up menu at the top of the Bills And Scheduled Transactions list. If you change your mind, you can choose Reconsider Rejected Scheduled Transactions from the Options menu to redisplay them.

Calendar

Quicken's Calendar, which has been reworked for Quicken 2003, keeps track of all your transactions—past and future—by date.

To open the Calendar, choose Tools | Calendar or press CTRL-K. The Calendar window, which is shown in Figure 7-3, appears.

Button Bar Options   You can use button bar options to work with the window's contents:

- **<Prev Month** and **Next Month>** enable you to move from one month to another.
- **Go To Date** enables you to go to a specific calendar date.
- **Add Note** enables you to enter a note for the selected date. The note you enter appears on the calendar (refer to the July 11 box in Figure 7-3). To view a note, click it.

Figure 7-3 • Use the Calendar to see transactions by date.

- **Select Accounts** displays a dialog you can use to specify which accounts should be included in the Calendar and its Account Balances area. Toggle check marks beside accounts you want to display and click OK to save your settings.
- **Print** prints the Calendar.
- **Options** offers additional commands for viewing and working with the Calendar window.
- **How Do I** provides additional information for completing tasks with the Calendar window.

Quicken Quick Tip

If you've been using Quicken for a while and are accustomed to seeing the Memorized Transaction List in the Calendar window, choose Show Memorized Transaction List from the Options menu in the Calendar's button bar to display it.

The Transactions Due Window   When you double-click a calendar date (or single-click a selected date), the Transactions Due window, which lists all the transactions for that date, appears:

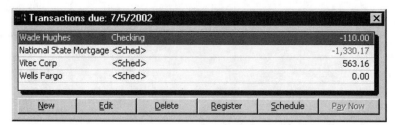

You can use buttons at the bottom of the window to work with transactions:

- **New** enables you to create a new transaction.
- **Edit** enables you to modify the currently selected transaction.
- **Delete** removes the selected transaction.
- **Register** opens the account register for the selected transaction. This option is only available for transactions that have already been entered in an account register.
- **Schedule** enables you to create a new scheduled transaction.
- **Pay Now** processes or records the selected transaction immediately. This option is only available for transactions scheduled for future dates.

Account Balances   The Account Balances area at the bottom of the Calendar is brand new in Quicken 2003. It displays the total account balances for the accounts displayed in the window, taking all payments into consideration. It works, in effect, like a simplified forecasting tool. I explain how to use Quicken's more powerful Cash Flow Forecast feature in Chapter 18.

Working with Scheduled Transactions

Scheduling a transaction was the hard part. (Not very hard, though, was it?) Entering, editing, and skipping a scheduled transaction is easy. Here's one way—in my opinion, the quickest and easiest—to work with scheduled transactions.

Click the Cash Flow Center button in the Account bar or choose Cash Flow | Cash Flow Center. If necessary, scroll down to the bottom of the window to view the Bills And Scheduled Transaction list shown earlier. This is the big list, the one with all of the transactions. Then use buttons in the Action column of the list to work with individual transactions:

Enter   The Enter button displays the Edit Current Transaction And Enter Into Register dialog. Use this dialog to finalize settings for a transaction. When you click Enter, the transaction is entered into the account register.

Edit   The Edit button displays the Edit All Future Transactions dialog. Use this dialog to modify settings for the transaction's future entries. This is the same dialog you'd use to create a scheduled transaction based on Schedule These? candidates, as discussed earlier.

Skip   The Skip button skips the next entry for the transaction. When you click this button, a confirmation dialog appears, asking if you want to skip the transaction that is due and telling you when the next transaction will be due. Click Yes to skip it. The transaction moves down in the list and its due date changes to the next due date.

Using Paycheck Setup

The Paycheck Setup feature offers yet another way to automate transactions. You use it to enter information about your regular payroll check and its deductions. Then, when payday comes along, Quicken automatically enters the payroll deposit information based on the Paycheck Setup transaction.

Although you can use Paycheck Setup to record payroll checks with varying amounts and deductions—such as a check with varying hourly wages or overtime pay—it can be a real timesaver if your paycheck is the same (or almost the same) every payday. If your paycheck does vary, be sure to include all possible deductions, even if their values are often zero. Then it'll be easy to just plug in different values when you need to.

Paycheck Setup has been completely reworked for Quicken 2003. It's now more complete and easier to use. And if you used Quicken Guided Setup to set up your Quicken data file, you may have already used Paycheck Setup to enter information about your paycheck.

Getting Started

Start by choosing Cash Flow | Banking Activities | Set Up Paycheck or click the Set Up Paycheck button in any Bills And Scheduled Transaction list. The Paycheck Setup dialog appears. The first screen provides general information about Paycheck Setup and how it works. Click Next to begin.

Note that if you have already set up a paycheck, following these instructions displays the Manage Paychecks dialog, which I discuss later. Click New in that dialog to display the Paycheck Setup dialog and create a new paycheck.

The first thing Quicken wants to know is whether the paycheck is yours or your spouse's (if applicable) and what the company name is. It uses this information to properly categorize the payroll deductions in each paycheck and to give the paycheck a name. After entering this information, click Next.

Next, Quicken asks what you want to track. You have two options:

- **I Want To Track All Earnings, Taxes, And Deductions** tells Quicken you want to keep track of all payroll deductions when recording a paycheck. This option makes it possible to take advantage of Quicken's tax planning features, which I discuss in Part Six of this book. If you select this option, continue following the instructions in the next section, "Tracking All Earnings and Deductions," after clicking Next.

- **I Want To Track Net Deposits Only** tells Quicken that you just want to track the net take-home pay, not the gross pay and deductions. This option makes setting up a paycheck a bit quicker, but it doesn't tap into Quicken's full power for automatically recording detailed information. If you select this option, continue following the instructions in the section titled "Tracking Net Deposits Only" after clicking Next.

Tracking All Earnings and Deductions

When you indicate that you want to track all earnings and deductions, Quicken displays a dialog like the one in Figure 7-4. Use this dialog to enter detailed information about the paycheck. It's a good idea to have a recent pay stub on hand when entering information because you'll want it to be as accurate as possible.

Setup Paycheck			☒

Company Name: Vitec Corp   Date: 7/2/2002 📅   [Done]

Memo (optional): Mike's Paycheck   [Cancel]
　　　　　　　　　　　　　　○ Prompt me to enter in register
How often: Weekly ▼   ○ Enter without prompting   [Help]

Account: Checking ▼

[Track Net Only<<]   Select this option if you only want to track net deposits from this paycheck.

Earnings

Name	Category	Amount		
Salary	**Salary Spouse**	750.00	[Edit]	[Delete]

[Add Earning ▼]

Pre-Tax Deductions

Name	Category/Account	Amount		
Employee Contribution Transfer	**[Mike's SARSEP]**	52.50	[Edit]	[Delete]

[Add Pre-Tax Deduction ▼]

Employer Match		**52.50**	[Edit]

Taxes

Name	Category	Amount		
Federal Tax	**Tax Spouse:Fed**	47.61	[Edit]	[Delete]
State Tax	**Tax Spouse:State**	10.77	[Edit]	[Delete]
Social Security (FICA)	**Tax Spouse:Soc Sec**	56.03	[Edit]	[Delete]
Medicare Tax	**Tax Spouse:Medicare**	17.62	[Edit]	[Delete]
Disability (SDI)	**Tax Spouse:SDI**	3.15	[Edit]	[Delete]

[Add Tax Item ▼]

After-Tax Deductions

What are your after-tax deductions?
Click the Add After-Tax Deduction button below to enter your after-tax deductions.

[Add After-Tax Deduction ▼]

Deposit Accounts

Account	Memo	Amount	
Checking	**Primary Account**	**562.32**	[Edit]

[Add Deposit Account]

Net Pay			**562.32**

W2 Gross			**697.50**

Figure 7-4 • The details for a paycheck in the Setup Paycheck dialog

Entering Amounts

You can enter an amount by clicking the default amount (0.00) and typing in a replacement value. Or, if you prefer, you can click the Edit button beside an item to display the Edit Earning dialog, which you can use to enter information.

To add another type of item to the dialog, use the Add pop-up menu in the appropriate section. For example, to add a pretax deduction, display the Add Pre-Tax Deduction pop-up menu (shown next) and choose an option. Then enter the details for that item in the dialog that appears. In some instances, choosing an option—such as 401(k)/403(b)/457 or Flex Spending—may display a dialog for creating a new Quicken account for the item. This may seem like a lot of work, but once the paycheck is set up properly, Quicken will take over and do all the hard work for you.

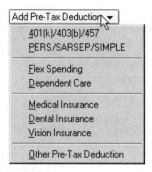

Go through the entire pay stub and enter all deductions into the dialog. Figure 7-4 shows an example; your check will probably have some different earnings and deductions. When you're finished, the Net Pay amount at the bottom of the dialog should match your take-home pay amount.

Setting Other Options

Before you click Done, make sure you set four very important options:

Date   Enter the date of the next paycheck (or the current paycheck, if you plan to enter this one after setting it up) in the Date field.

How Often   Use the How Often drop-down list to indicate the paycheck's frequency.

Account   Choose the account to which the net pay will be deposited. If the check will be deposited to more than one account—for example, if part of the paycheck is deposited to a company credit union savings account—make sure you indicate how much is deposited to each account in the Deposit Accounts area near the bottom of the dialog.

Entry Options   Select one of the two entry options:

- **Prompt Me To Enter In Register** includes the paycheck in Bills And Scheduled Transactions lists as a reminder to enter the transaction. You may want to use this option if the paycheck's amounts vary each payday or if you have the nasty habit of not depositing your paycheck on the day you get it.

- **Enter Without Prompting** automatically enters the paycheck in the appropriate account register when it's due. This is the best option to select if the paycheck is the same each payday, especially if you're lucky enough to have direct deposit.

Entering Year-to-Date Amounts

When you click Done, Quicken displays a dialog asking if you want to enter year-to-date information. If year-to-date totals appear on the pay stub you used to set up the paycheck, I highly recommend entering this information so all the earnings and deduction information is included in your Quicken data file.

Select I Want To Enter The Year-To-Date Information and click OK. The Paycheck Year-to-Date Amounts dialog, which is shown next, appears. Edit the values in the Year-to-Date column by clicking each one to select it and entering a replacement value. When you're finished, click Enter.

Tracking Net Deposits Only

When you indicate that you want to track just the net payroll deposits, Quicken displays a dialog like the one shown next. Use this dialog to enter information about the amount you expect to deposit. If you're not sure what the amount will be—like my royalty checks, which vary from one quarter to the next—you can leave the Amount field set to 0.00; if you do so, don't tell Quicken to enter the paycheck without prompting you or it will enter 0 each payday!

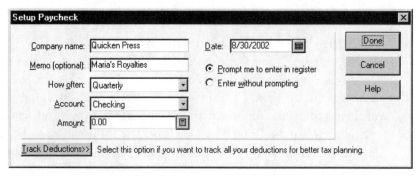

Be sure to set the correct options in the Date, How Often, and Account fields. Then select one of the two entry options: Prompt Me To Enter In Register or Enter Without Prompting. These options are discussed earlier in this chapter, in the section titled "Entry Options." When you're finished, click Done.

Managing Paychecks

Once you have at least one paycheck set up, you can use the Manage Paychecks dialog to modify it, delete it, or add another. Choose Cash Flow | Banking Activities | Set Up Paycheck or click the Set Up Paycheck button in any Bills And Scheduled Transaction list. The Manage Paychecks dialog, which lists all paychecks that have been set up in Quicken, appears. You can use the buttons on the bottom of the dialog to work with paychecks:

New   The New button displays the Paycheck Setup dialog, discussed earlier in this chapter, so you can set up a paycheck.

Edit   The Edit button displays the Edit Future Paychecks dialog for the currently selected paycheck. This dialog looks and works very much like the Paycheck Setup dialogs shown earlier, in which you enter paycheck information.

Delete   The Delete button deletes the selected paycheck. This does not delete any paycheck transactions already recorded—just the scheduled paycheck transaction. You'll have to click Yes in a confirmation dialog to remove the paycheck from Quicken.

Entering Paycheck Transactions

Entering a paycheck transaction is just as easy as entering a scheduled transaction. Display a Bills And Scheduled Transaction list in which the paycheck appears. Then click the Enter button beside it. The Edit Current Paycheck And Enter Into Register dialog appears. It displays all of the information you entered when you set up the paycheck. Modify values and options as necessary and click Enter. The paycheck's information is recorded.

Address Book

Quicken's Address Book feature automatically stores the address information you enter when using the Write Checks window. You can also use this feature to modify or delete existing information or add new records. Keeping track of addresses with the Address Book makes it easy to insert addresses when writing checks and to look up contact information when you need to follow up on transactions.

Quicken Quick Tip
Quicken's Address Book can handle most contact management needs—even those that have nothing to do with your personal finances. You can even use it to keep track of friends and family members and build holiday card lists.

Displaying the Address Book Window

Choose Tools | Address Book to display the Address Book window (see Figure 7-5). It lists all the records in the Address Book and offers button bar options to work with its contents:

- **New** enables you to create a new Address Book record.
- **Edit** enables you to edit the selected record.
- **Delete** removes the Address Book record. It does not affect transactions in which the record was used.
- **Modify** offers several commands for modifying the selected record or selecting multiple records.
- **Sort** enables you to change the order of records in the window.
- **Print** offers commands for printing Address Book record information.
- **How Do I** provides instructions for working with the Address Book window.

Figure 7-5 • Use the Address Book to keep track of the organizations and individuals you do business with.

Adding or Modifying Address Book Records

To add a new Address Book record, click New on the button bar of the Address Book window (see Figure 7-5). The Edit Address Book Record dialog appears.

You can also use the Edit Address Book Record dialog to edit an existing record. Simply select the record in the Address Book window and click the Edit button in the button bar.

The Edit Address Book Record dialog has five tabs for record information. Click a tab to display its options and then enter the information you want to store. Here's what you can enter in each of the five tabs:

- **Payee** is for the information that would normally appear in a Write Check window, as well as some additional contact information.
- **Contact** is for the name, title, phone numbers, and Web site of a specific person.
- **Secondary** is for a secondary mailing address and e-mail address.
- **Personal** is for personal information, such as spouse and children's names, birthday and anniversary, and still more phone numbers.
- **Miscellaneous** is for additional information, such as user-defined fields and notes.

Printing Entry Information

You can print the information in the list in three formats: list, labels, and envelopes.

Start by selecting a record or using the Group drop-down list at the top of the window to display the records that you want to print. Then choose one of the options on the Print menu on the button bar:

List   Choosing List displays a Print dialog just like the one that appears when printing Quicken reports. Use it to enter printing options and then click OK to print the list. Consult Chapter 9 for more information about printing lists and reports.

Labels   Choosing Labels displays the Print Labels dialog. It includes a list of commonly used Avery label products; be sure to select the right one before you click the Print button to print. To print a sheet of return address labels, choose an address from the drop-down list in the Return Address area and select the Return Address (Whole Sheet) option in the Print Selection area.

Envelope   Choosing Envelope displays the Print Envelope dialog. Use it to print #10 envelopes for Address Book records. Just set options in the dialog, put envelope stock into your printer, and click the Print button.

One Step Update and the PIN Vault

As discussed in Chapters 6 and 10, the bank account update, portfolio export, and WebEntry features use One Step Update to update information on the Web and download transactions entered on the Web. But that's not all One Step Update can do. This feature makes it possible to handle many of your connection chores at once. When used in conjunction with the PIN Vault feature, you can click a few buttons, enter a single password, and take a break while Quicken updates portfolio and account information for you. And now, in Quicken 2003, you can schedule updates to occur automatically when Quicken isn't even running.

Using One Step Update

The idea behind One Step Update is to use one command to handle multiple online activities. This eliminates the need to use update commands in a variety of locations throughout Quicken. One command does it all.

Setting Up the Update

Choose Online | One Step Update or click the Update button in the toolbar. If a dialog appears, asking if you want to set up the PIN Vault, click No for now; I explain how to use this feature later in this chapter. The One Step Update dialog, which is shown next, appears. It lists all the items that can be updated. Green check marks appear to the left of each item that will be updated when you connect. You can click in the first column to toggle the check marks there.

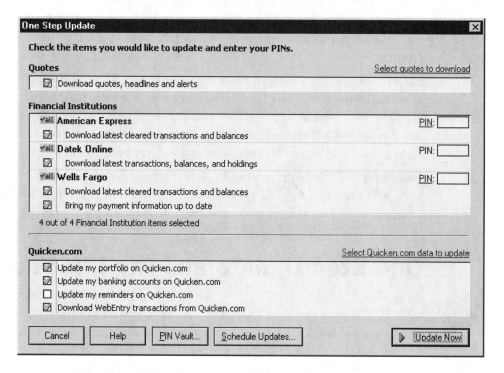

The dialog is split into three areas:

Quotes   The Quotes area offers one option, to download quotes, headlines, and alerts. You can select which quotes should be downloaded by clicking the Select Quotes To Download link. I tell you more about downloading quotes in Chapter 11.

Financial Institutions   The Financial Institutions area lists all the financial institutions for which online account services have been enabled. Your list will differ from the one shown here—unless you have the same financial institutions I have! You can enter your PIN in a box to the right of each institution name when you're ready to update your data.

Quicken.com   The Quicken.com area lists activities for uploading or exporting your Quicken data with Quicken.com. You can customize these options by clicking the Select Quicken.com Data To Update link. The options include:

- **Update My Portfolio On Quicken.com**, which I discuss in Chapter 11, copies information from the portfolio in your Quicken data file to the Web so you can view it on Quicken.com.
- **Update My Banking Accounts On Quicken.com** copies banking account information from your Quicken data file to the Web so you can view it on Quicken.com. I discuss this feature in Chapter 6.
- **Update My Reminders On Quicken.com** copies the information from your Quicken data file's alerts to the Web so you can view it on Quicken.com. I tell you about alerts in Chapter 9 and elsewhere in this book.
- **Download WebEntry Transactions From Quicken.com**, which I discuss in Chapter 6, downloads transactions you enter on Quicken.com to your Quicken data file.

Updating Information

Make sure check marks appear beside the items you want to update in the One Step Update dialog. If necessary, enter PINs in the text boxes beside financial institutions for which you want to update data. Then click Update Now.

Quicken establishes a connection to the Internet and begins transferring data. A Quicken One Step Update Status dialog appears as it works to show you where it is in the process. When the update is complete, the Online Update Summary dialog appears. As shown in Figure 7-6, it summarizes the activity for the update.

The PIN Vault

You might find it a nuisance to have to type in each PIN when you use the One Step Update feature—especially if you connect with more than one or two financial institutions. This is when the PIN Vault can help.

Quicken's PIN Vault feature enables you to store all your Quicken PINs in one central location. The PINs are then protected with a single password. When you use One Step Update, you enter just one password to access all financial institutions. You must have Online Account Access or Online Payment set up with two or more institutions to use the PIN Vault feature.

Setting Up the PIN Vault

Choose Online | PIN Vault | Setup. The PIN Vault Setup dialog appears. It provides some introductory information. Click Next to display the first window of the EasyStep tab.

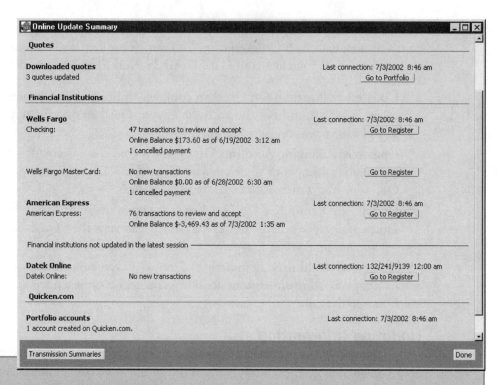

Figure 7-6 • The Online Update Summary dialog displays a summary of all activity that occurred during the One Step Update process.

Follow the instructions in each EasyStep tab to choose financial institutions and enter corresponding PINs. You'll enter each PIN twice because the characters you type do not appear onscreen; this is a secure way of making sure you enter the same thing both times. You can do this for any combination of financial institutions for which you have set up online access.

When you've finished, select the No option when asked whether you want to enter additional PINs. The PIN Vault Setup dialog appears. Use it to enter a master password to protect the PIN vault.

When you click Next, the Summary tab of the PIN Vault Setup window appears. As shown next, it displays a list of your financial institutions and indicates whether a PIN has been stored for each one.

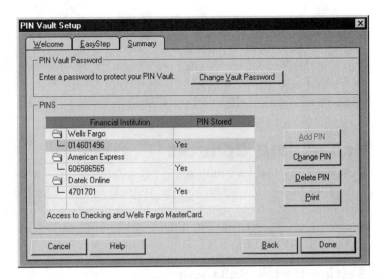

You can use buttons in this dialog to change or delete a selected PIN, print all PINs, or change the Vault password. When you've finished working with the window's contents, click Done. Quicken creates the PIN Vault.

Using the PIN Vault

Using the PIN Vault is easy. Simply choose Online I One Step Update or click the Update button in the toolbar. The PIN Vault Password dialog appears. Enter your password and click OK. Then continue using One Step Update in the usual way with one difference: You don't have to enter PINs for any of the financial institutions for which a PIN has been entered in the PIN Vault.

You can also use the PIN Vault in conjunction with the Update/Send button in the Online Center window, which is discussed in Chapters 6 and 11. Clicking that button automatically displays the PIN Vault Password dialog. Enter your password, click OK, and Quicken performs the update.

Editing the PIN Vault

Once you've created a PIN Vault, you can modify it to change PINs or add PINs for other financial institutions. Choose Online I PIN Vault I Edit. In the PIN Vault Password dialog that appears, enter the password that protects the PIN Vault and click OK.

The Modify PIN Vault dialog appears. It looks and works much like the Summary tab of the PIN Vault Setup dialog. Use it to make changes to the PIN Vault as desired. When you've finished, click Done.

Deleting the PIN Vault

You can delete the PIN Vault if you decide you no longer want to use it. Choose Online | PIN Vault | Delete. Then click Yes in the confirmation dialog that appears. Quicken deletes the PIN Vault. From then on, you'll have to enter PINs for each financial institution when you use One Step Update.

Scheduling Updates

Quicken 2003 enables you to schedule updates to occur when you're not using Quicken. Then, when you start Quicken, your data file is already updated with information from your financial institutions, ready to review and accept into your account registers. Your Quicken.com information can also be automatically updated based on information in your Quicken data file.

Setting Up the Schedule

To set up a schedule, begin by choosing Online | Schedule Updates. The Schedule Updates dialog, which is shown next, appears. Set options in each area of the dialog and click OK.

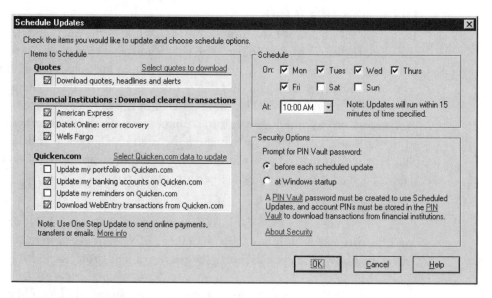

Here's a look at each of the options:

Items to Schedule   The Items To Schedule area lists all of the items in the One Step Update dialog I discussed earlier in this chapter. Click to toggle check marks beside each item you want to include in the schedule.

Schedule   The Schedule area determines when the updates will occur. Turn on check boxes for each day of the week you want the updates to occur, then choose a time from the At drop-down list. Since your computer must be running for the updates to take place, set options for when you know your computer will be turned on. Updates will not occur, however, if Quicken is running; this ensures that the automated feature does not interrupt your work with Quicken.

Security Options   Security options enable you to indicate when your computer should prompt you for the PIN Vault password. (The PIN Vault feature must be set up and used in conjunction with scheduled updates.) You have two options:

- **Before Each Scheduled Update** displays the PIN Vault Password dialog right before each update. You may want to select this option if the update is scheduled for a time when you expect to be at work at your computer. This is a more secure option, since it requires you to be present just before the update takes place. If you're not around, however, the update will not take place as scheduled.
- **At Windows Startup** displays the PIN Vault Password dialog when you start Windows. This option can make scheduled updates more convenient, since you don't have to be around when they occur.

Using the Schedule

Using the schedule is easy. First you must exit Quicken, since a scheduled update will not occur when Quicken is running. Eventually, the PIN Vault password dialog will appear. When it appears depends on the schedule and security options you set. Enter your password in the dialog and click Update. Quicken does the rest.

Changing the Schedule

To change the schedule, choose Online | Schedule Updates to display the Schedule Updates dialog. Make changes in the dialog as desired to modify settings. To cancel scheduled updates, turn off the check boxes beside each day of the week. When you're finished making changes, click OK.

Reconciling Your Accounts

In this Chapter:

- *The importance of reconciling accounts*

- *Starting a reconciliation*

- *Comparing transactions*

- *Making adjustments*

- *Reconciling credit card accounts*

- *Printing a reconciliation report*

One of the least pleasant tasks of manually maintaining a bank account is balancing or reconciling it monthly. If you're good about it, you faithfully turn over your bank statement each month and use the form your bank provides to balance the account. There's a lot of adding when it comes to totaling the outstanding checks and deposits, and the longer you wait to do the job, the more adding there is. And for some reason, it hardly ever comes out right the first time you try. Maybe you've even failed so many times that you've given up. I knew someone who'd open a new checking account once a year just so she could start fresh after 12 months of not being able to balance her account. That's *not* something I recommend.

In this chapter, I explain why you should reconcile your bank statements and how you can do it—quickly and easily—with Quicken.

The Importance of Reconciling Accounts

Reconciling your checking account is very important. It enables you to locate differences between what you think you have in the account and what the bank says you have. It can help you track down bank errors (which do happen once in a while) or personal errors (which, unfortunately, seem to happen more frequently). Completely balancing your checking account and making adjustments as necessary can prevent you from accidentally bouncing checks when you think you have more money than you really do. That can save you the cost of bank fees and a lot of embarrassment.

If you keep track of all bank account activity with Quicken, reconciling your bank accounts is easy. You don't need to use the form on the back of the bank statement. You don't even need a calculator. Just use Quicken's reconciliation feature to enter beginning and ending balances, check off cleared transactions, and enter the transactions you missed. You'll find you're successful a lot more often with Quicken helping you out.

You can use Quicken's reconciliation feature to balance any Quicken banking account—including credit card accounts. Although this chapter concentrates on checking accounts, I provide additional information for reconciling credit card accounts, too.

Reconciling Bank Accounts

Reconciling an account refers to the process of comparing transactions in your account register to transactions on the account statement sent to you by your bank. Transactions that match are simply checked off. Transactions that appear only in one place—your account register or the bank's account statement—need to be accounted for.

In this section, I cover the basics of reconciling a bank account with Quicken: comparing transactions, making adjustments, and finishing up.

Getting Started

To reconcile a bank account, you must have the statement for the account. Bank statements usually come monthly, so you won't have to wait long.

With statement in hand, open the account register for the account you want to reconcile. Then click the Reconcile button on the button bar. What happens next depends on whether the account is enabled for online access.

Accounts Without Online Account Access

If the account is not enabled for online access, the Statement Summary dialog, which is shown next, appears. It gathers basic statement information prior to reconciling the account. Enter information from your bank statement in the appropriate boxes. (Only enter service charge and interest earned information if you have not already entered it in the account register.) Then click OK to continue.

Accounts with Online Account Access

If the account is enabled for online account access, Quicken may begin by displaying a dialog that reminds you to download recent transactions or compare downloaded transactions to transactions in your register. If so, be sure to do this; it's the only way you can be sure that all transactions recorded by the bank are included in your account register.

Quicken displays the Reconcile Online Account dialog:

As you can see, this dialog offers two options for reconciling the account:

- **Paper Statement** enables you to reconcile the information in your Quicken account register to your bank statement. It is a traditional account reconciliation, and it works just like the account reconciliation you perform for an account without online account access. If you select this option, you must enter the bank statement ending date and ending balance in the appropriate boxes.

- **Online Balance** enables you to reconcile the account to the balance that was last downloaded for the account. If you select this option, you don't have to enter anything in the boxes. You can also enable a new Quicken feature: Auto Reconcile. Turning on the Auto Reconcile After Compare To Register check box tells Quicken to automatically reconcile the account to your financial institution's online balance each time you download and accept transactions. With this option turned on, you never have to reconcile the account again.

After setting options in this dialog, click OK to continue.

Quicken Quick Tip
Although Auto Reconcile is a great new feature that can save time and effort, I prefer reconciling to my paper bank statement. This prevents errors or confusion that could occur in the unlikely event of an error or omission in the downloaded data. It also forces me to keep a close eye on what appears on my printed statements.

Comparing Transactions

The next step in reconciling the account is to compare transactions that have cleared on the statement with transactions in your account register. For this, Quicken displays the Statement Summary window (shown in Figure 8-1), which displays all payments, checks, and deposits.

You can use button bar buttons within this window to work with its contents:

- **New** switches you to the account register window for the account you are reconciling so you can enter a new transaction.

- **Edit** switches you to the selected transaction in its account register window so you can modify it.

- **Delete** removes the selected transaction from the account register.

- **Back to Statement Summary** displays the Statement Summary dialog shown earlier or the Reconcile Paper Statement dialog (which is similar to the top half of the Reconcile Online Account dialog shown earlier) so you can check or change entries there.

- **View** offers options to change the sort order of the window's contents.

- **How Do I** provides instructions for completing specific tasks with the window.

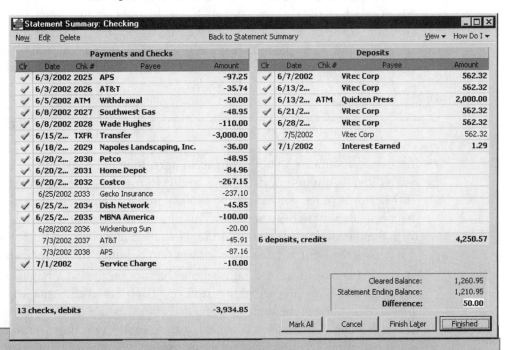

Figure 8-1 • Use the Statement Summary window to compare your register transactions to your bank statement transactions.

Reconciling to a Bank Statement

Your job is to check off the items in the window that also appear on your bank statement. While you're checking off items, be sure to check off the same items with a pen or pencil on your bank statement.

If the account is enabled for online account access and you have been downloading and comparing transactions regularly to accept them into your account register, many of the transactions in the Reconcile Bank Statement window may already be checked off. This speeds up the reconciliation process.

While you're checking off transactions in Quicken and on your bank statement, look for differences between them. Here are some of the differences you might encounter:

- An item that appears on the bank statement but not in your account register is an item that you did not enter. There are a number of reasons why you may have omitted the transaction. Perhaps it was a bank adjustment that you were not informed about. Or maybe you simply forgot. In Figure 8-1, the $50 difference between the Cleared Balance and the Statement Ending Balance is due to the failure to enter an ATM transaction—something many of us forget to do! To enter an omitted transaction, click New on the button bar to switch to the register window. Enter the transaction in the register as shown next and click the Return To Reconcile button to continue the reconciliation. Then click to place a check mark in the Clr column beside the item to mark it cleared.

6/20/2002	ATM	Withdrawal			50	00	*Deposit*		641	93
		[Pocket Money]					Enter	Edit ▼	Split	
							Return to Reconcile			

- An item that appears on both your account register and bank statement but has a different amount or date could be due to an error—yours or the bank's. If the error is yours, you can edit the transaction by double-clicking it in the Reconcile Bank Statement window. This displays the account register window with the transaction selected. Edit the transaction and click the Enter button. Then click the Return To Reconcile button to continue the reconciliation.

- Items that appear in your account register but not on the bank statement are items that have not cleared the bank yet. These are usually transactions prepared just before the bank's closing date, but they can be older. Do not check them off. Chances are, you'll check them off the next time you complete a reconciliation. If, during a bank reconciliation, you discover any uncleared items that are older than two or three months, you should investigate why they have not cleared the bank. You may discover that a check (or worse yet, a deposit) was lost in transit.

Reconciling to an Online Balance

If you've recently downloaded and accepted transactions for the account, reconciling to an online balance shouldn't take much effort. Items you've already reviewed and accepted will be checked off. Some more recent transactions may not be checked off because they haven't cleared your bank yet. Your job is to look for older transactions that appear in your Quicken account register that aren't checked off. These could represent stale payments that may have been lost in transit to the payee or errors (or duplications) you made when manually entering information into your Quicken account register. Follow up on all transactions more than 60 days old to see why they haven't been included with your downloaded transactions.

Finishing Up

When you reconcile a bank account with Quicken, your goal is to make the difference between the Cleared Balance and the Statement Ending Balance zero. You can monitor this progress at the bottom of the Statement Summary window, as shown in Figure 8-1.

When the Difference Is Zero

If you correctly checked off all bank statement items and the difference is zero, you've successfully reconciled the account. Congratulations. Click the Finished button.

If You Can't Get the Difference to Zero

Sometimes, try as you might, you just can't get the difference to zero. Here are a few last things to check before you give up:

- Make sure all the amounts you checked off in your account register are the same as the amounts on the bank statement.
- Make sure you included any bank charges or earned interest.
- Make sure the beginning and ending balances you entered are the same as those on the bank statement.

If you checked and rechecked all these things and still can't get the difference to zero, click Finished. Quicken displays a dialog like the one shown next that indicates the amount of the difference and offers to make an adjustment to your account register for the amount. Click Adjust to accept the adjustment. The amount of the adjustment will be recorded without a category.

But next month, don't give up!

First-Time Reconciliations

I was recently contacted by a reader who was having difficulties understanding how to reconcile an account for the first time. He seemed to think he needed to come up with some kind of "plug figure" to get the reconciliation to work. He hadn't even *tried* performing the reconciliation, too worried about what *might* happen. Oddly enough, he was an accountant. I suspect that he was over-thinking the situation, but I understand what he was concerned about and decided to address it in this edition of the book.

Suppose you have a checking account that you've been using for several years. Recently, you purchased and installed Quicken. You followed my instructions in Chapter 2 (and Chapter 5) to set up your checking account as a Quicken account, using the ending balance on your most recent bank statement—say it was dated 6/1/02—as the beginning balance in the account. After setting up the account, you entered all transactions dated after 6/1/02 into the account register.

July rolls along and you receive your 7/1/02 bank statement. Following the instructions in this chapter, you reconcile the account for the first time. But you discover that the 7/1/02 bank statement includes checks you wrote *before* 6/1/02 that were outstanding (had not cleared the bank) as of the 6/1/02 bank statement. If you don't consider these transactions in your reconciliation, there is a difference between the cleared balance and the statement ending balance. What do you do about these transactions?

This is what was confusing my accountant friend. He thought he needed to make some kind of adjusting entry in Quicken *before* starting the reconciliation. Instead, there are two options:

- If you want to record the transactions in your Quicken data file—perhaps to make charges to categories more complete—record them. You can do this during the reconciliation by clicking the New button on the Statement Summary window's button bar (refer to Figure 8-1). I explain how in this chapter. Once the transactions have been entered, be sure to check them off in the Statement Summary window. The difference should go away.
- If you don't want to record the transactions—perhaps you don't care about the categories that would be affected—let Quicken make an adjusting entry for you at the end of the reconciliation. That's the "plug figure" my accountant friend was looking for. He didn't realize that Quicken would take care of it for him.

Once that first reconciliation is complete, there should be no further problems—unless, of course, the 8/1/02 bank statement includes one or more very old checks from before 6/1/02. Then the same situation results, with the same options and resolution.

The moral of this story: trust Quicken. Even if you can't figure out the accounting procedures behind your finances, Quicken can.

Other Reconciliation Tasks and Features

Quicken offers a number of other reconciliation features that you might find useful. Here's a quick look at them.

Reconciling Credit Card Accounts

You can reconcile a credit card account the same way you reconcile a bank account. If you try to enter all credit card transactions as you make them throughout the month, it's a good idea to use the reconciliation feature to compare your entries to the credit card statement, just to make sure you didn't miss any. If you simply enter all credit card transactions when you get your statement, reconciling to the statement really isn't necessary.

When you begin the reconciliation process, Quicken displays either the Statement Summary dialog or the Reconcile Online Account dialog, depending on whether the credit card account has online account access features enabled. Both of these dialogs are shown next; they're very similar to the ones that appear when you reconcile a bank account.

Enter information in the appropriate text boxes and click OK to move on to the Statement Summary window, which looks and works almost exactly like the Statement Summary window that was shown in Figure 8-1.

If you can't successfully get the credit card reconciliation to work, Quicken offers to make adjustments. The following illustration shows the Adjusting Register To Agree With Statement dialog for a hopelessly messed-up account that needs adjustments to both payments and charges. Choose a category for each adjustment and click Adjust to make the adjusting entries.

At the conclusion of a credit card reconciliation, Quicken may display the Make Credit Card Payment dialog, offering to prepare a credit card payment for you. This is particularly handy if you like to pay your credit card bill after reconciling your statement to your entries. Select an account and payment method and click OK. Quicken prepares the transaction for you.

Re-reconciling an Account

Quicken remembers all of the transactions you check off as part of the reconciliation process. If you make a change to the amount or cleared status for a reconciled item, Quicken is smart enough to know that the reconciliation isn't correct anymore: the statement balance no longer matches the account balance. This activates Quicken's re-reconciliation feature.

If a dialog appears to warn you that manually reconciling an item will disable the re-reconciliation feature, think twice before continuing. Shutting off this feature could prevent you from resolving errors that could occur when you make improper changes to reconciled amounts.

The next time you reconcile the account, a dialog appears, telling you that the previously cleared items no longer match your bank statement. You have two options:

- **Resolve** displays a dialog like the one shown next. It lists the statements that are affected by the problem. You can re-reconcile the account for a particular statement by selecting the statement and clicking the Reconcile Again button or let Quicken create an adjusting entry by clicking the Adjust Register button.

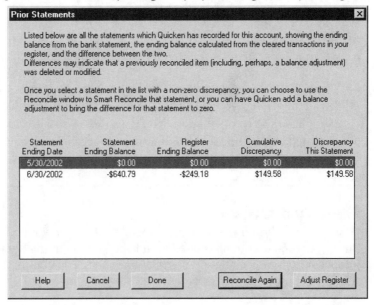

- **Ignore** enables you to continue with the reconciliation without resolving the problem. The same dialog will appear, however, the next time you reconcile the account.

Printing a Reconciliation Report

At the end of a reconciliation, Quicken displays a dialog that offers to create a reconciliation report. If you click Yes, the Reconciliation Report Setup dialog, shown next, appears. Set report options in the dialog and click Print to print the report.

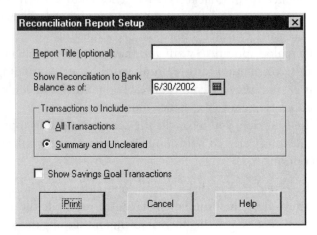

Identifying Reconciled Items

As shown in the next illustration, Quicken uses the Clr column in an account register to identify items that either have cleared the bank or have been reconciled:

- **c** indicates that the item has cleared the bank. You'll see a **c** in the Clr column beside items that you have checked off during a reconciliation if you have not completed the reconciliation. You'll also see a **c** beside items downloaded and accepted using Quicken's online account access feature, which I discuss in Chapter 6.

Quicken Quick Tip

I don't usually create Reconciliation reports. I have enough paper filed away! But if your reconciliation required an adjusting entry, it might be a good idea to document it by printing a reconciliation report. You can then file the report with your bank statement and canceled checks.

- **R** indicates that the item has been reconciled.

Checking	Register	Overview						
Delete Find Transfer Reconcile Write Checks Set Up Online						Report ▾ Options ▾ How Do I ▾		
Date	Num	Payee/Category/Memo	Payment		Clr	Deposit		Balance
6/28/2002		Vitec Corp			R	562	32	982 56
		--Form-- Mike's Paycheck						
6/28/2002	2036	Wickenburg Sun	20	00	c			962 56
		Subscriptions						
7/1/2002		Interest Earned			R	1	29	963 85
		Interest Inc						
7/1/2002		Service Charge	10	00	R			953 85
		Bank Charge						
7/3/2002	2037	AT&T	45	91				907 94
		Utilities:Telephone						

To prevent errors in your account registers, do not edit transactions that have been reconciled.

Examining Your Cash Flow

In this Chapter:

- *Cash Flow Center overview*

- *Using alerts*

- *Types of reports and graphs*

- *Creating reports and graphs*

- *Customizing and saving reports and graphs*

- *Printing reports and graphs*

At this point, you'll probably agree that entering financial information into Quicken is a great way to organize it. But sometimes organizing information isn't enough. Sometimes you need to see concise summaries of the information you entered, in the form of balances, activity reports, and graphs.

Quicken's Centers provide the kind of information you're looking for, in the form of snapshots, reports, and graphs. In this chapter, I conclude my discussion of Quicken's Cash Flow Center by telling you about the snapshots of information it offers and how you can take advantage of its Cash Flow alerts. I also explain how you can create, modify, and save standard and custom charts and graphs for all Quicken Centers.

A Closer Look at the Cash Flow Center

The previous chapters in this section have explored many aspects of Quicken's Cash Flow Center, including accounts, transaction entry, online account services, automation features, and reconciliations. But it's the Cash Flow Center window itself that offers a centralized place for examining the results of your work with Cash Flow Center accounts and features.

In this part of the chapter, I take you on a guided tour of the Cash Flow Center's two tabs so you can learn about the kind of information you can find there. To follow along with your data file, click the Cash Flow button on the Account bar or choose Cash Flow | Go To Cash Flow Center to display the Cash Flow Center window.

The My Data Tab

The Cash Flow Center's My Data tab (see Figure 9-1) displays a number of snapshots with useful information about your cash flow accounts. Most snapshots include buttons, an Options menu, or both that you can use to work with the snapshot. For example, the Banking Alerts snapshot at the top of the My Data tab has buttons and Option menu commands for showing, setting up, and deleting alerts. I discuss many of these options throughout this part of the book; you can explore the others on your own.

Here's a brief summary of each snapshot you'll find in the My Data tab of the Cash Flow Center.

Banking Alerts   The Banking Alerts snapshot lists Cash Flow Center alerts. You can click underlined links to go to the account or other item the alert applies to. I tell you how to set up and use Cash Flow Center alerts later in this chapter.

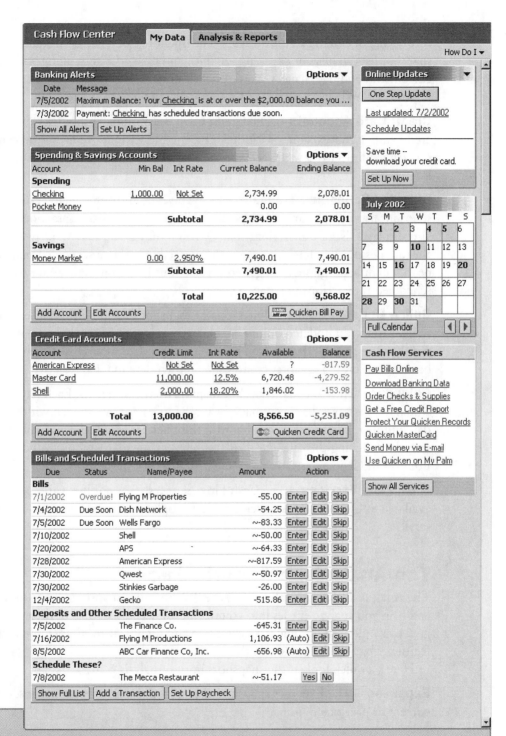

Figure 9-1 •The My Data tab of the Cash Flow Center includes many useful snapshots related to your cash flow accounts.

Spending & Savings Accounts   The Spending & Savings Accounts snapshot lists all of your checking, savings, and cash accounts, along with their current and ending balances. You can click underlined links to view the account register, set up balance alerts, and set interest rates.

Credit Card Accounts   The Credit Card Accounts snapshot lists all of your credit card accounts, along with their current and ending balances. You can click underlined links to view the account register, set the credit limit, and specify the interest rate.

Bills and Scheduled Transactions   The Bills and Scheduled Transactions snapshot lists all of your bills, deposits, and other scheduled transactions. It may also display a list of transactions that Quicken thinks you may want to schedule. Buttons beside each item enable you to enter, edit, or skip a scheduled transaction or to schedule or ignore a suggested transaction. I tell you more about using scheduled transactions in Chapter 7.

Online Updates   The Online Updates snapshot provides information about the last time you updated online-enabled accounts or Quicken.com. You can use the One Step Update button to initiate an update. I cover Quicken's online banking features in Chapter 6 and One Step Update in Chapter 7.

Calendar   The Calendar snapshot displays a small calendar. Each day for which a transaction has been made or is scheduled appears shaded with a bold date number. Clicking buttons beneath the calendar scrolls through different months. Clicking the calendar displays the full Calendar window, which I discuss in Chapter 7.

Cash Flow Services   The Cash Flow Services snapshot lists various services available to Quicken users. Clicking a link displays more information about the service.

The Analysis & Reports Tab

The Analysis & Reports tab (see Figure 9-2) includes snapshots that summarize and help you analyze entries into your cash flow accounts. Most of these snapshots give you a glimpse of Quicken's extensive and highly customizable reporting feature, which I discuss later in this chapter.

Here's a quick look at the snapshots in the Analysis & Reports tab:

Expenses   The Expenses snapshot displays a pie chart of your expenses for the current or previous month.

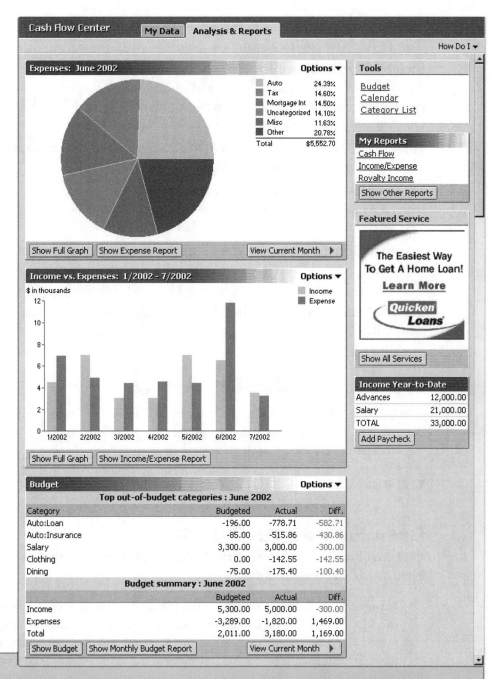

Figure 9-2 • The Analysis & Reports tab includes snapshots that help you understand your finances.

Income vs. Expenses The Income vs. Expenses snapshot displays a column chart of your year-to-date income and expenses.

Budget The Budget snapshot displays information from your budget, including the top five out-of-budget categories and a summary of your budgeted and actual income and expenses. To use this snapshot, you must set up a budget using Quicken's budgeting feature, as discussed in Chapter 18.

Tools The Tools area provides links to a number of Quicken features that you may find helpful when working with the Cash Flow Center.

My Reports The My Reports snapshot lists all of the reports and graphs you have created and saved for the Cash Flow Center. Click a link to display a report. I explain how to create and save reports later in this chapter.

Featured Service The Featured Service area contains an advertisement for a specific Quicken service. The ad changes each time you view the Analysis & Reports tab. To learn more about the service, click the graphic.

Income Year-to-Date The Income Year-to-Date snapshot summarizes your year-to-date income, by category.

Cash Flow Center Alerts

The Banking Alerts snapshot in the Cash Flow Center's My Data tab lists alerts about your Cash Flow accounts. Putting them right at the top of the window is a great way to make sure you don't miss them.

In this section, I tell you about the kinds of alerts Quicken offers for the Cash Flow Center and explain how to set them up.

Cash Flow Alerts Overview

Quicken offers seven different alerts that you can set up for Cash Flow accounts. Here's a look at each of them.

- **Account Min. Balances** enables you to set minimum balances for your checking and savings accounts. You can set a minimum amount and a reminder amount for each account. Quicken can alert you when the account balance falls below the reminder amount you specify. This option is especially useful if you have an account that requires a minimum balance.

- **Account Max. Balances** enables you to set maximum balances for your checking and savings accounts. Quicken alerts you when the account balance climbs above the amount you specify. You may find this useful if you like to keep excess cash in an interest-bearing account such as a savings account rather than a non-interest-bearing checking account.

- **Credit Card Limits** enables you to set limits for your credit card accounts. You can set a limit amount and a reminder amount. Quicken alerts you if the balance exceeds the reminder amount. This is a great way to keep credit card spending under control and avoid the embarrassment of having a card declined at the checkout counter.

- **Check Reorder Notice** tells Quicken to alert you when you reach a certain check number. You can set this option for checking and savings accounts. This feature can be used whether you use checks provided by your bank or another printer or checks you purchase exclusively for use with Quicken.

- **Monthly Expenses** enables you to specify maximum monthly spending amounts for any Quicken expense category. If you exceed the limit you specified, Quicken alerts you.

- **Savings Goals** tells Quicken to alert you when you fall behind on a savings goal. This option works directly with Quicken's Savings Goals feature, which I cover in Chapter 18.

- **Online Institution Now Offers Online Service** tells Quicken to alert you when one of your financial institutions supports online account services. Quicken can learn about new financial partners when you connect to the Internet to utilize other features. I tell you more about online account services in Chapter 6.

In addition, Quicken offers three other general reminders that appear in the Cash Flow Center:

- **Online Transactions** tells Quicken to remind you to download transactions from your financial institution if you haven't done so for 30 days or more.

- **Scheduled Transactions Reminder** tells Quicken to remind you in advance of any scheduled transactions that are due.

- **Sync with Qcom** tells Quicken to remind you to export your portfolio, account balances, and reminders with Quicken.com when balances change.

Setting Up Alerts

You set up alerts with the Setup tab of the Alerts Center window. To display this window, click the Set Up Alerts button in the Banking Alerts snapshot (refer to Figure 9-1) or choose Tools | Set Up Alerts. If necessary, click the plus sign (+) to the left of Cash Flow to display the Cash Flow Center alerts. You can then click the name of one of the alerts to view and set it. Figure 9-3 shows the Account Min. Balance alert being edited.

Setting Basic Options

To set an alert, begin by selecting the name of the alert on the left side of the window. If necessary, click the check box to place a green check mark within it. Then click the value you want to change on the right side of the window and enter a new value. Not all alerts have values you can change; for example, the Online Institution Now Offers Online Services alert is a simple on or off setting made with the green check mark.

Setting Other Options

There are two additional options you can set in the bottom half of the window:

Figure 9-3 • Use the Setup tab of the Alerts Center to set alerts for Cash Flow and other accounts.

Show Me The Alert As   There are two options for showing the alert:

- **Text In The Alert List** displays the alert as an item in the Banking Alerts snapshot only.
- **Urgent (Pop Up Dialog Box)** displays the alert in a dialog. This in-your-face alert must be dismissed by clicking the OK button in the dialog before continuing work with Quicken.

Keep The Alert In The List For   You can set the amount of time the alert should remain in the Banking Alerts snapshot. The default setting is One Month, but you can use the drop-down list to choose from One Day, One Week, One Month, One Quarter, or One Year.

Finishing Up

When you're finished setting options for an alert, click the Apply button to save them. You can then set other alerts in the same category or other categories.

When you're completely finished setting alerts, click Done to dismiss the Alerts Center window. The alerts will work quietly in the background, watching your finances. When it's time to go to work, they appear as you specified.

Working with Alerts

Once you've set up alerts, you can view, modify, or delete them as desired. Here's how.

Viewing Alerts

The Banking Alerts snapshot in the Cash Flow Center (refer to Figure 9-1) is one way to view alerts. But there are other ways.

Quicken Home   Quicken displays all alerts in the Alerts snapshot of the Quicken Home window—a good idea, since that's what Quicken displays first when you start it. Click the Quicken Home button at the top of the Account bar to view them. Here's what they might look like:

Alerts Center   You can also view alerts in the Show All tab of the Alerts Center window (see Figure 9-4). Click the Show All Alerts button in any Alerts snapshot or choose Tools | Show All Alerts to display them.

Modifying Alerts

You can change the way an alert works at any time. Choose Tools | Set Up Alerts to display the Setup tab of the Alerts Center (refer to Figure 9-3). Then follow the instructions in the section titled "Setting Up Alerts" to change alert settings.

Deleting an Alert

To delete an alert, choose Tools | Show All Alerts to display the Show All tab of the Alerts Center (refer to Figure 9-4). Turn on the check box beside each alert you want to delete and click the Delete button. A confirmation dialog appears. Click OK to delete the alert.

To prevent a deleted alert from appearing again in the future, use the Setup Tab of the Alerts Center window (refer to Figure 9-3) to turn off the check box for the alert in the list on the left side of the window.

Figure 9-4 • The Show All tab of the Alerts Center window enables you to view and delete alerts.

Quicken Reporting Overview

Quicken offers a variety of reports and graphs, each of which can be customized to meet your needs. I like to think of reports and graphs as the "fruits of my labor." I spend time entering data into Quicken so Quicken can crunch the numbers. I use the reports and graphs it creates to analyze my spending habits, find ways to save money, and submit information to financial institutions when I apply for loans.

In this section, I tell you about the types of reports and graphs Quicken offers. Then I explain how you can use a variety of techniques to quickly create reports and graphs based on the information in your Quicken data file. Although I'll concentrate on reports and graphs for the Cash Flow Center, the techniques in this part of the chapter apply to the reports and graphs you create for any Quicken data, regardless of the Center in which it appears.

Types of Reports and Graphs

Within Quicken are essentially three kinds of reports and graphs: saved, predefined, and EasyAnswer. Here's an overview of each one.

Saved

You can create custom reports and graphs by customizing the predefined reports and graphs. This multiplies your reporting capabilities, enabling you to create reports or graphs that show exactly what you need to show. When you save your custom reports and graphs, they can be created quickly, with just a few mouse clicks, to display current information. (Previous versions of Quicken referred to this feature as *memorized* reports.)

Quicken Quick Tip

Here's a real-life example of how Quicken's reporting features can help you. Not long ago, I applied by phone for a home equity line of credit. The bank representative asked a lot of questions about my finances, including balances on my accounts and the market value of my investments. Because I track all my finances in Quicken, all the information I needed was right in front of me, in Quicken windows and reports that I could generate within seconds. The application process took less than fifteen minutes, and I got preliminary approval right away.

Predefined

Quicken includes a number of predefined reports and graphs that are organized by topics that roughly correspond to Quicken's Centers. Each topic provides reports or graphs that answer a specific question:

- **Cash Flow** tells you how you are spending your money.
- **Investing** tells you how your investments are doing.
- **Tax** provides information on your tax situation.
- **Net Worth & Balances** tells you what you own and owe.
- **Business** shows you how your business is doing.

For example, the Cash Flow topic includes Banking Summary, Cash Flow, Income/Expense, Itemized Categories, Spending, Transaction, and Reconciliation, among others. These reports and graphs clearly show how you're spending your money.

EasyAnswer

EasyAnswer reports and graphs answer specific, predefined questions such as:

- Where did I spend my money during the period...?
- How much did I spend on...?
- How much did I pay to...?
- Am I saving more or less?

You select a question and then provide optional information such as a date range, payee, or account. Quicken gathers the information and generates the report or graph.

The Report Window

The window in which reports and graphs appear has been reworked for Quicken 2003. It now includes a navigation bar along the left side of the window which enables you to switch to various sub-reports you can create by customizing the original report. You can see an example of this in Figure 9-5. I explain how to customize reports to create sub-reports later in this chapter.

Another new feature in Quicken 2003 is the way the report window is automatically minimized to the Quicken task bar (right above the Windows task bar at the bottom of the application window) when you click outside the

Figure 9-5 • Here's a Cash Flow report for year-to-date activity. The navigation bar on the left side of the window includes sub-reports based on the original report.

window. To view the report again, click its name in the Quicken task bar and the window reappears.

Creating Reports and Graphs

With Quicken, creating a report or graph is as simple as clicking a few buttons. There are several techniques: choosing a report or graph from the Reports menu, setting options in the Reports and Graphs window, using the Report button or menu on button bars, and choosing commands from contextual menus. In this section, I explain how to use all of these techniques.

Reports and Graphs Window

The Reports and Graphs window (see Figure 9-6) offers one way to create reports and graphs. Choose Reports | Reports and Graphs to display it. Click one of the topics on the left side of the window to display a list of the available reports.

Figure 9-6 • You can use the Reports and Graphs window to create reports or graphs.

To create a report or graph, click its name on the right side of the window and then enter options in the settings area at the bottom of the window. Click Show Report or Show Graph to display the report or graph. (In some cases, only the Show Report button will appear.) Figure 9-7 shows an example.

The Reports Menu

Quicken's Reports menu, which is shown next, includes a number of submenus, each of which corresponds to a report category. To create a report or graph with the Reports menu, click a category submenu, then click a report option. Quicken creates a report for that option. If a graph is available, you can click the Graph tab at the top of the window to display it. (Figure 9-7 shows a graph window with the Report and Graph tabs displayed.)

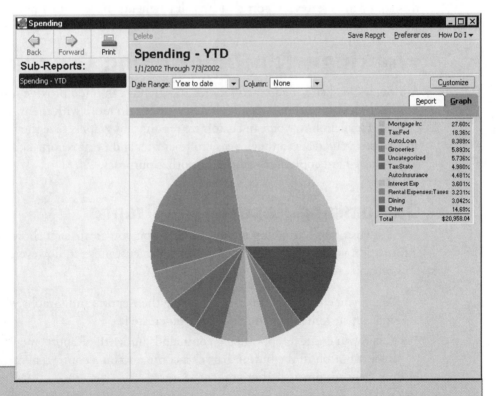

Figure 9-7 • Here's an example of a Spending graph. Clicking the Report tab displays the corresponding report.

Report Button

You can also create a report by using the Report button or menu on the button bar in some windows. This normally creates a report based on information selected within the window.

In a window that includes a Report button on the button bar, select one of the items in the window. Then click the Report button. A report appears in its own window. For example, you could create a Category Report by selecting a category in the Category & Transfer List window and then clicking the Report button.

Contextual Menus

The contextual menu that appears when you click the right mouse button while pointing to an item sometimes includes a command that will create a report for the item. For example, right-clicking the name of a payee in the account register window displays a menu that includes the Payments Made To command. Choosing this command creates a report that lists all payments made to that payee.

Working with Reports and Graphs

Although Quicken's predefined reports and graphs can often provide just the information you need onscreen, you may want to do more with them. In this section, I explain how you can customize reports and graphs, save the reports and graphs you create so they're easy to re-create, and print reports and graphs so you have hard copies for your files or other purposes.

Customizing Reports and Graphs

You can customize just about any report or graph you create so it shows only the information you want to display. When you can customize it, however, depends on how you create it:

- When you create a report or graph using the Reports and Graphs window, you can customize it before or after you create it.
- When you create a report using commands under the Reports menu, the Report button in the button bar, or a command on a contextual menu, you can only customize it after you create it.

Customization options vary from one type of report or graph to another. It's impossible to cover all variables in this chapter. I will, however, tell you about the most common options so you know what to expect. I'm sure you'll agree that Quicken's reporting feature is very flexible when you go beyond the basics.

Using the Customize Dialog

To customize a report or graph, click the Customize button at the bottom of the Reports and Graphs window or the Customize button at the top of the report or graph window. The Customize dialog appears. The dialog's full name includes the name of the report or graph.

The Customize Report dialog normally includes four tabs of options that you can set to customize the report:

- **Display** (shown in the previous illustration) enables you to set display options for the report, such as the title, row and column headings, organization, number formatting, and columns.
- **Accounts** enables you to select the accounts that should be included in the report.
- **Categories** enables you to select the categories to include in the report. If desired, you can use this tab to include only transactions for which the payee, category, or memo contains certain text.
- **Class** enables you to select the classes to include in the report. If desired, you can use this tab to include only transactions for which the payee, class, or memo contains certain text. This tab, which only appears if you have at least one class defined, makes it possible to generate reports by class. I tell you about classes in Chapter 3.
- **Category Groups** enables you to select the category groups to include in the report. I tell you about category groups in Chapters 3 and 18.
- **Advanced** enables you to set additional criteria for transactions to be included in the report, such as amount, status, and transaction type.

On each tab, you also have access to the Report Dates area, which you can use to specify a date or range of dates for the report.

Once you have set options as desired, click the Show Report, Show Graph, or OK button. If you are creating the report or graph from the Reports and Graphs window (refer to Figure 9-5), Quicken creates the report or graph to your specifications. If you are customizing an existing report or graph, Quicken creates a sub-report of the original report or graph and displays it in the same report window.

If the custom report or graph isn't exactly what you want, that's okay. Just click the Customize button in the report window and change settings in the

Customize dialog to fine-tune the report or graph. When you click OK, Quicken creates a new sub-report. You can repeat this process until the report or graph is exactly the way you want it.

Using the Customize Bar

The Customize bar near the top of a report window (see Figure 9-6) or graph window (see Figure 9-7) offers another way to customize a report or graph. Use it to change date ranges or modify subtotal settings for the report. After making a change in the Customize bar, click anywhere in the report or graph window to accept your settings. Quicken creates a sub-report based on your revised settings and displays it in the same report window.

Using QuickZoom

The QuickZoom feature enables you to create a report or graph on the fly. Simply double-click a report line item or a graph bar or legend item. Quicken generates a new sub-report for the item you double-clicked and displays it in the same report window.

Dragging Column Borders

You can change the width of columns on some reports by dragging the column markers. Column markers, when available, appear as paired vertical gray lines between column headings. Move the mouse pointer onto a column marker and a pair of black vertical lines with two arrows appears. Press the mouse button and drag to the right or left, as shown next. When you release the mouse button, the column's width changes.

Working with Sub-Reports

Quicken 2003 creates a sub-report each time you customize an existing report or graph or create a QuickZoom report. As you can imagine, it's easy to accumulate quite a few of these sub-reports when experimenting with Quicken's reporting features. Here's how to work with them.

Viewing a Sub-Report

To view a specific sub-report, click its name in the navigation bar on the left side of the report window (refer to Figure 9-6). The view changes to switch to the report.

You can also click the Back or Forward button at the top of the navigation bar to move among sub-reports you have already viewed.

Copying a Sub-Report

To copy a sub-report, display the sub-report you want to copy, then point to its name and click the right mouse button. A contextual menu appears. Choose Copy to copy the report to the Windows clipboard. You can then switch to a spreadsheet program (such as Excel) and use the Edit menu's Paste command to paste in the report.

Deleting a Sub-Report

To delete a sub-report, display the sub-report, then right-click its name to display a contextual menu like the one shown previously. Choose Delete This Sub-Report. To delete all sub-reports, choose Delete All Sub-Reports. You cannot use this technique to delete a main report—the report at the top of the Sub-Reports list.

Saving Reports and Graphs

You'll often create a predefined report and customize it to create a report you want to be able to see again and again. Rather than creating and customizing the report from scratch each time you want to see it, you can save the report's settings. Then, when you want to view the report again, just select it from a list, and it appears. You can do the same for graphs.

 A quick note here for experienced Quicken users. This feature was referred to as memorizing reports in previous versions of Quicken. As you'll see in this section, the feature got more than just a name change; it's now more convenient than ever to use.

Quicken Quick Tip

Why would you want to copy a report or sub-report? Well, perhaps you want to perform some additional calculations on the numbers. A spreadsheet program can do the job and the Copy button makes retyping all those numbers unnecessary. This feature only works for reports—not for graphs.

Saving a Report or Graph

To save a report or graph, start by creating, customizing, and displaying it. When it looks just the way you want, click the Save button on the report window's button bar. The Save Report dialog appears. Enter a name and description for the report or graph in the appropriate boxes. Then select the name of the Center in which you want it to be listed and click OK.

Viewing a Saved Report or Graph

When you save a report or graph, it appears a number of places throughout Quicken:

The Reports and Graphs Window   Saved reports and graphs appear in the Saved Reports topic in the Reports and Graphs window (see Figure 9-8). Double-click the name of the report or graph to display it.

The Saved Reports and Graphs Submenu   Saved reports and graphs also appear on the Saved Reports and Graphs submenu under the Reports menu, as shown next. Choose a report name to display it.

The My Reports Snapshot   Saved reports and graphs also appear in a list in the My Reports snapshot of a Center window. The Center in which a report or graph appears depends on the Center selected when the report was saved. Here's the Cash Flow Center's My Reports area with a few saved reports:

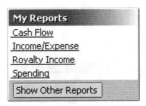

Printing Reports and Graphs

You can print reports and graphs. This enables you to create hard copies for your paper files or for use when applying for loans or completing your tax returns.

Printing a Report

To print a report or sub-report, begin by displaying it in the reports window. Then click the Print button at the top of the navigation bar on the left side of

Figure 9-8 • The Saved Reports topic lists all of your saved reports and graphs.

the window. The Print dialog, shown next, appears. Set options as desired and click OK.

Here's a look at the available options:

Print To Print To options determine the destination of the printed report or graph. There are four choices:

- **[Your Printer]** (the first option) prints to your printer. The wording of this option varies depending on the name of your default printer. This is the option you'll probably select most often.
- **ASCII Disk File** enables you to create a text file that includes all the information in the report. You can import the resulting file into a word processing program.
- **Tab-Delimited Disk File** enables you to create a tab-delimited text file that includes all the information in the report. In a tab-delimited text file, each column is separated by a tab character, making it easier to import the file into spreadsheet or database programs.
- **123 (.PRN) Disk File** enables you to create a comma-delimited text file that is easily recognized by Lotus 1-2-3 and other spreadsheet programs.

Orientation Orientation determines how the printed report will be viewed. The options are Portrait or Landscape. These are standard options offered by all programs. The icon beside each orientation illustrates the position of the paper.

Print Range The print range determines which pages will print. You can use this if the printout is expected to be more than one page. The default setting is

All, which prints all pages of the report. To print a range of pages, select Pages, then enter the first and last page number you want to print.

Fonts You can change the fonts used for the report by clicking the Heading Font and Body Font buttons. Each one displays a dialog that you can use to specify a font, font style, and font size, as shown here:

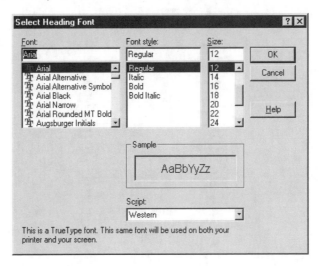

Additional Options There are three more options that can be toggled on or off with check boxes.

- **Print In Color** enables you to print in color—if you have a color printer.
- **Print In Draft Mode** substitutes a printer font for the fonts you may have selected for the report. This can speed printing. With this option turned on, the Print In Color and Fit To One Page Wide options are not available.
- **Fit To One Page Wide** scales the report so that it fits widthwise on the page. This sometimes involves changing the font size.

Previewing a Report You can click the Preview button in the Print dialog to see what the report will look like when printed. This gives you one last chance to check the appearance of the report before committing it to paper. Figure 9-9 shows what one of my saved reports looks like in the Print Preview window. You can click anywhere on the report to zoom in and see the details. If you want to print it, click the Print button at the top of the window. Otherwise, click Close to return to the report window.

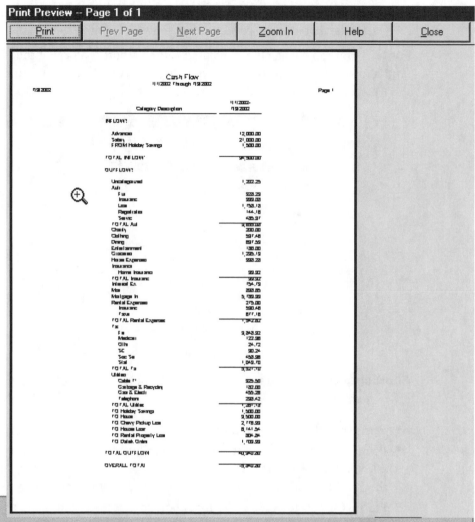

Figure 9-9 •You can preview a report to see what it will look like when printed.

Printing a Graph

Printing a graph is easy. Just click the Print button at the top of the window in which the graph is displayed. Quicken doesn't ask any questions. It simply sends the graph to the printer and prints it.

The Investing Center

This part of the book explains how you can use Quicken to track your investments. It begins by explaining the basics of tracking investments in Quicken, then goes on to explain how you can use Quicken's online investment tracking features to download investment information from your brokerage firm and exchange information with Quicken.com. Along the way, it provides a wealth of information you can use to invest wisely and maximize your investment returns. Finally, it explains how you can use Quicken's Investing Center and reporting features to keep an eye on your portfolio and investment returns. This part has three chapters:

Chapter 10: Entering Your Investment Transactions

Chapter 11: Using Online Investment Tracking and Research Tools

Chapter 12: Evaluating Your Position

Part Three

Entering Your Investment Transactions

In this Chapter:

- *Setting up investment accounts*

- *Recording investment transactions*

- *Adding and editing securities*

- *Using the Security Detail View window*

Chapter 10

Investments offer individuals a way to make their money grow. Although more risky than deposits made to an FDIC-insured bank, stocks, bonds, mutual funds, and other types of investments have the potential to earn more. That's why many people build investment portfolios as a way to save for future goals or retirement.

In this chapter, I tell you a little about investments and portfolio management and then explain how you can use Quicken to keep track of the money you invest.

Quicken Investment Basics

An *investment* is a security or asset that you expect to increase in value and/or generate income. There are many types of investments—Table 10-1 lists some of them. This chapter concentrates on the investments you can track with the features in Quicken's Investing Center.

Before learning how to use Quicken to track your investments, here's a review of Quicken's investment accounts and a more detailed explanation of why investment tracking is so important.

Your Quicken Portfolio

The term *portfolio* refers to the total of all of your investments. For example, if you have shares of one company's stock, shares in two mutual funds, and a 401(k) plan account, these are the items that make up your portfolio.

Types of Investment Accounts

Your Quicken portfolio can include four types of investment account. You can have as many investment accounts as you need to properly represent the investments that make up your portfolio.

Brokerage   A brokerage account is for tracking a wide variety of investments handled through a brokerage firm, including stocks, bonds, mutual funds, and annuities. Like the account at your brokerage firm, it can track income, capital gains, performance, market values, shares, and cash balances for multiple securities.

IRA or Keogh   An IRA or a Keogh account is for tracking a variety of retirement accounts, including standard IRA, Roth IRA, Education IRA, SEP-IRA, SIMPLE-IRA, and Keogh plans.

401(k) or 403(b)   A 401(k) or 403(b) account is for tracking 401(k), 403(b), or 457 plans, in which you make regularly scheduled, pre-tax contributions toward investments for your retirement. This type of account can track performance, market value, and distribution among investment choices. If you (and your spouse) have more than one plan, you should set up a separate account for each.

Single Mutual Fund   As the name implies, a single mutual fund account is for tracking one mutual fund. It can track the share balance, market value, income, capital gains, and performance of the fund. It can't, however, track interest, cash balances, or miscellaneous income or expenses.

Quicken 2003 simplifies the account creation process by offering two fewer account types. DRIP and Other Investment are no longer available. In most cases, you can use the Brokerage account type to account for dividend reinvestment program (DRIP) accounts and many other types of investments, as indicated in Table 10-1.

Choosing the Right Type of Account

Sometimes it's not clear which kind of account is best for a specific type of investment. Table 10-1 offers some guidance.

Type of Investment	Type of Account
CD	Savings account or brokerage account
Money market fund	Savings account or brokerage account
Stocks in your possession	Brokerage account
Brokerage account with one or more securities, with or without an associated cash, checking, or interest-earning account	Brokerage account
Employee Stock Options	Brokerage account
Employee Stock Purchase Plan (ESPP)	Brokerage account
Dividend Reinvestment Program (DRIP)	Brokerage account
Bonds, including U.S. Savings Bonds	Brokerage account
Treasury bills	Brokerage account
Single mutual fund with no cash balance	Single mutual fund account
Variable or fixed annuities	Brokerage account
401(k) or 403(b) plan	401(k) or 403(b) account
Traditional IRA, Roth IRA, Education IRA, Keogh Plan, SEP-IRA, or SIMPLE-IRA	IRA or Keogh account
Real estate	Asset account
Real estate investment trusts (REITs) or partnerships	Brokerage account

Table 10-1 • Quicken Accounts for Various Investment Types

Keep in mind that you can also track many types of investments in asset accounts. But Quicken's investment accounts enable you to better track and report on the income, capital gains, and performance of your investments.

This chapter concentrates on investment accounts tracked in brokerage, IRA or Keogh, 401(k) or 403(b), and single mutual fund accounts.

The Importance of Portfolio Management

At this point, you may be wondering why you should bother including investment information in your Quicken data file. After all, you may already get quarterly (or even monthly) statements from your broker or investment firm. What you may not realize, however, is how you can benefit from keeping a close eye on your investments. Take a look at what portfolio management with Quicken can do for you.

Centralizing Your Investment Records

Unless you have only one brokerage account for all your investments, you probably get multiple statements for the stocks, bonds, mutual funds, and other investments in your portfolio. No single statement can provide a complete picture of your portfolio's worth. Quicken can, however. By entering the transactions and values on each statement within Quicken, you can see the details of your entire portfolio in one place.

Knowing the Value of Your Portfolio on Any Day

Brokerage statements can tell you the value of your investments on the statement's ending date, but not what they're worth today. Or what they were worth on July 8, 2002. Quicken, however, can tell you what your portfolio is worth on any day for which you have entered security prices, and it can estimate values for dates without exact pricing information. If you like to keep your portfolio's value up to date with the latest security prices, you can retrieve prices online. I show you how to take advantage of this feature in Chapter 11.

Keeping Track of Performance History

Manually compiling a complete pricing and performance history for an investment is no small task, especially for periods spanning multiple statements. If you consistently enter investment information in your Quicken data file, however, preparing performance charts and reports is as easy as choosing a menu command or clicking a button.

Calculating Your Return on Investment

Return on investment varies from one investment to another. Quicken enables you to see the return on investment for each security you hold—all in one place.

You can use this feature to make better financial decisions. When you're ready to invest more money in your portfolio, it's easy to see which holding is best and may deserve more funding.

Calculating Capital Gains Quickly and Easily

Calculating the gain on the sale of an investment isn't always easy. Considerations include not only the purchase and selling prices, but commissions, fees, stock splits, and purchase lots. Quicken can take all the work out of calculating capital gains, even if you're just considering the sale and want to know what its impact will be. This is extremely helpful at tax time, as I discuss in Chapter 19.

Creating Investing Center Accounts

Before you can begin tracking your investments with Quicken, you must set up the investment accounts you'll need to do it right. I provide basic information about setting up accounts in Chapter 3. In this section, I provide the specifics for creating Investing Center accounts.

Creating a Standard Brokerage Account

Begin by displaying the Add New Investment Account dialog for a Brokerage or Standard Brokerage account as discussed in Chapter 2 or 3. The first screen should look like this:

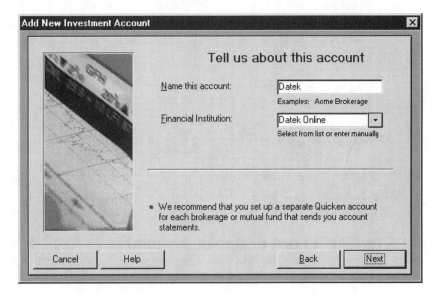

Enter a name for the account in the Name This Account box. Then enter your brokerage firm's name in the Financial Institution box. You can use the drop-down list to select a name or you can enter a name by typing it in. As you type, Quicken attempts to fill in a name from its list. Make sure the brokerage firm name is correct, especially if the account is enabled for online account services. Click Next.

If you entered the name of a brokerage firm that wasn't in the Financial Institution drop-down list, Quicken displays a dialog that lists brokerage firm names that are similar to what you typed. If your brokerage firm is in the list, select the top option and click the brokerage firm name. If it isn't, select the bottom option and make sure the correct name is entered in the box beneath it. Then click Next.

The next screen asks how you use cash in your investment account. You have two options:

- **I don't write checks or use a debit card from this account** tells Quicken that the account is not associated with a linked cash account.

- **I do write checks or use a debit card from this account** tells Quicken that the account is associated with a linked cash account, which you can access by writing checks or using a debit or ATM card. If you select this option, you must select one of two options. Add New Checking Account enables you to instruct Quicken to add a new checking account that will be linked to the account. Enter a name for the account in the box beside the option. Use Existing Checking Account tells Quicken that one of your existing checking accounts should be linked to the brokerage account. Choose an account from the drop-down list.

After setting options in the dialog, click Next. Quicken displays a summary of the information you set for the account. Click Done.

If your brokerage firm supports Online Account Services, the Online Account Activation dialog appears next. I explain in Chapter 11 how to activate online account services for brokerage accounts. For now, click Skip.

The Add Investment Account Data dialog appears next. I explain how to use this dialog to enter information about account holdings in the section titled "Adding Account Holdings Data" later in this chapter.

Creating an IRA or Keogh Account

Begin by displaying the Add New Investment Account dialog for an IRA or Keogh account as discussed in Chapter 2 or 3. The first screen should look like this:

Enter a name for the account in the Name This Account box. Then enter your investment firm's name in the Financial Institution box. Select an option to indicate whether the IRA is owned by you or your spouse. Then select one of the IRA types from the drop-down list at the bottom of the dialog. Click Next.

If you entered the name of an investment firm that wasn't in the Financial Institution drop-down list, Quicken displays a dialog that lists investment firm names that are similar to what you typed. If your investment firm is in the list, select the top option and click the investment firm name. If it isn't, select the bottom option and make sure the correct name is entered in the box beneath it. Then click Next.

Quicken displays a summary of the information you set for the account. Click Done.

The Add Investment Account Data dialog appears next. I explain how to use this dialog to enter information about account holdings in the section titled "Adding Account Holdings Data" later in this chapter.

Creating a 401(k) or 403(b) Account

When you create a 401(k) or 403(b) account, Quicken displays the 401(k)/ 403(b) Setup dialog, which you can use to enter information for the account and any loans you might have taken on it. This dialog uses Quicken's EasyStep approach to walk you through the process of entering information, then summarizes the information at the end of the setup process.

Begin by displaying the 401(k)/403(b) Setup dialog for a 401(k) or 403(b) account as discussed in Chapter 2 or 3. The first screen explains what the setup process does. Read this overview and click Next.

The next screen prompts you to enter basic information about the account. Enter a name for the account in the Account Name box. You can enter a brief description of the account in the Description box. Then enter your investment firm's name in the Financial Institution box. Click Next.

If you entered the name of an investment firm that wasn't in the Financial Institution drop-down list, Quicken displays a dialog that lists investment firm names that are similar to what you typed. If your investment firm is in the list, select the top option and click the investment firm name. If it isn't, select the bottom option and make sure the correct name is entered in the box beneath it. Then click Next.

Quicken prompts you for additional information about the account in the 401(k)/403(b) Setup dialog, shown next. Enter the name of the employer and whether it is a current or previous employer. Then indicate whether the account is yours or your spouse's. If the employer contributes to the account, say so and enter the vested percentage. You should have all of this information on your account statement or the paperwork you got when you started the account. Finally, to link the account to a paycheck transaction, turn on the Set Up A Withdrawal From My Paycheck For This Account check box. If you turn on this check box, the next screen will ask whether you have set up your paycheck in Quicken and, if so, which paycheck it is. Another dialog prompts you to enter your contribution and your employer's match contribution. If you haven't set up your paycheck in Quicken, Quicken will display Paycheck Setup when you're finished entering plan information. I explain how to use Paycheck Setup in Chapter 7.

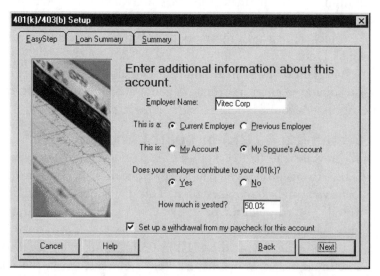

Clicking Next eventually displays a screen that asks if you have any loans against the account. If you do, indicate how many you have. When you click Next, Quicken will prompt you for information about each loan, including a description, the current balance, and the original loan amount. Check boxes enable you to specify whether you want Quicken to set up a loan account to track the loan balance as you make payments. I tell you how to track loans in Chapter 13. If your paycheck has been set up in Quicken, you can also tell Quicken to set up a paycheck withdrawal for loan payments and indicate the amount of the payment. Click Next to move through each of these screens.

When you're finished entering loan information, Quicken displays a screen that asks for general information about the securities in your account. Provide the statement date and number of securities (not number of shares) for the account. You'll also have to indicate whether your statement includes details about the number of shares held. When you're finished, click Next.

Quicken displays a series of screens and dialogs that enable you to enter information about the account holdings. You'll need your most recent statement to enter this information accurately.

The first screen that appears looks like the one shown next. Enter the name of a security in the Security Name box. If you enter a security name that isn't already set up in Quicken, Quicken displays the Set Up New Security dialog, which is similar to the Edit Security dialog I illustrate and discuss later in this chapter. Enter information about the new security in the dialog and click OK to save it and return to the 401(k)/403(b) Setup dialog. You can then enter the total number of shares of that security and the related ending balance on your statement. Click Next. If you have more than one security, you'll repeat this process for each one.

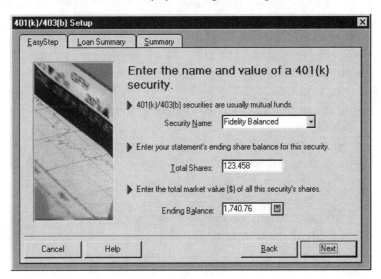

When you're finished entering holdings information, Quicken displays a summary of the information you set for the account. Click Done.

Creating a Single Mutual Fund Account

Begin by displaying the Add New Investment Account dialog for a Single Mutual Fund account as discussed in Chapter 2 or 3. The first screen should look like the following.

Enter a name for the account in the Name This Account box. Then enter your investment firm's name in the Financial Institution box. Specify whether the account is tax deferred by selecting the Yes or No option. Then click Next.

If you entered the name of an investment firm that wasn't in the Financial Institution drop-down list, Quicken displays a dialog that lists investment firm names that are similar to what you typed. If your investment firm is in the list, select the top option and click the investment firm name. If it isn't, select the bottom option and make sure the correct name is entered in the box beneath it. Then click Next.

Quicken displays a summary of the information you set for the account. Click Done.

Next, Quicken displays the Set Up Mutual Fund Security dialog. This dialog looks and works like the Set Up Security dialog, which I illustrate and discuss later in this chapter. Use the dialog to enter information about the mutual fund in the account and click OK.

The Add Investment Account Data dialog appears next. I explain how to use this dialog to enter information about account holdings in the following section.

Adding Account Holdings Data

When you create a new investment account, Quicken assumes that you have existing holdings that should be included in that account. It displays the Add Investment Account Data dialog's first screen, which is shown next. This dialog is new in Quicken 2003. It makes it easier to understand how the way you set up investment account balances affects Quicken's investment and tax reporting capabilities.

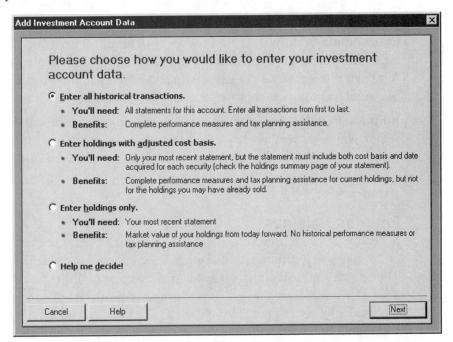

Choosing a Starting Balance Entry Method

The Add Investment Account Data dialog offers four options. Select the one you want and click Next.

Enter all historical transactions.   The most accurate yet time-consuming way to set up an investment account's beginning balances is to enter all transactions for the account, starting with the day it was opened. If the account is only a few weeks or months old, doing this may not be a big deal. But if you've had the account for years and it has dozens (or hundreds) of transactions, you may not think it's worth the effort. The benefit of this method is that Quicken will be able to generate accurate investment reports for all transactions in the account.

Enter holdings with adjusted cost basis. A quicker but less accurate way to set up an investment account's beginning balances is to take holdings information directly from the most recent account statement, including the cost and acquisition date for each security. This technique requires that your statement's holding summary includes cost basis and acquisition date information for each security. The benefit of this method is that Quicken can provide accurate investment reports for securities you hold now. It will not, however, be able to report on securities you sold before the statement date, even if they occurred within the same year.

Enter holdings only. The quickest way to set up an investment account's beginning balances is to enter the securities you own with today's market value. Although this technique can get you up and running in minutes, it makes it impossible for Quicken to generate accurate reports about any current holdings.

Help me decide! This option takes you through a question-and-answer session with Quicken, where you indicate what's important to you about tracking your investments. At the conclusion, Quicken redisplays the Add Investment Account Data screen shown previously with the option it suggests highlighted and selected.

Entering Holdings

No matter which option you select, when you click Next, Quicken will begin prompting you for information about the account and the securities within it. The screens and dialogs that appear vary depending on the information Quicken needs. Each screen in the Add Investment Account Data dialog provides an explanation of the requested information, making it easy to enter what's needed. You should be able to find all the information you need to enter on your brokerage or investment firm statements; be sure to have them handy.

Along the way, Quicken will display the Record Transaction dialog so you can enter security transaction details. The Set Up New Security dialog will appear each time you enter the name of a security that isn't already set up in Quicken. I explain how to use these dialogs in the next section and in the section titled "Working with Securities," later in this chapter.

When you're finished entering account holdings information, take a moment to check the account balances in Quicken with those on your investment account statement (if available). If you entered all requested information properly, the balances—especially the cash and share balances—should match. Market values may differ, depending on the method you used to enter the transactions and the source of your information.

Recording Investment Transactions

The most important part of properly tracking investments is recording all investment transactions. This includes purchases, sales, dividends, and other activity affecting your portfolio's value.

Before you enter a transaction, you must have all of its details. In most cases, you can find the information you need on a confirmation form or receipt you receive from your broker or investment firm. The information varies depending on the transaction, but it generally should include the security name, transaction date, number of shares, price per share, and commissions or fees.

In this section, I provide some information and advice for entering the most common transactions into investment accounts.

Account Register

The account register for an investment account, shown in Figure 10-1, looks similar to the account register window for any other type of account. It enables you to view, enter, and edit transactions for an investment account.

To open the account register window, click the name of the account in the Account bar or in the My Data tab of the Investing Center. If necessary, click the Register tab to display the account's transactions. (I tell you about the Overview tab in Chapter 12.)

Keep in mind that you can also enter transactions within the Security Detail View window (refer to Figure 10-3 later in this chapter) for the security that is affected. I tell you more about the Security Detail View window later in this chapter.

The button bar buttons and menus in the account register window enable you to enter investments and work with the register. The buttons and menus that appear vary depending on the type of account.

- **Record Transaction** is both a button and a menu. Clicking the button displays the Record Transaction dialog, which is discussed a little later in this chapter. Clicking the triangle displays a menu of actions that appear as forms in the Record Transaction dialog. This button/menu appears for all types of accounts except a 401(k) or 403(b) account.
- **Security View** displays the Security Detail View window (refer to Figure 10-3), which provides details about the securities set up in Quicken. I tell you more about the Security Detail View window later in this chapter.
- **Portfolio** opens the Investing Center's Portfolio tab. I tell you more about the Portfolio tab in Chapter 12.

Brokerage		Register	Overview					
Record Transaction ▾	Security View	Portfolio	Set Up Online	Analysis ▾		Checking Account	How Do I ▾	
Date	Action Memo	Security	Price	Shares	Amount Comm/Fee		Clr	Cash Bal
12/29/2000	BuyX	Apple Computer	14.875 [Brokerage-Cash]	100 1,497.49	1,497 49 9 99			0 00
3/2/2001	BuyX	Amazon.com	10 [Brokerage-Cash]	100 1,009.99	1,009 99 9 99			0 00
4/27/2001	BuyX	Intuit, Inc.	30.25 [Brokerage-Cash]	50 1,522.49	1,522 49 9 99			0 00
7/20/2001	SellX	Amazon.com	16.50 [Brokerage-Cash]	100 1,640.01	1,640 01 9 99			0 00
9/21/2001	BuyX	EBay	43.79 [Brokerage-Cash]	50 2,199.49	2,199 49 9 99			0 00
4/17/2002	SellX	Apple Computer	26 [Brokerage-Cash]	50 1,290.01	1,290 01 9 99			0 00
6/28/2002	SellX	Intuit, Inc.	50 [Brokerage-Cash]	50 2,490.01	2,490 01 9 99			0 00
7/8/2002	Action Memo	Security	Price	Shares	Amount Comm/Fee			

Enter	Edit ▾	Form

Linked Cash Bal: 4,190.57   **Ending Market Value:** 3,489.50

Download transactions from Datek Online!

Figure 10-1 • The account register window for a standard brokerage account shows all recorded transactions.

- **Set Up Online** displays the Online Account Activation dialog, which you can use to activate online account services for an investment account. This button only appears if the financial institution for the account supports online account services. I tell you how to set up online account access for investment accounts in Chapter 11.
- **Analysis** displays a menu of options to help you analyze your investments. I tell you about these options in Chapter 12.
- **Checking Account** opens the account register for a linked checking account. This option only appears if a linked checking account exists for the account.
- **How Do I** provides additional information about using the account register window and its options.

Using the Record Transaction Dialog

The easiest way to enter an investment transaction is with the Record Transaction dialog, which displays a custom form for virtually every kind of investment transaction. To open the Record Transaction dialog, click the Record Transaction button on the register window's button bar (refer to Figure 10-1). It looks like this when you first open it:

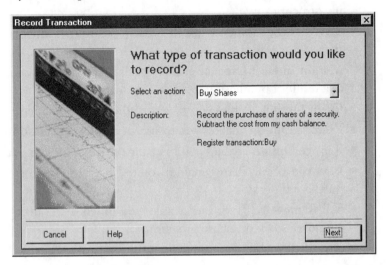

To use the Record Transaction dialog, you must begin by choosing an action from the drop-down list. Here's a list of the actions that are available. Note that Quicken 2003 added two types of transactions and changed the name of a handful of others.

- **Buy Shares** enables you to add shares to an investment account using a buy transaction.
- **Sell Shares** enables you to remove shares from an investment account with a sell transaction.

- **Add Shares** enables you to add shares to an investment account without an exchange of cash. You might use this option to add shares received as a gift.
- **Remove Shares** enables you to remove shares from an investment account without an exchange of cash. You might use this option to remove shares you have given to someone else as a gift.
- **Stock Split** enables you to record additional shares received as a result of a stock split.
- **Stock Dividend (non-cash)** enables you to add shares of a security paid as a dividend.
- **Reinvest Income** enables you to account for investment income (such as dividends) that are reinvested in the security. This is common with dividend reinvestment plans and mutual funds.

- **Record Income (dividend, interest)** enables you to record income from interest and dividends.
- **Return of Capital** enables you to record the return of part of your investment capital.
- **Miscellaneous Expense** enables you to record investment expenses other than commissions.
- **Margin Interest Expense** enables you to record the amount of interest paid as a result of purchasing securities on margin.
- **Grant Option** enables you to record the receipt of an employee stock option.
- **Exercise Option** enables you to use an employee stock option to buy stock.
- **Reprice Option** enables you to change pricing information for stock options.
- **Buy/Add ESPP Shares** enables you to buy shares in an employee stock purchase program.
- **Sell/Remove ESPP Shares** enables you to sell shares purchased through an employee stock purchase program.
- **Short Sell** enables you to record a short sale of a security.
- **Cover Short** enables you to record the purchase of stock to cover a short sale.
- **Corporate Name Change** enables you to record the change of the name of a company for which you own stock. This preserves the old name information; simply editing the security name in the Edit Security dialog does not.
- **Corporate Spin-Off** enables you to record securities obtained through a spin-off of a smaller company from one of the companies in which you own securities.
- **Corporate Acquisition (stock for stock)** enables you to record securities obtained in exchange for other securities you own, normally as a result of a corporate acquisition.
- **Transfer Shares** enables you to move shares from one Quicken investment account to another.
- **Reminder Transaction** enables you to enter an investment reminder that will appear each time you start Quicken. You may find this option useful if you want to conduct a transaction at a future date and are worried that you may forget to do it.

Record Transaction dialogs and forms are generally self-explanatory and easy to use. Here are a few common transactions to illustrate how they work.

Purchases

A security purchase normally involves the exchange of cash for security shares. In some cases, you may already own shares of the security or have it listed on your Watch List. In other cases, the security may not already exist in your Quicken data file, so you'll need to set up the security when you make the purchase.

Start by choosing Buy Shares in the Record Transaction dialog. When you click Next, the Buy Shares form appears. Enter information about the shares you have purchased:

- **Date** is the date of the transaction.
- **Security** is the name of the security. If you enter the name of a security that doesn't already exist in Quicken, the Set Up New Security dialog appears, which looks like the Edit Security dialog. (I explain how to use the Edit Security dialog later in this chapter.)
- **Account** is the name of the account in which the transaction should be recorded. You cannot change the option chosen from this drop-down list if you are entering a transaction from within the account register; if it's wrong, click Cancel, open the correct account register, and start over.
- **Number Of Shares** is the number of shares purchased.
- **Price Paid Per Share** is the per share price.
- **Commission** is the amount of commissions you paid to your brokerage or investment firm.
- **Total Cost** is calculated by Quicken. If you're recording the purchase of a fractional number of shares and this amount is off by a penny or two, use the Commission field to adjust the Total Cost. The net effect of tiny adjustments like this is negligible.
- **Use Cash For This Transaction** enables you to specify an account from which the total cost should be deducted. If the account has a linked cash account, that account is chosen by default and cannot be changed.

When you're finished entering information about the transaction, click Done. The transaction appears in the account register:

4/27/2001	BuyX	Intuit, Inc.	30.25	50		1,522	49		0	00
			[Brokerage-Cash]	1,522.49		9	99			

If you want to add security shares to an account without an exchange of cash, use the Add Shares action, which is new in Quicken 2003. Its form asks for most of the same information, but does not affect any cash balances.

Sales

A security sale also involves the exchange of cash for security shares. Normally, you dispose of shares you already own, but in some instances, you may sell shares you don't own. This is called *selling short,* and it is a risky investment technique sometimes used by experienced investors. (To record short sale transactions, use the Short Sale or Cover Short Sale action.)

To sell shares, choose Sell Shares in the Record Transaction dialog. When you click Next, the Sell Shares form, shown next, appears. Enter information about the shares you have sold:

- **Date** is the date of the transaction.
- **Security** is the name of the security. You can choose an option from the drop-down list.
- **Account** is the name of the account in which the transaction should be recorded. You cannot change the option chosen from this drop-down list if you are entering a transaction from within the account register. If it's wrong, click Cancel, open the correct account register, and start over.
- **Number Of Shares** is the number of shares sold.
- **Price Got Per Share** is the per share price.
- **Commission** is the amount of commissions you paid to your brokerage or investment firm.

- **Total Sale** is calculated by Quicken by multiplying the per share price by the number of shares and deducting the commission. This is the proceeds from the sale.
- **Cost Basis Method** enables you to choose one of two methods for calculating the cost per share sold:
  - **Average Cost** automatically averages the cost of all shares purchased and uses that average as a per share cost.
  - **Lot Identification** calculates the exact cost of the shares you are selling based on purchase lots. You can use this option for additional control over capital gains. For example, if you want to take advantage of long-term capital gains tax breaks, you could sell shares that have been in your possession for more than 12 months. If you want to record a loss, you could sell shares that cost more than the selling price. Obviously, your options will vary depending on the lots, their acquisition prices, and your selling price. If you select this option, click the Specify Lots button to display a dialog like the one shown next. Use the dialog to select the lots you are selling and click OK.

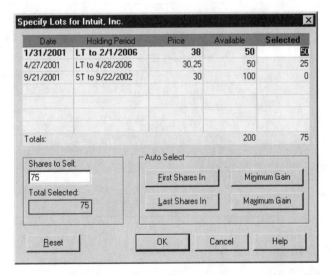

- **Record Proceeds?** enables you to specify an account to which the net proceeds should be added. If the account has a linked cash account, that account is chosen by default and cannot be changed.

When you click Done, the transaction is recorded. Here's what it might look like:

6/28/2002	SellX	Intuit, Inc.	50	75		3,740	01		0	00
			[Brokerage-Cash]	3,740.01			9	99		

Dividend Payments and Other Income

Many investments pay dividends, interest, or other income in cash. (That's why they're so attractive to an investor!) Recording this activity in the appropriate account register enables Quicken to accurately calculate performance, while keeping account balances up to date.

Keep in mind that many mutual funds are set up to reinvest income, rather than pay it in cash. Do not use the steps in this section to record a reinvestment of income. Instead, use the Reinvest Income action to enter transaction information.

To record dividend or interest income, choose Record Income (dividends, interest) from the drop-down list in the Record Transaction dialog, shown next. When you click Next, a Record An Income Event form appears. Use it to enter information about a cash payment on an investment:

- **Date** is the date of the transaction.
- **Account** is the name of the account in which the transaction should be recorded. You cannot change the option chosen from this drop-down list if you are entering a transaction from within the account register; if it's wrong, click Cancel, open the correct account register, and start over.
- **Security** is the name of the security. You can choose an option from the drop-down list. If the transaction isn't related to a specific security—for example, interest paid on a cash balance in a brokerage account—you can leave this field blank.

- **Category For Miscellaneous** is the category you want to use to record miscellaneous income. This field is only available if you enter a value in the Miscellaneous field.
- **Transfer Account** enables you to specify an account into which the income is deposited. If the investment account has a linked cash account, that account is chosen by default and cannot be changed.
- **Memo** enables you to enter a brief note about the transaction.
- **Dividend, Interest, Short-Term Cap Gain Dist, Mid-Term Cap Gain Dist, Long-Term Cap Gain Dist,** and **Miscellaneous** are fields for entering various types of income. In most cases, you'll use only one or two of these boxes.
- **Total Proceeds** is the total of all income amounts, calculated by Quicken.

When you click Done to record the transaction, it appears in the account register window for the account, like this:

7/8/2002	DivX	Automatic Data Prc			12	50		0	00
	.10/share dividend		[Brokerage-Cash]						

Other Transactions

Other transactions are just as easy to enter as purchases, sales, and dividends. Simply choose the appropriate option from the drop-down list in the Record Transaction dialog, and enter the transaction information in the form that appears. If you have the transaction confirmation or brokerage statement in front of you when you enter the transaction, you have all the information you need to enter it.

If you need additional guidance while entering a transaction, click the Help button in the Record Transaction dialog to learn more about the options that must be entered.

Editing Transactions

You can also use action forms to edit transactions. In the account register window, select the transaction you want to edit and click the Form button beneath it. Edit the transaction in the dialog that appears and click Done to save your changes.

Entering Transactions Directly into the Account Register

Experienced Quicken users may prefer to enter transactions directly into the account register. A drop-down list in the transaction's entry area offers appropriate transaction codes for all kinds of transactions. Explore this feature on your own once you're accustomed to entering investment transactions with the Record Transaction dialog's action forms.

Quicken Quick Tip

Frankly, I've been using Quicken for years now and I still prefer using action forms to enter transactions. It's the only way I'm confident that I'm entering all the information I need to, in the correct fields.

Adjusting Balances

Occasionally, you may need to adjust the cash balance or number of shares in an investment account or update the balance in a 401(k) account. Here's how.

Updating an Account's Cash Balance

You can adjust the balance in an investment account with a cash balance. Open the register window for the account you want to adjust and choose Investing | Investing Activities | Update Cash Balance. Then enter the adjustment date and correct balance in the dialog that appears, as shown next. When you click OK, Quicken creates an adjusting entry.

Updating an Account's Share Balance

You can adjust the number of shares in an investment account. Open the account register window for the account you want to adjust and choose Investing | Investing Activities | Update Share Balance. Enter the adjustment date, security, and correct number of shares in the dialog that appears, as shown next. When you click OK, Quicken creates an adjusting entry.

Updating 401(k) or 403(b) Balances

401(k) or 403(b) account balances change every time you make a contribution through your paycheck. To adjust the balance, click the name of the 401(k) or 403(b) account in the account bar to open it. If necessary, click its Overview tab. Click the Update Account button on the button bar. Then follow the prompts in the Update 401(k)/403(b) Account dialog that appears to update the information. The statement information screen from that dialog, which is shown next, gives you an idea of the kind of information you'll have to enter. When you're finished, check your entries in the Summary tab and click Done.

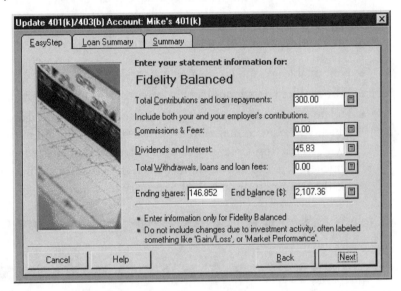

Remember, if you set up your paycheck as discussed in Chapter 7, Quicken will automatically record contributions to your 401(k) or 403(b) account every payday.

Working with Securities

This chapter talks a lot about securities. But exactly what are they?

In Quicken, a *security* is a single investment that has a share price. Examples of securities include stock shares for a specific company, bonds for a specific company, and mutual funds offered by investment firms. Normally, when you own a security, you own a certain number of shares. To calculate the total value of the security, you'd multiply the number of shares you own by the most recent per share price.

This part of the chapter explains how you can use the Security List, Add Security To Quicken, Edit Security, Security Type List, Investment Goal List, and Security Detail View windows to view, add, and work with securities.

Security List

The Security List window (see Figure 10-2) simply lists the securities in Quicken's data file. You can use this window to add, edit, delete, or hide securities, including *watch list securities*—securities you don't own but want to monitor. To open this window, choose Investing | Security List or press CTRL-Y.

Using the Button Bar

Button bar options enable you to work with the list's items:

- **New** enables you to create a new security.
- **Edit** enables you to modify the currently selected security.
- **Delete** removes the currently selected security. Do not delete a security for which you want to maintain historical information, even if you no longer own it. Deleting a security removes all record of the security from your Quicken data file. If you want to keep the information but don't want to see the security in lists, hide the security instead.

Figure 10-2 • Use the Security List window to view, add, edit, or remove securities that you own or watch.

- **Hide** (x) removes the currently selected security from all lists without actually deleting it. To view a hidden security, choose View Hidden Securities from the Options menu on the button bar. To unhide a security, view and select it, and then click the Hide button on the button bar.
- **Report** displays a Security Report for the selected security.
- **Options** displays a menu that enables you to toggle the view of hidden securities.
- **Print** prints a list of securities.

- **How Do I** provides additional instructions for using the Security List window.

Adding a New Security

To add a new security to your Quicken data file—either as a holding or a Watch List item—click the New button in the button bar of the Security List window (refer to Figure 10-2). The Add Security To Quicken dialog appears, displaying screens that prompt you for information about a security. This dialog uses a step-by-step approach to get the same information that you enter in the Set Up New Security dialog that appears when you enter a transaction for a security that has not yet been added to the Security List. The process is pretty straightforward, so I won't spend too much time providing detailed instructions. Instead, I'll explain what some of the less obvious options are all about.

Type of Security   The first thing you're prompted for is the type of security. There are eight options: Stock, Mutual Fund, Employee Stock Option, Employee Stock Purchase Plan, Bond, US Savings Bond, CD, Market Index, and Other. Market Index isn't really a security—it enables you to track popular market indexes, such as the Dow Jones Industrial Average or the S&P 500. Select the appropriate option and click Next.

Security Name   In most cases, Quicken prompts you for two pieces of information: the name of the security and the ticker symbol. Provide the full name of the security or a shorter name you use to refer to it. The ticker symbol is required if you want to use Quicken's online features to download security values; I tell you more about that in Chapter 11. If you have an Internet connection, you can use the Lookup button to look up the ticker symbol for securities.

Employee Stock Options   If you are creating an employee stock option, you can create a new security or select a security that you already track. Each screen in the Add Security To Quicken dialog prompts you for information about the stock option—such as the date it was granted, grant number, number of shares, exercise price, vesting schedule, and expiration date—so you may want to have the related paperwork handy to consult to ensure that your entries are correct. Once set up, Quicken will track the value of the stock and its option and automatically enter necessary vesting transactions in your account register.

ESPP Security Type   If you are creating an employee stock purchase plan type, Quicken offers to display the action form for purchasing ESPP shares. Doing so automatically creates the shares. If you don't use the form to create the shares, the security is not created.

Market Indexes   If you selected Market Index as the type of security, Quicken displays a dialog like the one that follows, asking which market indexes you want to track. Place a check mark beside the desired indexes. Quicken will add them to your watch list, which I discuss later in this chapter.

Asset Class   Asset class information works with Quicken's Asset Allocation feature to help you diversify your portfolio so it best meets your investment goals. There are eight asset class options: Domestic Bonds, Global Bonds, Large Cap Stocks, Small Cap Stocks, International Stocks, Cash, Other, and Unclassified. If you know which asset class the security belongs to, select it. Because mutual funds are usually a mixture of asset classes, Quicken supports class mixtures. The Asset Class Mixture dialog, shown next, allows you to specify the exact mixture. If you don't know a security's asset class and have access to the Internet, you can have Quicken automatically download asset class information when you connect. I tell you how in Chapter 11.

Investment Goal   An investment goal is how the security fits into your investment scheme. There are six predefined options: None, College Fund, Growth, High Risk, Income, and Low Risk. Specifying an investment goal enables you to group securities by goal onscreen and in printed reports. You can modify the list of investment goals. I explain how a little later in this chapter.

Cost Basis   Quicken supports two methods of tracking the cost of your securities. Although you can switch methods at any time, the IRS requires that you stick to a method for a security once you have reported your first capital gain. The two options are:

- **Lot Identification** enables you to track the cost of each security by its purchase lot. This is the most accurate way to track investment costs and performance. It also enables you to control capital gains timing by allowing you to choose the lots you sell.
- **Average Cost** enables you to average the cost of all the purchases of a security. This method is commonly used for mutual funds reporting and has less bookkeeping requirements for tax purposes.

Holdings vs. Watch List Securities   Quicken enables you to track the securities you own—your holdings—as well as the ones you want to watch. The securities you don't own but want to watch are referred to as *watch list securities*.

- **Track My Holdings** enables you to enter holdings information for the security at the end of the setup process.

- **Put It On The Watch List** enables you to watch a security, even if you don't own it. Although the Watch List feature does not require Internet access, it's a heck of a lot more useful if you regularly download stock prices using the Online Quotes feature of Quicken. I tell you about Online Quotes in Chapter 11.

Tracking Start Date If you are setting up a security for which you want to track holdings (one you own), there are three options for setting the tracking start date:

- **Today** begins tracking an investment as of the current date. This is the quickest option.
- **The End Of Last Year** begins tracking an investment as of the last day of the previous year. This enables you to generate accurate reports for the current year and the future. This is the compromise option.
- **The Date You Purchased This Security** begins tracking an investment from the date you enter. Although this option may require a bit more work on your part, you should select it if you are using lot identification and want to generate accurate reports—including capital gain/loss tax reports— for all years. This is the most accurate option.

Investment Account To enter holdings information for a security, Quicken needs to know which account it should be recorded in. Choose an account from the drop-down list.

Holdings Information As illustrated next, for each security, Quicken prompts you to enter the number of shares, cost per share, and commission or fee for the purchase transaction. Quicken will automatically calculate the total cost and display it in the window.

Downloading Security Values When you're finished adding securities, Quicken will ask if you want to download security values. I explain how to do this in Chapter 11.

Editing a Security

You can edit a security to correct or clarify information you previously entered for it. Select the security's name in the Security List window (Figure 10-2) and click the Edit button on the button bar. The Edit Security dialog, which is shown next, appears. Enter or edit information in the dialog and click OK to save your changes.

This dialog is virtually the same as the Set Up New Security dialog that appears when you enter a transaction for a new security. It offers several additional options that aren't available when you set up a security with the Add Security To Quicken dialog discussed earlier.

Est. Income Estimated income is the amount you expect to earn per year per share of the security. Normally, this field is used for expected annual dividends per share.

Back Load If the security is a mutual fund and it has a back load (a fee for selling fund shares), enter the load percentage in this box. This enables Quicken to accurately estimate capital gains. I tell you about Quicken's Capital Gains Estimator in Chapter 12.

Download Asset Class Information Turn on this check box if you want Quicken to automatically download asset class information when it connects to the Internet to download quotes and other security information. This option is especially useful for mutual funds, which normally have a mixture of asset classes. I explain how to download asset class information in Chapter 11.

Tax Free   Turn on the Tax Free check box if income from this security is not taxable. An example would be a tax-free municipal bond.

Use Average Cost   If you don't want to track the security by lot, turn on the Use Average Cost check box. As discussed earlier in this chapter, this affects the way Quicken calculates the cost of securities.

Show In Watch List   Turning on the Show In Watch List check box adds the security to your Watch List so you can track its prices even if you don't own it.

Other Info   Clicking the Other Info button displays a dialog you can use to enter additional information about the security, such as the broker name and phone number, security rating, and comments.

Security Type List

The Security Type List, which is shown next, displays a list of security types. To display this list, choose Investing | Security Type List.

You can use button bar buttons to modify the list:

- **New** enables you to create a new security type. Clicking this button displays the Set Up Security Type dialog, which you can use to enter a name for the security type.
- **Edit** enables you to change the name of the currently selected security type.
- **Delete** enables you to remove the currently selected security type from the list.

- **Print** prints the Security Type List.
- **How Do I** provides instructions for working with the Security Type List window.

Adding or removing security types does not affect the first screen of the Add Security To Quicken dialog, which lists standard security types.

Investment Goal List

As illustrated next, the Investment Goal List window displays a list of all investment goals. You may find investment goals useful for organizing your investments based on what you expect them to do for you. To show the Investment Goal List, choose Investing | Investment Goal List.

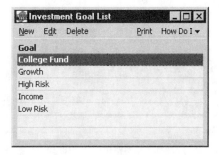

You can use button bar buttons to modify the list if desired:

- **New** enables you to create a new investment goal. Clicking this button displays the Set Up Investment Goal dialog, which you can use to enter a name for the goal.
- **Edit** enables you to change the name of the currently selected investment goal.
- **Delete** enables you to remove the currently selected investment goal from the list.
- **Print** prints the Investment Goal List.

- **How Do I** provides instructions for working with the Investment Goal List window.

Security Detail View

The Security Detail View window (see Figure 10-3) provides a wealth of information about a specific security, including value and performance information, transactions, and price or market value history. You can use this window to

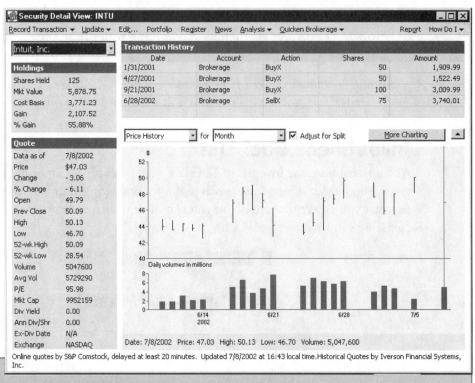

Figure 10-3 • The Security Detail View window displays all kinds of information about a security you own or watch.

enter transactions, update prices, edit a security, or open the Portfolio or account register windows.

To open the Security Detail View window, choose Investing | Security Detail View or click the Security View button in the account register window for an investment account (refer to Figure 10-1). To switch from one security to another, use the drop-down list in the upper-left corner of the window.

The button bar buttons in the Security Detail View window enable you to enter investments and switch to other views:

- **Record Transaction** is both a button and a menu. Clicking the button displays the Record Transaction dialog, which is discussed earlier in this chapter. Clicking the triangle displays a menu of actions that appear as forms in the Record Transaction dialog.

- **Update** is a menu full of options for using an Internet connection to update current and historical price information for securities you own or watch. These options can be a real timesaver, as I discuss in Chapter 11.

- **Edit** displays the Edit Security dialog I discussed earlier in this chapter, which you can use to change information about the security.

- **Portfolio** opens the Investing Center's Portfolio tab. I tell you more about the Portfolio tab in Chapter 12.

- **Register** opens the account register window (see Figure 10-1), which I discussed earlier in this chapter.

- **News** connects to the Internet to display the Quicken.com News page, with news and other information about the security.

- **Analysis** displays a menu of options to help you analyze your investments. I tell you about these options in Chapter 12.

- **Quicken Brokerage** is a menu that appears only in Quicken Premier. It enables you to access features for a new Quicken service, Quicken Brokerage powered by Siebert. This service enables you to initiate trades from right within Quicken.

- **Report** displays a Security Report, which summarizes all activity for the security.

- **How Do I** provides additional information about using the Security Detail View window and its options.

Using Transaction Download and Research Tools

In this Chapter:

- *Setting up transaction download*

- *Downloading transactions*

- *Comparing downloaded transactions to register transactions*

- *Reviewing account balance details*

- *Comparing downloaded holdings to recorded holdings*

- *Downloading stock quotes and news headlines*

- *Exporting your portfolio to Quicken.com*

- *Using online research tools*

Quicken offers three separate features for tracking investments online:

- **Transaction Download** enables you to download transactions and balances for your investment accounts. This helps automate the entry of investment transactions and keeps your Quicken records in sync with your brokerage firm's records.
- **Online Quotes, Headlines, and Alerts** enables you to obtain current and historical quotes, asset allocation information, and news headlines about individual stocks, mutual funds, and other investments. This automates the tracking of market values and provides valuable information you can use to make better investment decisions. This feature can also alert you to important information about securities you own or watch.
- **Portfolio Export** enables you to put a copy of your investment portfolio on the Quicken.com Web site, where you can track its value from any computer connected to the Internet—without Quicken.

In this chapter, I tell you about each of these features and explain how they can help you save time and stay informed about your investments. I also tell you about some of the features on Quicken.com that can help you research investments.

The instructions in this chapter assume that you have already configured your computer for an Internet connection. If you have not done so, do it now. Chapter 4 provides the information you need to set up and test an Internet connection for Quicken. This chapter also assumes that you understand the topics and procedures discussed in Chapters 3 and 7, and builds on many of the basic concepts discussed in those chapters.

Transaction Download

Transaction Download enables you to download transactions, balance details, and holdings information directly from the financial institutions with which you maintain investment accounts. Each transaction can then be entered into your Quicken investment account with the click of a mouse button. You can also review downloaded account balance details and compare downloaded holdings information to the information recorded in your portfolio.

Transaction Download is supported by many of the brokerage or investment firms that appear in the drop-down list when you create a brokerage account. You can learn if your brokerage firm supports this feature by checking the Account

Attributes area in the Overview tab for the account. Click the name of the brokerage account in the Account bar and, if necessary, click the Overview tab. As shown next, the word Available appears beside Transaction Download if your brokerage firm supports this feature.

Account Attributes	Options ▼
Account Name	Datek
Description	
Financial Institution	Datek Online
Account Number	
Transaction Download	Available
View on Quicken.com	Available

[Edit Account Details] [Change Online Services]

Setting Up Transaction Download

To use Transaction Download, you must configure the appropriate Quicken accounts. This requires that you enter information about your financial institution and the account(s) you want to track.

Applying for Transaction Download

Before you can use Transaction Download, you may need to apply for it. I tell you how at the end of Chapter 4. Normally, all it takes is a phone call, although some brokerage and investment firms do allow you to apply online. Another way to apply or get application information is to click the Sign Up Now button that appears in the Online Account Activation dialog shown later in this chapter.

Not all brokerage firms have an application process. My broker, for example, provides Quicken access information on its Web site. To access my account with Quicken, I simply configure Quicken with my account number and the same PIN I use to access my account via the Web. There's no need to wait for an application to be processed and additional information to be sent.

If you do need to apply, it may take up to a week for the application to be processed. You'll know that you're ready to go online when you get a letter with setup information. The setup information consists of the following:

Customer ID   This may be your account number, Social Security number, or some other ID the brokerage firm provides.

PIN (Personal Identification Number)   You'll have to enter this code into Quicken when you download transactions. If this information is sent by your brokerage firm, it may be sent separately for additional security.

Setting Up the Account

Setting up Transaction Download is similar to setting up Online Account
Services for a bank account or credit card account. Open the register for the
brokerage account you want to set up Transaction Download for. Click the Set
Up Online button on the button bar to display the Online Account Activation
dialog. Enter your Customer ID and PIN in the appropriate boxes and click Next.

Quicken connects to the Internet again to get more information about your
brokerage firm and account. After a moment, it displays a dialog like the one shown
next that lists all of your accounts at the brokerage firm that are online-enabled.
Use this dialog like the one shown next to match your accounts at the brokerage
firm with your Quicken accounts. Select an account in the scrolling list, then
select one of the options beneath the list:

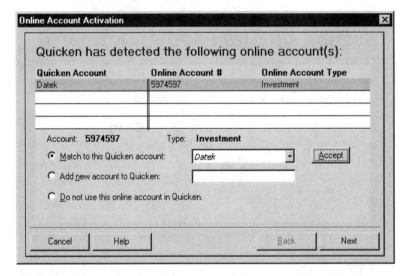

- **Match To This Quicken Account** enables you to select an existing Quicken
  account from the drop-down list.
- **Add New Account To Quicken** enables you to enter a name for a new
  Quicken account.
- **Do Not Use This Online Account In Quicken** ignores the online account
  and does not match or create a Quicken account for it.

After selecting an account and an option, click the Accept button to assign the
online account to the Quicken account. You can repeat this process for all accounts
that appear in the dialog. This makes it possible to set up a bunch of accounts at
once, thus speeding up the setup process.

When you're finished matching accounts, click Next. A summary dialog summarizes the accounts that have been activated and the services they have been activated for. Click Done.

A little Service Agreement Information dialog may appear next. It tells you that online financial services are provided by your financial institution and not Intuit. Read the contents of the dialog and click OK. You're now ready to download transactions.

Using the Online Center Window

When you enable Transaction Download, you can use the Online Center to download account information, compare it to data in your Quicken file, and enter new transactions and adjustments. Choose Investing | Online Center. If necessary, choose the name of your brokerage firm from the Financial Institution drop-down list near the top of the window. Figure 11-1 shows what this window looks like for a Datek Online investment account.

The button bar offers a number of options you can use for investment tracking:

- **Payees** displays the Online Payee List window, which I discuss in Chapter 6.
- **Contact Info** displays the Contact Information dialog for the currently selected financial institution. You can use the information in the dialog to contact the bank or credit card company by phone, Web site, or e-mail.

Figure 11-1 • Use the Online Center window to download investment transactions, check balances, and holdings.

- **PIN Vault** gives you access to Quicken's PIN Vault feature, which I discuss in Chapter 7. (This option only appears if you have online account services enabled for accounts at more than one financial institution.)
- **Trade** connects to the Internet and displays your brokerage firm's home page in an Internet window. You can then log in to make online trades.
- **Print** prints the transactions listed in the window.
- **Options** displays a menu of commands for working with the current account or window.
- **How Do I** provides additional instructions for working with the Online Center window.

Downloading Transactions

To download transactions, you must connect to your financial institution. Make sure the brokerage firm is selected in the Online Center window (see Figure 11-1) and click the Update/Send button. The Online Update For This Account window appears.

Enter your PIN and click Update Now. Wait while Quicken connects to your financial institution. A Quicken One Step Update Status window appears during the connection.

When Quicken is finished exchanging information, the status window disappears. Quicken attempts to match securities in the downloaded Transaction List to securities in the Security List within Quicken. It displays the Matching Security dialog, shown next, for each security it doesn't recognize.

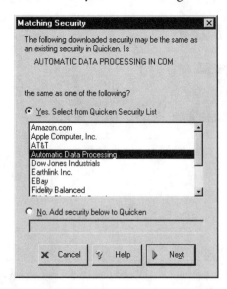

Choose an option for the security and click Next to continue:

- **Yes. Select From Quicken Security List.** This option tells Quicken that the security is already in Quicken's data file. If you select this option, you must select a security from the list below it.
- **No. Add Security Below To Quicken.** This option tells Quicken that the security is new to the Quicken data file. If you select this option, you must enter a name for the security in the text box below it.

An Online Update Summary window appears next to summarize the activity that took place while you waited. Click Done. If you display the Online Center window again, you'll see the transactions you downloaded in the bottom half of the window's Transactions tab, as shown next. Because your investment firm knows exactly what you bought and sold, all transaction details appear in the window.

Transactions	Balances	Holdings				

Downloaded transactions as of 7/1/2002 4:35:06 AM · Compare to Register...

Account		Transactions				
Datek		**14**				

Date	Activity	Description	Price	Quantity	Amount
4/4/2002	Shares In	AUTOMATIC DATA PROCESSING IN COM	$0	116.0000	
4/4/2002	Shares In	AUTOMATIC DATA PROCESSING IN COM	$0	83.0000	
5/16/2002	Sell	AUTOMATIC DATA PROCESSING IN COM	$55	-99	$5434.92
6/28/2002	Buy	LUCENT TECHNOLOGIES INC	$1.50	200	$-309.99
6/28/2002	Buy	QWEST COMMUNICATIONS INTL INC	$2.50	200	$-509.99
7/1/2002	Dividend	AUTOMATIC DATA PROCESSING IN COM			$11.50
1/16/2002	Credit				$0.02
2/20/2002	Credit				$0.04
3/18/2002	Credit				$0.04
4/16/2002	Credit				$0.04

The first time you connect, your financial institution sends all transactions from the past 60 days or more—mine sent two years' worth! After that, only new transactions will be downloaded.

Reviewing Transactions

To compare downloaded transactions to register transactions, click the Compare To Register button in the Online Center window (shown previously) or simply switch to the register window for the account. The account register window opens with the downloaded Transaction List in the bottom half of its window. Figure 11-2 shows what the window might look like with two transactions matched and another already accepted.

Reviewing and Accepting Transactions The split register window in Figure 11-2 looks and works very much like the split window that appears when you accept downloaded bank and credit card account transactions into Quicken.

Figure 11-2 • Use this window to compare downloaded transactions to transactions in your account register.

Consult the section titled "Comparing Downloaded Transactions to Register Transactions" in Chapter 6 for details. In most cases, you'll simply select a new or matched transaction and click the Accept button to accept it or to enter and accept it. If a transaction has a status of Near Match, you can edit the transaction in the account register window so it matches before you accept it. Because Quicken will automatically enter most transaction information, using this method to enter an investment transaction can be much faster than entering it manually in the account register window.

Entering and Accepting a Sale Transaction   When you try to accept a transaction marked Sell, Quicken displays the Sell Shares dialog, shown next. Specify whether you want to sell shares based on Average Cost or Lot Identification. If you select Lot Identification, click the Specify Lots button and use the dialog that appears to choose the lots you want to sell. I tell you about cost basis and specifying lots in Chapter 10.

Entering and Accepting a Transfer In or Transfer Out Transaction

Transactions that display XIn or XOut in the Action column are for cash transfers into or out of the account. When you select one of these transactions, Quicken displays the Add New Cash Transaction dialog, shown next. You have three options:

- **Create A Transfer From Another Account.** This option enables you to record the transaction as a transfer from another Quicken account. If you select this option, be sure to choose the right account from the drop-down list beside it.

- **Assign An Income Or Expense Category.** This option enables you to record the transaction as an income or expense item. This is commonly used for interest income (a transfer in) or margin interest expense (a transfer out), but may be related to other income or fees. If you select this option, be sure to choose a category from the drop-down list beside it.

- **Neither. Create A Transfer From Within This Account.** This option enables you to record the transfer in or out without affecting any other Quicken accounts or categories. You might use this option to record a transfer that occurred before you began recording transactions with Quicken.

Finishing Up   When you're finished working with transactions, click the Done button in the bottom half of the window. If you haven't accepted all transactions, a dialog asks whether you want to finish now or later. Remember, downloaded transactions that have not been accepted may not be entered in your investment register. Thus, your register and portfolio balances may be misstated until you accept all downloaded transactions.

Comparing Holdings   If your Quicken portfolio and brokerage portfolio don't match, Quicken displays a dialog to tell you. Click Yes in that dialog to display the Add Adjustments Into Register pane (shown later in this chapter) in the bottom half of the register window. I explain how to compare portfolios in the section "When Holdings Don't Match," a little later in this chapter.

Reviewing Balances

When you download transactions from your financial institution, you also receive detailed account balance information. To review this information, click the Balances tab in the Online Center window. Here's what it might look like:

Transactions	**Balances**	Holdings

Datek

Balances at Datek Online as of 7/1/2002 4:35:06 AM

Balance	Amount	Description
Cash	$0.00	Available Cash
Margin	$0.00	Margin Balance
Short	$0.00	Market Value of Securities Held Short
Cash Balance	$-268.00	Cash Balance
Long Stock Value	$4879.00	Long Stock Value
Short Stock Value	$0.00	Short Stock Value
Long Option Value	$0.00	Long Option Value
Short Option Value	$0.00	Short Option Value
Account Value	$4611.00	Account Value

Reviewing Holdings

The financial institution also sends you information about your individual holdings. You can review this information in the Online Center window and compare it to the information in your portfolio.

To review holdings, click the Holdings tab in the Online Center window. Here's the Holdings tab for the same account shown in the previous illustration:

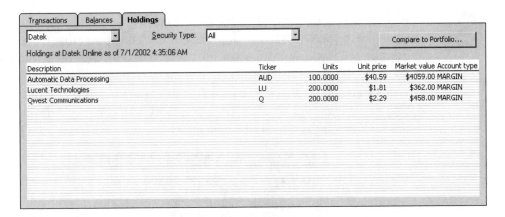

To compare downloaded holdings to holdings in your portfolio, click the Compare To Portfolio button. Quicken compares the holdings information. What happens next depends on whether the holdings information matches.

When Holdings Match   When downloaded holdings match the holdings recorded in your portfolio, Quicken displays a dialog telling you that your Quicken account and your Brokerage Holdings are in agreement. Click OK to dismiss it and continue working with Quicken.

When Holdings Don't Match   When downloaded holdings don't match the holdings recorded in your portfolio, the investment register window for the account appears. A list of discrepancies between the downloaded and recorded holdings is included in the bottom half of the window, as shown next.

When you select a discrepancy item and click the Add Adjustment button, a dialog like the one shown next appears. Choose the option that represents the amount of detail you want to show for the transaction. When you click OK, Quicken displays the appropriate action form to record the adjustment. Do this for each discrepancy listed in the bottom half of the investment account register. When you have finished, Quicken displays a dialog confirming that the information matches. Click OK to dismiss the dialog and continue working with Quicken.

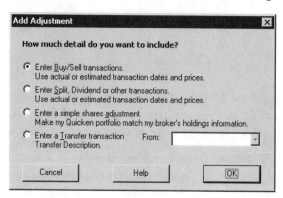

Downloading Quotes, Headlines, and Alerts

Quicken enables you to download up-to-date stock quotes, news headlines, and alerts for the securities in your portfolio and on your Watch List. You set it up once and then update the information as often as desired. You can even download historical price information so you can review price trends for a security that only recently caught your eye.

Quicken Quick Tip

Because the quote and headline download feature is built into Quicken, it doesn't rely on your brokerage firm for information. That means you can download quotes, headlines, and alerts even if your brokerage firm doesn't offer Transaction Download. All you need is Internet access.

Setting Up the Download

Before you can get quotes online, you must set up the feature. Choose Edit |
Preferences | Customize Online Updates. If necessary, click the Quotes tab in
the Customize Online Updates dialog that appears, as shown next. Toggle the
green check marks to the left of each security for which you want to download
quotes, headlines, and alerts. Then click OK.

Updating Information

You can update quotes and information any time you like. Choose Investing |
Online Activities | Get Online Quotes. Quicken connects to the Internet and
begins downloading information. While it works, a Quicken One Step Update
Status dialog shows you what's going on. When it has finished, Quicken displays
the Online Update Summary window, which tells you how many securities were
updated. Click Done to dismiss it.

You can also update quotes using One Step Update, which I discuss in Chapter 7.
It enables you to download quotes when you perform other tasks online.

Viewing Downloaded Quotes and Headlines

You can view quotes and news headlines for a security in two places:

- **Security Detail View** window (see Figure 11-3), which I introduce in Chapter 10, displays quote information for individual securities. To open this window, choose Investing | Security Detail View.

- **Portfolio** window (see Figure 11-4), which I discuss in greater detail in Chapter 12, displays quotes and news headlines for all securities you own or watch. To display this window, choose Investing | Portfolio or press CTRL-U.

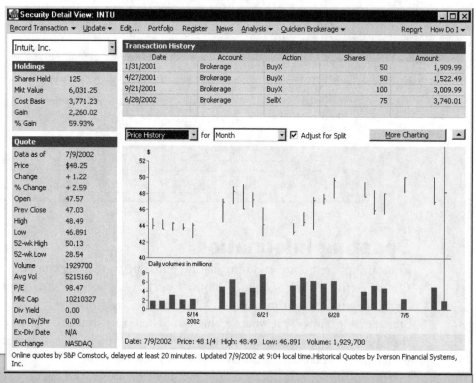

Figure 11-3 • The Security Detail View window shows information about securities, including quotes.

Figure 11-4 • You can view quotes with the Quotes view in the Portfolio window.

Viewing Stock Quotes

The Security Detail View window (see Figure 11-3) offers the most detailed quote information. You can find it down the left side of the window. If you have been faithfully downloading quotes for your securities (or have downloaded historical quotes, as discussed in the next section), a chart of the price history appears in the body of the window. You can use the drop-down list in the top-left corner of the window to switch from one security to another.

In the Portfolio window, downloaded quotes appear beside the security name or ticker symbol. Stock quotes are delayed 20 minutes during the trading day.

Quotes for mutual funds are updated once a day by around 6:00 P.M. eastern time. Prior to that, you'll see the previous day's prices with *est* beside the price indicating that the price has not been updated. Choose Quotes from the View drop-down list near the top of the window to see more quote details, as shown in Figure 11-4.

You can also view stock quotes by selecting the security in the Security Detail View or Portfolio window and choosing Edit Price History from the Update menu on the button bar. This displays the Price History window, which displays all of the recorded stock quotes for the security, as shown here:

Date	Price	High	Low	Volume
7/9/2002	48	48.49	46.891	2,002,500
7/8/2002	47.03	50.13	46.70	5,047,600
7/5/2002	50.09	50.09	48.11	2,339,500
7/3/2002	48.07	48.10	45.45	4,685,300
7/2/2002	46	48.44	45.49	5,319,400
7/1/2002	47.63	49.45	47.61	4,024,600
6/28/2002	49.72	50.01	47.44	6,257,700
6/27/2002	47.44	47.97	46.65	5,703,900
6/26/2002	47.15	47.55	43.50	6,320,000
6/25/2002	44.49	45.73	44.02	7,088,700
6/24/2002	43.25	44.33	42.95	5,364,900
6/21/2002	44.20	46.30	42.70	7,789,800
6/20/2002	47.24	48.18	46.25	4,738,600
6/19/2002	46.13	49.09	46.02	3,733,200
6/18/2002	48.34	48.86	46.70	6,674,900

Price History for: Intuit, Inc. — New, Edit, Delete, Print, Close

Viewing News Headlines

To view news headlines for a security, point to the newspaper icon that appears beside the ticker symbol for any security with news stories in the Portfolio window (refer to Figure 11-4). As shown next, a window pops up with links to recent news stories. When you click a link, Quicken uses its internal Web browser to connect to the Internet and display the news story.

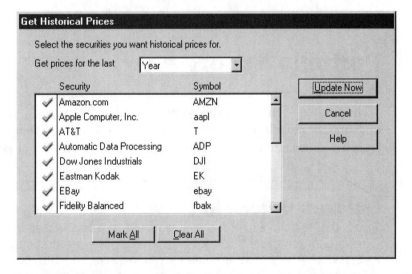

Name	Price	Chg	% Chg	Ind%Chg	Ind
📁 Brokerage					
⊞ aapl 📊	17.75	↓ - 0.26	-1.44%	-4.60%	Pers
⊞ ebay 📊	57.18	↑ + 0.94	+1.67%	-3.55%	Inter
⊞ INTU	48	↑ + 0.97	+2.06%	+7.59%	App
⊞ T					g
Cash					
📁 Datek					
⊞ ADP					3iz
⊞ LU					ce
⊞ Q 📊	2.66	↑ + 0.56	+26.67%	+1.49%	U.S.

LUCENT TECHNOLOGIES INC (LU)
MedcoHealth IPO may price late Tuesday
Hosted by CBS MarketWatch, 10:57 AM EDT
Schaeffer's Option Activity Watch Features CTXS, CIEN, BVF
PR Newswire, 10:56 AM EDT
Sector edges higher ahead of earnings
Hosted by CBS MarketWatch, 10:26 AM EDT

Downloading Historical Quote Information

Quicken enables you to download up to five years of historical quotes for any security you own or watch. Choose Investing | Online Activities | Download Historical Prices. Quicken displays the Get Historical Prices dialog:

Choose a time period from the drop-down list at the top of the dialog. Make sure check marks appear beside all securities for which you want to get historical quotes. Then click the Update Now button. Quicken connects to the Internet and retrieves the information you requested. When it is done, it displays the Online Update Summary dialog. Click Done to dismiss the dialog. You can review the quotes that were downloaded in the Security Detail View window (refer to Figure 11-3).

Downloading Asset Class Information

For each security you own or watch, you can include asset class information. This enables you to create accurate asset allocation reports and graphs. I explain how to manually enter asset class information in Chapter 10 and how you can use this information to diversify your portfolio to best meet your investment goals in Chapter 12.

The trouble is, most mutual funds consist of many investments in a variety of asset classes. Manually looking up and entering this information is time consuming and tedious. Fortunately, Quicken can download this information from the Internet and enter it for you.

Choose Investing | Online Activities | Download Asset Classes. Quicken displays the Download Security Asset Classes dialog, which looks and works very much like the Get Historical Prices dialog shown in the previous illustration. Make sure check marks appear beside all securities for which you want to download asset class information, and then click the Update Now button. Quicken connects to the Internet and retrieves the information you requested. When it is done, it displays the Online Update Summary dialog. Click Done to dismiss the dialog. The asset classes are automatically entered for each security.

Portfolio Export

The Portfolio Export feature enables you to track your portfolio's value on the Web. Although you can do this without Quicken by manually customizing and updating the default portfolio Web page at Quicken.com, it's a lot easier to have Quicken automatically send updated portfolio information to Quicken.com for you.

Quicken Quick Tip

To use the Portfolio Export feature, you must register Quicken. (Quicken will remind you if you haven't completed this step.) The registration process sets up a private Quicken.com account for you to store your portfolio data. This same account is used for other Quicken.com features, including WebEntry and bank account update, which I discuss in Chapter 6.

Exporting Your Portfolio

In Quicken, choose Investing I Online Activities I Update Portfolio on Quicken.com. The Portfolio tab of the Customize Quicken Updates dialog appears, as shown next. If this dialog does not appear, you can display it by choosing Edit I Preferences I Customize Online Updates and then clicking the Portfolio tab in the dialog that appears.

Click to toggle the check marks beside each account that you want to track on the Web. If you also want to track Watch List items on the Web, turn on the Track My Watch List On Quicken.com check box. Finally, select one of the upload options:

- **Send My Shares** exports the ticker symbols and the number of shares of each security you own for your portfolio. This enables you to track both prices and portfolio values.
- **Send Only My Symbols** exports just the ticker symbols for your portfolio. This enables you to track prices but not portfolio values.

When you're finished, click OK. The One Step Update dialog appears. Make sure the check mark beside Update My Portfolio On Quicken.com is turned on, and then click Update Now. (I tell you more about using One Step Update in Chapter 7.)

A Quicken.com login dialog may appear. Use it to log in to Quicken.com and click the Update Now button. Quicken establishes a connection to the Internet, and displays a status dialog while it updates information. When it's finished, it displays the Online Update Summary dialog. Click Done to dismiss it.

Checking Your Portfolio on the Web

Once your portfolio has been updated, you can view it at any time from any computer with Web access. (Figure 11-5 shows an example.) Use a Web browser to navigate to http://www .quicken.com/investments/portfolio/.

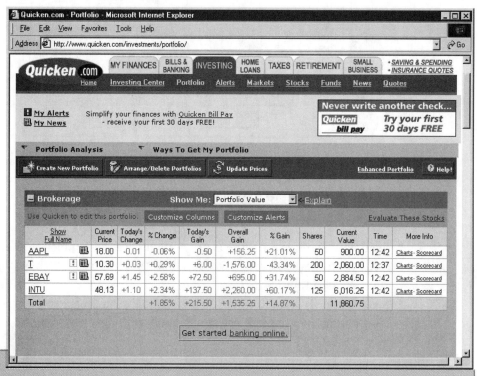

Figure 11-5 • Once your portfolio has been exported, it can be viewed on the Web from any computer.

Quicken Quick Tip

If your computer is set to save your Quicken.com login information or you have manually logged in to Quicken.com, an abbreviated version of your portfolio (called a Mini Portfolio) appears right on the Quicken.com home page, in place of the default portfolio.

(Or simply click the My Portfolio link on the Quicken.com home page, http://www.quicken.com/.) If prompted to log in, do so. The contents of your portfolio appear on the page.

Using Online Research Tools

Quicken offers access to a number of research tools on Quicken.com. You can use these tools to find and learn about securities before you invest.

In this part of the chapter, I tell you a little about Quicken's online research tools so you can explore them on your own. I think you'll find them valuable resources for making wise investment decisions.

Quote Lookup

The Quote Lookup feature enables you to look up stock ticker symbols. These symbols are required to use Quicken's Quote, News, and Alerts Download feature, as well as other features that obtain information about securities on the Web.

Choose Online | Online Research Tools | Quote Lookup. Quicken displays the Ticker Search page in a Web browser window. Select a security type option, then enter all or part of the security name in the edit box. Click Search.

As shown in Figure 11-6, Quicken displays all of the securities it found that matched the criteria you entered. You can note the ticker symbol or click underlined links in the Links column to get more information about the security.

Multiple Security Charting

Quicken displays a chart of a security's prices right in the Security Detail View window. This is a great way to see trends in a single security's values. But what if you want to compare that security to another one? Or to a popular index? That's where Multiple Security Charting comes in.

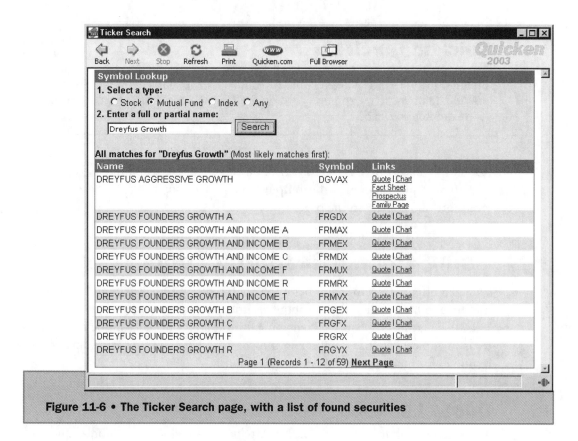

Figure 11-6 • The Ticker Search page, with a list of found securities

To begin, choose Investing | Online Research Tools | Multiple Security Charting. The Multiple Security Charting window, which is shown next, appears. Use it to set options and select securities for the chart you want to create. To select more than one security, hold down CTRL while clicking each security name. When you click the Go Online To Chart button, Quicken connects you to the Internet and displays a Quicken.com page with the chart you requested (see Figure 11-7).

Figure 11-7 • A multiple-security chart created on Quicken.com, displayed in a Quicken Internet window

One-Click Scorecard

One-Click Scorecard instantly prepares reports that help you evaluate a security before you invest, using a variety of well-known analysis techniques and strategies.

To get started, Online | Online Research Tools | One-Click Scorecard. Quicken connects to the Internet and displays the Getting Started page of the One-Click Scorecard on Quicken.com. Enter the ticker symbol for the security you want to evaluate and click Go. After a moment, Quicken displays the recommended strategy report page for the security (see Figure 11-8).

The report that appears automatically displays the results based on the recommended investing strategy for that type of investment. For example, because Intuit is a stock with strong growth and value characteristics, the recommended strategy is Robert Hagstrom's *The Warren Buffet Way*. You can change the strategy by choosing a different one from the drop-down list; just be aware that the strategy you choose may not be the best one for evaluating that security. Read through the report to learn more about the analysis. Pay close attention to the

Figure 11-8 • The One-Click Scorecard report for Intuit as of July 9, 2002, displayed in a Quicken Internet window

Next Steps area at the end of the report if you think you want to invest in the company.

Evaluator

One-Click Scorecard instantly prepares reports that help you evaluate a security before you invest, using a variety of well-known analysis techniques and strategies.

To get started, choose Online | Online Research Tools | Evaluator. Quicken connects to the Internet and displays the Getting Started page of the Security Evaluator on Quicken.com. Enter the ticker symbol for the security you want to evaluate and click Go. After a moment, Quicken displays a detailed analysis page full of information for the security.

Mutual Fund Finder

Quicken's Mutual Fund Finder enables you to search for mutual funds based on criteria you provide. It offers several types of searches:

- **Popular Searches** enable you to find funds that match popular investing strategies.
- **EasyStep Search** walks you through the process of setting up custom search criteria. This option helps you learn about funds as you search.
- **Full Search** puts all search criteria on one page, so you can see and set them all at once. This option includes more advanced variables that may be of interest to knowledgeable investors.

To get started, choose Online | Online Research Tools | Mutual Fund Finder. Quicken connects to the Internet and displays the Getting Started page of the Mutual Fund Finder on Quicken.com. Click a link for one of the search types and follow the instructions that appear onscreen to enter search criteria. Figure 11-9 shows an example of the first page in the EasyStep search. When you're finished entering criteria, the results appear in an Internet window, like the one in Figure 11-10. You can use the Quote link for a fund to learn more about it.

Figure 11-9 • One way to search for mutual funds is with the EasyStep Search.

Figure 11-10 • Mutual Fund Finder search results appear in a window like this one.

Evaluating Your Position

Chapter 12

In this Chapter:

- *The Investing Center*

- *Investment alerts*

- *Investment analysis and reports*

- *The Portfolio window*

- *Investor's Reference Guide*

- *Asset Allocation Guide*

- *Portfolio Rebalancer*

- *Portfolio Analyzer*

- *Buy/Sell Preview*

- *Capital Gains Estimator*

As you enter transactions into Quicken—whether manually or via transaction download—Quicken builds a portrait of your investment portfolio and performance. If you're serious about investing, you can use this information to evaluate your investing position and fine-tune your portfolio to diversify and maximize returns.

Quicken's Investing Center offers a wide range of tools you can use to evaluate and strengthen your investment positions, including reports, graphs, alerts, analysis tools, and reference materials. This chapter takes a closer look at the features that can make you a better investor.

The Investing Center

The Investing Center window should be your first stop for evaluating your investment position. Each of its three tabs includes snapshots with calculated information and links to more information on Quicken and Quicken.com features.

To open the Investing Center window, click the Investing Center button in the Account bar. One of the Investing Center's three tabs appears. Click the tab for the window you want to view.

In this part of the chapter, I take you on a guided tour of Quicken's Investing Center window, so you know exactly how you can use it to monitor your investments.

My Data

The My Data tab, which is shown in Figure 12-1, offers snapshots with general information about your investment accounts and investments.

Investment Alerts

Investment alerts are automatically downloaded with quotes and news headlines, as discussed in Chapter 11. They appear in the Investment Alerts area near the top of the window. You can click a link within an alert to view additional information, either in your Quicken data file or on the Web.

There are ten investment alerts:

- **Price And Volume** consists of three alerts. Price alerts notify you when a security's price rises above or falls below values you specify. Volume alerts notify you when the sales volume of a security exceeds a value you specify. News alerts notify you when news stories are available for a security. You must set options for these alerts on Quicken.com.

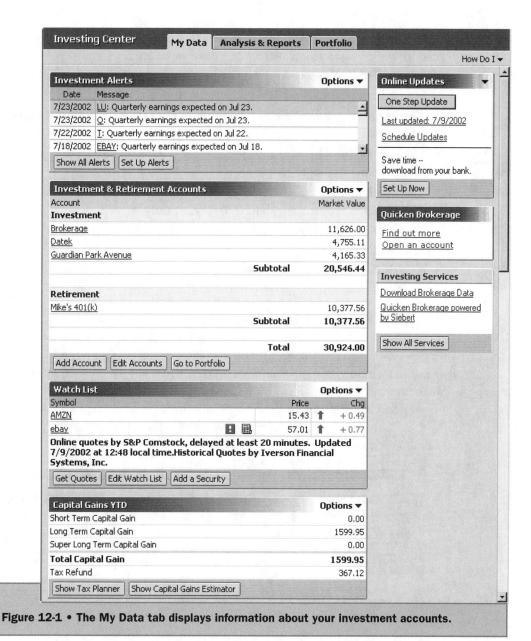

Figure 12-1 • The My Data tab displays information about your investment accounts.

- **Download Quotes Reminder** reminds you to download quotes from Quicken.com.

- **Maturity Date Reminder** reminds you when a CD or bond reaches its maturity date.

- **Stocks Ratings And Analysis** notifies you when ratings and analysis information becomes available for stocks you track.
- **Mutual Funds Ratings And Analysis** notifies you when ratings and analysis information becomes available for mutual funds you track.
- **Tax Implications On Sale** notifies you of your tax implications when you sell a security.
- **Cap. Gains For The Year** notifies you if you exceed your capital gains limit for the year.
- **Tax Efficient Investments** provides you with information about investments that are more tax efficient than those you already have.
- **Mutual Fund Distributions** provides you with information about mutual fund distributions.
- **Securities Holding Period** provides you with information about holding periods for securities you own.

Setting Up Alerts To set up investment alerts, click the Set Up Alerts button in the Investment Alerts area. Quicken displays the Setup tab of the Alerts Center window, shown next, which I discuss in greater detail in Chapter 9. On the left side of the window, click the name of an alert you want to set, then set options for the alert in the right side of the window. (Some alerts, such as the Price and Volume alert, must be set on Quicken.com.) You can disable an alert by removing the green check mark beside its name. When you are finished making changes, click Done to save them.

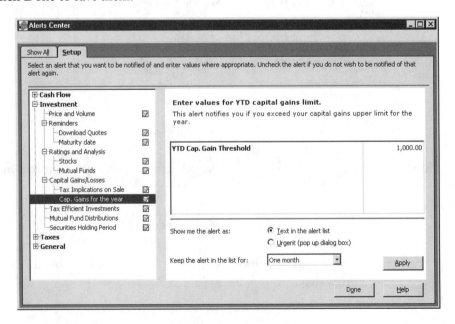

> ## Quicken Quick Tip
> The alerts I find most useful are Price, Maturity Date Reminder, Stocks Ratings And Analysis, and Capital Gains For The Year. These alerts give me timely information that I need to know without subjecting me to information overload.

Deleting Alerts   To remove an alert from the Investment Alerts area, select the alert and choose Delete from the Options button on the Investment Alerts area button bar. Select an option in the Delete Alert(s)! dialog, shown next, that appears and click OK. You can also use the Delete All command on the Options menu to delete all alerts in the Investment Alerts area.

Investment & Retirement Accounts
The Investment & Retirement Accounts snapshot lists all of your investment accounts, including those for retirement, along with their current market values. (Market value is determined by the most recently downloaded or entered security values.) You can click the name of an account to view its register.

Watch List
The Watch List snapshot lists all of the securities on your Watch List, along with the most recently entered or downloaded quotes. Click a security's symbol to open the Security Detail View window for it. Two icons beside a ticker symbol display alerts and news headlines for a security when you point to them.

The Options menu on the Watch List snapshot's button bar offers commands for working with securities and your Watch List.

Capital Gains YTD

As you buy and sell securities, Quicken keeps track of your capital gains. In Quicken Premier, it displays year-to-date capital gain calculations in the Capital Gains YTD snapshot. This snapshot also works with the tax planner to calculate your total taxes, including your capital gains or losses. You can use Option menu commands and buttons in the snapshot to access the Tax Planner and Capital Gains Estimator and to create a report for Schedule D of your tax return.

Online Updates

Online Updates offers links and buttons to update your investing information by downloading transactions and quotes and updating your Quicken.com portfolio. I discuss these features in Chapter 11.

Quicken Brokerage

Quicken Brokerage powered by Siebert enables you to access your brokerage account from within Quicken. You can use links in this area to learn more about Quicken Brokerage powered by Siebert or, if you're already signed up, to access its features.

Investing Services

The Investing Services area offers links that you can use to learn more about various Quicken services.

Analysis & Reports

The Analysis & Reports tab of the Investing Center displays a number of customizable graphs of your investment data, along with a few snapshots with links to other features.

Each of the graphs that appear in the Analysis & Reports tab can be customized, using commands on the graph's Option menu. Buttons beneath each chart enable you to go to a full-sized graph in a report window or view a related report.

Portfolio Value Graph By Account

The Portfolio Value Graph By Account displays your portfolio as a stacked column chart, with each account represented by a different color. The total bar height represents the total value of your portfolio and the different colored bar portions show what makes up the portfolio. Ideally, you want this chart to have a steady increase in value, but with today's investing environment, anything other than a steady decrease is welcome!

Portfolio Value & Cost Basis

The Portfolio Value & Cost Basis graph uses a line graph to illustrate the cost of your portfolio—what you've invested—and the market value. Ideally, you want the line with the beige points to appear above the line with the orange points.

Returns By Account

The Returns By Account graph displays columns for each of your investment accounts. Columns above the 0 line are making money, while those below the 0 line are losing money. A mustard-colored line indicates the total internal rate of return for your entire portfolio. Let's hope that line is above the 0 line!

Asset Allocation

Asset Allocation, which I cover in detail later in this chapter, refers to the way your investment dollars are distributed among different types of investments. It's a measure of how well your portfolio is diversified.

The Asset Allocation graph displays two pie charts: Current Allocation and Target Allocation. Current Allocation indicates your portfolio's current diversification. Target Allocation is the allocation you set up with Quicken's Portfolio Rebalancer, which is discussed later in this chapter. If you have not yet used the Portfolio Rebalancer, the Target Allocation pie won't have any slices.

Market Value Allocation

The Market Value Allocation graph indicates how your portfolio's market value is distributed among different securities. This is also a measure of diversification. The more pie slices and the more even the slices are, the better your portfolio is diversified among securities.

Tools

The Tools area offers links to Quicken features to help you manage and analyze your portfolio. I cover most of these features in this chapter and the Security Detail View window in Chapters 10 and 11.

My Reports

The My Reports area lists your investment reports. I explain how to create, modify, and save reports in Chapter 9.

Featured Service

Featured Service is an ad for one of the Quicken services. This ad changes each time you open this window.

Quotes & Research

The Quotes & Research area offers a quick and easy way to get quotes and other investment information from Quicken.com.

Enter a ticker symbol in the box. If you don't know the ticker symbol, you can click the Don't Know The Symbol? link and use the Ticker Search window that appears to look up the symbol. Then select one of the three options to determine which Quicken.com research page you want to display. When you click Go, Quicken connects to the Internet and displays the information in an Internet window. I tell you about the Quote, One-Click Scorecard, and Evaluator pages on Quicken.com in Chapter 11.

Portfolio

The Portfolio tab of the Investing Center (see Figure 12-2) displays all of your investments in one place. Information can be viewed in a wide variety of ways

Quicken Quick Tip

Quicken's Portfolio window is my favorite source of "How am I doing?" investing information. I consult this window each time I use Quicken, and find myself using the quotes download feature to keep the window up to date several times during a Quicken session. To make the most of this feature, be sure to customize it as discussed later in this chapter.

to show you exactly what you need to see to understand the performance, value, or components of your portfolio.

You can open the Portfolio window by clicking the Portfolio tab in the Investing Center, by choosing Investing | Portfolio, by pressing CTRL-U, or by clicking the Portfolio button in the button bar of the account register or Security Detail View window.

Name	Price	Shares	Mkt Value	Cost Basis	Pre-Tax Gain	% Gain
Brokerage			8,584.89	7,252.55	1,332.34	18.37
Apple Computer, ...	17.651	50	882.55	748.74	133.81	17.87
AT&T	10.12	200	2,024.00	3,636.00	-1,612.00	-44.33
EBay	59.40	50	2,970.00	2,199.49	770.51	35.03
Intuit, Inc.	46.49	125	5,811.25	3,771.23	2,040.02	54.09
Cash			-3,102.91	-3,102.91		
Datek			4,775.74	6,081.72	-1,305.98	-21.47
Automatic Data P...	40.54	100	4,054.00	5,500.00	-1,446.00	-26.29
Lucent Techn...	2.02	200	404.00	309.99	94.01	30.33
Qwest C...	2.78	200	556.00	509.99	46.01	9.02
Cash			-238.26	-238.26		
Guardian Park Avenue			4,054.32	3,969.16	85.16	2.15
Guardian Park Av... est.	26.66	152.075	4,054.32	3,969.16	85.16	2.15
Mike's 401(k)			10,115.77	10,279.53	-163.76	-1.59
Fidelity Balanced est.	13.73	123.458	1,695.08	1,740.76	-45.68	-2.62
Fidelity Blue Chip ... est.	34.27	245.716	8,420.69	8,538.77	-118.08	-1.38
Watch List			0.00	0.00	0.00	0.0
Amazon.com	15.25					
EBay	59.40					
Indexes			0.00	0.00	0.00	0.0
Dow Jones Industrials	9,082.0...					
NASDAQ Composite	1,376.62					
S&P 500 Index	949.16998					
Totals:			27,530.72	27,582.96	-52.24	-0.19

Online quotes by S&P Comstock, delayed at least 20 minutes. Updated 7/10/2002 at 7:10 local time. Historical Quotes by Iverson Financial Systems, Inc.

Figure 12-2 • The Portfolio tab of the Investing Center shows all of your investments in one place.

Using Button Bar Options

The button bar in the Portfolio window offers several options to change the view of your portfolio:

- **Record Transaction** enables you to enter investment transactions with action forms, as discussed in Chapter 10.
- **Update** is a menu full of options for using an Internet connection to update current and historical price information for securities you own or watch. These options can be real timesavers, as I discuss in Chapter 11.
- **Security View** opens the Security Detail View window for the currently selected security. I tell you about the Security Detail View window in Chapters 10 and 11.
- **Register** opens the account register window for the currently selected investment account. If no account is selected, a dialog asks which account you want to view. I tell you about the account register in Chapter 10.
- **Analysis** offers a number of commands for features to help you analyze your portfolio's performance and value, including Portfolio Analyzer, Capital Gains Estimator, and Multiple Security Charting. These features are discussed in this chapter and Chapter 11.

- **Quicken Brokerage** enables you to use features available through Quicken Brokerage powered by Siebert. Although Quicken Brokerage powered by Siebert can be used by any Quicken user, the Quicken Brokerage menu only appears in Quicken Premier.
- **Customize** offers options for customizing the window's display. I discuss these options later in this chapter.
- **How Do I** provides additional information about using the Portfolio View window and its options.

Using Portfolio View Options

You can quickly customize the Portfolio window's view by using the Group By, View, and As Of options right beneath the button bar. There are many view combinations—far too many to illustrate in this book. Here's a brief overview so you can explore these options on your own.

Group By Options   The Group By options enable you to select the order in which securities appear. The drop-down list offers seven options: Accounts, Industry, Security, Security Type, Investment Goal, Asset Class, and Sector. These options correspond to information entered as part of a security's definition, either manually, when you create the security, or automatically, when you download asset class information. I explain how to create securities in Chapter 10 and how to download security information in Chapter 11.

View Options   The View drop-down list enables you to specify the view that should be used to display the information. Each of the nine predefined views can be customized with the Customize View dialog shown later in this chapter. There are also nine "custom" views that you can customize to make your own views of the data.

Portfolio Date   You can use the As Of box to set the date for which you want to view the portfolio. For example, suppose you want to see what your portfolio looked like a month ago, before a particularly volatile market period. Enter that date in the text box. Or click the calendar button beside the text box to display a calendar of dates, and then click the date you want to display. The view changes to show your portfolio as of the date you specified.

Customizing a View

Quicken offers an incredible amount of flexibility when it comes to displaying information in the Portfolio window. Not only does it come preconfigured with nine different views you can choose from the View drop-down list, but it enables you to create nine other custom views. You can customize any of these views.

To customize a view, begin by using the View drop-down list to choose the view you want to customize. Then choose Customize Current View from the Customize menu on the button bar. The Customize Current View dialog appears, as shown next. Set options as desired in the dialog and click OK to change the view.

Changing the View Name   To change the name of the view, enter a new name in the Name box.

Including Closed Lots   To include sold security lots in the view, turn on the Show Closed Lots check box. Keep in mind that this may greatly increase the number of lines of information that appear in the Portfolio window.

Selecting Columns to Show   To display a column of information, select it in the Available Columns list and click the Add button beside it. To hide a column of information, select it in the Displayed column list and click the Remove button. You can change the order in which columns appear by selecting a column name in the Displayed Columns list and using the Move Up or Move Down button to change its order in the list.

Displaying Symbols Rather Than Names   To display a security's ticker symbol rather than its name, turn on the Show Symbols In Name Column check box.

Selecting Accounts to Include   To specify which accounts should appear, toggle the green check marks to the left of the account name in the Accounts To Include list. Only those accounts that are checked will appear. You can change the order in which accounts appear by selecting an account name in the Accounts To Include list and using the Move Up or Move Down button to change its order in the list.

Selecting Securities to Include   To specify which securities should appear, toggle the green check marks to the left of the security name in the Securities To Include list. Only those securities that are checked will appear.

Setting Portfolio View Options

Quicken also enables you to specify the period for return calculations and the tax rate used in the Portfolio window. Setting these options enables you to fine-tune the way Quicken makes Portfolio window calculations.

Choose Options from the Customize menu on the Portfolio window's button bar. Use the Portfolio View Options dialog that appears to set options and click OK. Your options are as follows:

Show Return Calculations For   The Show Return Calculations For area offers two options for determining the period for which Quicken calculates the return on investment:

- **Entire History** includes all transactions in the calculations.
- **From** enables you to enter a starting date for calculations. All transactions between that starting date and the current date are included in the calculations.

Tax Rate Used In Portfolio View   Use the Tax Bracket drop-down list to choose tax rates that should be used in tax calculations for capital gains. If you are utilizing Quicken's Tax Planner, which I cover in Chapter 20, choose Use Tax Planner Rate. Otherwise, choose the rates that are appropriate for your financial situation.

Tracking Security Values

As the individual tabs within the Investing Center illustrate, Quicken can automatically do all the math to tell you what your investments are worth— *if* you take the time to enter the per share prices of each of your securities.

When you record transactions, Quicken automatically records the security price. It uses the most recently entered price as an estimate to calculate the current value of the investment. You can see this in the Portfolio window (see Figure 12-2)—those gray *est* characters indicate that the price is an estimate. The *est* characters appear if the current date is on a weekend or holiday or you haven't entered or downloaded the current day's prices. Of course, the Portfolio window and all of Quicken's investing reports and charts are a lot more valuable with up-to-date security price information and a history of prices.

You can enter price information two ways: manually (the hard way) and automatically (the easy way). I show you how to manually enter security prices in this chapter; to learn how to automatically enter prices via Internet download, consult Chapter 11.

Manually Entering Security Prices

Manually entering security prices isn't really difficult. It's just time consuming. And the more securities you track, the more time consuming it is. But without an Internet connection, this may be the only way you can enter prices into Quicken.

Quicken Quick Tip
If you track more than one or two securities and want to update price information more often than once a week, don't read this section. You don't want to enter security prices manually. Trust me. It's an extremely tedious task. Quicken's capability to download stock prices directly from the Internet—even five-year price histories—can save you tons of time and prevent data entry errors. And best of all, it's free. All you need is an Internet connection. Learn about setting up an Internet connection in Chapter 4 and about downloading quotes in Chapter 11.

To manually enter a security's price, start by displaying either the Portfolio window (refer to Figure 12-2) or the Security Detail View window, which I discuss in Chapters 10 and 11. Select or display the security for which you want to enter price information. Then choose Edit Price History from the Update button on the button bar. The Price History window for the security appears, as shown next. It shows all the price information stored within the Quicken data file for the security.

Date	Price	High	Low	Volume
7/10/2002	46.49	47.16	46.31	233,200
7/9/2002	46.40	48.49	46.35	4,137,300
7/8/2002	47.03	50.13	46.70	5,047,600
7/5/2002	50.09	50.09	48.11	2,339,500
7/3/2002	48.07	48.10	45.45	4,685,300
7/2/2002	46	48.44	45.49	5,319,400
7/1/2002	47.63	49.45	47.61	4,024,600
6/28/2002	49.72	50.01	47.44	6,257,700
6/27/2002	47.44	47.97	46.65	5,703,900
6/26/2002	47.15	47.55	43.50	6,320,000
6/25/2002	44.49	45.73	44.02	7,088,700
6/24/2002	43.25	44.33	42.95	5,364,900
6/21/2002	44.20	46.30	42.70	7,789,800
6/20/2002	47.24	48.18	46.25	4,738,600
6/19/2002	46.13	49.09	46.02	3,733,200

Price History for: Intuit, Inc. — New Edit Delete Print Close

You can use buttons on the window's button bar to add, edit, delete, and print the price history:

- **New** displays the New Price dialog. Use it to enter the date and closing price for the security. If you're really dedicated to entering data, you can even enter the daily high, low, and volume.
- **Edit** displays the Edit Price dialog for the currently selected price. This dialog looks and works just like the New Price dialog.
- **Delete** removes the selected price. When you click this button, a confirmation dialog appears. You must click OK to delete the price.
- **Print** prints the price list.
- **Close** closes the Price History window.

Viewing Market Values and Performance

Once you've entered price information for your securities, you can view their market value and performance information in the Portfolio window (see Figure 12-2) and Security Detail View window. Use options within the windows to modify the information that is displayed. I explain how earlier in this chapter and in Chapter 10.

Investment Analysis Tools

In addition to the Quicken.com-based investment research tools discussed in Chapter 11, Quicken offers a number of built-in tools that can help you learn more about investing and analyze your investment portfolio.

In this part of the chapter, I introduce these analysis tools so you can explore them more fully on your own.

Investor's Reference Guide

If you're new to investing, you probably have lots of questions. Although I provide some basic investment information in Chapter 10, if you're a Quicken Premier user, you have access to a much more thorough guide: the Investor's Reference Guide.

Choose Investing | Investor's Reference Guide. The Investor's Reference Guide window, which is shown in Figure 12-3, appears. Its main window provides some basic information about the guide. You can click underlined links on the left side of the window to display topics. Then follow the instructions on the right side of the window to read through each topic. You can even click the Print button in the button bar to print information from the Guide for later reference. The Guide is extremely informative and can help you become a better investor.

Asset Allocation

Many investment gurus say that an investor's goals should determine his or her asset allocation. If you're not sure what your asset allocation should be, Quicken

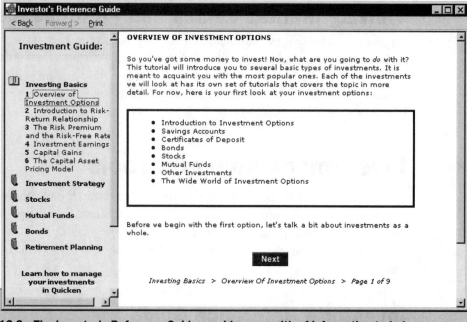

Figure 12-3 • The Investor's Reference Guide provides a wealth of information to help you become a better investor.

can help. It includes a wealth of information about asset allocation, including sample portfolios with their corresponding allocations. You can use this feature to learn what your target asset allocation should be to meet your investing goals. Then you monitor your asset allocation and, if necessary, rebalance your portfolio to keep it in line with what it should be.

Using the Asset Allocation Guide

The Asset Allocation Guide explains what asset allocation is, why it's important, and how Quicken can help monitor it in your portfolio. Choose Investing | Asset Allocation Guide. The Asset Allocation Guide window appears (see Figure 12-4).

To take full advantage of this feature, read the information on the right side of the window. You can click links within the text or in the left column to learn more about a specific topic. If you're new to asset allocation, you may find the See Model Portfolios link especially useful. It shows suggested asset allocations based on risk and returns for a number of portfolios.

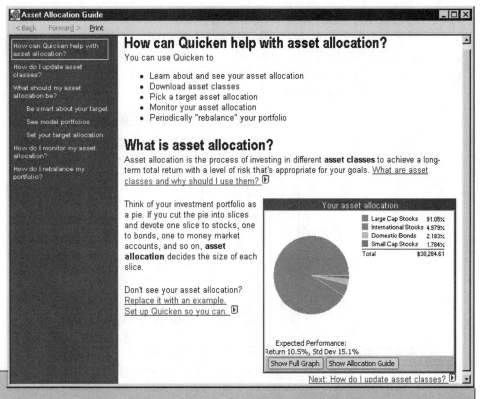

Figure 12-4 • The Asset Allocation Guide explains what asset allocation is and how it can help you meet your investment goals.

Monitoring Your Asset Allocation

To monitor the asset allocation of your portfolio, you must enter asset class information for each of your investments. There are two ways to do this:

- **Manually enter asset class information**. Although this isn't difficult for stocks, it can be time consuming for investments that have an asset class mixture, such as mutual funds. I explain how to manually enter asset class information in Chapter 10.
- **Download asset class information**. If you have a connection to the Internet, this is the best way to enter this information. With a few clicks, Quicken does all of the work in seconds. The information is complete and accurate. I explain how to download asset class information in Chapter 11.

Viewing Your Asset Allocation

A pie chart of your asset allocation appears right in the Asset Allocation Guide window (see Figure 12-4) as well as in the Analysis & Reports tab of the Investing Center. To get more information about a piece of the pie, click it. A yellow box with details appears:

Setting Your Target Asset Allocation

If you know what you want your asset allocation to be, you can set up a target asset allocation. Quicken can then display your target in the pie chart beside the current asset allocation chart on the Investing Center's Analysis & Reports window so you can monitor how close you are to your target.

Choose Change Target Allocations from the Options menu in the Asset Allocation area of the Investing Center's Analysis & Reports window. The Set Target Asset Allocation dialog appears. Here's what it looks like with a sample allocation already entered:

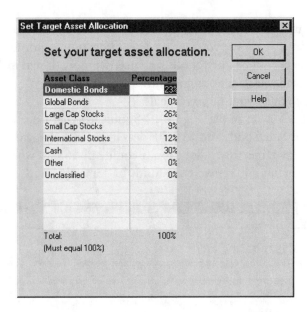

Enter the desired percentages for each class of asset. When the total of all percentages equals 100, click OK to save your settings. The Target chart in the Asset Allocation area of the Investing Center window reflects your settings.

Using the Portfolio Rebalancer

If your current asset allocation deviates from your target asset allocation, you may want to rebalance your portfolio. This means buying and selling investments to bring you closer to your target asset allocation.

Keep in mind that brokerage fees and capital gains impacts often are related to buying and selling securities. For this reason, you should carefully evaluate your investment situation to determine how you can minimize costs and capital gains while rebalancing your portfolio. If small adjustments are necessary to bring you to your target asset allocation, you may not find it worth the cost to make the changes. Use this information as a guideline only!

Quicken can tell you exactly how you must change your current asset allocation to meet your target asset allocation. Choose Investing | Portfolio Rebalancer. The Portfolio Rebalancer window shown in Figure 12-5 appears. It provides instructions and shows you how much you must adjust each asset class to meet your targeted goals.

Here's an example. Figure 12-5 indicates that I need $6,304 more invested in domestic bonds and $19,701 less invested in large cap stock. If I wanted to meet my target asset allocation, I could sell $6,000 worth of my large cap stock investments and reinvest the funds in domestic bonds. This would change my

Figure 12-5 • The Portfolio Rebalancer window tells you what adjustments you need to make to bring your asset allocation closer to target.

asset allocation, bringing it closer to target, without changing the total value of my portfolio.

Portfolio Analyzer

Quicken's Portfolio Analyzer enables you to look at your portfolio a number of ways:

- **Performance** shows your portfolio's average annual rate of return, compared to market indexes like the Dow Jones Industrial Average and the S&P 500 index. It also shows your top five best and worst performers, so you can see how individual securities are doing.

- **Holdings** lists your investment accounts, then shows a pie chart of your top ten holdings. Because most experts recommend that no single security take up more than 10 percent of your portfolio (remember Farmer Joe and his basket of eggs?), you may find the percentage distribution helpful when considering diversification.

- **Asset Allocation** displays your current and target asset allocation so you can see how close you are to your target. I explain how to set up a target allocation earlier in this chapter.

- **Risk Profile** shows how "risky" your portfolio is when compared to the risk associated with specific classes of investments.

- **Tax Implications** summarizes your realized and unrealized year-to-date capital gains or losses. Capital gains and losses are broken down into three categories: short term, long term, and super long term.

What's great about the Portfolio Analyzer is that it provides tables and charts to show information about your portfolio, then explains everything in plain English so you know what the tables and charts mean. Using this feature regularly can really help you learn about the world of investing and how your portfolio measures up.

Buy/Sell Preview

Quicken Premier includes a brand new feature called Buy/Sell Preview. It offers a quick and easy way to see the impact of a securities purchase or sale on your finances—including your taxes.

Choose Investing | Buy/Sell Preview. In the top half of the Buy/Sell Preview window that appears, enter information about the proposed purchase or sale. Quicken automatically enters the most recent price information for a security you own or watch, but you can override that amount if necessary. When you're finished setting options, click Calculate. Quicken displays its results in the bottom half of the window. Here are two examples—one for a purchase and the other for a sale.

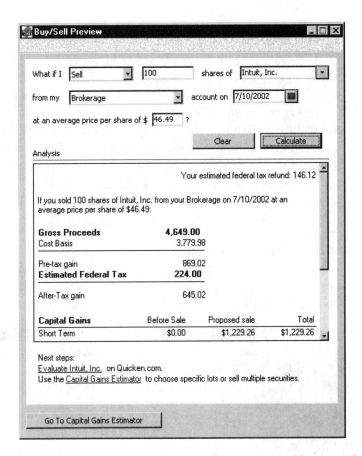

The Buy/Sell Preview feature works with Quicken's Tax Planner, which I discuss in Chapter 20, to calculate the net effect of a sale on your expected tax bill or refund. You can find this information in the window for a sale calculation.

Capital Gains Estimator

Quicken's Capital Gains Estimator enables you to estimate capital gains or losses and their related tax implications *before* you sell a security. The information it provides can help you make an informed decision about which security to sell.

Getting Started

Choose Investing | Capital Gains Estimator. The Capital Gains Estimator's welcome window appears.

Start by reading the information in the right side of the window. It explains what the Capital Gains Estimator does and offers links for learning more about specific terms and topics. Then click each of the links in the left side of the window, in turn, to step through the process of setting up the Capital Gains Estimator for your situation. You'll be prompted to name and choose a scenario, select taxable investment accounts to include, set your tax rate, and enter capital loss carryover information. By entering complete and accurate information, Quicken can provide a more accurate indication of tax impacts.

Deciding What to Sell

Quicken Premier users can tap into a brand new feature in the Capital Gains Estimator which enables Quicken to help you decide which securities to sell. Follow instructions in the What Should I Sell? screen (see Figure 12-6) to tell

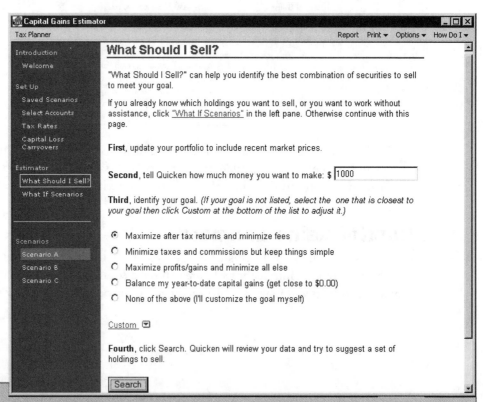

Figure 12-6 • Quicken can help you decide what to sell if you tell it what your goals are.

Quicken your goals for the sale and click the Search button at the bottom of
the window.

A dialog appears while Quicken makes complex calculations to meet your
goals. When it's finished, you can click the Show Results button in the dialog
to display the What If Scenarios with Quicken's recommendation and the results
(see Figure 12-7).

Manually Adding Proposed Sales

If you prefer, you can manually indicate proposed sales in the What If Scenario
screen (refer to Figure 12-7). The Step 1 area shows all the securities you hold
in the accounts you selected during the setup process. There are two ways to add
a proposed sale:

- Double-click the name of the security you want to sell. Then enter the
  number of shares and sales price in the Add To Scenario dialog that appears,
  shown next, and click OK. If you have multiple purchase lots for the security,
  this automatically sells the oldest lots first.

- If necessary, click once on the plus sign (+) to the left of the security that
  you want to sell to display the purchase lots. Then click on the lot you
  want to sell. This enables you to specify exactly which lots are to be sold.

No matter which method you use, the sale is added to the Step 2 area of the
window, which lists all of the proposed sales (see Figure 12-7).

To adjust the number of shares to be sold, click in the shares field for the
proposed sale (in the Step 2 area) and enter a new value. The value you enter
must be less than or equal to the number of shares purchased in that lot.

You can set up proposed sales for up to three scenarios—just click the
Scenario link on the left side of the window to see and set that scenario's
options. You can mix and match any sales you like to reach your goal.

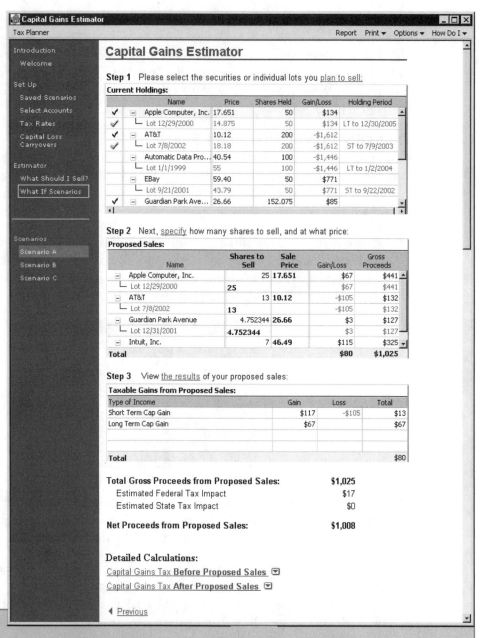

Figure 12-7 • Quicken displays its recommendation as a What If Scenario.

Reading the Results

When all information has been entered, you can see the true power of the Capital Gains Estimator. It tells you about the proceeds from the sales, as well as the gain or loss. If you scroll down in the What If Scenario screen (refer to Figure 12-7), you'll find more information about the proposed sale and its tax implications in the Step 3 area, including the gross profit and net proceeds from proposed sales. You can click links to view the results of additional calculations, such as the tax situation before and after executing the proposed sales and gain or loss on the proposed sales. Do the same for each scenario to see how they compare—then make your selling decision.

The Property & Debt Center

This part of the book explains how you can use the features of Quicken's Property & Debt Center to keep track of your property and loans. It starts with coverage of assets, such as a car and home, and the loans that you may have used to finance them. Then it moves on to some Quicken tools that can help you organize and keep track of important household information. Finally, it tells you how you can use the Property & Debt Center window and other Quicken features to keep tabs on expenses related to your assets and debt. This part of the book has three chapters:

Chapter 13:   *Monitoring Assets and Loans*

Chapter 14:   *Managing Household Records*

Chapter 15:   *Keeping Tabs on Your Property and Debt Expenses*

Part Four

Monitoring Assets and Loans

In this Chapter:

- *Assets and liabilities defined*

- *Loan basics*

- *Setting up asset and loan accounts*

- *Tracking a loan*

- *Adjusting asset values*

Assets and loans (or liabilities) make up your net worth. Bank and investment accounts, which I cover in Chapters 5 and 10, are examples of assets. Credit card accounts, which I cover in Chapter 5, are examples of liabilities. But there are other assets and liabilities you may want to track with Quicken, including a home, car, recreational vehicle, and related loans. By including these items in your Quicken data file, you can quickly and accurately calculate your net worth and financial fitness.

In this chapter, I explain how to set up asset and liability accounts to track your possessions and any outstanding loans you used to purchase them.

The Basics

Before you begin, it's a good idea to have a clear understanding of what assets, liabilities, and loans are and how they work together in your Quicken data file.

Assets and Liabilities

An *asset* is something you own. Common examples might be your house, car, camper, computer, television set, and patio furniture. Most assets have value—you can sell them for cash or trade them for another asset.

Although you can use Quicken to track every single asset you own in its own asset account, doing so would be very cumbersome. Instead, you'll normally account for high-value assets in individual accounts and lower-value assets in a Home Inventory asset account. For example, you may create separate asset accounts for your home and your car, but group personal possessions such as your computer, television, and stamp collection in a single Home Inventory asset account. This makes it easy to track all your assets, so you have accurate records for insurance and other purposes.

A *liability* is something you owe—often to buy one of your assets! For example, if you buy a house, chances are you'll use a mortgage to finance it. The mortgage, which is a loan that is secured by your home, is a liability. You can use Quicken to track all of your liabilities, so you know exactly how much you owe at any given time.

Loans

A *loan* is a promise to pay money. Loans are commonly used to buy assets, although some folks often turn to debt consolidation loans to pay off other liabilities—I tell you more about that in Chapter 18.

Here's how it works: the lender gives the borrower money in exchange for the borrower's promise to pay it back. (The promise is usually in writing, with lots of signatures and initials.) The borrower normally pays back the loan with periodic payments to the lender that include interest on the loan balance or *principal*. The amount of the loan is reduced after each payment. The borrower incurs interest expense while the lender earns interest income.

While most people think of a loan as something you owe (a liability), a loan can also be something you own (an asset). For example, say you borrow money from your brother to buy a car. In your Quicken data file, the loan is related to a liability—money that you owe your brother. In your brother's Quicken data file, the loan is related to an asset—money that is due to him from you.

Types of Loans

There are several types of loans, some of which are designed for specific purposes. Here's a quick summary of what's available, along with their pros and cons.

Mortgage

A *mortgage* is a long-term loan secured by real estate. Most mortgages require a 10 percent or higher down payment on the property. Monthly payments are based on the term of the loan and the interest rate applied to the principal. The interest you pay on a mortgage for a first or second home is tax deductible. If you fail to make mortgage payments, your house could be sold to pay back the mortgage.

A *balloon* mortgage is a special type of short-term mortgage. Rather than make monthly payments over the full typical mortgage term, at the end of the fifth, seventh, or tenth year, you pay the balance of the mortgage in one big "balloon" payment. Some balloon mortgages offer the option of refinancing when the balloon payment is due.

Home Equity Loans or Lines of Credit

A *home equity loan* or *second mortgage* is a line of credit secured by the equity in your home—the difference between its market value and the amount of outstanding debt. Your equity rises when you make mortgage payments or property values increase. It declines when you borrow against your equity or property values decrease. A home equity loan lets you borrow against this equity.

There are two benefits to a home equity loan: interest rates are usually lower than other credit, and interest may be tax deductible. For these reasons, many people use home equity loans to pay off credit card debt; renovate their homes; or buy cars, boats, or other recreational vehicles. (I used a home equity line of credit in 1999 to buy a new Jeep. Not only did I get a low rate, but the interest I paid on the loan is tax deductible.) But, as with a mortgage, if you fail to pay a home equity reserve, your house could be sold to satisfy the debt.

Reverse Equity Loans

A *reverse equity loan* provides homeowners who own their homes in full with a regular monthly income. Instead of you paying the lender, the lender pays you. This type of loan is attractive to retirees who live on a fixed income. The loan is paid back when the home is sold—often after the death of the homeowner. (You can imagine how the next of kin feel about that.)

Car Loans

A *car loan* is a loan secured by a vehicle such as a car, truck, or motor home. Normally, you make a down payment and use the loan to pay the balance of the car's purchase price. Monthly payments are based on the term of the loan and the interest rate applied to the principal. Interest on car loans is not tax deductible.

Personal Loans

A *personal loan* is an unsecured loan—a loan that requires no collateral. Monthly payments are based on the term of the loan and the interest rate applied to the principal. You can use a personal loan for just about anything. Some people use them to pay off multiple smaller debts so they have only one monthly payment. Interest on personal loans is not tax deductible.

Loan Considerations

When applying for a loan, a number of variables have a direct impact on what the loan costs you now and in the future. Be sure to ask about all these things *before* applying for any loan.

Interest Rate

The *interest rate* is the annual percentage applied to the loan principal. Several factors affect the interest rate you may be offered:

- **Your credit record** affects the interest rate offered because a borrower with a good credit record can usually get a better rate than one with a bad credit record. Of course, if your credit record is really bad, you might not be able to borrow money at any rate.
- **The type of loan** affects the interest rate offered because, generally speaking, personal loans have the highest interest rates, whereas mortgages have the lowest. From highest to lowest between these two types are a used car loan, a new car loan, and a home equity reserve or line of credit.
- **The loan term** affects the interest rate offered because the length of a loan can vary the interest within a specific loan type. For example, for car loans, the longer the term, the lower the rate.

- **The amount of the down payment** has an effect on the interest rate offered because the more money you put down on the purchase, the lower the rate may be.
- **Your location** affects the interest rate offered because rates vary from one area of the country to another.
- **The lender** affects the interest rates because rates also vary from one lender to another. Certain types of lenders have lower rates than others.

Two kinds of interest rates can apply to a loan: fixed and variable.

- **Fixed rate** applies the same rate to the principal throughout the loan term.
- **Variable rate** applies a different rate to the loan throughout the loan term. For example, the loan may start with one rate and, each year, switch to a different rate. The rate is usually established by adding a certain number of percentage points to a national index, such as treasury bill rates. A cap limits the amount the rate can change. Mortgages with this type of rate are referred to as *adjustable rate mortgages,* or *ARMs.*

Although ARMs usually offer a lower initial interest rate than fixed rate mortgages, you should consider the overall economic conditions before deciding on one. For example, when we purchased our first home, in the mid-1980s when interest rates were high, we selected an ARM. When interest rates dropped, so did the rate on our mortgage. If we'd selected a fixed-rate mortgage when we bought that home, we would have had to refinance to get the same savings. But because rates were much lower when we bought our current home, we selected a fixed rate to protect us from possible rate increases in the future. That was five years ago and the rate we locked in at is still lower than what many banks are offering.

Term

A loan's *term* is the period of time between the loan date and the date payment is due in full. Loan terms vary depending on the type of loan:

- Mortgage loan and home equity reserve loan terms are typically 10, 15, 20, or 30 years.
- Balloon mortgage loan terms are typically 5, 7, or 10 years.
- Car loan terms are typically 3, 4, or 5 years.

Down Payment

A *down payment* is an up-front payment toward the purchase of a home or car. Most mortgages require at least 10 percent down; 20 percent down is preferred.

Keep in mind that if you make only a 10 percent down payment on a home, you may be required to pay for the cost of private mortgage insurance. This protects the lender from loss if you fail to pay your mortgage, but increases your monthly mortgage payments.

Application Fees

Most lenders require you to pay an application fee to process your loan application. This usually includes the cost of obtaining a property appraisal and credit report. These fees are usually not refundable—even if you are turned down.

Mortgage Closing Costs

In addition to the application fee and down payment, many other costs are involved in securing a mortgage and purchasing a home. These are known as *closing costs*. The Real Estate Settlement Procedures Act of 1974 requires that your lender provide a Good Faith Estimate of closing costs. This document summarizes all of the costs of closing on a home based on the mortgage the lender is offering.

Here's a brief list of the types of costs you may encounter. Because they vary from lender to lender, they could be a deciding factor when shopping for a mortgage. Note that most of these fees are not negotiable.

- **Origination fee** covers the administrative costs of processing a loan.
- **Discount or "points"** is a fee based on a percentage rate applied to the loan amount. For example, 1 point on a $150,000 mortgage is $1,500.
- **Appraisal fee** covers the cost of a market-value appraisal of the property by a licensed, certified appraiser.
- **Credit report fee** covers the cost of obtaining a credit history of the prospective borrower(s) to determine credit worthiness.
- **Underwriting fee** covers the cost of underwriting the loan. This is the process of determining loan risks and establishing terms and conditions.
- **Document preparation fee** covers the cost of preparing legal and other documents required to process the loan.
- **Title insurance fee** covers the cost of title insurance, which protects the lender and buyer against loss due to disputes over ownership and possession of the property.
- **Recording fee** covers the cost of entering the sale of a property into public records.
- **Prepaid items** are taxes, insurance, and assessments paid in advance of their due dates. These expenses are not paid to the lender but are due at the closing date.

Setting Up Accounts

To track an asset or liability with Quicken, you must set up an appropriate account. All transactions related to the asset or liability will be recorded in the account's register.

In this section, I tell you about the types of accounts you can use to track your assets and liabilities and explain how to set up each type of account.

Choosing the Right Account

Quicken offers four property and loan account types for tracking assets and liabilities.

- **House (with or without Mortgage)**   A house account is for recording the value of a house, condominium, or other real estate. When you create a house account, Quicken asks whether there is a mortgage on the property. If there is, you can have Quicken create a related liability account for you or associate the house account with an existing liability account. This makes it possible to set up both your house asset account and mortgage liability account at the same time.

- **Vehicle (with or without Loan)**   A vehicle account is similar to a house account, but it's designed for vehicles, including cars, trucks, and recreational vehicles. Quicken asks if there is a loan on the vehicle; if there is, it can create a related liability account or link to an existing liability account.

- **Asset**   An asset account is for recording the value of other assets, such as personal property. For example, my Quicken data file includes asset accounts for my horses, art and antiques, and my personal possessions.

- **Liability**   A liability account is for recording money you owe to others. As mentioned earlier, when you create a house or vehicle account, Quicken can automatically create a corresponding liability account for you. You can create a liability account to record other debts that are not related to the purchase of a specific asset.

Creating Asset and Liability Accounts

You create asset and liability accounts with the Account Setup dialog, which walks you through the process of creating the account. Quicken offers a number of ways to open this dialog for an asset or liability account. Here are some suggestions:

- Click the Setup button on the toolbar to display Quicken Guided Setup. Click the Property & Debt item under Add Accounts. As shown next, Quicken

Guided Setup displays buttons for each type of asset and liability account. Click the button for the type of account you want to create.

Add every property and debt account that you want to track in Quicken.

House	Add Account	Accounts for homes you own such as your primary residence or rental properties.
Vehicle	Add Account	Accounts for vehicles you own, such as cars, trucks, or boats.
Asset	Add Account	Accounts for things you own besides homes or vehicles such as art, collectibles, or business assets.
Liability	Add Account	Accounts for money you owe besides credit card debt. (Track credit card debt in Cash Flow).

- Click the Add Account button in the Property & Debt Accounts area of the Property & Debt Center window. In the Add New Account dialog that appears (shown next), select the option for the type of account you want to create and click Next.

Add New Account

Choose the type of account to create.

- **House (with or without Mortgage)**
  Accounts for homes you own such as your primary residence or rental properties.

- **Vehicle (with or without Loan)**
  Accounts for vehicles you own, such as cars, trucks, or boats.

- **Asset**
  Accounts for things you own besides homes or vehicles such as art, collectibles, or business assets.

- **Liability**
  Accounts for money you owe besides credit card debt. (Track credit card debt in Cash Flow).

Cancel | Help | Next

- Choose Property & Debt | Property & Debt Accounts | Add Account. In the Add New Account dialog that appears (just shown), select the option for the type of account you want to create and click Next.

- Choose Tools | Account List or press CTRL-A to display the Account List window. Then click the Add Account button in the button bar. Select the option for the type of account you want to create and click Next.

Chapter 3 explains how to use the Account Setup dialog to create new Quicken accounts. In this section, I provide information about the kinds of data you'll have to enter to create asset and liability accounts.

Account Name and Other Information

Give the account a name that clearly identifies the asset or liability. For example, if you have two cars and plan to track them in separate asset accounts, consider naming the account with the make and model of the car. *Jeep Wrangler* and *Chevy Pickup* do a better job identifying the cars than *Auto 1* and *Auto 2*. When creating a liability account, you may want to include the word *mortgage* or *loan* in the account name so you don't confuse it with a related asset.

For a vehicle account, Quicken will also ask for the make, model, and year of the car. Quicken stores this information in the Account Details dialog for the asset. (You can view and edit this information after the account has been created by clicking the Edit Account Details button in the Overview tab of the asset's account register.)

Starting Point Information

For house and vehicle accounts, Quicken prompts you to enter information about the asset's purchase, including the acquisition date and purchase price. You can find this information on your original purchase receipts. Quicken also asks for an estimate of the current value. For a house, this number will (hopefully) be higher than the purchase price; for a car, this number will probably be lower. This is the amount that will appear as the asset account balance.

For assets and liabilities, Quicken prompts you for a starting date and value (asset) or amount owed (liability). If you don't know how much to enter now, you can leave it set to zero and enter a value when you know what to enter. I explain how to adjust asset values later in this chapter.

Optional Tax Information

For asset and liability accounts, you can click a Tax button to enter tax schedule information for transfers in and out of the account. This is completely optional and, in most cases, unnecessary. I explain how to set up Quicken accounts and categories to simplify tax preparation in Chapter 19.

Related Mortgage or Loan

When creating a house or vehicle account, Quicken asks whether there is a related mortgage or loan. You have three options:

- **Yes, create a liability account for me.** This option tells Quicken that there is a loan and that it should create a liability account.
- **There is a mortgage/loan and I'm already tracking it in Quicken.** This option enables you to select an existing liability account to link to the loan.
- **The house/vehicle is paid for, so I don't need a liability account.** This option tells Quicken that there is no loan so no liability account is necessary. (Lucky you!)

Loan Information

If you indicated that Quicken should create a liability account for a house or vehicle, it automatically displays the Edit Loan dialog, which you can use to enter information about the loan. If you set up a liability account, Quicken asks if you want to set up an amortized loan to be associated with the liability. I explain how to set up a loan later in this chapter.

The Account Register

When you're finished setting up an asset or liability account (and related loans and loan payments, if applicable), Quicken automatically displays the account's register. Figure 13-1 shows what a house account might look like. The first transaction, dated 10/15/1997, shows the opening balance, which is the amount paid for the house. The second transaction, dated 6/5/2002, shows an adjustment automatically made by Quicken to increase the account's balance based on my estimate of its worth on the day I created the account.

All transactions that affect an asset or liability account's balance appear in the account register. I tell you more about using account registers for asset and liability accounts later in this chapter.

Asset : House	**Register**	**Overview**						
Delete Find Transfer Update Balance					Report ▾ Options ▾ How Do I ▾			
Date	Ref	Payee/Category/Memo		Decrease	Clr	Increase	Balance	▲
10/15/1997		Opening Balance				207,500 00	207,500 00	
		[House]						
6/5/2002		Balance Adjustment			R	22,500 00	230,000 00	
		[House]						
3/6/2002 ▦	Ref	Payee		Decrease		Increase		
		Category	Memo			Enter Edit ▾ Split		
								▼

Ending Balance: 230,000.00

Figure 13-1 • The account register for a newly created asset shows what you paid for the asset, as well as the estimated market value as of the account creation date.

Tips for Minimizing Loan Expenses

Borrowing money costs money. It's as simple as that. But there are some things you can do to minimize the cost of a loan:

Shop for the lowest rate.   This may seem like a no-brainer, but a surprising number of people simply go to a local bank and accept whatever terms they offer. You don't have to use a local bank to borrow money for a home, car, or other major purchase. Check the financial pages of your local newspaper or the Bills & Banking channel on Quicken.com. And if you're shopping for a car, keep an eye out for low-interest financing deals. Sometimes, you can save a lot of money in interest by buying when the time is right. For example, suppose you have a choice of two five-year car loans for $20,000, one at 6.15 percent and the other at 8.4 percent. Over the course of five years, you'll pay $1,279 less if you go with the lower rate. That can buy a lot of gas.

Minimize the loan term.   The shorter the loan term, the less interest you'll pay over the life of the loan. The savings can be quite substantial. For example, suppose you have a choice of two loan terms for a $100,000, 7.25 percent mortgage: 15 years or 30 years. If you choose the 15-year mortgage, you'll pay $64,315 in interest, but if you choose the 30-year mortgage, you'll pay a whopping $145,583 in interest— $81,000 more! Neither option is appealing, but the shorter term mortgage is certainly easier to swallow. The drawback? The monthly payment for the 15-year mortgage is $913, while the payment for the 30-year mortgage is only $682. Obviously, your monthly spending budget will weigh heavily into the decision.

Maximize the down payment.   The less you borrow, the less you'll pay in interest—and the less your monthly payments will be. Take the loan term example just shown. Suppose your budget won't allow you to go with the shorter term loan—you just can't make those monthly payments. But if you cashed in an IRA worth $10,000 and put that toward the down payment (talk to your tax advisor; you may be able to do this without penalty for the purchase of a first home), you could knock almost $100 per month off the 15-year loan's monthly payment, which might be enough to fit it into your budget—and save another $13,000 in interest!

Make extra loan payments.   If you can't go for a shorter term loan, consider making extra payments towards the loan's principal. Take another look at the 30-year mortgage example just shown. If you pay an additional $50 per month (increasing your monthly payment to $732), you can save more than $33,000 in interest and pay off the loan almost six years early! Or perhaps you get a generous holiday bonus each year. If you put $1,000 of that bonus toward the mortgage each January as an extra payment, you can save almost $46,000 in interest and pay off the loan eight years early!

Clean up your credit *before* applying for a loan.   Loan terms vary based on credit history. To get the best deal, your credit should be as clean as possible. If you think there might be problems in your credit report, get a copy—you can learn how in the Credit area of Quicken.com's Bills & Banking channel. (You might also want to try the myFICO credit score service available for a fee through Quicken; choose Property & Debt | Quicken Services | Check Your FICO Credit Score to learn more.) Then do what you need to get things cleaned up.

When evaluating the dollar impact of different loan deals, use Quicken's Loan Calculator. It'll make complex loan payment calculations for you. I explain how to use Quicken's financial calculators, including the Loan Calculator and Refinance Calculator, in Chapter 17.

Tracking a Loan

Quicken makes it easy to track the principal, interest, and payments for a loan. Once you set up a loan and corresponding liability or asset accounts, you can make payments with Quicken using QuickFill (see Chapter 7), scheduled transactions (see Chapter 7), or online payments (see Chapter 6). The Loan feature keeps track of all the details so you don't have to.

Before I explain how to use the loan feature, let me take a moment to make something clear. A loan is not the same as an asset or liability account. A loan, in Quicken, is information that Quicken uses to calculate the amount of interest and principal due for each payment of an amortized loan, such as a mortgage or car loan. A loan must be associated with an asset account (if you are a lender) or a liability account (if you are a borrower), as well as an income or expense category to record interest income or expense. Loan transactions are recorded in the associated asset or liability account—not in Quicken's loan records. It's possible to delete a loan without losing any transaction data, as I explain later in this section. But you can't delete an asset or liability account that has a loan associated with it unless the loan is deleted first.

Setting Up a Loan

There are three ways to set up a loan:

- Create a house, vehicle, or liability account with a related mortgage or loan as discussed earlier in this chapter. Quicken automatically prompts you for loan information.
- Click the Add Loan button in the Loan Accounts Summary area of the Property & Debt Center window.
- Choose Property & Debt | Loans or press CTRL-H to display the View Loans window (shown later in this chapter). Then click New in the window's button bar.

The method you use determines what dialogs and prompts appear. For example, if you create a loan when you create a house account, Quicken displays the Edit Loan dialog that summarizes all loan information in two screens. If you create a loan by clicking the New button in the View Loans window, Quicken displays the Loan Setup dialog with EasyStep screens that walk you through the loan creation process. It doesn't matter which method you use; the information you need to enter is basically the same. Here's what you can expect.

Type of Loan   The Loan Setup dialog starts by prompting you for a loan type. You have two options:

- **Borrow Money** is for loans for which you're borrowing money from a lender, such as a car loan, mortgage, or personal loan. Quicken uses a liability account to record the loan.
- **Lend Money** is for loans for which you're the lender. Quicken uses an asset account to record the money owed from the borrower.

Loan Account   The Loan Setup dialog prompts you to enter the account for the loan. Again, you have two options:

- **New Account** enables you to set up a brand-new account for the loan. Be sure to enter a name for the account.
- **Existing Account** enables you to select one of your existing liability accounts for the loan. This option is only available if you have already created a liability account that isn't already linked to a loan.

Loan Details   No matter how you create the loan, you'll be prompted for information about the loan creation, amount, and payments. It's important to be accurate; get the numbers directly from a loan statement or agreement if possible.

Quicken can calculate some of the values—such as the loan balance and monthly payments—for you. It does this automatically based on answers to questions in the Set Up Loan dialog. If you're using the Edit Loan dialog, select the Calculate option in the Payment area. When you click Done, Quicken displays a dialog telling you that it has calculated the values. Click OK to return to the Edit Loan dialog to see the calculated amount. Keep in mind, however, that Quicken's calculated amounts may not exactly match those calculated by your bank or finance company.

When you've finished entering loan information in the Setup Loan dialog, a series of Summary tab windows display entered and calculated values. Here's what the Edit Loan dialog screens look like for a $32,000, five-year car loan started on May 15, 2001; these windows are virtually identical to the last two screens that appear in the Loan Setup dialog when you create a loan from the View Loans window:

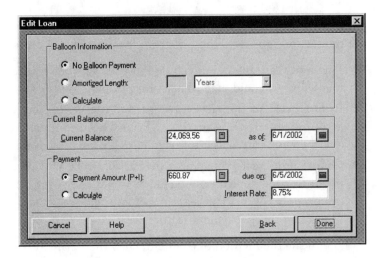

Setting Up Payments

When you set up a loan, Quicken automatically prompts you to set up payment information by displaying the Edit Loan Payment (or Set Up Loan Payment) dialog:

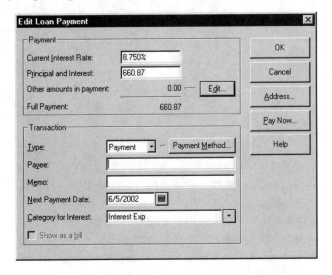

   Enter information in this dialog to set up the payment. If the total payment should include additional amounts for property taxes, insurance, or other escrow items, click the Edit button. This displays the Split Transaction window, which you can use to enter categories, memos, and amounts to be added to the payment.

In the Transaction area of the dialog, you can specify the type and method for the transaction. For type, there are three options on the drop-down list:

- **Payment** is a transaction recorded in your account register only. You must manually write and mail a check for payment. This is covered in Chapter 5.
- **Print Check** is a transaction recorded in the Write Checks dialog and account register. You can use the Print Check command to print the check, and then you can mail it for payment. This is also covered in Chapter 5.
- **Online Pmt** creates a payment instruction to be processed by your financial institution for use with online payment. This is covered in Chapter 6. This option only appears if at least one of your bank accounts is enabled for Quicken's online payment feature.

To indicate the method of payment, click the Payment Method button. The Select Payment Method dialog appears:

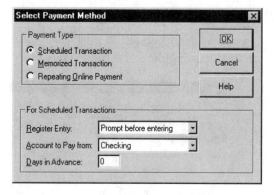

This dialog offers three Payment Type options:

- **Scheduled Transaction** is a transaction scheduled for the future. If you select this option, you must also choose options and enter values to specify how Quicken should enter the transaction, which account should be used to pay, and how many days in advance it should be entered and paid. All this is covered in Chapter 7.
- **Memorized Transaction** is a transaction memorized for use with QuickFill or the Quicken Financial Calendar. This is also covered in Chapter 7.
- **Repeating Online Payment** is a recurring online payment instruction processed by your financial institution. If you select this option, you must also select a repeating online payment transaction from a drop-down list. If you have not already created a transaction to link to this loan payment, select one of the other options and return to this dialog after you have created the required transaction. Consult Chapter 6 for complete instructions.

Creating an Associated Asset Account

At the conclusion of the payment setup process, Quicken may display a dialog asking if you want to create an asset to go with the loan. This enables you to set up an asset account for the full purchase price of your new home or car. Click Yes to create a new account; click No if you have already created one. I discussed creating an asset account earlier in this chapter.

Reviewing Loan Information

The View Loans window displays information about your loans, as shown next. You can open this window by choosing Property & Debt | Loans or by pressing CTRL-H.

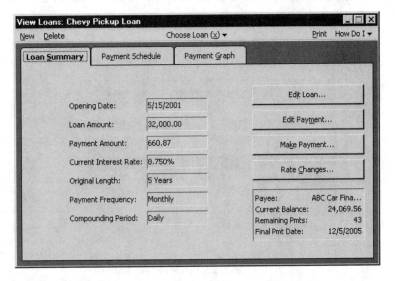

Button Bar Options

The View Loans window's button bar offers options for working with loans:

- **New** enables you to create a new loan. I explained how this option works earlier in this chapter.
- **Delete** removes the currently displayed loan. If you click this button, a dialog appears, asking if you want to save the associated account for your records. If you click Yes, Quicken removes the loan information, but keeps the liability account and all of its transactions. If you click No, Quicken deletes the loan information and the liability account. This causes any related transactions in other accounts—such as payments made from your checking account—to be uncategorized. (I recommend that you click Yes. You can always hide the account if you don't want to see it; I explain how in Chapter 3.)

- **Choose Loan** displays a menu of your current loans. Use it to choose the loan you want to display in the window.

- **Print** prints a loan payment schedule for the currently displayed loan. The printout includes all of the information in the Payment Schedule tab of the View Loans window, which is shown and discussed momentarily.

- **How Do I** provides instructions for working with the View Loans window.

Window Tabs

The tabs along the top of the window's information area enable you to view various pieces of information about a loan.

Loan Summary   Loan Summary, shown earlier, summarizes the loan information.

Payment Schedule   Payment Schedule, shown next, displays a schedule of past and future payments. You can turn on the Show Running Totals check box to display cumulative totals, rather than individual payment information.

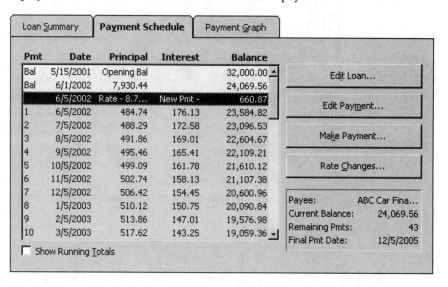

Payment Graph   Payment Graph, shown next, displays a graph of the loan payments. Where the two lines meet indicates the point at which you start paying more toward the loan principal than for interest. You can point to a position on a graph line to display its value.

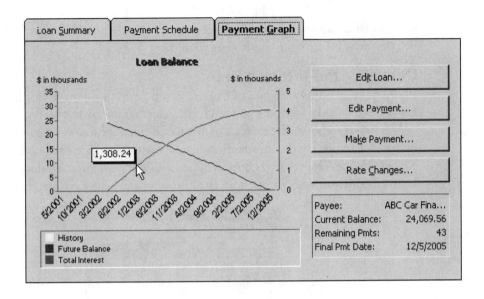

Modifying Loan Information

Once you've created a loan, you can modify it as necessary to record corrections, changes in the interest rate, or changes in payment methods. You can do all these things with buttons in the View Loans window.

Changing Loan Information

If you discover a discrepancy between the loan information in the View Loans window and information on statements or loan agreement papers, you can change the loan information in Quicken.

If necessary, choose the loan account's name from the Choose Loan menu in the button bar to display the information for the loan you want to modify. Then click the Edit Loan button. A pair of Edit Loan windows enables you to change just about any information for the loan. Modify values and select different options as desired. Click Done in the last window to save your changes. Quicken automatically makes any necessary entries to update the account.

Changing Payment Information

Occasionally, you may want to make changes to a loan's payment information. For example, suppose the real estate taxes on your property are reduced (you can always hope!) and the resulting escrow amount, which is included in the payment, changes. Or you decide to switch payment method from a scheduled transaction to a repeating online payment.

If necessary, choose the loan account's name from the Choose Loan menu in the button bar to display the information for the loan payment you want to modify. Then click the Edit Payment button. The Edit Loan Payment dialog, shown earlier, appears. Make changes as desired and click OK. Quicken updates the payment information with your changes.

Changing the Interest Rate

If you have an adjustable rate mortgage, you'll periodically have to adjust the rate for the loan within Quicken to match the rate charged by the lender.

If necessary, choose the loan account's name from the Choose Loan menu in the button bar to display the information for the loan whose rate you want to change. Then click the Rate Changes button. The Loan Rate Changes window appears. It lists all the loan rates throughout the history of the loan, as shown here:

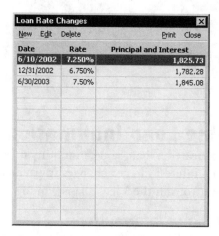

To insert a rate change, click New in the window's button bar. The Insert An Interest Rate Change dialog appears:

Enter the effective date and new rate in the appropriate text boxes. Quicken automatically calculates the new loan payment. When you click OK, the rate appears in the Loan Rate Changes window. Click the Close button to dismiss the window. Quicken recalculates the loan payment schedule for you.

Making a Loan Payment

Although it's usually more convenient to set up a loan payment as a scheduled transaction or repeating online payment instruction as discussed earlier, you can also use the View Loans window to make a loan payment. This method is especially useful for making extra loan payments—payments in addition to your normal periodic payments.

If necessary, choose the loan account's name from the Choose Loan menu in the button bar to display the information for the loan for which you want to make a payment. Then click the Make Payment button. A Loan Payment dialog appears, asking whether you are making a regularly scheduled payment or an extra payment. Click the appropriate button.

Making a Regular Loan Payment

If you click the Regular button, the Make Regular Payment dialog, which is shown next, appears. Set options to specify the bank account from which the payment should be made, the type of transaction, the payee information, the date, and a memo for the transaction. If the type of transaction is set to Payment, you can enter a check number or use one of the options on the drop-down list to set a number option. The Category and Amount are already set using values calculated by Quicken—you shouldn't have to change them. Click OK to enter the transaction.

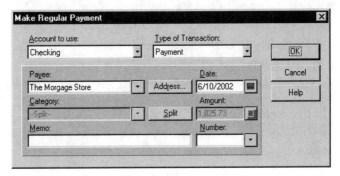

Making an Extra Loan Payment

If you click the Extra button, the Make Extra Payment dialog appears. As you can see in the following illustration, it's almost identical to the Make Regular Payment dialog. There are only two differences: the loan account is automatically set as the transfer account in the Category field and the Amount field is left blank. Set options in the dialog to specify payment information, including the amount. Then click OK to enter the transaction.

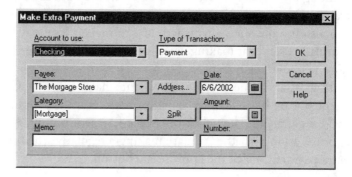

Recording Other Asset Transactions

Part of tracking assets is keeping track of their current values and modifying account balances when necessary. Like a bank or investment account, which I discuss in Chapters 5 and 10, activity for an asset account appears in its account register.

As usual, Quicken offers several ways to open an asset account's register:

- Click the name of the account in the Property & Debt Accounts area of the Account Bar or the Property & Debt Center.
- Choose the name of the account from the Property & Debt Accounts submenu under the Property & Debt menu.
- Double-click the name of the account in the Account List window.

The Account Register, which is shown in Figure 13-1, appears in the Property & Debt Center. You can use button bar buttons to work with the register and its entries:

- **Delete** removes the currently selected transaction.
- **Find** enables you to search for transactions in the window. I discuss searching for transactions in Chapter 5.
- **Transfer** enables you to create a transfer transaction. I cover transfers in Chapter 5, too.
- **Update Balance** enables you to create a transaction to update the value of the asset. I discuss this option later in this section.
- **Report** is a menu that offers a variety of reporting options for account information.

- **Options** is a menu that offers a variety of options for changing the view of the window.
- **How Do I** provides instructions for completing tasks with the Account Register window.

In this section, I explain how you can record changes in asset values due to acquisitions and disposals, improvements, market values, and depreciation.

Adding and Disposing of Assets

The most obvious change in an asset's value occurs when you add or remove part of the asset. For example, I have a single asset account in which I record the value of my horses and related equipment. When I buy a new horse, it increases the value of the account. Similarly, when I sell one of my saddles, it decreases the value of the account.

In many instances, when you add or dispose of an asset, money is exchanged. In that case, recording the transaction is easy: simply use the appropriate bank account register to record the purchase or sale and use the asset account as a transfer account in the category field. Here's what the purchase of a new horse might look like in my checking account:

6/24/01	5028	Jules The Horse Trader		3,000 00		1,289 26
		[Horses & Tack]	Cherokee			

And here's the same transaction in my Horses and Tack asset account:

6/24/01		Jules The Horse Trader			3,000 00	10,500 00
		[Checking]	Cherokee			

If the asset was acquired without an exchange of cash, you can enter the transaction directly into the asset account, using the Gift Received category (or a similar category of your choice) to categorize the income. Similarly, if the asset was disposed of without an exchange of cash, you can enter the transaction into the asset account register using the Gifts Given or Charity (or other appropriate category) to categorize the write-off.

If you have completely disposed of the asset and no longer need the account, don't delete the account! Doing so will remove all income and expense category transactions and uncategorize all transfer transactions related to the account. Instead, consider hiding the account to get it off account lists. I explain how in Chapter 3.

Updating Asset Values

A variety of situations can change the value of a single asset. The type of situation will determine how the value is adjusted. Here are three common examples.

Recording Improvements

Certain home-related expenditures can be considered improvements that increase the value of your home. It's important to keep track of improvements because they raise the property's tax basis, thus reducing the amount of capital gains you have to record (and pay tax on) when you sell the house. Your tax advisor can help you determine which expenditures can be capitalized as home improvements.

Since most home improvements involve an expenditure, use the appropriate cash flow account register to record the transaction. Be sure to enter the appropriate asset account (House, Condo, Land, and so on) as a transfer account in the Category field. Here's what a home improvement transaction might look like in my checking account:

6/5/2002	1259	Dan The Man Home Improvements	3,500	00			2,641	79
		[House] Patio						

And here's the same transaction in my House asset account:

6/5/2002		Dan The Man Home Improvements			3,500	00	233,500	00
		[Checking] Patio						

Adjusting for Market Value

Real estate, vehicles, and other large-ticket item assets are also affected by market values. Generally speaking, real estate values go up, vehicle values go down, and other item values can vary either way depending on what they are.

To adjust for market value, click the Update Balance button in the button bar of the account register for the asset you want to adjust. The Update Account Balance dialog, which is shown here, appears:

Use this dialog to enter the date and market value for the asset. Then select a category or transfer account to record the gain or loss of value. When you click OK, the entry is added to the account register as shown here:

6/6/2002	Balance Adjustment		R	2,950	00	18,450	00
	Misc						

If you don't want the adjustment to affect any category or account other than the asset, choose the same asset account as a transfer account. When you click OK, a dialog will warn you that you are trying to record a transfer into the same account. Click OK again. You can see an example of an adjustment like this in Figure 13-1.

Recording Depreciation

Depreciation is a calculated reduction in the value of an asset. Depreciation expense can be calculated using a variety of acceptable methods, including straight line, sum of the year's digits, and declining balance. Normally, it reduces the asset's value regularly, with monthly, quarterly, or annual adjustments.

Depreciation is commonly applied to property used for business purposes since depreciation expense on those assets may be tax deductible. If you think depreciation on an asset you own may be tax deductible, use Quicken to track the depreciation expense. Otherwise, depreciation probably isn't worth the extra effort it requires to track.

To record depreciation, create an entry in the asset account that reduces the value by the amount of the depreciation. Use a Depreciation Expense category to record the expense. The transaction might look something like this:

6/1/01	Jeep Depreciation	200	00			17,800	00
	Auto:Depreciation						

Keep in mind that you can set up monthly, quarterly, or annual depreciation transactions as scheduled transactions. This automates the process of recording them when they are due. I tell you about scheduled transactions in Chapter 7.

Quicken Quick Tip

I update the value of all my assets once a year. Whenever possible, I use documented values—for example, I can estimate the value of my vehicles using the Kelly Blue Book Web site at http://www.kbb.com/. If I can't get a documented value for an asset—such as my house—I use an estimate. I then use the Update Account Balance dialog to bring each asset account up to date. It doesn't take long to do, and I benefit by having accurate values in my Quicken data file.

Managing Household Records

In this Chapter:

- *Tracking the value of personal possessions*

- *Organizing emergency records*

When most people think of assets, they think of homes, cars, and other big-ticket items. But personal possessions—such as the furniture and electronics equipment in your home, the bicycle and golf clubs in your garage, and the stamp collection on the shelf in your hall closet—are also a part of your assets. Quicken Home Inventory makes it easy to record and track the value of these things. Similarly, Quicken's Emergency Record Organizer enables you to keep track of information that's good to have on hand, especially in the event of an emergency. Together, these Quicken features help you keep your household records manageable.

In this chapter, I explain how to use Quicken Home Inventory and the Emergency Records Organizer to create detailed records of your belongings and other important information.

Quicken Home Inventory

Quicken Home Inventory is a separate program that comes with Quicken Deluxe. You can open it from within Quicken, enter or edit information about the things in your home, and then update your Quicken data file with item valuations. You can also use Quicken Home Inventory to keep track of your insurance policies and any insurance claims you might make.

Quicken Home Inventory is excellent for providing detailed information about your possessions. This information is extremely valuable in the event of a burglary, fire, or other loss when you need to provide details to the police and/or insurance company. Enter this information and print reports to keep in a safe place. Then, once a year or so—or right after a big yard sale—update the entries and prepare a fresh report so your printed files are up to date.

Entering Basic Information

To start, choose Property & Debt | Quicken Home Inventory. The Quicken Home Inventory program starts and appears onscreen, over your Quicken program window (see Figure 14-1). You can use this List View window to add or modify summary information about each inventory item.

To add an item to the home inventory, begin by choosing a home location from the drop-down list near the top of the window. Click New at the bottom of the window or click anywhere in the first empty line to start a new line. Then enter basic information about the item on the line and press ENTER.

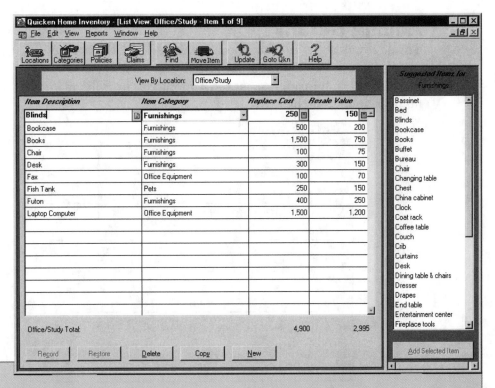

Figure 14-1 • **Quicken Home Inventory enables you to report the value of everything in your home, room by room.**

A quick way to enter a standard item is to choose the item category and then double-click one of the suggested items in the list on the right side of the window. Modify the values if desired and press ENTER.

Quicken Quick Tip

Don't get carried away! Although you can use Quicken Home Inventory to track every possession in every room, from the ceiling lamp to the carpeting, entering that kind of detail isn't really necessary. Instead, enter the most valuable items, the ones that would be most difficult or costly to replace. This will save you time while enabling you to record your most important belongings.

Adding Details

To add details about an item, select it and then click the icon beside it in the Item Description column. Use the Detail View window, which is illustrated next, to enter more information about the item, such as its make and model, its serial number, and its purchase date.

Clicking the Receipts & Records button displays the Receipts And Records dialog, shown next. You can toggle check boxes to indicate the types of records you have for the item, as well as where those records can be found.

Clicking the Resale Value History button displays the Resale Value History dialog, shown next, which you can use to record changes in the item's resale value. Click the New button in the dialog to create a new value entry. You may find this feature useful for keeping track of the value of collectible items, especially those you hold as "investments."

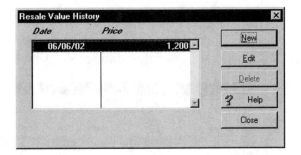

When you're finished adding item details, click the Return To List View button at the top of the window. If a dialog appears asking if you want to record changes to the item, click Yes.

Using the Toolbar

The toolbar along the top of the Quicken Home Inventory window (see Figure 14-1) offers a number of options you can use to customize and work with the program and its data.

Locations

The Locations button displays the Locations dialog, which is shown next. It enables you to add, modify, or remove names for rooms in your home. It also displays a list of entered items by location.

Location	Items	Replace Cost	Resale Value
Bedroom	8	3,210	1,605
Closets			
Dining Room	1	1,200	600
Family Room			
Garage	13	4,165	2,083
Halls and Entry			
Kitchen	6	2,350	1,175
Laundry/Utility Room			
Living Room	1	400	200
Office/Study	9	4,900	2,995

Categories

The Categories button displays the Categories dialog, shown next, which enables you to add, modify, or remove names for categories of items. It also displays a list of entered items by category.

A quick note here: Don't confuse "categories" in Quicken Home Inventory with "categories" in Quicken. The two terms are used differently. Quicken Home Inventory categories have nothing to do with Quicken categories.

Category	Items	Replace Cost	Resale Value
Appliances	8	3,150	1,575
Bath			
Clothing			
Decorations & Art			
Electronics	2	60	30
Emergency supplies	1	25	13
Furnishings	12	6,450	3,275
Garage & Yard	7	2,450	1,225
Hobbies & Crafts			
Jewelry & Valuables	1	1,000	500

Policies

The Policies button displays the Policies dialog, shown next, which enables you to add, modify, or remove insurance policies. It also displays a list of entered items by insurance policy. (You can set the insurance policy for an item in the Detail View window, shown earlier.)

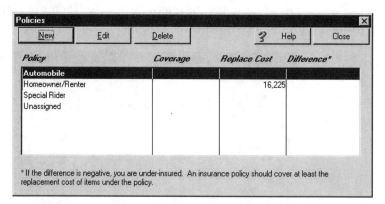

Policy	Coverage	Replace Cost	Difference*
Automobile			
Homeowner/Renter		16,225	
Special Rider			
Unassigned			

* If the difference is negative, you are under-insured. An insurance policy should cover at least the replacement cost of items under the policy.

When you click the dialog's New button to create a new policy or Edit button to edit an existing policy, a dialog like the one shown next appears. Enter details about the policy, including the contact information for making changes or claims. If you enter a dollar amount in the Coverage box, Quicken displays the amount in the Policies dialog, along with the difference between the coverage amount and the value of insured items. A negative number indicates that you don't have enough insurance to cover all items.

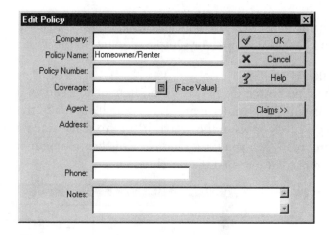

Claims

The Claims button displays the Insurance Claims dialog, which lists any claims you have entered into Quicken Home Inventory.

To create a new claim, click the New button in the dialog. A new Claim Instructions dialog appears, with information about creating a claim. Read the instructions and click OK to dismiss it. Then fill out the fields in the New Claim dialog, which is shown next, to enter details about the claim. You can click the Items button to display a list of all items entered in Quicken Home Inventory for the policy you selected. Then select each item you want to include in your claim and click OK.

When you're finished entering information in the New Claim dialog, click OK. A dialog appears, asking if you want to create a report showing the claim information. Click Yes to create the report onscreen, then click Print to print it and Close to return to the Quicken Home Inventory List View window.

Find

The Find button displays the Find Item dialog, shown next, which you can use to search for inventory items. Enter search criteria in the Search For box, then toggle check boxes in the Search In area to determine where the text should be matched. When you click Find All, Quicken Home Inventory displays a list of all items that matched the search criteria.

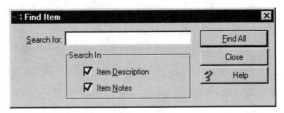

Move Item

The Move Item button enables you to change the location of an item. Click the button to display the Move Item dialog, shown next. Choose a location from the Current Location drop-down list to view a list of items in that location. Select the item(s) you want to move in the Items list, then select the location you want to move it to in the Move To This Location list. Click the Move button to change the item's location. (I wish it were this easy to move a refrigerator from the kitchen to the garage!)

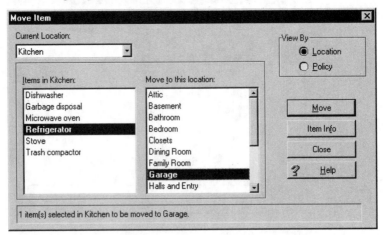

You can repeat this process for each item you want to move. When you're finished, click Close.

Update

The Update button updates the home inventory information in Quicken to reflect any changes you made while working with Quicken Home Inventory. I explain how this works a little later in this chapter.

Goto Qkn

The Goto Qkn (go to Quicken) button switches you back to Quicken without closing Quicken Home Inventory. You can use the Windows task bar or choose Property & Debt | Quicken Home Inventory to return to Quicken Home Inventory.

Help

The Help button changes the mouse pointer into a help pointer—a pointer with a question mark. Click the item you want to learn more about. A window appears with information. You can click the window's close button to dismiss it when you're finished reading it.

Printing Home Inventory Reports

The Reports menu in the Quicken Home Inventory program window offers a number of basic reports you can use to print inventory information, as shown next. This is extremely useful when applying for homeowner or home office insurance, especially when the insurance company requires detailed information about certain types of belongings.

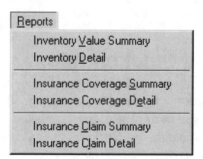

To create a report, choose its name from the menu. The report appears onscreen—Figure 14-2 shows an example. You can use the View drop-down list to change the way information is presented in the report. Click the Print button to print the report and the Close button to close the report and return to Quicken Home Inventory's List View window.

Figure 14-2 • A Quicken Home Inventory Report can provide information about all the items you entered in your home inventory.

Updating Quicken Information

When you've finished entering or modifying information in Quicken Home Inventory, click the Update button on its toolbar. A small dialog appears, asking you whether you want to send inventory data to the Home Inventory account in your Quicken data file. Click Yes. Then choose File | Exit to close Quicken Home Inventory.

When you switch back to Quicken, you'll see a Home Inventory account—even if you didn't create one—with a balance corresponding to the resale value of home inventory items. When you open the account, Quicken Home Inventory automatically launches, enabling you to add or update information.

Property & Debt Accounts	Options ▼
Account	Ending Balance
Property (Assets)	
Art & Antiques	18,450.00
Chevy Pickup	36,000.00
Home Inventory	8,657.50
House	233,500.00
Jeep	18,000.00
Subtotal	**314,607.50**
Debt (Liabilities)	
Chevy Pickup Loan	-24,069.56
HELOC	-51,423.20
House Loan	-102,491.97
Subtotal	**-177,984.73**
Total	**136,622.77**

[Add Account] [Edit Accounts]

Emergency Records Organizer

The Emergency Records Organizer (ERO) enables you to track personal, financial, and legal information that may come in handy in the event of an emergency. It consists of a number of forms you can fill in with information. You can enter as much or as little information as you like. You can go into great detail on subjects that are important to you and completely ignore others. You can update and print the information at any time. It's this flexibility—and the fact that all information can be stored in one place—that makes the ERO a useful tool.

To open the ERO, choose Property & Debt | Emergency Records Organizer. Its main window, which provides an introduction to its features, appears. Read what's in the window or click the Getting Started link to learn more.

Creating and Updating Records

To create or modify ERO records, click the ERO's Create/Update Records tab to display the entry window, which is shown in Figure 14-3. The window has three parts: the area drop-down list, the topic list, and the entry form.

To enter the information you want to organize, follow the steps as they appear in the window, and click Save. You can then click New Record to add another record for the same area and topic, or repeat the steps to add records for other areas or topics.

Figure 14-3 • The main entry window of the Emergency Records Organizer

Areas and Topics

The ERO offers 11 different areas of information, each with its own set of topics:

- **Adults' Emergency Info** is information you may need in the event of an adult's health-related emergency. Topics include Contact List (refer to Figure 14-3), Physicians/Dentists, Medical History, and Hospital Information.

- **Children's Emergency Info** is information you may need in the event of a child's health-related emergency. Topics include Contact List, Physicians/ Dentists, Medical History, and Hospital Information.

- **Adults' Important Info** is important information about the adults in your home or family. Topics include Summary (for birth date, Social Security number, driver's license number, and so on), Residence, Employment/ Business, Business Partners, Education, Marriage Info, and Military Record.

- **Children's Important Info** is important information about the children in your home or family. Topics include Child's Summary (for birth date, school, grade, and Social Security number), School, Caretaker, Schedules, and Guardian.

- **Personal & Legal Docs** is for information about important personal and legal documents. Topics include Will, Living Will, Funeral Arrangements, Powers of Attorney, Birth Certificate, Passport, and Tax Records.

- **Accounts** is for bank and other account information. Topics include Quicken Bank Acct., Quicken Credit Acct., Quicken Asset Acct., Quicken Liability Acct., Checking, Savings, Credit/Debit, and Other Accounts. Some of this information may be filled in for you based on accounts you created with Quicken.

- **Income** is for information about sources of income. Topics include Salary, Dividends, Interest, Rental Income, Annuity, Trust Fund, Alimony, Child Support, and Other.

- **Invest. and Retirement** is for information about regular and retirement investments. Topics include Quicken Invest. Acct., IRA Account, 401(k) Account, Money Market, Cert. of Deposit, Stocks, Bonds, Mutual Funds, Keogh/SEP Plan, Pension, and Social Security. Some of this information may be filled in for you based on accounts you created with Quicken.

- **Auto/Home/Property** is for general information about your property and vehicles. Topics include Property, Prev. Residence, Safe Deposit Box, Post Office Box, Safe, Alarm Information, Storage, Pets, Automobile, Motorcycle, and Recreational.

- **Insurance** is for insurance information. Topics include Life Insurance, Medical Insurance, Dental Insurance, Auto Insurance, Property Insurance, Disability Insurance, and Other Insurance.

- **Mortgage/Loans** is for information about loans. Topics include Mortgage, Personal Loans, Auto Loans, and School Loans.

At this point, you might be wondering about the wisdom of keeping all kinds of important—and often private—information in one place. After all, the burglar who took your stamp collection and fax machine could also take your computer. Fortunately, you can back up and password-protect your Quicken data file. I show you how in Appendix A.

Entry Form

The entry form that appears when you choose an area and select a topic (see Figure 14-3) varies with the area and topic. Each form offers labeled text boxes for entering appropriate information. You can enter as much information as you like and skip over as many fields as you like. You won't get an error message for entering "wrong" information.

When you've finished filling in a form for a topic, click the Save button in the entry form part of the window. Then, to create a new record in the same area, click the New Record button and fill in a fresh form. You can view and edit other records at any time by clicking the Prev or Next button.

When a topic has one or more records stored for it, a green check mark appears to the left of the topic name. This makes it easy to locate completed records.

Printing Reports

The ERO includes its own reporting feature, which makes it easy to generate reports for a variety of purposes based on the information you entered. You can give printed reports to people who may need them and lock others up in a secure place for when you need them.

Click the Report tab on the ERO window to display the report options (see Figure 14-4). You can select a report from the drop-down list at the top of the window and preview it in the area below. Then click the Print button on the button bar to print the currently selected report. It's as simple as that.

Here's a quick list of the reports so you know what's available:

- **Emergency Report** (shown in Figure 14-4) is to give to someone in case of a family emergency.
- **Caretaker Report** is for someone taking care of your home or pet while you are away.
- **Survivor's Report** is for your lawyer or heirs in the event of your death.
- **Summary of Records Entered Report** lists the areas, topics, and record names you've entered in the ERO. It does not provide any detailed information.
- **Detail Report** lists everything you've entered into the ERO. As the name implies, it provides detail and can be used as a kind of master list.

Quicken Quick Tip

The Survivor's Report is a very useful document to have around. My life is extremely complex, with many responsibilities that I juggle on a daily basis. If something happened to me, whoever got stuck taking care of my responsibilities until I was able to get back to them (or until my estate was closed), would be completely lost without this document to help them. It's better to create a helpful document that may never be used than to need a document that was never created.

Figure 14-4 • The Report tab of the ERO window enables you to select predefined reports to view onscreen or print.

Keeping Tabs on Your Property & Debt

Chapter 15

In this Chapter:

- *The Property & Debt Center*

- *Property & Debt alerts*

- *Asset & Liability account details*

- *Reports and graphs*

When you create asset and liability accounts and enter related transactions into Quicken, as discussed in the previous two chapters, Quicken summarizes your entries and calculates balances. It displays this information in a number of places: the account bar, the Property & Debt Center, account registers and overviews, and reports and graphs. You can consult Quicken's calculated balances and totals at any time to learn about your equity and the expenses associated with your debt and automobile.

In this chapter, I explain how to use Quicken's reporting features to keep tabs on your property and debt. As you'll learn in these pages, there's a wealth of information about your net worth just a mouse click away.

The Property & Debt Center

Asset and liability accounts are part of Quicken's Property & Debt Center. You can open the Property & Debt Center by clicking its button on the account bar or by choosing Property & Debt | Go to Property & Debt Center. Figure 15-1 shows what it might look like.

This part of the chapter takes a closer look at the Property & Debt Center, so you know exactly what you can find there and how you can customize it for your own use.

Account Balances

The Property & Debt Accounts area (refer to Figure 15-1) lists all of your asset and liability accounts and displays each account's ending balance. (This information is also available in the account bar, as discussed in Chapter 1.) You can click the name of an account to view its account register or overview—I tell you about those windows later in this chapter.

One of the nice things about the Property & Debt Accounts area is that it separates assets from liabilities and provides subtotals for each. The total at the bottom is the net of the two. If this is a negative number, your finances are in some serious trouble.

The Options pop-up menu at the top of the Property & Debt Accounts area and two buttons at the bottom of the area offer several options for working with accounts:

- **Create an account** (menu option) and **Add Account** (button) display the Add New Account dialog, which you can use to create an asset or liability account. I explain how to create accounts in Chapter 3 and provide details specific to asset and liability accounts in Chapter 13.

- **Reconcile an account** (menu option) displays a dialog you can use to choose any of your accounts and perform a reconciliation. I explain how to reconcile accounts in Chapter 8.

- **Get transactions online** (menu option) displays the Online Center window, which you can use to download transactions from your financial institution. I explain how to use the Online Center in Chapters 6 and 11.

- **Set up alerts** (menu option) displays the Setup tab of the Alerts Center window, so you can set up alerts. I explain how to set up property and debt related alerts later in this chapter.

- **View Account List** (menu option) and **Edit Accounts** (button) display the Account List window, which you can use to view and manage accounts. The Account List is covered in detail in Chapter 3.

Figure 15-1 • The Property & Debt Center displays information about assets and liabilities.

Loan Accounts Summary

The Loan Accounts Summary is farther down in the Property & Debt Center—you may have to scroll to see it. It lists all of your amortized loans—the ones you set up in the View Loans dialog, as instructed in Chapter 13. Here's an example:

Loan Accounts Summary					Options ▼
Account	Balance	Int Rate	Principal Pd	Interest Pd	Pmts Left
Chevy Pickup Loan	25,700.61	8.50	6,299.39	2,898.33	46
House Loan	96,998.80	6.88	33,001.20	36,342.25	115
Total	122,699.41		39,300.59	39,240.58	

Add Loan | Make a Payment | | | | Quicken Loans

The Loan Accounts Summary includes several columns of information for each loan:

- **Account** is the name of the account. You can click the account name to view its register or overview, which I discuss later in this chapter.
- **Balance** is the ending balance for the account.
- **Int Rate** is the current interest rate.
- **Principal Pd** is the total of the payments made toward the loan balance.
- **Interest Pd** is the total of the interest paid for the loan.
- **Pmts Left** is the number of payments left on the loan. This does not take into consideration any extra payments you may have made that will reduce the loan term.

The Balance, Principal Pd, and Interest Pd columns contain information calculated by Quicken based on transactions entered in your Quicken data file. It's important to note that the Interest Pd column only totals the amount of interest entered in Quicken. If you set up an existing loan for which payments (including interest) had already been made, Quicken adds interest already paid on the loan in the totals.

The Options pop-up menu at the top of the Loan Accounts Summary area and three buttons at the bottom of the area offers several loan-related options:

- **Set up a new loan** (menu option) and **Add Loan** (button) display the Loan Setup dialog, so you can create a new loan. I explain how to use this dialog in Chapter 13.
- **Make a payment** (menu option) and **Make a Payment** (button) display the Loan Summary tab of the View Loans window. To make a payment

on a loan, choose the loan name from the Choose Loan pop-up menu and then click the Make Payment button. I explain how to use the View Loans window and make payments in Chapter 13.

- **Plan to reduce my debt** (menu option) displays the Debt Reduction dialog, which you can use to develop a debt reduction plan. I cover this planning feature in Chapter 17.
- **Quicken Loans** (button) displays information about Quicken Loans, one of the services available through Quicken.

Auto Expenses

The Auto Expenses area, at the bottom of the Property & Debt Center, offers a customizable summary of expenses related to your automobile:

Auto Expenses			Options ▼
Category	YTD Expenses	MTD Expenses	Monthly Avg
Auto:Fuel	328.29	25.66	54.71
Auto:Insurance	939.08	515.86	156.51
Auto:Loan	1,758.18	778.71	293.03
Auto:Registration	144.16	0.00	24.02
Auto:Service	485.37	34.10	80.89
Show Auto Expense Report			

There are four columns of information:

- **Category** is the full name of the category (including subcategory, if applicable) of expense.
- **YTD Expenses** is the total year-to-date amount for that category.
- **MTD Expenses** is the total month-to-date amount for that category.
- **Monthly Avg** is the monthly average expenditure for that category.

You can customize the Auto Expenses report by choosing Customize This Report from its Options pop-up menu. The Customize Auto Expenses Component dialog appears. It has two tabs: Accounts and Categories (shown next). Click a tab, then toggle check marks beside account or category names to include or exclude them from the report. By default, the report includes all accounts and just the Auto category (with its subcategories). But you can make the report include anything you like. When you're finished making changes, click OK to save them. The Auto Expenses area refreshes to reflect your changes.

Alerts

Property & Debt alerts appear at the top of the Property & Debt Center, right where you can see them. This area displays any alerts you have created for your assets or liabilities, when it's time to alert you.

Setting Up Property & Debt Alerts

To set up an alert, begin by clicking the Setup Alerts button in the Property & Debt Alerts area. The Setup tab of the Alerts Center window appears. Click the name of the alert you want to set on the left side of the window to display its options on the right. Figure 15-2 shows what the Insurance Reappraisal alert settings might look like with two alerts already set.

There are two alerts that apply to property and debt:

- **Insurance Reappraisal** notifies you before an insurance policy expires so you can either reevaluate coverage or shop for a new policy.

- **Mortgage Reappraisal** notifies you before a mortgage changes from variable to fixed (or fixed to variable) so you can consider refinancing. Even if your mortgage doesn't convert, you can use this alert to remind you to periodically check for better mortgage deals.

Both alerts work pretty much the same way. For each alert, enter a name and date in the far right column. Select one of the options at the bottom of

Figure 15-2 • Setting up Insurance Reappraisal alerts

the window to indicate how you want the alert to appear: as text in the alert list (refer to Figure 15-1) or as a pop-up dialog like the one shown next. Finally, use the drop-down list to specify the length of time the alert should remain in the list and click Apply.

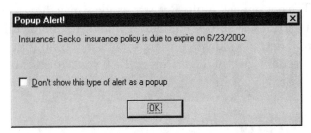

Repeat this process for each alert you want to set. When you're finished, click Done.

Working with Property & Debt Alerts

The Options pop-up menu at the top of the Property & Debt Alerts area and two buttons at the bottom of the area offer several options for working with alerts:

- **Show All Alerts** (menu option and button) displays the Show All tab of the Alerts Center window, so you can see all alerts set up in Quicken.
- **Set Up Alerts** (menu option and button) displays the Setup Alerts tab of the Alerts Center window, so you can add an alert.
- **Delete** and **Delete All** (menu options) display the Delete Alert(s) dialog, which you can use to delete either the selected alert (and all alerts like it) or all alerts.

Account Details

To learn more about the transactions and balances for a specific account, you can view account details in the Register and Overview windows. Click the name of an account (other than a Home Inventory account, as discussed in Chapter 14) in the account bar or Property & Debt Center to open these windows—click a tab at the top of the window to display the one you want (refer to Figures 15-3 and 15-4).

Register

An account's Register window (see Figure 15-3) lists all transactions entered into that account, as well as the ending balance. As I explain in Chapter 13, you can enter transactions right into the register. Other transactions—such as principal payments for a mortgage or other loan—are automatically calculated and entered by Quicken.

The bottom half of the Register window may show a list of Bills and Scheduled Transactions, as shown in Figure 15-3. You can hide this list by clicking the close button on the window's bottom scroll bar. This fills the window with register transactions, so you can see more. I tell you about scheduled transactions in Chapter 7.

Overview

An account's Overview window (see Figure 15-4) is split into three different areas of information about the account: Attributes, Status, and Balance.

Figure 15-3 • The Register window for a mortgage

Account Attributes

The Account Attributes area (refer to Figure 15-4) provides basic information about the account, including its name and description and whether it can be viewed on Quicken.com.

The Option menu at the top of the area offers several related commands:

- **Create a new account** displays the Add New Account dialog, which enables you to create any kind of Quicken account. I explain how to create accounts in Chapter 3.
- **View/edit comments** displays the Account Comments dialog, which you can use to enter comments about the account.

Figure 15-4 • The Overview window for a mortgage

- **Set tax attributes** displays the Tax Schedule Information dialog, which you can use to choose tax return schedules and lines to associate with transfers in and out of the account. I explain how this feature works in Chapter 19.

- **Set Web pages** displays the Bookmark Web Pages dialog. You can use this dialog to enter the Web addresses (or URLs) for Web pages related to the account; the addresses you enter appear in the Account Attributes area. For example, you can include a link to your mortgage company's Home page or Login page in the Account Attributes area of your mortgage account so you can quickly jump to that page when working with Quicken. Both the Bookmark Web Pages dialog and Account Attributes area are shown next.

- **Browse Web pages** displays a submenu that lists the Web pages you entered in the Bookmark Web Pages dialog previously shown. Choose an option to launch Quicken's internal browser and view that page on the Internet.

Clicking the Edit Account Details button at the bottom of the Account Attributes area displays the Account Details window, which you can use to enter general information about the account. The fields that appear in this dialog vary depending on the type of account that is displayed. The following illustration shows what it looks like for a liability account.

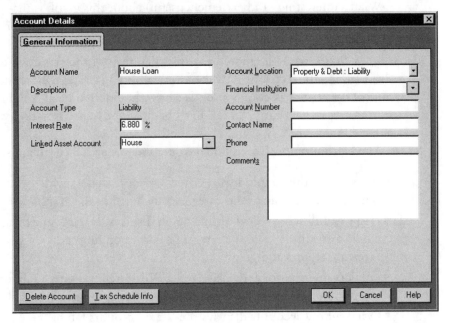

Account Status

The Account Status area (refer to Figure 15-4) provides information about the status of the account, including balance, linked account, and equity information. You can click underlined text in the Account Status area to view the details behind linked information or perform reconciliations.

The Options pop-up menu offers three related commands:

- **Update my account balance** displays the Update Account Balance dialog, which you can use to change the balance of the account. I explain how to modify an account's balance with this dialog in Chapter 13.
- **Manage my loans** displays the View Loans dialog, which you can use to add, modify, or delete loans. I explain how this dialog works in Chapter 13, too.
- **View all my accounts** displays the View Accounts tab of the Account List window, which I cover in Chapter 3.

Account Balance

The Account Balance area (refer to Figure 15-4) displays a graphical representation of the balance of the account. You can click on a column to see its exact value.

What's interesting (and extremely useful) about this graph is that if the account is linked to another account, both accounts are displayed on the graph, and your equity—the difference between what an asset is worth and what you still owe on its loan—is charted as a line. Figure 15-4 shows a good example. Although it's the Account Balance for a liability (a mortgage), it shows the value of the related asset (a house). See how the Equity line and Value Of Asset column rise in February 2002? That's because the house's market value was updated that month, thus increasing both.

The Options pop-up menu offers a number of related commands:

- **Customize this graph** displays the Customize dialog, which you can use to change the date range and categories included in the graph.
- **Go to a full screen view of this graph** displays the Account Balance graph in its own window, with a tab for its corresponding report. I tell you about creating reports and graphs later in this chapter.
- **Report my net worth** displays a Net Worth report, with a tab for its corresponding graph. I discuss reports and graphs later in this chapter.
- **View all my accounts** displays the View Accounts tab of the Account List window, which I cover in Chapter 3.

- **Help reduce my debt** displays the Debt Reduction dialog, which I discuss in Chapter 18.
- **Forecast my future account balances** starts Quicken's forecasting feature, which I discuss in detail in Chapter 18.

Reports and Graphs

The information you enter in Property & Debt Center accounts appears on two reports and their corresponding graphs: Account Balances and Net Worth. These reports provide the same information with slight differences in the order and wording of the presentation.

Creating Reports

To create a report, choose its name from the appropriate submenu—in this case, Net Worth & Balances—under the Reports menu. Quicken makes its calculations and displays the report (see Figure 15-5) in a report window. You can click the Graph tab in the window to display the corresponding graph.

Another way to create a report is to click its link in the My Reports area of the Property & Debt Center. As shown next, this area lists all the reports you have saved to this Center, using the Save Report button in the report window's button bar. I explain how to save reports in Chapter 9.

Quicken Quick Tip

I found the Net Worth report extremely helpful the last time I applied for a loan. Rather than manually filling out the form that the bank sent me, I used Quicken to create a Net Worth report that included only the accounts that really mattered. (I also created a few investment reports to provide details of my investments.) It took me just minutes to complete the application process. And yes, I got the loan.

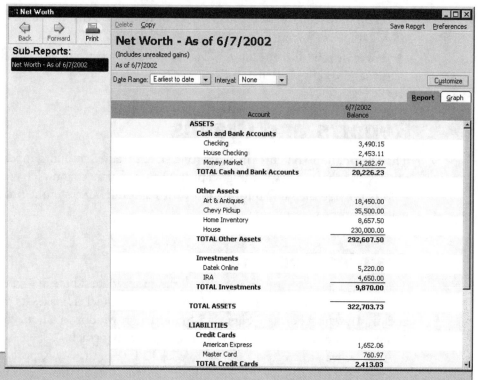

Figure 15-5 • A Net Worth report summarizes the balances in all of your accounts.

Working with the Report Window

The report window works the same for the Account Balances and Net Worth reports as it does for any other Quicken report. I explain how to use buttons and other options in the report window to customize reports, create subreports, and save reports in Chapter 9; consult that chapter for details.

The Planning Center

This part of the book tells you about Quicken's planning features, which you can use to plan for your retirement, major purchases, and other life events. It covers Quicken's built-in financial calculators, as well as features that can help you save money and make your dreams come true. Its three chapters are:

Chapter 16: *Planning for the Future*

Chapter 17: *Using Financial Calculators*

Chapter 18: *Reducing Debt and Saving Money*

Planning for the Future

In this Chapter:

- *Quicken planning overview*

- *Life event planners*

- *Playing "what if"*

Chapter 16

To many people, the future is an unknown, a mystery. After all, who can say what will happen tomorrow, next year, or ten years from now? But if you think about your future, you can usually come up with a few events that you can plan for: your marriage, the purchase of a new home, the birth of your children (and their education years later), and your retirement. (These are just examples—everyone's life runs a different course.) These events, as well as many unforeseen events, all have one thing in common: they affect your finances. In this chapter, I tell you about planning for future events and how tools within Quicken and on Quicken.com can help.

Getting Started with the Quicken Planner

The Planning Center offers access to all of Quicken's built-in planning features, including the Quicken Planner's main plan assumptions and individual financial planners. Once you have set up your plan, the Planning Center provides an up-to-date view of how well your plan is working.

Here's how it works. You start by entering plan assumptions, which include information about you and your current finances, as well as your tax rate. Quicken makes calculations based on what you entered to display plan results. As you continue to work with Quicken, entering transactions that affect your finances, Quicken updates the result of the plan. It also takes into consideration your entries in any of Quicken's other planners, such as the College Planner or Special Purchase Planner.

In this section, I explain how to set assumptions for the Quicken Planner and how to view the results of your plan in the Planning Center.

Setting Plan Assumptions

The easiest way to see what plan assumptions need to be made is to view the Plan Assumptions area of the Planning Center. Click the Planning Center button in

> ### Quicken Quick Tip
> I won't lie to you: setting up Quicken Planner assumptions can be time consuming. But I think that the benefit of using this feature far outweighs the cost (in time) of setting it up. This is especially true if you're settled down and are raising a family—Quicken can help you plan for the major events of your life so you're prepared for them. If you don't have the time to set up the Quicken Planner now, make time in the future.

the tool bar or choose Planning | Go to Planning Center. When you first start out, the Plan Assumptions area may look like this:

Plan Assumptions	Options ▼
Click on the links below to set or change your plan assumptions.	
About You	Tell Quicken about yourself and your family.
Income	Enter your salary and other income.
Tax Rate	What tax rate do you expect to pay?
Inflation	How much inflation do you expect?
Savings & Investments	How much do you save and invest?
Homes and Assets	Total assets: $292,608
Loans and Debt	Do you have any loans?
Expenses	Enter your living expenses and plan for future expenses.

Change Assumptions   Explore What If's

To set details for an assumption category, click its underlined link. This displays a dialog you can use to enter information. Here's a look at each category.

About You
Clicking the About You link displays the About You dialog, which is shown next. Its fields are pretty self-explanatory, so I won't go into much detail. (After all,

you should be able to figure out how to enter your name and date of birth!) When you're finished entering information in the dialog, click Done to save it.

Here are some less obvious things to consider when entering data into the About You dialog.

Include Spouse   If you turn on the Include Spouse check box, you can enter information into the Spouse column of the dialog. If you don't have a spouse or don't want to include him or her in your plan, leave that check box turned off.

Life Expectancy   You can either enter what you think might be your life expectancy or click the Calculate button to display the Calculate Life Expectancy dialog, shown next. Set options in the dialog and Quicken tells you how long you may live. Of course, this is an estimate based on current research into life expectancy; you may or may not live to reach the age Quicken suggests.

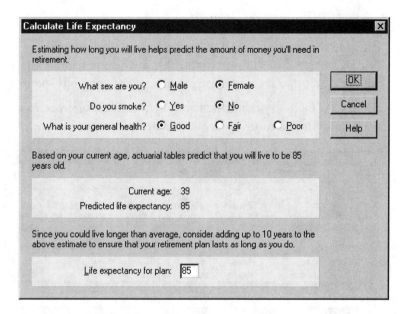

Children and Dependents   To enter information about children or other dependents, click the New button at the bottom of the dialog. This displays the Add Child/Dependent dialog, shown next, in which you can enter the name and date of birth for a dependent. When you click OK, the person is added to the list. Repeat this process for each child or dependent you need to add. Once a child or dependent has been added, you can select his or her name and click the Edit button to change information about him or her (although I can't see why a name or birth date would change), click the Delete button to remove him or her permanently from the plan, or turn on the Exclude From Plan check box so Quicken doesn't use him or her in its calculations.

Income

Clicking the Income link displays the Income dialog, which is organized into three separate tabs of information. This is where you enter salary, retirement benefit, and other income information for you and your spouse.

Salary   The Salary tab, which is shown next, enables you to record information about current and future salary and self-employment income.

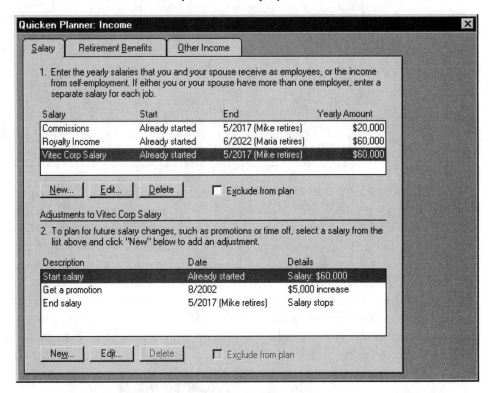

To add an income item, click the New button to display the Add Salary dialog. Then set options to enter information about the income item. As you can see in the following illustration, the dialog is extremely flexible, enabling you to enter start and end dates for a salary—which is useful for income from seasonal employment. (If you don't need to enter specific dates, choose Already Started from the Salary Start drop-down list and one of the retirement options from the Salary End drop-down list.) When you click OK, the item is added to the list.

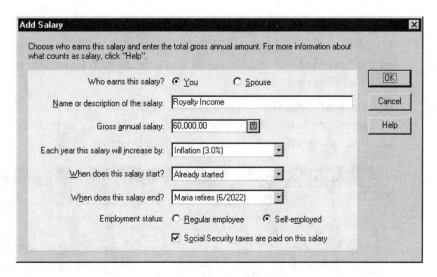

For each item you add, Quicken automatically includes adjustments that specify when the item begins and ends. But you can add other adjustments if you know about changes in the future. Select the item in the top half of the dialog, then click the New button at the bottom of the dialog. Enter information in the Add Salary Adjustment dialog that appears (shown next) and click OK. The information is added to the bottom half of the Salary tab of the Income dialog.

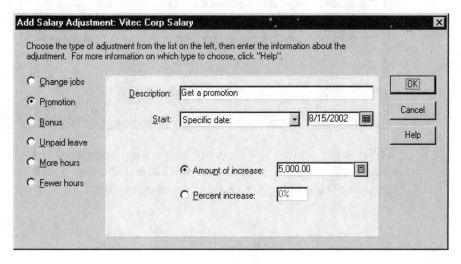

You can select any of the salary or adjustment items and click the Edit or Delete button to change or remove it. You can also select an item and turn on the Exclude From Plan check box to exclude its information from the Quicken Planner.

Retirement Benefits The Retirement Benefits tab, which is shown next, enables you to enter information about Social Security or pension benefits you are currently receiving or to estimate future benefits.

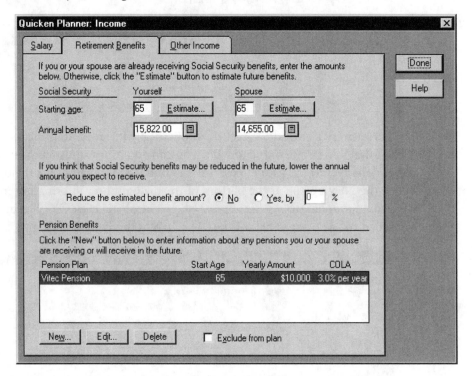

To estimate future Social Security benefits, enter the age at which you expect to begin collecting benefits and click the Estimate button. The Estimate Social Security Benefits dialog, which is shown next, appears.

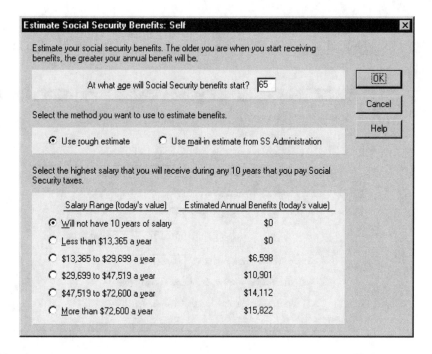

You have two options:

- **Use rough estimate** (shown previously) enables you to select a salary range option to estimate benefits.
- **Use mail-in estimate from SS Administration** enables you to enter the amount provided by the Social Security Administration on your annual Social Security Statement.

When you click OK, the amount is automatically entered in the Retirement Benefits tab.

To add a pension, click the New button at the bottom of the dialog. This displays the Add Pension dialog, which is shown next. Enter information about the pension and click OK to add it to the Retirement Benefits tab. You can always select the pension and click Edit or Delete to change or remove it, or turn on the Exclude From Plan check box to exclude it from the Quicken Planner's calculations.

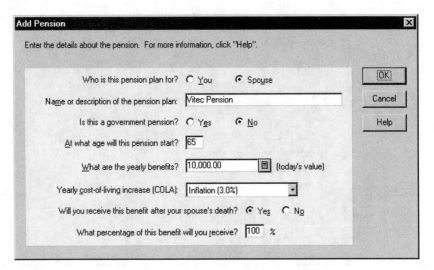

Other Income   The Other Income tab, shown next, enables you to enter income from other sources, such as gifts, child support, and inheritances. Don't use this tab to enter income from investments or rental properties; the Quicken Planner provides other places to enter this information.

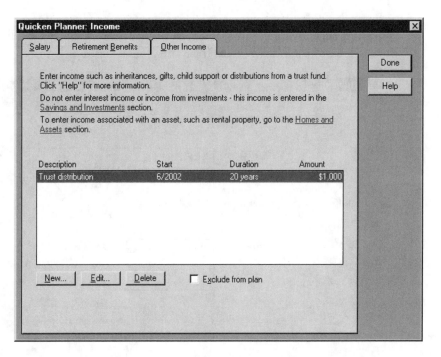

To enter an income item, click the New button. Enter information in the Add Other Income dialog, which is shown next. An interesting option in this dialog is the ability to specify how the money will be used: either saved and invested or used to pay expenses. The option you select determines how this income is used in the plan. If you're not sure what to select, leave it set to the default option.

When you click OK, the item is added to the Other Income tab's list. You can edit, delete, or exclude the item from the plan as desired.

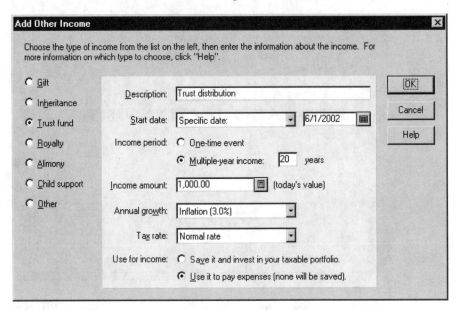

Tax Rate

Clicking the Tax Rate link displays the Average Tax Rate dialog. You have two options:

- **Demographic average** (shown next) enables you to estimate your tax rate based on where you live and what your income is.

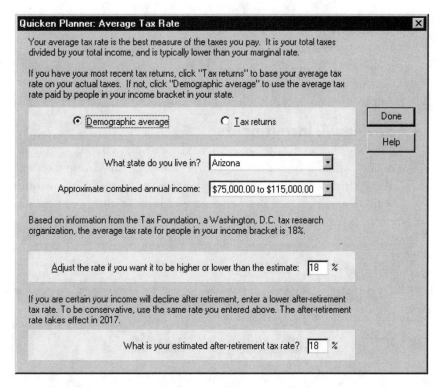

- **Tax returns** enables you to estimate your tax rate based on the total income, total federal taxes, and total state taxes from your most recent tax returns.

No matter how you estimate the tax rate, you can adjust it by entering a preferred value. You can also enter an estimate of your post-retirement tax rate, which may be lower.

Inflation

Clicking the Inflation link displays the Estimated Inflation dialog, which includes a graphic depiction of the inflation trend from 1927 through 1995. Quicken suggests an inflation rate of 3 percent, but you can enter any rate you think is correct in the text box. Click Done to save your estimate.

Savings & Investments

Clicking the Savings & Investments link displays the Savings and Investments dialog, which is organized into three tabs. Use this dialog to enter information about current bank and investment accounts, as well as contributions you or your spouse make regularly to accounts and the return you expect to earn on your investments.

Savings   The Savings tab, which is shown next, lists all of the bank accounts you have set up in Quicken, along with their current balances.

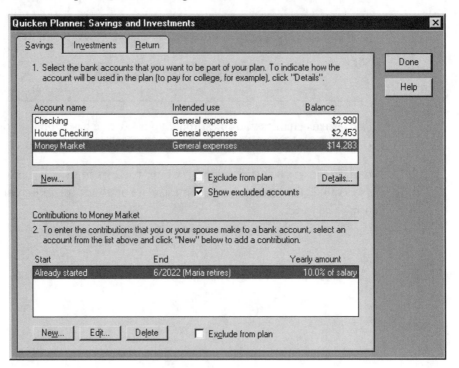

If you have omitted any accounts from Quicken, now is a good time to add them if you want them to be part of your plan. Click the New button to display the Add New Account dialog; I explain how to use this dialog to create new accounts in Chapter 3.

Quicken automatically assumes that each bank account will be used for General expenses. You can change this assumption by selecting an account and clicking the Details button. Choose a new purpose from the drop-down list in the Account Details dialog that appears (shown next) and click OK. You'll find that until you use Quicken's other planners, General expenses is the only offered option. But if you use another planner—for example, the College Planner—an option for that planner's expense appears in the drop-down list.

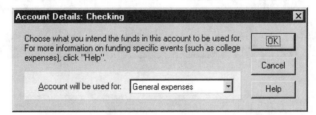

If you or your spouse make regular contributions to one of your bank accounts, you can enter information about that contribution in the dialog. In the top half of the dialog, select the account that receives the contribution. Then click the New button at the bottom of the dialog. Use the Add Contribution dialog that appears to indicate how much you contribute. The dialog will walk you through the process of entering information based on whether the contribution is a percentage of a salary or a base amount that increases each year.

Investments   The Investments tab, which is shown next, lists all of the investment accounts you have set up in Quicken, along with their current market values. Remember, since market value is determined by security prices, the market value is only as up to date as the most recently entered or downloaded security prices.

This tab works just like the Savings tab. You can click the New button in the top half of the dialog to add another investment account or click the New tab in the bottom half of the dialog to enter regular contribution information for any selected investment account. You can also specify the intended use for any account by selecting the account name and clicking the Details button.

Return   The Return tab, shown next, enables you to specify your expected rates of return for pre-retirement and post-retirement investments. If you turn on the check box near the top of the dialog, additional text boxes appear, enabling you to enter different rates of return for taxable and tax-deferred investments. At the bottom of the dialog, you can enter the percentage of the taxable return that is subject to taxes. This is normally 100 percent, but for your situation, the percentage may be different.

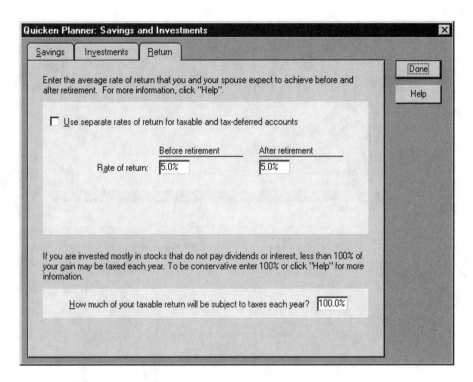

Homes and Assets

Clicking the Homes and Assets link displays the Homes and Assets dialog, which is organized into two tabs. This is where you can enter information about currently owned assets and assets you plan to purchase in the future.

Asset Accounts The Asset Accounts tab, which is shown next, lists all of the asset accounts you have created in Quicken, including accounts for your home, vehicle, home inventory, and other assets. If you have additional assets that have not yet been entered in Quicken and you want to include them in your plan, click the New button and use the Add New Account dialog that appears to create the new account; I explain how in Chapter 3.

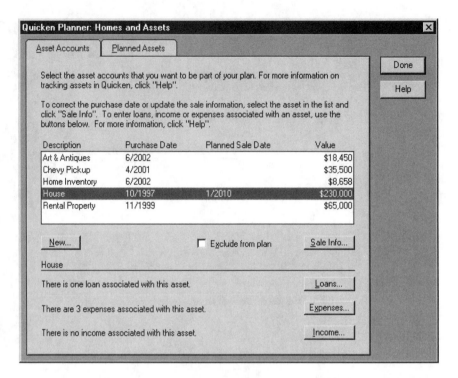

If you plan to sell an asset, you can enter selling information for it. Select the asset in the top half of the dialog, then click the Sale Info button. A series of dialogs prompts you for information about the asset's purchase and sale date and price, as well as other information that affects how much money you can expect to receive and pay taxes on. This information is then added to your plan.

Three buttons at the bottom of the dialog enable you to associate loans, expenses, and income with a selected asset. This is especially important when working with assets you plan to sell, since the sale of the asset should also end associated debt, expenses, and income.

- **Loans** enables you to link existing loans to the asset or add new loans, including home equity loans. It also enables you to enter information about planned loans—for example, if you plan to use a home equity loan to build an addition on your house sometime next year. You can also enter information about planned payoffs—perhaps you're expecting a big trust fund check (lucky you!) and plan to use it to pay off your house.

- **Expenses** enables you to enter property tax information as well as other expenses related to the asset. For a home, this might include association fees, homeowner's insurance, and estimated maintenance and utility costs. For a car, this might include registration, fuel, service, and insurance. For each expense you add, Quicken prompts you for information about the expense, including how you expect to pay for it—with money in a specific bank account or with a loan. It even enables you to set up a monthly savings target to pay for the item.

- **Income** enables you to enter information about income you expect to earn from the asset. This is especially useful if you own rental property. The dialog that appears when you add an income item is almost the same as the Add Other Income dialog shown earlier in this chapter. It even allows you to specify how you plan to use the income: for investment or to pay expenses.

Planned Assets   The Planned Assets tab enables you to enter information about any assets you plan to purchase in the future. For example, suppose you indicated in the Asset Accounts tab that you planned to sell your home or car on a specific date. If you plan to replace it with another home or car, this is where you'd enter information about the replacement. Quicken uses dialogs that walk you through the process of entering details about the future purchase. Once you've entered planned asset information, you can select the asset in the list and add loans, expenses, and income for it, as well as choose the accounts you plan to use to pay for it.

Loans and Debt

Clicking the Loans and Debt link in the Plan Assumptions area displays the Loans and Debt dialog, which is organized into three tabs. This is where you enter information about current and planned loans, as well as information from your debt reduction plan.

Loan Accounts   The Loan Accounts tab, which is shown next, displays information about current loans. This information comes from loans you have set up within Quicken. To add another loan that isn't already recorded in Quicken, click the New button to display the Loan Setup dialog, which I cover in Chapter 13. If you plan to pay off a loan before its last payment date, you can click the Payoff button to enter future payoff information.

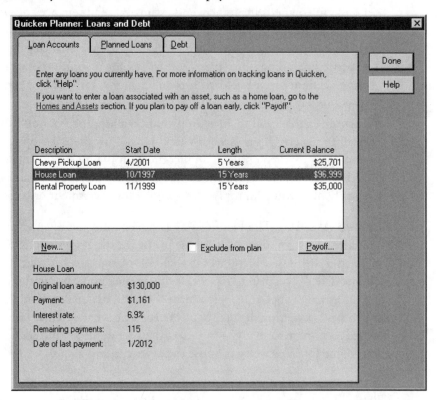

Planned Loans The Planned Loans tab enables you to enter information about loans you plan to make in the future. This does not include any loans you may have already planned in the Homes and Assets dialog discussed earlier. Instead, this is for loans that are not associated with any particular asset, such as a personal loan you plan to pay for flying lessons or a really special vacation.

Debt The Debt tab includes information from the Debt Reduction Planner. I cover that in detail in Chapter 18.

Expenses

Clicking the Expenses link displays the Expenses dialog, which is organized into four tabs. This is where you enter information about your living expenses, as well as any adjustments to expenses, and the expenses for college or other special events.

Living Expenses   The Living Expenses tab, which is shown next, enables you to enter your estimated living expenses using one of two techniques:

- **Rough estimate** (shown previously) enables you to enter an estimate of your annual living expenses. Using this technique is quicker, but may not be as accurate.
- **Category detail** enables you to have Quicken calculate an estimate of your annual living expenses based on transactions already entered in your Quicken data file. This technique is more accurate, especially if you have been using

Quicken for a while and have a good history of transactions. If you select this method, you can click the Details button that appears in the middle of the dialog to display the Living Expense Category Detail dialog (shown next). Toggle check marks to include or exclude specific categories and enter monthly amounts as desired. When you click OK, Quicken annualizes the amounts and enters them in the Living Expenses tab.

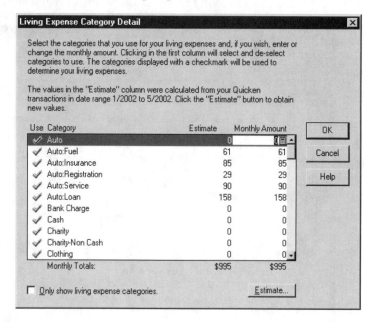

One thing to keep in mind here: don't include expenses that you may have already included for an asset. For example, if you included car insurance expenses in the Homes and Assets dialog, don't include them again here. Doing so would duplicate the expense and overstate your annual expenses.

At the bottom of the dialog, you can enter a percentage of surplus cash—cash left over after paying living expenses—that you want to put into savings.

Adjustments　The Adjustments tab enables you to enter any adjustments to your expenses that are related to planned changes in your life. For example, perhaps you plan to hire a nanny to take care of your newborn child while you go back to work. You can add this planned expense as an adjustment for a predefined period of time. When you click the New button in the Adjustments tab, the Add Living Expense Adjustment appears. Here's how it might look if I hired a nanny to take care of my [fictional] child, Nathaniel, while I continued to write computer books:

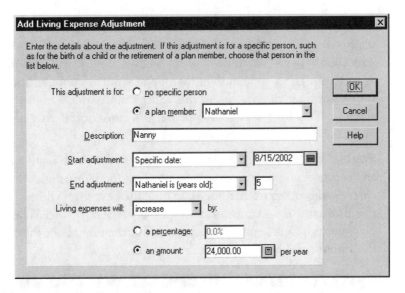

College Expenses   The College Expenses tab enables you to plan for the education of your children—or yourself! Clicking the New button in this tab displays the Add College Expense dialog, which walks you through the process of entering expected college expenses for a plan member. Don't know what college will cost? No problem. Quicken has a built-in database of college expenses for public, private, and specialized schools throughout the country. Since Nathaniel is going to be a pilot (like his mother wishes she'd become), I looked up the cost of Embry-Riddle Aeronautical University here in Arizona for this shocking news:

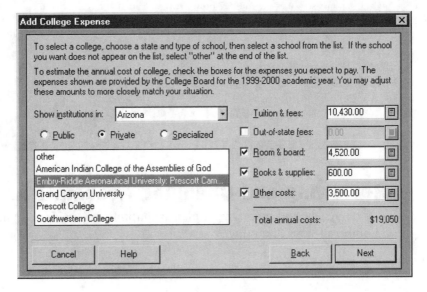

Of course, you can override any of the amounts Quicken displays or enter your own amounts. Just remember to be realistic. If you underestimate expenses, your plan won't be accurate. The dialog also prompts you for information about expected financial aid, student loans, and student contributions to cover all sources of financing. If you have a college fund—such as an educational IRA—already set up for the college expense, you can associate it with the expense to indicate how it will be paid for.

Special Expenses   The Special Expenses tab, which is shown next, includes any expenses you may have already added in the Homes and Assets dialog and enables you to enter other one-time or annual expenses you expect to incur. Use this for items like a vacation, wedding, or large purchase. When you click the New button, Quicken prompts you for information about the expense, including the amount and how you expect to finance it.

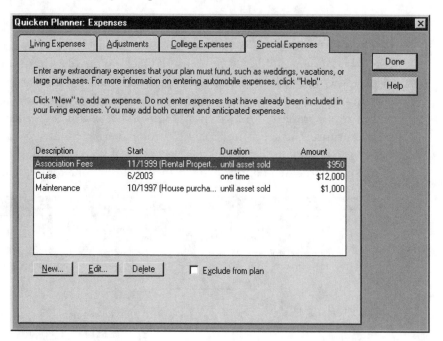

Reviewing and Changing Assumptions

You can review and modify your plan assumptions at any time. Quicken offers a number of ways to do this.

The Plan Assumptions Area

Once you enter assumptions into the Quicken Planner, a brief summary of the assumptions appears in the Plan Assumptions area in the Planning Center. It might look something like this:

Plan Assumptions	Options ▼
Click on the links below to set or change your plan assumptions.	
About You	Maria & Mike 1 dependent.
Income	Combined yearly salaries: $140,000
Tax Rate	Effective tax rate: 18% After-retirement tax rate: 18% starting in 2017
Inflation	Inflation rate: 3.0%
Savings & Investments	Current savings: $19,726 Current investments: $9,870
Homes and Assets	Total assets: $357,608
Loans and Debt	You have 3 loan accounts in your plan.
Expenses	Current yearly living expenses: $25,000.

| Change Assumptions | Explore What If's |

You can click links in the Plan Assumption area to open the same dialogs discussed earlier in this chapter. Review and change plan assumptions as desired and click Done in the dialog to save them.

The Planning Assumptions Window

A better way to review plan assumptions is in the Planning Assumptions window (see Figure 16-1). To open this window, choose Planning | Planning Assumptions or click the Change Assumptions button in the Plan Assumptions or Plan: Results area of the Planning Center.

You can use links on the left side of the window to quickly navigate from one category of assumption to another. The details appear in the main part of the window. For each category of assumption, there are two links:

- **How is this used?** explains how the information in that category of assumption is used in the plan.
- **Edit** enables you to edit the assumptions for that category, using the same dialogs discussed earlier in this chapter.

Figure 16-1 • The Planning Assumptions window displays details about your Quicken Plan assumptions.

Saved Plans

The Saved Plans area of the Planning Center lists individual plans you have added to the Quicken Planner, whether with the various Assumptions dialogs or individual planners. Click a link to open the associated planner and change data as desired. I discuss Quicken's planners later in this chapter in the section "Using Quicken's Planners." Here's what this area looks like with my assumptions set:

Saved Plans

My Retirement Plan
College expense for
Nathaniel
New Home
Maintenance
Association Fees
Cruise

Planners

As I discuss later in this chapter, each individual planner can also be used to add assumptions to your plan. Follow the instructions within the planner to enter data and the data is added to the Quicken Planner's data.

Viewing Plan Results

When Quicken has enough data about your assumptions to calculate plan results, it displays them graphically in the Plan: Results area of the Planning Center. Here's what my plan looks like:

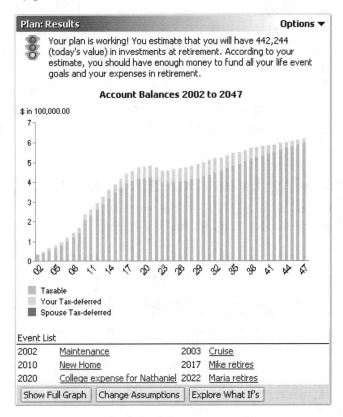

The very top of the Plan: Results area tells you whether your plan is working and how much you should have in investments at retirement. Amounts are in today's dollars; to view them in future dollars, choose Show Amounts In Future Value from the Options pop-up menu at the top of the area.

The graph beneath this summary shows your taxable and tax deferred savings. The ideal shape of this graph shows a steady increase until the year you retire, then a gradual decrease. You can point to a column to display a yellow box with the exact value in it. You can also display a full-page version of the Plan: Results area by clicking the Show Full Graph button at the bottom of the area or by choosing Show Full Screen from the Options pop-up menu at the top of the area.

Plan results change automatically based on a variety of changes within your Quicken data file:

- When the account balances referred to in the plan change, the plan changes accordingly.
- When you change plan assumptions, the plan changes accordingly.
- When you use Quicken's planners to plan for major purchases, college, retirement, and other events that affect your finances, the plan changes to include these events.
- When you play "what if" with assumptions and save the changes as your plan, the plan changes accordingly. I tell you about playing "what if" a little later in this chapter.

Viewing Event Status and Savings Targets

Quicken also keeps track of your progress toward certain events and savings targets. It displays this information in the Planning Center.

- **Event Status**, which is shown next, displays information about events in your plan that are funded with specific accounts.

Event Status		Options ▼
Review the status of events that are funded by specific accounts. The current savings for your retirement plan shows the balances of your retirement accounts.		
Expense	**Current Savings**	**Status**
Your retirement plan	$4,650	On track

- **Monthly Savings Targets**, which is shown next, displays information about your savings toward events in your plan. Clicking a link for an expense displays the summary area of the appropriate planner.

Monthly Savings Targets		Options ▼
Compare your current monthly savings targets to your recent actual savings.		
Expense	**Calculated Target**	**Savings Target**
Retirement contribution		$250
College expense for Nathaniel (202...	$292	$292
Cruise (2003)	$978	$978
Monthly total:	$1,270	$1,520
Savings last month:		$3,747
Average monthly savings (last 6 m...		$1,002

Clicking a link for an expense displays the summary area of the appropriate planner. As discussed next, you can use the planner to review and modify event information.

Using Quicken's Planners

Quicken's planners offer another way to add financial planning information to Quicken. Rather than enter general assumptions, most planners concentrate on specific events or goals, such as buying a home or sending a child to college. Unlike the plan assumptions dialogs discussed earlier in this chapter, the individual planners provide more information about the event or item you are planning for.

In this part of the chapter, I introduce the individual planners and give you an idea of how their interface works. You can then explore each of the planners on your own.

A Look at the Planners

Quicken 2003 includes five planners, all of which can be accessed through commands on the Planning menu or links in the Planning Center:

- **Retirement Planner** is the most comprehensive planner. It looks at all of your current financial information, as well as the results of other planners, to help you plan for retirement. It basically reviews all data entered for Quicken Planner assumptions, as discussed earlier in this chapter.

- **College Planner** helps you plan for your children's college education. It gathers the same information you could enter for a new college expense in the College Expenses tab of the Expenses dialog.
- **Home Purchase Planner** helps you plan for the purchase of a new home. It gathers the same information you could enter for a new home in the Planned Assets tab of the Homes and Assets dialog.
- **Debt Reduction Planner** helps you save money while getting out of debt as quickly as possible. I cover this planner in detail in Chapter 18.
- **Special Purchase Planner** helps you plan for special purchases, such as vacations, vehicles, and other large expenditures. It gathers the same information you could enter for major expenditures in the Special Expenses tab of the Expenses dialog.

All of these planners work pretty much the same way. You enter information about your current financial situation or let Quicken enter the information for you based on account balances and category transactions. Then you tell the planner a little about the event you're planning for. For example, the College Planner needs to know how old your children are now and when you expect them to go to college. It also needs to know how much you expect the education to cost. When you enter all this information into Quicken, it performs calculations and shows you results. Planning information is saved within your Quicken data file so you can view or update it at any time.

Adding Plan Details with Quicken's Planners

You can add details to the assumptions of your financial plan by using Quicken's planners to add specific events to the plan. The information you enter into these plans becomes part of your overall financial plan, thus changing the Plan Results. When you use any of these planners to create plans, each individual plan appears in the Planning Center window and on submenus that appear on the Planning menu. This makes it easy to view and change plans.

Here's a look at four of Quicken's planners; the other one (the Debt Reduction Planner) is covered in Chapter 18.

Retirement Planner

The Retirement Planner enables you to plan for your retirement. It is, by far, the most exhaustive planner, primarily because it requires all the information entered as plan assumptions. In fact, if you have already entered plan assumptions, you can go through the Retirement Planner very quickly; if not, it'll take you about

30 minutes to enter all the information it requires. (That information will be saved for use by other planners.)

To start, choose Planning | Retirement Planner or click the Retirement Planner link in the Planners area of the Planning Center. The My Retirement Plan window (see Figure 16-2). Read the information in the window, then click the Next link to begin entering information. Follow the prompts that appear to open dialogs and enter data for a number of topics, many of which may already include information from plan assumptions or other planners. The items you complete are checked off in the navigation bar on the left side of the window; you can also click links for items there to complete them in any order you like.

When you have finished entering information, the Your Plan screen shows your financial plan. Subsequent windows enable you to check your plan for problems, play "what if" with your plan (as I discuss later in this chapter in the section "Playing 'What If'"), and view a summary of your plan.

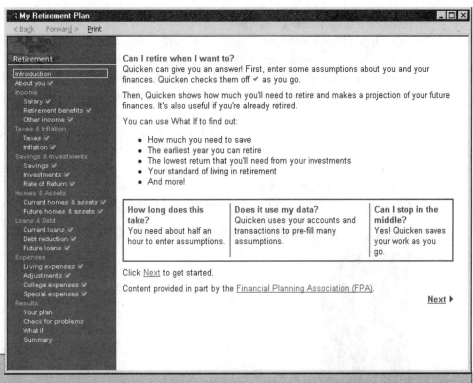

Figure 16-2 • The Retirement Planner can help you determine whether you can retire when you want to.

College Planner

The College Planner enables you to plan for your child's college education. It uses information already entered as plan assumptions, as well as new information you enter about your child's college plans.

Choose Planning | College Planner or click the College Planner link in the Planners area of the Planning Center to display the College Planner window (see Figure 16-3). Read the information in the introduction screen and click the Next link to get started. Then follow the prompts to add or edit information about a dependent's college education.

When you have finished entering information in the planner windows, the Results screen shows your financial plan with your child's college education included. Subsequent screens offer you a chance to play "what if" with your financial plan, summarize cost and funding information, and allow you to connect to the Internet for other resources, including college and financial aid information.

Home Purchase Planner

The Home Purchase Planner enables you to plan for the purchase of a home—either a primary residence or vacation home. Like the other planners, it prompts you for information about a specific event, but it also has built-in calculators to help you determine affordability so you can understand how a home would fit into your budget.

To get started, choose Planning | Home Purchase Planner or click the Home Purchase Planner link in the Planners area of the Planning Center to display the Can I Afford That House? window. Read the information on the introduction screen and click the Next link. Then follow the prompts to enter information about your finances (see Figure 16-4) and the proposed purchase. In some cases,

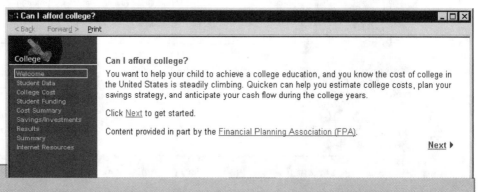

Figure 16-3 •**The College Planner makes it easy to enter complete information to plan for a college education.**

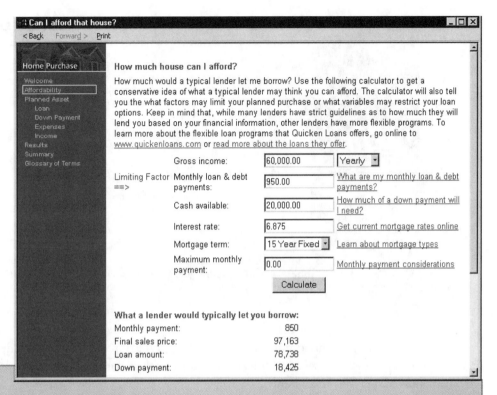

Figure 16-4 • The Home Purchase Planner even helps you determine whether you can afford to buy a home.

you can get information from your Quicken data file and from the Internet by clicking links within the window. When you're finished entering information, the planner displays its results. Subsequent screens summarize the information and display a glossary of terms you should know when purchasing a home.

Special Purchase Planner

The Special Purchase Planner enables you to plan for a major purchase, such as a new car or recreational vehicle or a costly vacation. It uses information already entered as plan assumptions, as well as new information you enter about the special purchase.

Choose Planning | Special Purchase Planner or click the Special Purchase Planner link in the Planners area of the Planning Center to display the Special Purchase Planner window (see Figure 16-5). Read the information in the window and follow the prompts that appear to enter all information about the purchase. When you are finished, the results window shows your financial

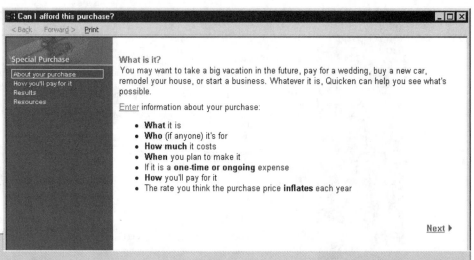

Figure 16-5 • The Special Purchase Planner helps you determine whether you can afford to buy high-ticket items.

plan with the planned purchase included. The Resources window provides links to other resources within Quicken and on Quicken.com to learn more about purchasing big-ticket items.

Playing "What If"

Once you've entered assumptions, created plans for specific events, and viewed your plan results, you might wonder how a change in one or more assumptions would affect the plan. You can use the What If Event Scenarios feature to see how the changes would affect the plan without changing the plan itself.

Here's an example. Say you've been offered a job in another state. The job pays about the same salary, but you can move to a town where your living expenses would be greatly reduced. You can see how the job change would affect your financial plans for the future by playing "what if" to modify existing assumptions, and then see the old and new plan results side by side.

Setting "What If" Options

Choose Planning | "What If" Event Scenarios or click the Explore What If's button in the Plan: Results area. The What If window, which is shown in

Figure 16-6, appears. The first time you use it, it displays the account balances shown in your Plan Results.

Choose a goal option from the drop-down list in the top-left of the window. Then click appropriate links on the left side of the window to open dialogs to change assumptions.

In our example, you might use the following links:

- Click Current Homes & Assets to add proposed sale information about your current home.
- Click Current Loans to record the proposed payoff of your mortgage when you sell your current home.
- Click Future Homes & Assets to add proposed purchase information about your new home and its associated mortgage.
- Click Adjustments to add a proposed adjustment for the reduced living expenses when you move to your new home.

Get the idea? Each time you make a change, the Plan Comparison chart changes. Here's what it might look like for our example:

Figure 16-6 • The What If window enables you to play "what if" with your financial plan.

Using "What If" Results

When you've finished changing assumptions and viewing results, you can click one of the three buttons at the top of the What If window:

- **Reset What If** clears all the assumptions you changed while playing "what if." This enables you to start over.
- **Save What If as Plan** saves the assumptions you changed while playing "what if" as your actual financial plan. When the window closes, you'll see the results in the Planning Center window change accordingly.
- **Close Without Saving** simply closes the window so you can continue working with Quicken. Your settings are not saved.

Using Financial Calculators

In this Chapter:

- *Financial calculator overview*

- *Retirement Calculator*

- *College Calculator*

- *Refinance Calculator*

- *Investment Savings Calculator*

- *Loan Calculator*

Chapter 17

Sometimes, the hardest part about financial planning is making the calculations you need quickly, to determine the feasibility of a potential plan. For example, suppose you're thinking about refinancing your home because today's interest rates are lower than the rate you locked into six years ago. You know your monthly payment can decrease, but you're not sure if you'll save enough money to cover the fees involved in the refinancing. The calculations seem complex and you're not sure what to do. That's where one of Quicken's financial calculators—the Refinance Calculator—can help. It can take raw data about your current mortgage and the one you're considering, and crunch the number in a flash to tell you whether it's worthwhile to take the next step.

In this chapter, I tell you about each of Quicken's financial calculators. I'm sure you'll find them handy tools for making the quick calculations you need to start the decision-making process with your financial plans.

A Look at Quicken's Financial Calculators

Quicken includes five financial calculators you can use to make quick financial calculations: the Retirement Calculator, the College Calculator, the Refinance Calculator, the Investment Savings Calculator, and the Loan Calculator. These calculators make complex calculations simple.

How the Calculators Work

All five of the financial calculators share the same basic interface. But although they are similar in appearance, each is designed for a specific purpose. It's important to pick the correct calculator to get the job done.

Quicken Quick Tip

I've been called an Excel guru. (About 20 years ago, I was called a Lotus jockey, but that's going back a bit further than we need to.) Before I started working with Quicken's calculators, I'd whip out Excel and build a worksheet every time I needed to perform loan payment calculations or estimate the value of savings at some future date. If I were smart, I'd save these worksheets in a safe place so I could access them again and again, but I always wound up deleting or losing them. So every time I needed to make a calculation, I'd spend ten to fifteen minutes just setting it up. Thanks to Quicken, those days are gone. Whenever I need to perform a complex financial calculation, I simply fire up Quicken and open the calculator of my choice. It saves a lot of time and effort.

In most instances, you begin by telling the calculator what part of the formula you want to calculate. For example, when calculating a loan, you can calculate the loan amount or the periodic payment. Then you enter values and set other options in the calculator's dialog to give Quicken the information it needs to make its calculations. Clicking a Calculate button completes the process. Quicken is very fast; the results appear as soon as you click Calculate—if not sooner.

Accessing the Financial Calculators

All of Quicken's financial calculators can be opened at least two ways:

- Choose the name of the calculator from the Financial Calculators submenu under the Planning Menu:

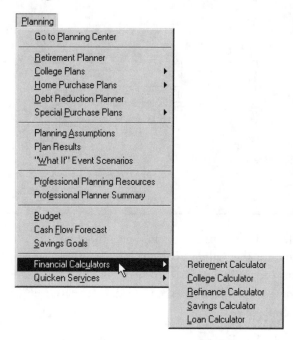

- Click the name of the calculator in the Calculators area of the Planning Center:

Using the Financial Calculators

Ready to give Quicken's financial calculators a try? The rest of this chapter provides some detailed instructions for using each of them.

Retirement Calculator

The Retirement Calculator can help you calculate some of the numbers you need to plan for your retirement. To open it, choose Planning | Financial Calculators | Retirement Calculator or click the Retirement Calculator link in the calculators area of the Planning Center. The Retirement Calculator appears:

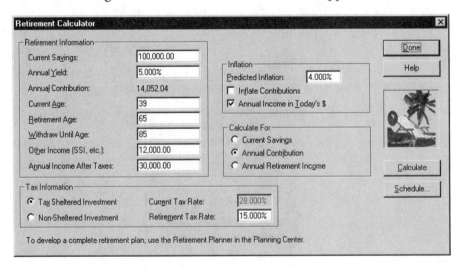

Select a Calculate For option, and then enter or select values and options throughout the dialog. Most options are pretty straightforward and easy to understand. When you're finished, click the Calculate button to see the results.

Here's a closer look at the options in the Retirement Calculator.

Calculate For

The Calculate For option affects which value is calculated by Quicken:

- **Current Savings** calculates the amount of money you should currently have saved based on the values you enter.
- **Annual Contribution** calculates the minimum amount you should contribute to a retirement account based on the values you enter.
- **Annual Retirement Income** calculates the annual amount of retirement income you'll have based on the values you enter.

Retirement Information

Retirement Information options enable you to enter the values Quicken should use in its calculations. The values you must enter vary depending on the Calculate For option you select.

Tax Information

Tax Information options enable you to indicate whether your retirement savings are in a tax sheltered investment or a non-sheltered investment. If you select the Non-Sheltered Investment option, you can enter your current tax rate and Quicken will automatically calculate the effect of taxes on your investment income. By experimenting with this feature, you can clearly see why it's a good idea to use tax sheltered or tax deferred investments whenever possible.

Inflation

Inflation options make complex calculations to account for the effect of inflation on your savings dollars. To use this feature, enter an inflation rate in the Predicted Inflation box, then toggle check marks for the two options below it:

- **Inflate contributions** makes calculations assuming that the annual contributions will rise with the inflation rate.
- **Annual Income in Today's $** makes calculations assuming that the Annual Income After Taxes entry is in today's dollars and not inflated.

Schedule

Clicking the Schedule button displays a printable list of deposits made and income withdrawn, with a running balance total. Here's what it looks like with the calculations shown earlier:

Deposit Schedule			☒
Print			Close

This deposit schedule assumes that your retirement income keeps pace with a 4.0% annual inflation rate. Note that income is in future, pre-tax dollars.

Age	Deposit	Income	Balance
0	0.00	0.00	100,000.00
39	14,052.04	0.00	119,052.04
40	14,052.04	0.00	139,056.68
41	14,052.04	0.00	160,061.56
42	14,052.04	0.00	182,116.67
43	14,052.04	0.00	205,274.55
44	14,052.04	0.00	229,590.31
45	14,052.04	0.00	255,121.87
46	14,052.04	0.00	281,930.00
47	14,052.04	0.00	310,078.54
48	14,052.04	0.00	339,634.51

College Calculator

The College Calculator enables you to calculate savings for the cost of a college education. Choose Planning | Financial Calculators | College Calculator or click the College Calculator link in the Calculators area of the Planning Center. The College Calculator, shown next, appears:

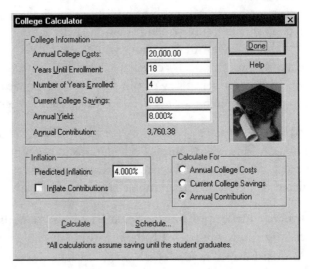

Select a Calculate For option, and then enter or select values and options throughout the dialog. Most options are pretty straightforward and easy to understand. When you click Calculate, Quicken calculates the results.

Here's a look at the options in the College Calculator:

Calculate For

The Calculate For option affects which value is calculated by Quicken:

- **Annual College Costs** calculates the annual tuition you'll be able to afford based on the values you enter.
- **Current College Savings** calculates the amount of money you should currently have saved based on the values you enter.
- **Annual Contribution** calculates the minimum amount you should contribute to college savings based on the values you enter.

College Information

The College Information area enables you to enter the values Quicken should use in its calculations. The values you must enter vary depending on the Calculate For option you select.

Inflation

Inflation options make complex calculations to account for the effect of inflation on your savings dollars. To use this feature, enter an inflation rate in the Predicted Inflation box. You can then toggle the Inflate Contributions check box, which makes calculations assuming that the annual contributions will rise with the inflation rate. Quicken automatically inflates the amount of tuition no matter how you set the Inflate Contributions check box.

Schedule

Clicking the Schedule button displays a printable list of deposits made and money withdrawn for tuition, with a running balance total. Here's what it looks like with the calculations shown earlier:

Deposit Schedule

Print   Close

Year	Deposit	Tuition	Balance
0	0.00	0.00	0.00
2002	3,760.38	0.00	3,760.38
2003	3,760.38	0.00	7,821.59
2004	3,760.38	0.00	12,207.70
2005	3,760.38	0.00	16,944.69
2006	3,760.38	0.00	22,060.65
2007	3,760.38	0.00	27,585.88
2008	3,760.38	0.00	33,553.13
2009	3,760.38	0.00	39,997.76
2010	3,760.38	0.00	46,957.96
2011	3,760.38	0.00	54,474.98

Refinance Calculator

If you own a home and are thinking about refinancing, you can try the Refinance Calculator to see whether refinancing will really save you money and, if so, how much. Choose Planning | Financial Calculators | Refinance Calculator or click the Refinance Calculator link in the Calculators area of the Planning Center. The Refinance Calculator dialog appears:

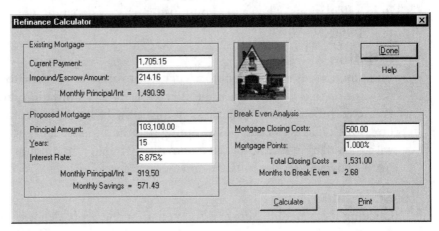

Enter values for your current mortgage and proposed mortgage in the text boxes to calculate your monthly savings with the new mortgage. Here's a closer look at the entries:

Existing Mortgage

Existing Mortgage options enable you to enter your current total monthly mortgage payment and the amount of that payment that is applied to property taxes and other escrow items. Quicken automatically calculates the amount of principal and interest for each payment. If you already know the principal and interest amount, you can enter that in the Current Payment box and leave the Impound/Escrow Amount box empty. The result is the same.

Proposed Mortgage

Proposed Mortgage options enable you to enter information about the mortgage you are considering to replace your current mortgage. The Principal Amount may be the balance on your current mortgage, but it could be more or less depending on whether you want to refinance for more or less money. (Refinancing often offers a good opportunity to exchange equity for cash.)

Break Even Analysis

Break Even Analysis options are optional. If you enter the closing costs and points for the proposed mortgage, Quicken will automatically calculate how long it will take to cover those costs based on your monthly savings. As you can see in the previous illustration, it will take 2.68 months for the savings to pay for the closing costs and points on the new mortgage.

Print

Clicking the Print button displays the Print dialog, which you can use to print the results of your calculations.

Investment Savings Calculator

The Investment Savings Calculator enables you to calculate savings annuities—periodic payments to a savings account or investment. Choose Planning | Financial Calculators | Savings Calculator or click the Savings Calculator link in the Calculators area of the Planning Center. The Investment Savings Calculator appears:

Select a Calculate For option and then enter or select values and options throughout the dialog. Most options are pretty straightforward and easy to understand. When you click Calculate, Quicken displays the results.

Here's a closer look at each of the entry options:

Calculate For

The Calculate For option affects which value is calculated by Quicken:

- **Opening Savings Balance** calculates the amount of money you should currently have saved based on the values you enter.
- **Regular Contribution** calculates the minimum amount you should regularly contribute to savings based on the values you enter.

- **Ending Savings Balance** calculates the total amount saved at the end of the savings period based on the values you enter.

Savings Information

Savings Information enables you to enter values for Quicken to use in its calculations. The option you choose from the Number Of drop-down list will determine how interest is compounded; in most cases, you'll probably set this to Months.

Inflation

Inflation options make complex calculations to account for the effect of inflation on your savings dollars. To use this feature, enter an inflation rate in the Predicted Inflation box, then toggle check boxes for the two options below it:

- **Inflate contributions** makes calculations assuming that the annual contributions will rise with the inflation rate.
- **Ending Balance in Today's $** makes calculations assuming that the Ending Savings Balance is in today's dollars and not inflated.

When you click Calculate, Quicken displays the results. You can click the Schedule button to see a printable list of deposits, with a running balance total.

Schedule

Clicking the Schedule button displays a printable list of deposits made, with a running balance total. Here's what it looks like with the calculations shown earlier:

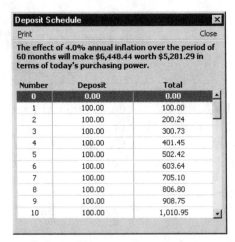

Deposit Schedule

Print   Close

The effect of 4.0% annual inflation over the period of 60 months will make $6,448.44 worth $5,281.29 in terms of today's purchasing power.

Number	Deposit	Total
0	0.00	0.00
1	100.00	100.00
2	100.00	200.24
3	100.00	300.73
4	100.00	401.45
5	100.00	502.42
6	100.00	603.64
7	100.00	705.10
8	100.00	806.80
9	100.00	908.75
10	100.00	1,010.95

Loan Calculator

Quicken's Loan Calculator can quickly calculate the principal or periodic payment for a loan. Choose Planning | Financial Calculators | Loan Calculator or click the Loan Calculator link in the Calculators area of the Planning Center. The Loan Calculator dialog appears:

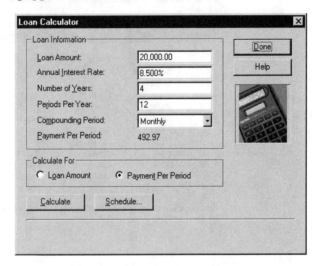

Select one of the Calculate For options, enter information in the remainder of the dialog, and click Calculate. Getting the answer is a lot quicker and easier with the Loan Calculator than using one of those loan books or building an Excel spreadsheet to do the job.

Here's a look at the Loan Calculator options:

Calculate For

The Calculate For options determine what Quicken calculates:

- **Loan Amount** enables you to calculate the amount of a loan based on specific periodic payments.
- **Payment Per Period** enables you to calculate the periodic loan payment based on the loan amount.

Loan Information

Loan Information options enable you to enter values for Quicken to use in its calculations. The information you must enter varies depending on the Calculate For option you select. Be sure to set the Periods Per Year and Compounding Period options correctly; an incorrect entry will misstate the results.

Schedule

Clicking the Schedule button displays a printable amortization table that lists the payment number, the amount of the principal and interest paid at each payment, and the ending balance for the loan:

Pmt	Principal	Interest	Balance
		8.50%	20,000.00
1	351.30	141.67	19,648.70
2	353.79	139.18	19,294.91
3	356.30	136.67	18,938.61
4	358.82	134.15	18,579.79
5	361.36	131.61	18,218.43
6	363.92	129.05	17,854.51
7	366.50	126.47	17,488.01
8	369.10	123.87	17,118.91
9	371.71	121.26	16,747.20
10	374.34	118.63	16,372.86
11	377.00	115.97	15,995.86
12	379.67	113.30	15,616.19
13	382.36	110.61	15,233.83
14	385.06	107.91	14,848.77

Approximate Future Payment Schedule

Print   Close

Reducing Debt and Saving Money

In this Chapter:

- *Reducing debt*

- *Budgeting and forecasting*

- *Setting up savings goals*

Chapter 18

The best way to prepare for life events is to build up your savings. Saving money is an important part of financial management. Savings enable you to take vacations and make major purchases without increasing debt, help your kids through college, handle emergencies, and have a comfortable retirement.

In this chapter, I tell you about saving money and how tools within Quicken can help. If you're in debt and can't even think about saving until you dig your way out, this chapter can help you, too. It starts by covering Quicken tools for reducing your debt.

Debt Reduction Planner

It's not easy to save money if most of your income is spent paying credit card bills and loan payments. If you're heavily in debt, you might even be having trouble keeping up with all your payments. If that's the case, it's time to think about reducing your debt.

Quicken's Debt Reduction Planner is a tool for helping you reduce your debt. You enter information about your financial situation, and Quicken develops a debt reduction plan for you. The Debt Reduction Planner is thorough, easy to use, and an excellent tool for teaching people how they can get out of debt as quickly as possible, saving hundreds (if not thousands) of dollars in interest charges.

To get started, choose Planning | Debt Reduction Planner or click the Debt Reduction Planner link in the Planners area of the Planning Center. If you have explored this feature before, the Debt Reduction window appears with a chart showing the information you previously entered (refer to Figure 18-1 later in this chapter). If you have never used it before, the Debt Reduction dialog appears, enabling you to create a new debt reduction plan.

Creating a New Debt Reduction Plan

If necessary, click the New Plan button on the button bar of the Debt Reduction window. If a dialog warns that you will overwrite your current plan, click Yes. The Debt Reduction dialog appears, displaying its Welcome screen. Insert your

Quicken Deluxe CD in your CD-ROM drive and click Next to continue. An introductory movie plays to tell you what the Debt Reduction Planner can do for you. (If you don't have your Quicken Deluxe CD-ROM available, you can skip the movie. But I do recommend viewing it the first time you use the Debt Reduction Planner.) When the movie has finished, click Next to begin.

Entering Debt Information

When you click Next after viewing the movie, the Debts tab of the window appears. It should look something like this:

This tab lists all of your current debts, as they are recorded in Quicken. Use the buttons to the right of the list to modify the list:

- If the debt list is not up to date or complete, click the Update Debts button to import current debt information from your Quicken data file.
- To add a debt that you do not track in Quicken, click the Add button. The Edit Debt Reduction dialog, shown next, appears. Use it to enter information about the debt and click OK to add it to the list.

- To modify information about a debt, select it and click the Edit button to display the Edit Debt Reduction dialog just shown. Make changes as desired and click OK to save the changes.

- To remove a debt from the list, select it and click the Remove button. In the confirmation dialog that appears, click Yes. This removes the debt from the Debt Reduction Planner, but does not remove it from your Quicken data file. You may want to use this feature to remove a long-term debt such as a mortgage so you can concentrate on higher interest, short-term debt, such as credit cards and personal loans.

When the debt list shows all of your debts, click Next to continue.

If required information is missing from one or more debts, Quicken will tell you and then display the Edit Debt Reduction dialog for each debt so you can update the information. You must complete this process before you can continue.

Next, Quicken tells you about your current debt situation, including your total debt, your total monthly payments, and a projection of when you will be debt-free based on the debt information you provided. Click Next to continue.

Setting the Order of Debts

The Order tab of the Debt Reduction dialog begins with a movie. When it has finished, click Next to continue. Quicken puts your debts in the order of cost, with the highest at the top. It might look something like this:

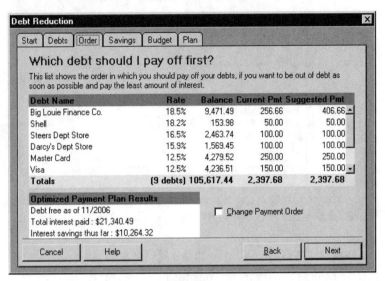

This tab sets the debt payoff order so that the most expensive debt is paid off first, thus saving you interest charges. The Suggested Pmt column offers a suggested payment amount; following the suggestion makes it possible to pay off the debts faster without increasing your total monthly payments. If desired, you can turn on the Change Payment Order check box to change the order in which debts are paid off—this, however, will cost you more and increase the payoff time. Click Next to continue.

If you turn on the Change Payment Order check box and click the Next button, the dialog changes to enable you to change the order of debts. Click a debt to select it and then click Move Up or Move Down to change its location in the list. When you've finished, click Next.

Using Savings to Pay Off Debt

The Savings tab begins by playing a movie that tells you why you might want to use savings and investments to pay off your debt. Listen carefully—the movie is full of good information! When the movie is finished, click Next.

Quicken summarizes your current savings and investments and enables you to specify how much of your savings should be applied to your debt, as shown next.

Enter a value in the text box and click the Recalculate button. The Results area shows the effect of your change. Click Next to continue.

Adjusting Your Budget

The Budget tab offers options for helping you reduce your spending, which can, in turn, help you reduce your debt. It begins by displaying a movie with tips and instructions. When the movie is finished, click Next to continue.

As shown next, Quicken displays a list of your top four expenses, with text boxes for entering the amount by which you can cut back on each one every month:

Enter the amounts by which you can cut back for the categories that appear or for different categories you select from the drop-down lists. Quicken automatically suggests that you apply the savings to the debt, thus adjusting the Results area for your entries. Click Next to continue.

Reviewing the Plan

The Plan tab (shown next) displays your custom debt reduction action plan:

Scroll through the debt reduction plan to see what it recommends. Better yet, click the Print This Action Plan button to print a copy you can refer to throughout the coming months. Click Next to continue.

Next, Quicken offers to track your debt reduction plan for you. You can toggle the settings for two different check boxes to enable this feature:

- **Alert Me If I Fall Behind** tells Quicken to alert you if you fall behind on debt reduction and to include your debt in budgeting and forecasting models. (I tell you about Planning Center alerts, budgeting, and forecasting later in this chapter.)

- **Set Up Scheduled Transactions for My Monthly Payments** tells Quicken to schedule transactions for the monthly payments included in your debt reduction plan. This makes it impossible for you to forget about debt reduction payments. (I tell you about scheduling payments in Chapter 7.)

Turn on the check box for each option that you want to enable and then click Next. Quicken plays another movie. When it is finished, click Done.

Viewing the Debt Reduction Plan Results

When you click Done in the final screen of the Debt Reduction dialog, the Debt Reduction window appears (see Figure 18-1). It uses a graph to compare debt reduction using your current method (the blue line) with that of your new debt reduction plan (the green line).

To see the results of your plan on a month-to-month basis, click the Payment Schedule button at the top of the Debt Reduction window. The Debt Reduction Payment Schedule dialog, which is shown on the following page, appears. It lists the payments you should make for each month, according to the plan and your account balances at month-end.

Figure 18-1 • The Debt Reduction plan window clearly illustrates how quickly you can get out of debt and save interest costs by using Quicken's plan.

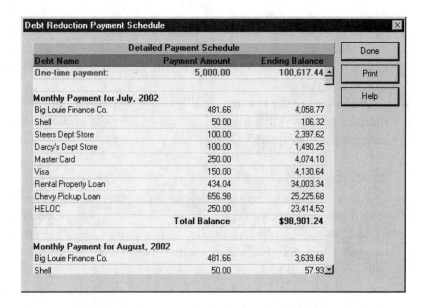

Modifying the Plan

Once you have a debt reduction plan, you can modify it in a number of ways:

- Click the Update Debt Balances button on the button bar to import the current balances of your debt into the Debt Reduction Planner.
- Enter new values in the Current Plan area at the bottom of the Debt Reduction window.
- Click the New Plan button on the button bar to create a new plan from scratch.

No matter which method you choose, Quicken will automatically revise the graph and other information to reflect your changes.

Budgeting and Forecasting

When money is tight or you're interested in meeting financial goals, it's time to create a budget and monitor your spending. But if you're serious about managing your money, you might want to create a budget before you need one. While Quicken's categories give you a clear understanding of where money comes from and where it goes, budgets enable you to set up predefined amounts for each category, thus helping you to control spending.

Budgets also make it easier to create forecasts of your future financial position. This makes it possible to see how much cash will be available at a future date—before the holidays, for summer vacation, or for the day you plan to put down a deposit on a new car.

In this part of the chapter, I tell you how to create a budget and use it to monitor your spending habits. I also explain how to create a forecast so you can glimpse your financial future.

Budgeting

The idea behind a budget is to determine expected income amounts and specify maximum amounts for expenditures. This helps prevent you from spending more than you earn. It also enables you to control your spending in certain categories. For example, say you realize that you go out for dinner a lot more often than you should. You can set a budget for the Dining category and track your spending to make sure you don't exceed the budget. You'll eat at home more often and save money.

In this section, I explain how to set up a budget and use it to keep track of your spending. I think you'll agree that budgeting is a great way to keep spending under control.

Organizing Categories into Groups

Budgets are based on transactions recorded for categories and subcategories. (That's why it's important to categorize all your transactions—and not to the Misc category!) Quicken also enables you to organize categories by category groups. Although you don't have to use the Groups feature when creating your budget—it's entirely optional—grouping similar categories together can simplify your budget.

You can see the group to which each category is assigned in the Group column of the Category List window (see Figure 18-2). Choose Tools | Category List to display it. If the Group column does not appear in your list, choose Show Category Group from the window's Options menu to display it.

The Default Groups By default, Quicken includes several category groups that it assigns to the categories it creates when you first set up your Quicken data file:

- **Discretionary** is for expenses you can avoid (or at least minimize), such as entertainment, subscriptions, and vacation.
- **Income** is for earned income, such as your salary, and miscellaneous income items, such as interest, dividends, and gifts received.
- **Mandatory Expenses** are expenses you can't avoid, such as fuel for your car, groceries, rent, and insurance.

Category	Type	Description	Group	Tax	Tax Line Item
Advances	Income	Book Advances		✓	Schedule C:Gross receipts or sales
Bonus	Income	Bonus Income	Income	✓	W-2:Salary or wages, self
Div Income	Income	Dividend Income	Income	✓	Schedule B:Dividend income
Employer Benefit	Income	Employer Benefit	Income	✓	W-2:Salary or wages, self
Dental	Sub	Dental Plan Employer Benefit	Income	✓	W-2:Salary or wages, self
Medical	Sub	Medical Plan Employer Benefit	Income	✓	W-2:Salary or wages, self
Vision	Sub	Vision Plan Employer Benefit	Income	✓	W-2:Salary or wages, self
Gift Received	Income	Gift Received	Income		
Interest Inc	Income	Interest Income	Income	✓	Schedule B:Interest income
Invest Inc	Income	Investment Income	Income	✓	

Figure 18-2 • The Category List window displays all categories and the names of the groups to which they are assigned.

In addition, if you indicated that you use Quicken to track the activity of a small business when you first set up your Quicken data file, Quicken includes Business Income and Business Expenses groups to track the income and expenses from your business.

Assigning Groups to Categories   You can assign a group to a category when you create or edit the category. In the Category List window (see Figure 18-2), either click New or select an existing category and click Edit. The Set Up Category or Edit Category dialog appears. Click the arrow next to the Group box to display the Group drop-down list, which looks like this:

You have three options:

- Click the name of an existing group to assign it to a category.
- Click New to display a dialog for creating a new group. When you enter a group name and click OK in the dialog to save it, the new group is assigned to the category and appears in all group lists.
- Click Edit to display the Manage Category Groups dialog, which you can use to create, edit, or delete groups.

When you have assigned a group to the category, click OK to save it with the category. It appears in the Category List window.

Creating a Budget

Quicken can automatically generate a budget for you based on past transactions. You can edit the budget it creates to meet your needs. Or you can create a budget from scratch.

To start creating a budget, choose Planning | Budget. The Setup tab of the Budget window, which is shown in Figure 18-3, appears.

Creating a Budget Automatically   The quickest and easiest way to create a budget is to let Quicken do it for you based on your income and expenditures. For Quicken to create an accurate budget, however, you must have several months of transactions in your Quicken data file. Otherwise, the budget may not reflect all regular income and expenses.

Figure 18-3 • The Setup tab of the Budget window

Select the Automatic option in the Setup tab of the Budget window (refer to Figure 18-3) and click Create Budget. The Create Budget: Automatic dialog, which is shown next, appears. Use this dialog to set options for the budget.

In the date range area, enter the starting and ending dates for the transactions on which you want to base the budget. Whenever possible, the date range should be the most recent 12-month period. But if you have less than 12 months of data, enter the date range for the period for which you have data.

Next, select a budget method option:

- **Average Amounts** enters monthly averages based on the period in the date range. If you select this option, choose a frequency from the drop-down list.
- **Monthly Detail** copies the total values for each month to the corresponding month in the budget.
- **Quarterly Detail** copies the total values for each quarter to the corresponding quarter in the budget.

If you're not sure which to select, consider this advice. Select Monthly Detail or Quarterly Detail if you have a full year of transactions (or close to it) and you have seasonal income (such as a teaching job) or expenses (such as a vacation home). Select Average if you have less than six months of transactions or don't have seasonal income or expenses.

Toggle check boxes in the Options area as desired:

- **Round values to nearest** enables you to round calculated values to the nearest $1, $10, or $100. If you enable this option, choose a value from the drop-down list beside it.

- **Exclude one-time transactions** tells Quicken not to consider one-time transactions when creating the budget. For example, suppose you made a single large payment to a furniture company to buy living room furniture. If that transaction is considered for budgeting purposes, Quicken will automatically assume that you make payments like that every year and include it in the budget. (Of course, you can always edit a budget to exclude such items after the budget has been created.)

Clicking the Categories button displays the Choose Categories dialog, shown next. You can use this dialog to select specific categories to budget. You may find this useful if you only want to budget certain categories, such as dining, clothing, and entertainment. Click to toggle the check boxes beside each category name. The categories with check marks will be included in the budget when you click OK.

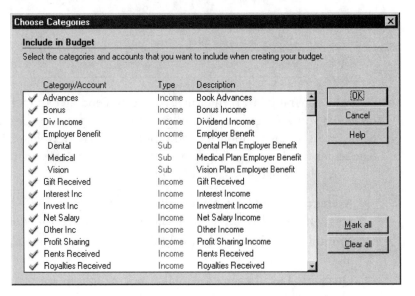

When you click OK in the Create Budget: Automatic dialog, Quicken displays a dialog telling you that the new budget has been created. Click OK to dismiss this dialog. The Income tab of the Budget window appears next.

Creating a Budget Manually   If you prefer, you can create a budget from scratch. This is more time consuming, but it forces you to look at each category carefully to estimate future expenses.

Select the Manual option in the Setup tab of the Budget window (refer to Figure 18-3) and click Create Budget. A dialog appears with instructions for completing your budget. Click OK to dismiss the dialog. The Income tab of the Budget window appears next.

Completing a Budget

Once you have created a budget, you can fine-tune it to set the categories and amounts that should appear. If you created your budget automatically, this is a matter of reviewing budget income, expense, and savings items and making changes you deem necessary. If you created a budget manually, however, you must manually add categories and set amounts for each one. You do this in the Income, Expenses, and Savings tabs of the Budget window. Because these windows all look and work pretty much the same way, only one is illustrated: the Expenses tab, which is shown in Figure 18-4.

Adding a Category   To add a category, click the Choose Categories button at the bottom of the Budget window. This displays the Choose Categories dialog shown earlier. Click to place a check mark beside each category you want to include in the budget.

By default, when you create a budget automatically, Quicken only includes the categories for which transactions exist. When you create a budget manually,

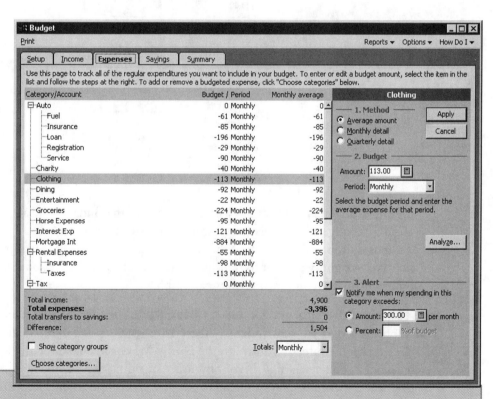

Figure 18-4 • The Expenses tab of the Budget window, with several expense categories entered

Quicken does not include any categories at all; all categories must be added manually.

Changing the Budget for a Category   To change the budget method and amount for a category, click its name in the Budget window, then set options on the right side of the window. If you change the method to Monthly Detail or Quarterly Detail, the right side of the window changes so you can enter monthly (as shown next) or quarterly values. When you make a change, click the Apply button to save it.

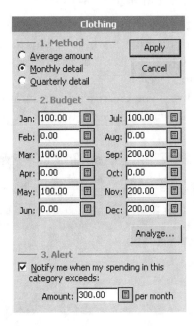

Adding a Savings Transfer   The Savings tab of the Budget window enables you to add budgeted transfers to investment or savings accounts. Click the Choose Accounts button at the bottom of the window and use the dialog that appears to select the accounts you want to transfer money to. Then set Budget options for the account as instructed in the previous paragraph.

Setting an Alert for an Expense Category   The Alert area in the Expenses tab of the Budget window (refer to Figure 18-4) enables you to set an alert for a selected expense category. Turn on the Notify Me check box and enter a value in the Amount box beneath it. If your monthly spending exceeds the amount you specified, Quicken displays a dialog to tell you. (This option only appears in the Expenses tab of the Budget window.)

Analyzing Actual Category Amounts Clicking the Analyze button in the Budget window displays a column chart, like the one shown next, of actual expenditures for the selected category. This helps you visualize the actual pattern of income, expense, or savings.

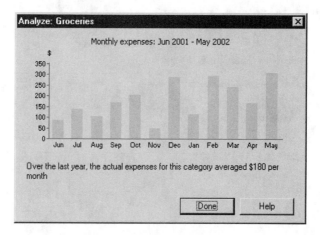

Viewing Amounts by Category Group To organize categories by group, turn on the Show Category Groups check box at the bottom of the Budget window. A dialog may appear, telling you that some category groups contain both income and expense items; click OK to dismiss it. The view changes to sort categories by group, as shown in Figure 18-5, and the separate Income, Expenses, and Savings tabs are replaced by a single Budget tab. To return to the default view, turn off the Show Category Groups check box and choose Separate View from the Options menu on the window's button bar.

Viewing a Completed Budget

When you're finished setting options in the Income, Expenses, and Savings tabs of the Budget window, click the Summary tab. This displays the budget summary, which is shown in Figure 18-6.

Working with Budgets

Here are a few additional things you might want to do with Quicken's budgeting feature. All of these things can be done from the Setup tab of the Budget window. Here's what the tab looks like when you've created one budget (left) and when you've created multiple budgets (right):

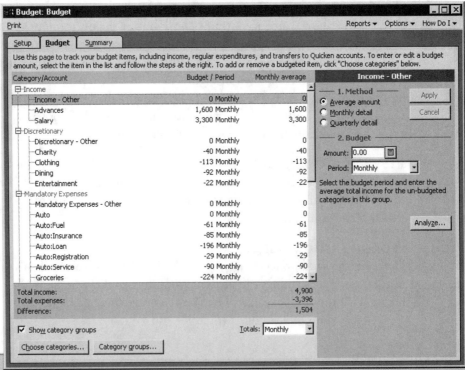

Figure 18-5 • You can view a budget's categories by group.

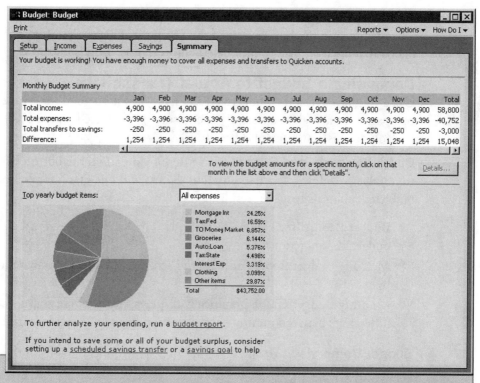

Figure 18-6 • The Summary tab of the Budget window summarizes your budget information.

Creating Another Budget   Quicken enables you to have more than one budget. In the Setup tab, select the method you want to use to create the new budget and click Create Budget. If you selected Automatic, the Create Budget: Automatic dialog that appears includes a place to enter a name for the budget. If you selected Manual or Copy Current, the Budget Name dialog appears so you can name the budget. Enter the requested information and click OK. Then fine-tune your new budget as discussed earlier in this section.

Opening a Specific Budget   To open a specific budget, select the budget name in the middle part of the Setup tab and click Open.

Renaming a Budget   To rename the current budget, click the Rename button in the top part of the Setup tab. To rename another budget, select the budget name and click the Rename button in the middle part of the Setup tab. Enter a name and description in the Rename Budget dialog that appears and click OK.

Deleting a Budget To delete a budget, select the budget name and click the Delete button in the middle part of the Setup tab. Click Yes in the confirmation dialog that appears. You cannot delete the currently open budget.

Comparing a Budget to Actual Transactions

Once you have created a budget you can live with, it's a good idea to periodically compare your actual income and expenditures to budgeted amounts. Quicken lets you do this a number of different ways.

Budget Reports and Graphs The Reports menu on the button bar in the Budget window offers two different reports and one graph for comparing budgeted amounts to actual results:

- **Budget Report** (see Figure 18-7) displays the year-to-date actual and budgeted transactions.
- **Monthly Budget Report** displays the actual and budgeted transactions by month.
- **Monthly Budget Graph** graphically displays the favorable and unfavorable differences between monthly actual and budgeted income amounts.

Budget Comparison Graphs You can display budget graphs in the Quicken Home window. This feature enables you to keep an eye on the budget categories and groups that interest you most.

To use this feature, switch to the Quicken Home window and customize it as instructed in Appendix B. The items or snapshots that provide budget information are:

- **Budget** displays a chart that compares your actual to budgeted income and expenses.
- **Budget Goal Progress** tracks spending for a single category's budget. This helps you monitor spending for a specific category that's important to you.

Quicken Quick Tip

Make sure you compare budgeted amounts to actual results for the period for which you have recorded data. For example, don't view a year-to-date Budget Report if you began entering data into Quicken in March. Instead, customize the report to show actual transactions beginning in March. I provide details about creating and customizing reports and graphs in Chapter 9.

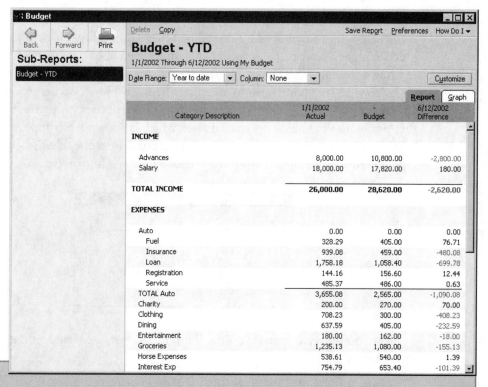

Figure 18-7 • A Budget Report compares actual to budgeted amounts.

- **Budgeted Categories** compares actual category amounts with your budget.
- **Budgeted Net Income** displays a chart that compares your budgeted to actual net income.
- **Category Group Budget** tracks progress against your budget by category group.

You can customize any of the graphs by right-clicking them and choosing the Customize This Chart or Customize This Graph command from the contextual menu that appears. I explain how to customize reports and graphs in Chapter 9.

Forecasting

Forecasting uses known and estimated transactions to provide a general overview of your future financial situation. This "crystal ball" can help you spot potential cash flow problems (or surpluses) so you can prepare for them.

Creating a Forecast

A forecast without data is like a crystal ball that's full of fog—it doesn't show you much. To get a clear picture, you need to enter data about future transactions by creating a forecast.

To create a forecast, begin by opening the Cash Flow Forecast window. Choose Planning | Cash Flow Forecast. If you have not yet created a forecast, the Automatically Create Forecast dialog, which is shown next, appears. If you have already created a forecast and want to create a new one, choose Options | Update Forecast on the Cash Flow Forecast window's button bar.

How you proceed depends on the kind of data you use—budget data or register data:

Creating a Forecast with Budget Data   To create a forecast with budget data, enter beginning and ending dates for which you have a budget. This will normally be the current year. Click the Advanced button to display the Advanced AutoCreate dialog, shown next. Select Create Both in the top part of the dialog and From Budget Data in the bottom part of the dialog. Click Done to save your settings and then click OK in the Automatically Create Forecast dialog to create the forecast. Figure 18-8 illustrates a forecast based on a budget.

Figure 18-8 • This forecast was based on a budget, with known expenses included. (This example looks a bit like an EKG, doesn't it?)

Creating a Forecast with Register Data   To create a forecast based on register data, enter beginning and ending dates for which you have register data. The time span should cover at least six months, and for best results, it should cover a full year. Click the Advanced button to display the Advanced AutoCreate dialog. Select Create Both in the top part of the dialog and From Register Data in the bottom part of the dialog. Click Done to save your settings and then click OK in the Automatically Create Forecast dialog to create the forecast.

Entering Income and Expense Items

Once you've created a forecast, you can fine-tune it by entering or modifying known or estimated events. Click the Income Items or Expense Items button in the Cash Flow Forecast window (see Figure 18-8). The Forecast Income Items or

Forecast Expense Items window appears, as shown next; use this window to add, modify, or delete items:

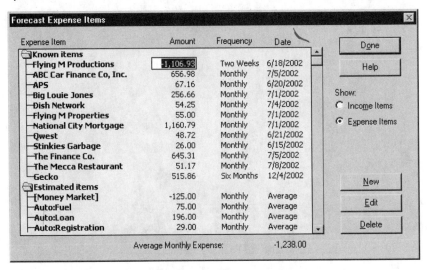

- To display either income or expense items, select one of the Show options.
- To edit an item, click it to select it and enter a new value.
- To add, modify, or remove items, click the New, Edit, or Delete button.

When you click New or Edit, the Create New Income/Expense Item or Edit Income/Expense Item dialog appears (see the following illustration). Use this dialog to enter or edit information for a forecast item. The exact name of the dialog varies, depending on how you're using it, but the options are the same.

Start by selecting the Income or Expense option to determine the type of item you are creating. Then fill in the remaining fields with information about the item. You can click More to select a category for the item and set the total number of entries for a recurring item. When you're finished, click OK.

Working with Scenarios

When you create a single forecast, you create a forecast for the *base scenario*. Just as you can have multiple budgets, you can also have multiple forecast scenarios.

Creating a New Scenario   To create a new scenario, choose Manage Scenarios from the Options menu on the Cash Flow Forecast window's button bar. The Manage Forecast Scenarios dialog, which is shown next, appears. Click New to display a dialog in which you can enter a scenario name and choose to copy the existing scenario. When you click OK, the new scenario's name appears as the selected scenario on the Scenario Data drop-down list.

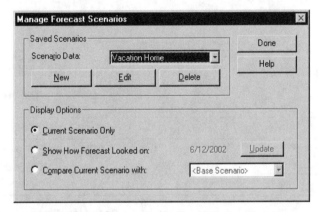

Changing a Scenario's Display   The Display Options in the Manage Forecast Scenarios dialog let you change the display of a selected scenario:

- **Current Scenario Only**, which is the default option, displays only one scenario in the Forecasting window.
- **Show How Forecast Looked on** enables you to update the scenario for the current date. Select this option and then click the Update button.
- **Compare Current Scenario with** enables you to include two scenarios in the Forecasting window (see Figure 18-9). This makes it easy to see how one differs from the other.

Select the option you want and click Done to apply it.

Savings Goals

Quicken's Savings Goals feature helps you save money by "hiding" funds in an account. You set up a savings goal and make contributions to it using the Savings Goals window. Although the money never leaves the source bank account, it is

Figure 18-9 • By including two scenarios in the Cash Flow Forecast window, you can see how they compare.

deducted in the account register, thus reducing the account balance in Quicken. If you can't see the money in your account, you're less likely to spend it.

Open the Savings Goals window by choosing Planning | Savings Goals. Figure 18-10 shows what the window looks like with one savings goal already created.

Quicken Quick Tip

The Savings Goals feature really works. I used this technique with a paper check register years ago. Not only did it help me save money, but it prevented me from bouncing checks in the days when I kept a dangerously low checking account balance. Having this feature built into Quicken certainly makes using this technique easier.

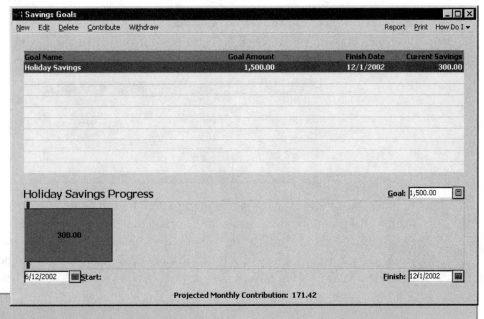

Figure 18-10 • Use the Savings Goals window to create and work with savings goals.

The top half of the Savings Goals window lists the savings goals you have created with Quicken. The bottom half shows the progress for the selected goal. You can use button bar options to work with window contents:

- **New** enables you to create a savings goal.
- **Edit** enables you to modify the selected savings goal.
- **Delete** removes the selected savings goal.
- **Contribute** enables you to contribute funds from a Quicken account to the selected savings goal.
- **Withdraw** enables you to remove funds from a savings goal and return them to a Quicken account.
- **Report** creates a report of the activity for savings goals.
- **How Do I** provides instructions for performing specific tasks with the Savings Goals window.

Creating a Savings Goal

To create a savings goal, click New on the button bar in the Savings Goals window. The Create New Savings Goal dialog, which is shown next, appears:

Enter the information for your savings goal in the text boxes. The name of the savings goal cannot be the same as any Quicken category or account. For the Finish Date, enter the date by which you want to have the money saved. For example, if you're using savings goals to plan for a vacation, the Finish Date should be shortly before the date you want to start the vacation. When you've finished, click OK to add the savings goal to the list in the Savings Goals window.

Contributing Funds to a Savings Goal

To contribute funds to a savings goal, select the savings goal in the Savings Goals window and click the Contribute button on the button bar. The Contribute To Goal dialog (shown next) appears:

Select the account from which you want to transfer the money from the drop-down list. The balance of the account appears in the bottom of the dialog. Then enter the amount of the transfer in the Amount box. By default, Quicken suggests the projected monthly contribution amount, but you can enter any amount you like. When you've finished, click OK.

As shown in the next illustration, Quicken creates an entry in the account register of the account from which the money was contributed. It also updates the progress bar and information in the Savings Goals dialog.

| 6/10/2002 | | Contribution towards goal | 300 | 00 | | | | | 6,900 | 00 |
| | | [Holiday Saving: | | | | | | | | |

When you create a savings goal, Quicken creates an asset account to record the goal's transactions and balance. To automate contributions to the goal, you can create a scheduled transaction to periodically transfer money from one of your bank accounts to the savings goal asset account. I tell you about scheduled transactions in Chapter 7.

Meeting Your Goal

Once you have met your savings goal, you can either withdraw the funds from the savings goal so they appear in a Quicken account or delete the savings goal to put the money back where it came from.

Withdrawing Money

In the Savings Goals window, select the savings goal from which you want to withdraw money. Click the Withdraw button on the button bar. The Withdraw From Goal dialog (shown next), which works very much like the Contribute To Goal dialog, appears. Use it to remove funds from the savings goal and put them back into the account from which they were contributed:

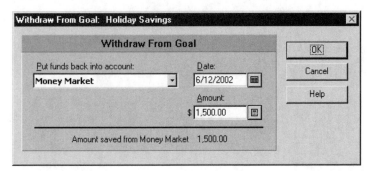

Deleting a Savings Goal

In the Savings Goals window, select the savings goal you want to delete and click the Delete button on the button bar. A dialog appears, asking if you want to keep the savings goal account for your records:

- Click Yes to transfer the funds back to the original account(s) and keep the savings goal account.
- Click No to transfer funds back to the original account(s) and delete the savings goal account.

The Tax Center

This part of the book explores the features of Quicken's Tax Center, which can make tax preparation quicker and easier, enable you to plan for tax time, and even help you save money on your income taxes. Its two chapters are:

Chapter 19:   *Simplifying Tax Preparation*

Chapter 20:   *Planning for Tax Time*

Part Six

Simplifying Tax Preparation

In this Chapter:

- *Including tax information in accounts and categories*

- *Tax reports*

- *Online Tax Tools*

- *Exporting to TurboTax*

Chapter 19

Tax time is no fun. It can force you to spend hours sifting through financial records and filling out complex forms. When you're done with the hard part, you may be rewarded with the knowledge that you can expect a refund. But it is more likely that your reward will be the privilege of writing a check to the federal, state, or local government—or worse yet, all three.

Fortunately, Quicken can help. Its reporting features can save you time. By using the tax tools that are part of Quicken or available on Quicken.com, the next tax season may be a little less stressful. In this chapter, I show you how.

Tax Information in Accounts and Categories

As discussed briefly in Chapter 3, Quicken accounts and categories can include information that will help you at tax time. In this section, I tell you more about this feature, including why you should use it and how you can set it up.

Why Enter Tax Information?

By including tax information in Quicken accounts and categories, you make it possible for Quicken to do several things:

- **Prepare tax reports** that summarize information by tax category or schedule
- **Display tax information in the Tax Center window**, which shows an up-to-date summary of your tax situation
- **Save time using the Tax Planner**, a Quicken feature that can import information from your Quicken data file based on tax information you enter
- **Distinguish between taxable and nontaxable investments**, which enables you to create accurate reports on capital gains, interest, and dividends
- **Use TurboTax to prepare your tax return,** enabling you to import Quicken information into TurboTax based on tax form and line items, thus eliminating the need to manually prepare tax returns or manually enter data into TurboTax

By spending a few minutes setting up tax information for your accounts and categories, you can save hours compiling information for your returns.

Including Tax Information in Accounts

You enter an account's tax information in the Tax Schedule Information dialog
for the account. Choose Tools | Account List or press CTRL-A to display the
Account List window. Select the name of the account in the View Accounts tab
and click the Edit button on the button bar. In the General Information tab of
the Account Details dialog that appears, click the Tax Schedule Info button.
The Tax Schedule Information dialog appears:

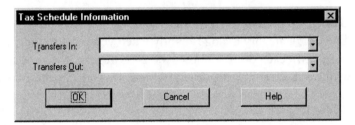

Use the Transfers In and Transfers Out drop-down lists to map account
activity to specific lines on tax return forms and schedules. When you're finished,
click OK. Repeat this process for all accounts for which you want to enter tax
information.

Including Tax Information in Categories

There are two ways to enter tax line item information for Quicken categories:

- Enter tax line item information for a single category in the Edit Category dialog
- Match multiple categories to tax line items with the Tax Line Item
  Assignment pane

Quicken Quick Tip
In previous versions of Quicken, the tax information feature for accounts was
used primarily to keep track of 401(k) investments and other tax-deferred
deductions from payroll checks. If you use the Payroll Setup feature to account
for all payroll deductions, including retirement plan contributions, you shouldn't
have to change the settings for any of your accounts.

Keep in mind that Quicken automatically sets tax information for many of the categories it creates. You can see which categories are tax related and which tax form lines have been assigned to them right in the Category List window. Concentrate on the categories without tax assignments; some of these may require tax information, depending on your situation.

You can also enter tax information when you first create a category. The Set Up Category dialog looks and works very much like the Edit Category dialog, shown next. I tell you more about the Set Up Category dialog in Chapter 3.

Using the Edit Category Dialog

The Edit Category dialog is handy when you need to set tax information for just one or two categories. Choose Tools | Category List to open the Category List window. Select the category for which you want to enter tax information. Then click the Edit button on the button bar to display the Edit Category dialog, shown here:

If the category's transactions should be included on your tax return as either income or a deductible expense, turn on the Tax-Related check box. Then use the Tax Line Item drop-down list to choose the form or schedule and line for the item. (You can expand this list by selecting the Extended Line Item List option.)

A description of the tax line item you chose appears at the bottom of the dialog. Click OK. Repeat this process for all categories that should be included on your tax return.

Using the Tax Line Item Assignment Pane

The Tax Line Item Assignment pane offers a quick and easy way to set tax information for multiple categories, all in one place. Choose Tax | Tax Line Item Assignment. The Category List window appears, with the Tax Line Item Assignment pane showing in the bottom half of the window (see Figure 19-1). Use this area to assign tax line information to Quicken categories.

To assign a tax line item to a category, select the category in the top half of the window. Then use the Tax Item drop-down list to choose the form or schedule and line for the item. (You can expand this list by selecting the Extended List option.) A description of the tax line item you chose appears on the right side of the Tax Line Item Assignment pane. Click Apply. Repeat this process for all categories that should be included on your tax return.

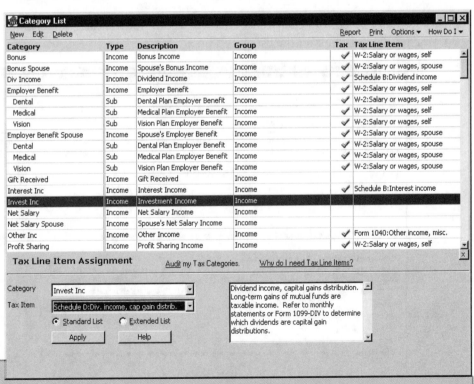

Figure 19-1 • The Tax Line Item Assignment pane appears in the bottom of the Category List window.

It is not necessary to match all categories—just the ones that should appear on your tax return. When you've finished, you can click the close button in the top-right corner of the Tax Line Item Assignment pane to dismiss it. The information is recorded for each category.

Auditing Your Tax Line Assignments

Quicken can "audit" the tax line information associated with categories and tell you where there may be problems with the assignments. This feature helps ensure that you have properly set up your categories to take advantage of Quicken's tax features.

Choose Tax | Tax Category Audit or click the Audit link in the Tax Line Item Assignment pane (refer to Figure 19-1). Quicken quickly reviews all your categories. If it finds potential problems, it displays them in the Tax Category Audit window (see Figure 19-2).

You have three choices for working with the items Quicken finds:

• To accept Quicken's suggested correction for the category, click the Change link on the category's line.

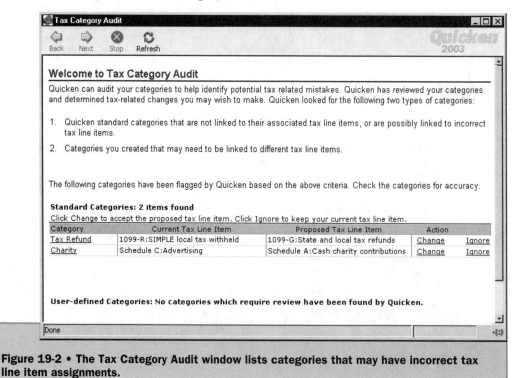

Figure 19-2 • The Tax Category Audit window lists categories that may have incorrect tax line item assignments.

- To ignore the possible problem, click the Ignore link on the category's line.
- To manually change the tax line assignment, click the category name link and make the desired changes in the Edit Selected Tax Audit Category dialog that appears. (This dialog looks and works just like the Edit Category dialog shown earlier in this chapter.)

If Quicken doesn't find any problems with your categories, it displays a dialog that tells you so.

Tax Reports

Quicken offers several different tax reports that can make tax time easier by providing the information you need to prepare your taxes. All of these reports are based on the tax information settings for the accounts and categories in your Quicken data file. You can learn more about Quicken's reporting feature in Chapter 14.

To create a report, select Reports | Tax and choose the name of the report from the submenu:

- **Capital Gains** summarizes gains and losses on the sales of investments, organized by the term of the investment (short or long) and the investment account.
- **Schedule A-Itemized Deductions** summarizes the itemized deductions that appear on Schedule A of a 1040 tax return.
- **Schedule B-Interest And Dividends** summarizes interest and dividends income that is reported on Schedule B of a 1040 tax return.
- **Schedule D-Capital Gains And Losses** summarizes the capital gains and losses from the sale of investments that is reported on Schedule D of a 1040 tax return.
- **Tax Schedule** summarizes tax-related transactions, organized by tax form or schedule and line item.
- **Tax Summary** summarizes tax-related transactions, organized by category and date.

Quicken Quick Tip

If you pay a tax preparation specialist, be sure to furnish him or her with accurate tax reports from Quicken. Doing so should save the preparer time and reduce your tax preparation bill.

Online Tax Tools

The Online Tax Tools submenu under the Tax menu offers access to a number of tax-related features on Quicken.com that can help you with your taxes. All you need to take advantage of these features is an Internet connection.

Here's a quick look at Quicken's tax tools. The next time you're thinking about taxes, be sure to check these out.

Tax Calculators   The Tax Calculators command displays the Tax Tools page on Quicken.com where you can find dozens of tools for making tax and other financial calculations. Just click a link on the page to work with the calculator.

Common Tax Questions   The Common Tax Questions command displays the Tax FAQs page on Quicken.com. This page lists dozens of tax-related questions, organized by topic. To get an answer to a question, click its link.

Tax Forms   The Tax Forms command displays the Tax Forms page on Quicken.com, which offers links to various categories of tax forms. Click a link to display additional information and links to forms. When you click a form link, Quicken downloads the form as an Acrobat PDF file that either appears in a Web browser window or in an Adobe Acrobat Reader window. (You must have the freely distributed Adobe Acrobat Reader software to open and use these forms.) Print the form to fill it out manually.

Federal Tax Publications   The Federal Tax Publications command displays the IRS Publications page on Quicken.com. This page is full of links to IRS publications available on the Web. You'll find these publications extremely helpful when trying to figure out tax laws—provided you can understand the publication!

TurboTax

If you're tired of paying a tax preparer to fill out your tax return for you, but you're not quite confident enough about your tax knowledge to manually prepare your own return, it's time to check out TurboTax tax preparation software. It's the best way to simplify tax preparation.

Intuit offers two versions of TurboTax for Windows PC users. You can learn more about both of them by choosing Tax | Quicken Services | TurboTax – Special Offers.

TurboTax Premier Software   TurboTax Premier is software that works seamlessly with Quicken to prepare your taxes. Just follow the instructions in this chapter to set up your accounts and categories with tax information. Then import your Quicken data into TurboTax. You can go through an easy interview process to make sure you haven't left anything out—much like the interview you might go through with a paid tax preparer. TurboTax calculates the bottom line and enables you to either print your returns or file them electronically.

TurboTax for the Web   TurboTax for the Web enables you to fill out your tax forms online, using the same kind of interview process you'd find in TurboTax Premier. When you're finished preparing your return, you can print out the forms or file electronically.

Quicken Quick Tip

I absolutely refuse to pay someone to prepare my taxes. After all, I have an accounting degree. I should use it for *something* other than writing Quicken books, shouldn't I? Unfortunately, about seven years ago, my tax situation—and the tax laws—started getting very complex. Neither my brain nor my calculator were able to come up with the answers I needed to get the job done right. So I gave TurboTax a try. It takes something that is incredibly difficult—tax preparation—and makes it relatively easy. If you're sick of dealing with tax preparers and tax returns, do yourself a favor and try TurboTax. My only regret is that I didn't start using it sooner.

Planning for Tax Time

In this Chapter:

- *Tax planning basics*

- *Tax Planner*

- *Tax Withholding Estimator*

- *Tax Center*

- *Deduction Finder*

- *Itemized Deduction Estimator*

- *Tax-Exempt Investment Yield Comparison*

Chapter 20

Surprises can make life interesting. But not all surprises are good ones. Consider the surprise you may get one April when your tax preparer announces that you'll have to write a rather large check to your Uncle Sam and his friends in your state revenue department.

Quicken's tax planning features, like the Tax Planner and Tax Withholding Estimator, can help you avoid nasty surprises. Other built-in tax tools, like the Deduction Finder, Itemized Deduction Estimator, and Tax-Exempt Investment Yield Comparison, can save you money and help you make smarter financial decisions. All these features can be found in the Tax Center, which is full of snapshots to help you monitor your tax situation. In this chapter, I tell you all about Quicken's tax planning and monitoring features.

Planning to Avoid Surprises

One of the best reasons to think about taxes before tax time is to avoid surprises on April 15. Knowing what you'll owe before you owe it can help ensure that you pay just the right amount of taxes up front—through proper deductions or estimated tax payments—so you don't get hit with a big tax bill or tax refund.

Quicken offers two built-in tax planning tools that you can use to keep track of your tax situation throughout the year. The Tax Planner helps you estimate your federal income tax bill for the 2002 and 2003 tax years. The Tax Withholding Estimator helps you determine whether your withholding taxes are correctly calculated. Finally, the Tax Center, summarizes your tax situation with a number of useful snapshots. Here's a closer look at each of these features.

Using the Tax Planner

Quicken's Tax Planner includes features from Intuit's TurboTax product to help you estimate your federal income tax bill for the 2002 and 2003 tax years. While this can help you avoid surprises, it can also help you see how various changes to income and expenses can affect your estimated tax bill.

Quicken Quick Tip

You may think of a big tax refund as a gift from Uncle Sam. Well, it isn't. It's your money that Uncle Sam has been using, interest free, for months. When you overpay your taxes, you're giving up money that you could be using to reduce interest-bearing debt or earn interest or investment income. Make sure you don't overpay taxes throughout the year so you can keep your money where it'll do you the most good.

Opening the Quicken Tax Planner Window

To open the Tax Planner, choose Tax | Tax Planner. The first time you open the Tax Planner, it may display a dialog that offers to import TurboTax data into Quicken for tax planning purposes. If you click Yes, follow the instructions that appear on screen to complete the import. If you click No, or when the import process is complete, the Tax Planner Summary screen for the Projected scenario appears (see Figure 20-1).

Entering Tax Planner Data

Data can be entered into the Tax Planner from three different sources:

- **TurboTax** data can be imported into Quicken. Choose File | Import | TurboTax. Then use the dialog that appears to locate and import your TurboTax data. This information can be used to project current year amounts in the Tax Planner.

Figure 20-1 • **The Tax Planner Summary screen displays a summary of all information stored in the Tax Planner.**

- **User Entered** data can override any automatic entries. Use this to enter data that isn't entered any other way or has not yet been entered into Quicken—such as expected year-end bonuses or tax-deductible expenses.
- **Quicken Data** can be automatically entered into the Tax Planner. This works only if you have properly set up your tax-related Quicken categories with appropriate tax return line items as discussed earlier in this chapter.

Here's how it works. Click a link in the navigation bar on the left side of the Tax Planner window or in the Tax Planner Summary screen (refer to Figure 20-1) to view a specific type of income or expense. Then click a link within the window for a specific item. Details for the item appear in the bottom of the window, as shown in Figure 20-2. (You may have to click the Show Details link to expand the window and show the details.) If desired, change the source option and, if necessary, enter an amount.

The options you can choose from vary depending on whether TurboTax data is available or the item has transactions recorded in Quicken. For example, in Figure 20-2, TurboTax data is not available, but transactions have been entered in Quicken. You can either select the User Entered option and enter a value in the Annual Total column or select the Quicken Data option and enter an adjusting value in the Adjustment column. This makes it easy to manually override any automatic source entries.

Repeat this process for any Tax Planner items you want to check or change. The tax planner automatically recalculates the impact of your changes.

To quickly reset values to amounts automatically entered by Quicken, choose Reset To Quicken Default Values from the Reset menu on the Tax Planner's button bar.

Using Scenarios

The scenarios feature of the Tax Planner enables you to enter data for multiple scenarios—a "what if" capability that you can use to see tax impacts based on various changes in entry data. For example, suppose you're planning to get married and want to see the impact of the additional income and deductions related to your new spouse. You can use a scenario to see the tax impact without changing your Projected scenario.

To use this feature, click the Scenario link in the navigation bar on the left side of the Tax Planner window (refer to Figure 20-1 or 20-2). The Tax Planner Options screen, which is shown next, appears. Choose a different scenario from

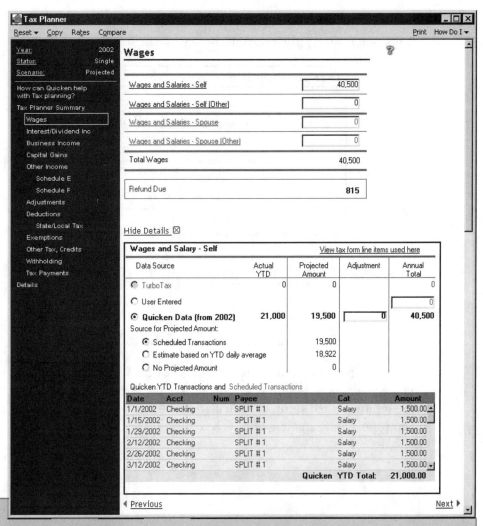

Figure 20-2 • You can enter additional information into the Tax Planner.

the Scenarios drop-down list. If Quicken asks whether you want to copy the current scenario to the scenario you chose, click Yes if that other scenario hasn't been set up yet. Choose options from the Tax Year and Filing Status drop-down list to set the scenario options. Then click the Next link in the bottom of the window to return to the Tax Planner Summary window. If necessary, change the values in the new scenario.

```
Tax Planner Options                                          ?

Select the Tax Year, Filing Status and Scenario you'd like to use:


              Tax Year:  |2002                        |▼|
         Filing Status:  |Married Filing Jointly       |▼|
             Scenarios:  |1                           |▼|


Note:  When changing options above, be sure to select the
Scenario first before changing the Year or Filing Status. Check
your settings for the open Scenario in the upper left navigation
bar.

Next ▶
```

To compare one scenario to another, click the Compare button in the Tax Planner window's button bar. A dialog like the one shown next appears, showing the results of each scenario's calculations. When you're finished viewing the comparative information, click OK to dismiss the dialog.

Tax Scenario Comparisons								☒
	Projected		Scenario 1		Scenario 2		Scenario 3	
Filing Status		Single		Married-Joint		Married-Sep		Single
Tax Year		2002		2002		2002		2002
Adjusted Gross Income		68,140		128,140		68,140		0
Deductions and Exemptions		12,636		19,851		12,636		0
Taxable Income		55,503		108,288		55,503		0
Total Tax		14,607		26,309		15,159		0
Marginal, Avg. Tax Rates	27.0%	21.4%	27.0%	20.5%	27.0%	22.2%	0.0%	0.0%

OK   Help

Finishing Up

When you're finished using the Tax Planner, click the close button on the button bar or switch to another window. This saves the information you entered and updates the Projected Tax calculations in the Tax Center. (I tell you about the Tax Center window later in this chapter.)

Tax Withholding Estimator

Quicken's Tax Withholding Estimator feature helps you determine whether your W-4 form has been correctly completed. It does this by comparing your estimated tax bill from the Tax Planner to the amount of withholding tax deducted from your paychecks.

Using the Tax Withholding Estimator Feature

To get started, choose Tax | Tax Withholding Estimator. The Am I Under Or Over Withholding? window appears, as shown in Figure 20-3.

Read the information and follow the instructions in the middle column of the window. You'll be prompted to enter information related to withholding taxes. The instructions are very clear and easy to follow, so I won't repeat them here. Each time you enter data and click the Adjust Tax Projection button, the Projected Refund Due or Projected Tax Due amount in the lower-right corner of the window changes. Your goal is to get the amount as close to zero as possible, which you can do by adjusting the number of W-4 allowances and additional withholding per pay period.

Figure 20-3 • Use the Tax Withholding Estimator to determine whether your federal withholding taxes are correct.

None of the entries you make in the Tax Withholding Estimator feature will affect your Quicken data or any other tax planning feature within Quicken, so don't be afraid to experiment.

Acting on the Results of Tax Withholding Estimator Calculations

What do you do with this information once you have it? Well, suppose your work with the Tax Withholding Estimator feature tells you that you should change your W-4 allowances from 2 to 3 to avoid overpaying federal withholding taxes. You can act on this information by completing a new W-4 form at work. This will decrease the amount of withholding tax in each paycheck. The result is that you reduce your tax overpayment and potential refund.

The Tax Center

Quicken summarizes all information about your tax situation in the Tax Center (see Figure 20-4). Here's a quick look at what you can find in the Tax Center window.

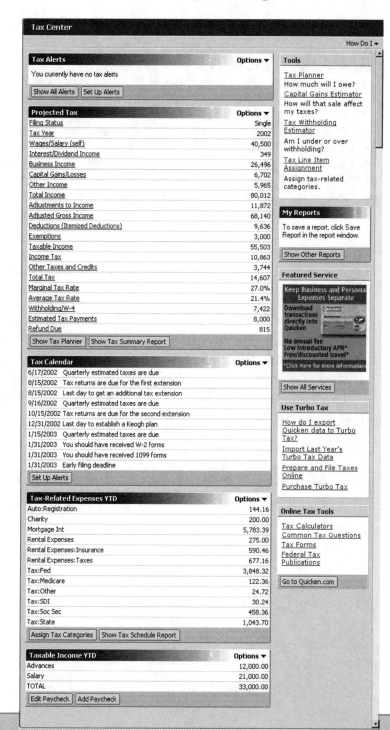

Figure 20-4 • The Tax Center window is full of snapshots of your tax situation.

Quicken Quick Tip

In my discussion of the Tax Withholding Estimator, I tell you that your goal is to get the Projected Tax Due amount as close to zero as possible. A *Quicken 2002: The Official Guide* reader had a problem with that. He pointed out that your goal should be to pay as little taxes as possible throughout the year without getting an underpayment penalty on April 15. His logic is to hold on to your money as long as you can. While his strategy is good and legal— remember, if there's no penalty, you couldn't have done anything wrong—I personally don't like to write a check on April 15. So I aim for zero. It's your choice.

Tax Alerts

The Tax Alerts snapshot displays alerts related to your tax situation. Quicken offers three tax alerts:

- **Over/Under Withholding** enables you to set a threshold value to alert you if your payroll withholding is too much or not enough.
- **Itemized Deductions** (Schedule A Reminder) displays information about the types of personal deductions you can claim on Schedule A of your tax return.
- **Important Tax Dates** notifies you in advance of tax calendar events, such as estimated tax due dates and extension deadlines.

To set tax alerts, click the Set Up Alerts button at the bottom of the Tax Alerts snapshot. Then use the Setup tab of the Alerts Center window that appears (shown next) to set alert options. I tell you more about setting alerts in Chapter 9.

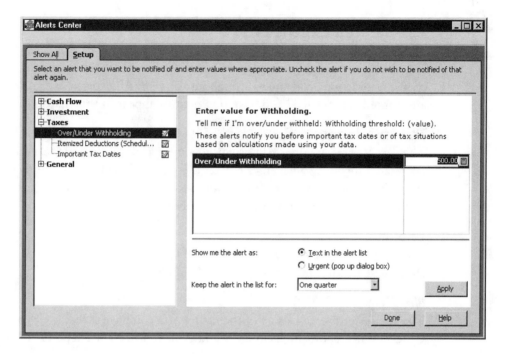

Projected Tax

The Projected Tax snapshot provides a summary of your upcoming projected tax return, including the amount you'll have to pay or get back as a refund. The information in this snapshot is based on the Tax Planner's Projected scenario. I discuss the Tax Planner earlier in this chapter.

Tax Calendar

The Tax Calendar lists recent and upcoming events on the IRS tax calendar. You can use the Options menu to set up alerts or visit an online tax calendar.

Quicken Quick Tip

It's a good idea to use the Tax Withholding Estimator feature periodically to make sure actual amounts are in line with projections throughout the year. (I recommend using it once every three months or so.) Whenever possible, use actual values rather than estimates in your calculations. And be sure to act on the results of the calculations by filing a new W-4 form, especially if the amount of your Projected Refund Due or Projected Tax Due is greater than a few hundred dollars.

Tax-Related Expenses YTD

The Tax-Related Expenses YTD snapshot summarizes all of your year-to-date tax-related expenses. Quicken automatically calculates this information based on the transactions you enter throughout the year. All expense categories that are marked "tax-related" and have transactions appear in this snapshot.

Taxable Income YTD

The Tax-Related Income YTD snapshot summarizes all of your year-to-date tax-related income. Quicken calculates these totals based on the transactions you enter throughout the year. All income categories that are marked "tax-related" and have transactions appear in this snapshot.

Tools

The Tools area offers links to a number of Quicken tax-related features. I discuss all of these features in this chapter and Chapter 19.

My Reports

The My Reports area lists all of the tax reports you have saved. I tell you about Quicken's tax reports in Chapter 19 and explain how to save reports in Chapter 9.

Featured Service

The Featured Service area is an advertisement for one of Quicken's services. The Featured Service changes each time you open the Tax Center, so it may appear different when you view it.

Use TurboTax

The Use TurboTax area provides links for working with TurboTax tax preparation software. I tell you a little about TurboTax in Chapter 19.

Online Tax Tools

Online Tax Tools provides links to tax tools on Quicken.com. I discuss the online tax tools in Chapter 19.

Minimizing Taxes by Maximizing Deductions

One way to minimize taxes is to maximize your deductions. While Quicken can't help you spend money on tax-deductible items—that's up to you—it can help you identify expenses that may be tax deductible, so you don't forget to include them on your tax returns.

Quicken offers two features to help maximize your deductions. Deduction Finder asks you questions about expenditures to determine whether they may be tax deductible. Itemized Deduction Estimator helps make sure you don't forget about commonly overlooked itemized deductions.

Deduction Finder

The Deduction Finder uses another TurboTax feature to help you learn which expenses are deductible. Its question-and-answer interface gathers information from you and then provides information about the deductibility of items based on your answers.

Working with the Deduction Finder Window

To open the Deduction Finder, choose Tax | Deduction Finder. An Introduction dialog may appear. Read its contents to learn more about Deduction Finder and then click OK. Figure 20-5 shows what the Deductions tab of the Deduction

Figure 20-5 • The Deduction Finder helps you identify expenses that may be tax deductible.

Finder window says about the Godiva chocolates I sent my editors for the holidays last year.

You can use button bar options to work with the Deduction Finder window:

- **See Introduction** displays the Introduction window, so you can learn more about how Deduction Finder works.
- **Clear Checkmarks** removes the check marks from items for which you have already answered questions.
- **Print** prints a summary of deduction information about all the deductions for which you have answered questions.
- **How Do I** provides instructions for completing tasks within the Deduction Finder window.

Finding Deductions

As you can see in Figure 20-5, the Deductions tab of the Deduction Finder window uses clearly numbered steps to walk you through the process of selecting deduction types and deductions and then answering questions. It's easy to use. You don't have to answer questions about all the deductions—only the deductions you think may apply to you. When you've finished answering questions about a deduction, the result appears near the bottom of the window. You can then move on to another deduction.

The Summary tab of the window, shown next, summarizes the number of deductions available in each category, the number for which you answered questions, and the number for which you may be eligible to take deductions based on your answers to the questions.

Deductions	Summary	Action Plan			
Deduction types			**# Available**	**# Answered**	**# Eligible**
Employee type			28	0	0
Homeowner type			5	2	2
Individual type			23	7	5
Investor type			7	2	2
Medical type			11	3	3
Self-Employed type			33	10	9

When you've finished answering questions, you can click the Action Plan tab to get more information about the deductions and the things you need to do to claim them. Although you can read the Action Plan information onscreen, if you answered many questions, you may want to use the Print button on the button bar to print the information for reference.

Itemized Deduction Estimator

The Itemized Deduction Estimator feature helps make sure you don't overlook any itemized deductions—the deductions on Schedule A of your tax return—that you might qualify for. It does this by guiding you through a review of deduction ideas and providing the information you need to know whether you may qualify.

To get started, choose Tax | Itemized Deduction Estimator. The How Can I Maximize My Deductions? window appears, as shown in Figure 20-6.

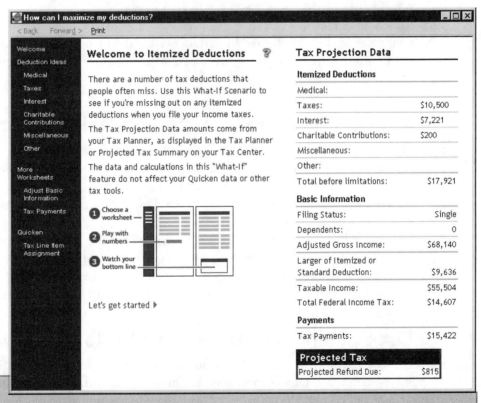

Figure 20-6 • With the Itemized Deduction Estimator feature, you won't miss out on any Schedule A deductions.

Read the information and follow the instructions in the middle column of the window. You'll be prompted to enter information related to itemized deductions for medical expenses, taxes paid, interest paid, charitable contributions, and other items. The instructions are clear and easy to follow. Each time you enter information and click the Calculate Total button, the Projected Refund Due or Projected Tax Due amount in the lower-right corner of the window changes. Your goal is to get a Projected Refund Due amount as high as possible or a Projected Tax Due amount as low as possible.

Again, none of the entries you make in the Itemized Deduction Estimator feature will affect your Quicken data or any other tax planning feature within Quicken. Experiment as much as you like.

Making Smart Decisions

Your taxes can also be affected by certain taxable transactions, such as the sale of securities or the income you earn on your investments. Quicken offers several tools to show you the tax impact of these events:

Buy/Sell Preview and Capital Gains Estimator

The Buy/Sell Preview and Capital Gains Estimator help you determine which investment to sell based on capital gains tax rules. You enter information about a proposed security sale or your goal for selling a security, and Quicken calculates the tax impact or recommends specific sales. Using these features can minimize your capital gains taxes.

Buy/Sell Preview is available only in Quicken Premier. Although the Capital Gains Estimator is available in both Quicken Premier and Deluxe, the Premier version offers optimization features not available in the Deluxe version. I explain how to use the Buy/Sell Preview and Capital Gains Estimator in Chapter 12.

Tax-Exempt Investment Yield Comparison

The Tax-Exempt Investment Yield Comparison shows you the post-tax earnings of tax-exempt and taxable investments. This can help you understand how your tax rate and investment return rates work together to influence your return on investment.

To access this feature, choose Tax | Tax-Exempt Investment Yield Comparison. The Tax-Exempt Investment Equivalent Yield dialog, illustrated next, appears.

To use it, find the yield of a tax-exempt investment in the leftmost column. Then move across the row to the column for your tax bracket. The rate there is the equivalent rate for a taxable investment—the rate a taxable investment must beat to earn more than the tax-exempt investment.

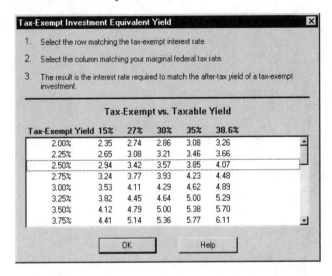

For example, if I have a tax-exempt investment earning 2.5 percent and I'm in the 30 percent tax bracket, a taxable investment must earn more than 3.57 percent to be better than the tax-exempt investment.

Appendixes

This part of the book provides some additional information you may find helpful when using Quicken. These two appendixes explain how to work with Quicken data files and how to customize Quicken.

Part Seven

Managing Quicken Files

In this Appendix:

- *Creating and opening data files*

- *Backing up and restoring data files*

- *Importing and exporting data*

- *Performing other file management tasks*

- *Password-protecting Quicken data*

All the data you enter in Quicken is stored in a Quicken data file. This file includes all account and category setup information, transactions, and other data you have entered into Quicken.

Technically speaking, your Quicken data file really consists of a number of files with the same name and different extensions. Manipulating these files without using Quicken's built-in file management tools can cause errors.

Commands under Quicken's File menu enable you to perform a number of file management tasks, including creating, opening, backing up, restoring, importing, exporting, renaming, deleting, and password-protecting data files. In this appendix, I cover all of these tasks.

Working with Multiple Data Files

Chances are, you won't need more than one Quicken data file—the one that's created as part of the Quicken Guided Setup process covered in Chapter 2. But, just in case you do, here's how you can create and open another one.

Creating a Data File

Start by choosing File | New. A dialog appears, asking whether you want to create a new Quicken file or a new Quicken account. (Some users confuse the two and try to use the File menu's New command to create a new account. I tell you the correct way to create an account in Chapters 2 and 3.) Select New Quicken File and click OK.

A Create Quicken File dialog like the one shown next appears. Use it to enter a name for the data file. Although you can also change the default directory location, it's easier to find the data file if it's in the C:\Program Files\QUICKENW\ subdirectory with other Quicken data files. Click OK.

Quicken Guided Setup appears next. It walks you through the process of specifying information about yourself and your financial goals so Quicken can help you set up the correct categories and accounts for your financial management needs. I explain how to use Quicken Guided Setup in Chapter 2; turn to that chapter if you need assistance working with it.

Opening a Different Data File

If you have more than one Quicken data file, it's important that you enter transactions into the right one. You can see which data file is currently open by looking at the file name in the application window's title bar:

To open a different data file, choose File | Open, or press CTRL-O, and use the standard Open dialog that appears to select and open a different file. Only one Quicken data file can be open at a time.

Backing Up Your Quicken Data File

Imagine this: you set up Quicken to track all of your finances, and you record transactions regularly so the Quicken data file is always up to date. Then one evening, when you start your computer to surf the Net, you find that your hard drive has died. Not only have your plans for the evening been ruined, but your Quicken data file is also a casualty of your hard drive's untimely death.

If you back up your Quicken data as regularly as you update its information, the loss of your Quicken data file would be a minor inconvenience, rather than a catastrophe. In this section, I explain how to back up your Quicken data file and how to restore it if the original file is lost or damaged.

Backing Up to Disk

Quicken makes it very difficult to forget backing up. Every third time you exit the Quicken program, it displays the Automatic Backup dialog shown next, which prompts you to back up your data file. Click the Backup button to display the Quicken Backup dialog.

You can also begin the backup process by choosing File | Backup or pressing CTRL-B at any time while using Quicken. This displays the Quicken Backup dialog, which is shown next.

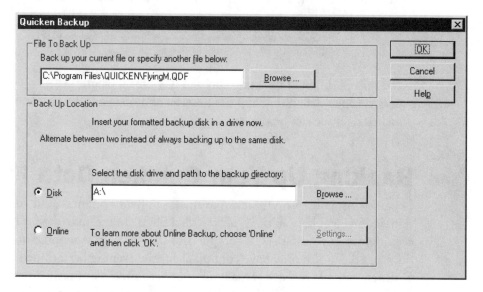

Begin by specifying which Quicken data file you want to back up. Quicken assumes you want to back up the currently open file and displays its pathname in the File To Back Up area. But you can click the Browse button and use the dialog that appears to select another data file.

Next, select one of the Back Up Location options:

- **Disk** enables you to back up to another disk, either on your computer or one that's accessible via a network. If you select this option, you can use the Browse button to locate and select a backup disk and directory. As the dialog recommends, it's a good idea to alternate between two disks for backup purposes. This means you'll always have two versions backed up, in case one version is bad. It's a good idea to choose a backup location other than your hard disk, such as a floppy disk (for small data files), Zip disk, or Jaz disk. (Backing up to your hard disk defeats the purpose of backing up!) These instructions assume you have selected Disk.

- **Online** enables you to back up to a server on the Internet, using Quicken's Online Backup service, which is available for a nominal fee. You can learn more about this service by selecting Online and then clicking OK to display the Quicken Services window for the Quicken Online Backup service.

After selecting Disk and indicating a backup directory in the Quicken Backup dialog, click OK. If you are backing up the currently open Quicken data file, it disappears and a small gray window appears, telling you that Quicken is backing up your data. When the backup is complete, the data file's windows reappear and a dialog informs you that the file was backed up successfully. Click OK.

If your Quicken data file is too large to fit on the disk you indicated in the Quicken Backup dialog, Quicken will prompt you to insert additional formatted disks until the backup is complete. Follow the instructions that appear onscreen to complete the backup.

Restoring

In the event of loss or damage to your data file, you can restore from backup. Start Quicken and then choose File | Restore Backup File. The Select Restore Drive dialog, which is shown next, appears:

Select Restore Drive

Please insert your disk containing previously backed up Quicken data in a drive now. Then select the letter of the drive.

Restore files from Drive: A:

OK
Cancel
Help

Choose the drive designation letter for the drive containing the backup files from the drop-down list and click OK. The Restore Quicken File dialog appears next:

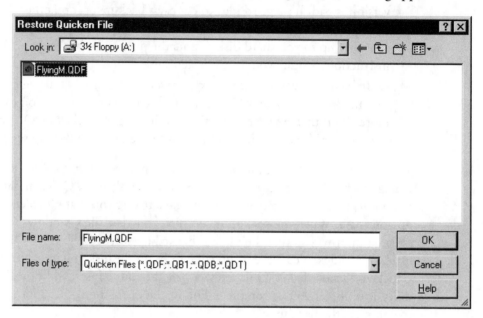

Use this dialog to locate and select the data file that you want to restore. Then click OK. One of two things may happen:

- If the file has the same name as the Quicken data file currently in use, a dialog appears, asking if you want to overwrite the file in use. To replace the current file with the backup copy, click OK.
- If the file has the same name as another Quicken data file in the QUICKEN directory on your hard disk, a dialog appears, warning you that you will overwrite the existing file. If you're sure you want to restore the backup and overwrite the existing file with the same name, click OK.

Quicken restores the file from the backup copy. It places a copy of the restored file in the QUICKEN directory on your hard disk, displaying a status window as it works. When it has finished, it displays a dialog telling you that the file has been restored successfully. Click OK.

Moving a Quicken Data File Between Two Computers

Intuit's Technical Support staff is often asked how to move a Quicken data file from one computer to another. In fact, this question is so common that Intuit asked me to address it in this book.

The best way to move a data file from one computer to another is with the Backup and Restore Backup File commands. Begin by opening the file with Quicken on the computer on which it resides. Then follow the instructions in this appendix to back up the file to removable media, such as a floppy disk, Zip or Jaz disk, or CD-ROM disc, or a network drive (preferably one that the other computer is connected to). Then fire up Quicken on the other computer and follow the restoring instructions in this appendix to restore the backup copy. When you're finished, the Quicken data file is ready to use on the new computer.

It's important to remember that once you begin making changes to the file on the new computer, the file on the old computer will no longer be up-to-date. That means that if you want to use the file on the old computer again, you need to complete the backup and restore process to move the file back to that computer. As you can imagine, if you often move the file from one computer to another and back, it can be difficult to keep track of which version of the file is the most up-to-date.

Although you can make your Quicken data file "portable" by keeping it on removable media so you can access it from any computer, neither Intuit nor I recommend doing so. Removable media is more susceptible to data loss and damage than an internal or networked hard disk. Quicken users have reported numerous problems using this technique; don't add your own problems to the list.

Importing and Exporting Data

Quicken supports its QIF format for importing data from other versions of Quicken to Quicken 2003, or for exporting Quicken 2003 for Windows data for use with other versions of Quicken.

Importing .QIF File Data

You can import data saved in Quicken QIF format into Quicken 2003 for Windows. You might find this useful when converting Quicken for Macintosh or QuickBooks files to Quicken format. Simply use the program's Export command to create the QIF format file. Then import the data into Quicken.

Before you import a QIF format file into your Quicken data file, back up the data file. Remember, Quicken automatically saves all changes to a data file. If something goes wrong with the import, your original data file could be damaged or could contain some incorrect transactions. I explain how to back up a data file in the section "Backing Up Your Quicken Data File" earlier in this appendix.

To import a QIF format file, choose File | Import | QIF File. The QIF Import dialog appears. Click the Browse button to display the Import From QIF File dialog, which is shown next. Use it to locate and select the QIF format file you want to import.

Click OK to go back to the QIF Import dialog, which is shown next. Choose All Accounts or a specific account from the drop-down list. Then turn on check boxes for the items you want to include in the import. If you are importing into a brand-new Quicken file that does not include any accounts or categories, be sure to turn on the Account List, Category List, and Security List check boxes. When you have finished, click OK to begin the import.

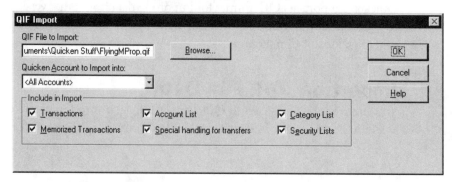

As Quicken imports data, it may display dialogs asking if you want to create and import data for specific accounts and categories. Click Yes to have Quicken create categories and classes as necessary. Quicken displays a status dialog as it imports the transactions. Another dialog tells you when the import is finished. Click OK.

Open the account register for one of the accounts that data has been imported into. The window appears with a split, as shown in Figure A-1. Imported transactions involving a transfer account are automatically entered into the account register, as shown in the top half of the window. Transactions involving a category are not entered into the register and appear in the bottom half of the window. Adding imported transactions in the bottom half of the window to the account register is just like adding downloaded transactions to your Quicken data file; you can learn how in Chapter 6. Be sure to do this for each account into which data was imported.

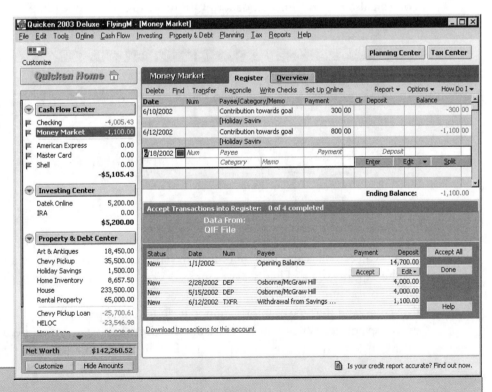

Figure A-1 • Imported items may appear in the bottom half of the account register window

Importing Other Data

Quicken 2003 can automatically open files created with most versions of Quicken for Windows (.QDF extension) and Quicken for DOS (.QDF extension). In most cases, you don't need to use the Import command for these files; use the Open command instead. Additional converters and conversion instructions are available on the Quicken technical support Web site (http://www.intuit.com/support/quicken/). That's also where you can find a wealth of troubleshooting and advanced how-to information, including specific instructions for converting Microsoft Money and Quicken for Macintosh data files.

The Import submenu under the File menu also offers options for importing TurboTax files and WebConnect files. I tell you about TurboTax in Chapter 19 and about WebConnect in Chapter 6.

Exporting Quicken Data to a .QIF File

You can also export Quicken data to QIF format. Choose File | Export | QIF File to display the QIF Export dialog, which is shown next:

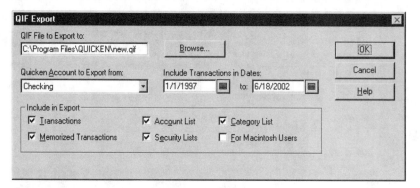

Start by entering a pathname for the QIF file you want to export to. If you prefer, you can click the Browse button to select a directory and enter a file name for the exported data. Then set options as desired for the export, including the Quicken account to export from (a specific account or all accounts), the transaction date range, and the type of information to include. Each option changes the amount of data exported. When you have the options set the way you want them, click OK. Quicken exports the data, creating a file with the name you specified.

Exporting Quicken Data to Other Formats

You can also use options in the Print dialog to save report data as a file on disk. The file can then be imported into other applications such as word processors, spreadsheets, or databases. I explain how to use the Print command to save data to a file in Chapter 9.

Other File Management Tasks

The File Operations submenu under Quicken's File menu enables you to perform several other tasks with Quicken data files. Here's a quick summary of each command, with tips for when you may find them useful.

Copying the Current Data File

The Copy command enables you to copy the current data file to a different disk or save a copy with a different name. When you choose File | File Operations | Copy, the Copy File dialog, shown next, appears. Use it to enter a pathname for the copy and specify which transactions should be included. Click OK to make the copy.

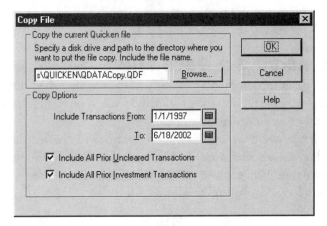

When the copy is finished, a dialog asks if you want to continue working with the original data file or the new copy. Select the appropriate option and click OK to continue working with Quicken.

Deleting a Data File

The Delete command enables you to delete a data file. When you choose File |
File Operations | Delete, the Delete Quicken File dialog, which is shown next,
appears. Use it to locate and select the data file you want to delete.

When you click OK, another dialog appears, asking you to confirm that you
want to delete the file. You must type in **Yes** to delete the file.

Remember, deleting a Quicken data file permanently deletes all of its data.
Use this command with care!

Renaming a Data File

The Rename command enables you to rename a data file. This is the best way to
rename a data file and the only method you should use. Renaming files in Windows
could cause information to be lost.

When you choose File | File Operations | Rename, the Rename Quicken File
dialog, shown next, appears. Use it to select the file you want to rename and enter a
new name. When you click OK, Quicken changes the name of the main data file
you selected and all of its support files.

Checking the Integrity of a Data File

The Validate command enables you to check the integrity of a Quicken data file. This command is particularly useful if you believe that a file has been damaged.

When you choose File | File Operations | Validate, the Validate Quicken File dialog appears. It looks very much like the Delete Quicken File dialog, illustrated earlier in this chapter. Use it to locate and select the file you want to validate. When you click OK, Quicken checks the data file's integrity.

If the file has a problem, Quicken displays one of these dialogs:

If the file does not appear to have any problems, Quicken displays this dialog:

Sometimes you can repair a damaged file by simply opening it in Quicken. Use the Open command as discussed near the beginning of the chapter. If Quicken can't open the file, it tells you. That's when it's time to reach for that backup file. You *did* make one recently, didn't you?

Making a Year-End Copy of a Data File

The Year-End Copy command enables you to create two different types of file copies suitable for year-end data storage: Archive and Start New Year. When you choose File | File Operations | Year-End Copy, the Year-End Copy dialog, which is shown next, appears. Select a Year-End Action and click OK.

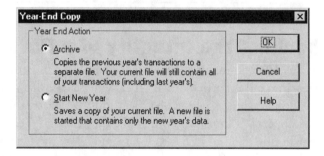

Creating an Archive

An *archive* is a copy of the previous year's transactions saved in a separate file. All transactions remain in the current file. Use this if you want a separate record of a year's transactions, but you want to continue working with the data in your current data file.

When you select this option, the Archive File dialog shown next appears:

If necessary, use the Browse button to enter the pathname for the archive file. Then enter the ending date for the transactions to include and click OK. Quicken creates the archive file as specified. When it has finished, it displays a dialog that enables you to select the file you want to work with: the Current file or the Archive file. Select the appropriate option and click OK to continue working with Quicken.

Creating a New Year File

The Start New Year option in the Year-End File dialog saves a copy of the current file and then creates a new file with just the transactions from the current year. Use this if you want to keep your current file small.

When you select this option, the Start New Year dialog shown next appears:

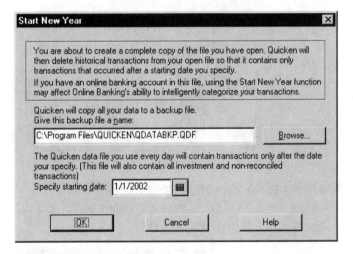

If necessary, use the Browse button to enter a pathname for the current file's backup. Then enter the starting date for the file you want to create and click OK. Quicken copies the current file and saves it with the name you specified. It then deletes all prior year transactions and saves the file as the current file. When it's finished, it displays a dialog that enables you to select the file you want to work with: the old file or the file for the new year. Select the option for the file you want and click OK to continue working with Quicken.

Password-Protecting Quicken Data

Quicken offers two types of password protection for your data: file passwords and transaction passwords. In this section, I tell you how these options work.

Protecting a Data File

When you password-protect a data file, the file cannot be opened without the password. This is the ultimate in protection—it prevents unauthorized users from even seeing your data.

Setting Up the Password

Choose File | Passwords | File to display the Quicken File Password dialog, which is illustrated next. Enter the same password in each text box and click OK.

Opening a Password-Protected Data File

When you open a data file that is password-protected, the Quicken Password dialog, which is shown next, appears:

You must correctly enter your password and then click OK to open the file.

Changing or Removing a Password

Choose File | Passwords | File to display the Quicken File Password dialog, which is illustrated next. Enter the current password in the Old Password box, then enter the same new password in the two boxes beneath it. (To remove a password, leave the two bottom boxes empty.) Click OK.

Protecting Existing Transactions

When you password-protect existing transactions, the transactions cannot be modified unless the password is properly entered. This prevents unauthorized or accidental alterations to data.

Setting Up the Password

Choose File | Passwords | Transaction to display the Password To Modify Existing Transactions dialog, shown next. Enter the same password in the top two text boxes. Then enter a date before which the transactions cannot be modified and click OK.

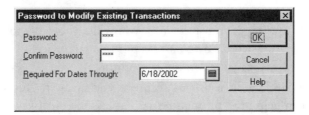

Modifying a Password-Protected Transaction

When you attempt to modify a transaction that is protected with a password, the Quicken Password dialog, shown next, appears. You must correctly enter your password and then click OK to modify the transaction.

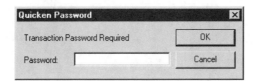

Changing or Removing a Password

Choose File | Passwords | Transaction to display the Change Transaction Password dialog, which is illustrated next. Enter the current password in the Old Password box, then enter the same new password in the two boxes beneath it. (To remove a password, leave the two bottom boxes empty.) Click OK.

Password Tips

Here are a few things to keep in mind when working with passwords:

- Passwords can be up to 16 characters in length and can contain any character, including a space.
- Passwords are case sensitive. That means, for example, that *PassWord* is not the same as *password*.
- If you forget your password, you will not be able to access the data file. Write your password down and keep it in a safe place—but not on a sticky note attached to your computer monitor.
- Your data file is only as secure as you make it. Quicken's password protection can help prevent unauthorized access to your Quicken data files.

Customizing Quicken

In this Appendix:

- *Customizing the Quicken Home window*

- *Customizing the toolbar*

- *Setting Quicken preferences*

Once you've worked with Quicken for a while, you may want to fine-tune the way it looks and works to best suit your needs. Some customization options—like selecting securities for online quotes and selecting accounts to synchronize with Quicken.com—are an integral part of using Quicken. Most of these options are discussed elsewhere in this book. Other customization options—like customizing the toolbar and setting Web Connect—are less commonly used. In this appendix, I explain all the customization options available for Quicken and provide cross-references to other chapters in the book where you can learn more about the features they work with.

Customizing Quicken's Interface

Quicken offers a number of ways to customize its interface to best meet your needs. In this part of the chapter, I explain how to customize the Quicken Home window and toolbar.

Customizing the Quicken Home Window

As discussed in Chapter 1, the Quicken Home window is the first thing that appears when you start Quicken. It displays a number of snapshots full of information about your finances and links to Quicken features.

Although you cannot customize the default Quicken Home window, you can create new views of the window and customize them. This makes it possible to include only the information you think is important in the window.

Creating a New View

By creating multiple views, you can make several versions of the Quicken Home window, each with a specific set of information. You can then switch from one view to another to quickly see the information you want.

In the Quicken Home window, choose Create A New View from the Customize menu on the button bar. The Customize View dialog appears:

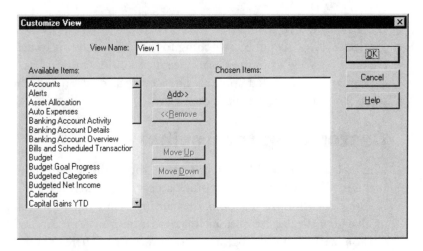

Enter a name for the view in the View Name box. Then follow the instructions in the next section to add items to the view and click OK. The new Quicken Home window view is created to your specifications and appears onscreen.

Modifying the Current View

You can modify the current view with the Customize View dialog, shown previously. If it's not showing, choose Customize This View from the Customize menu on the button bar. Make changes as desired and click OK to save them.

Adding an Item   To add an item to the view, select it in the Available Items list and click Add. Its name appears in the Chosen Items list. You can include up to 16 items in the Quicken Home window.

Removing an Item   To remove an item from the view, select it in the Chosen Items list and click Remove.

Rearranging Items   To rearrange the order of items in the Chosen Items list, select an item and click Move Up or Move Down. Repeat this process until the items appear in the order you want.

Switching from One View to Another

If you have created more than one view for the Quicken Home window, each view has its own tab at the top of the Quicken Home window, as shown next. To switch from one view to another, simply click its tab.

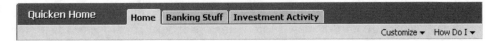

Deleting a View

To delete a view, begin by switching to the view you want to delete. Then choose Delete This View from the Customize menu on the button bar. Click OK in the confirmation dialog that appears. The view is deleted, and another view takes its place. You cannot delete the Home view.

Customizing the Toolbar

The toolbar is a row of buttons along the top of the screen, right beneath the menu bar. These buttons offer quick access to Quicken features.

You can customize the toolbar by adding, removing, or rearranging buttons, or changing the display options for toolbar buttons. You can do all this with the Customize Tool Bar dialog, which is shown next. There are two ways to open this dialog: click the Customize button on the toolbar (if you haven't already removed it), or choose Edit | Customize Tool Bar.

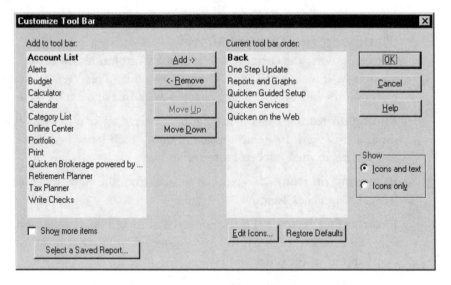

To customize the toolbar, make changes in this dialog and click OK. The toolbar is redrawn to your specifications.

Adding Buttons

To add a button, select it in the Add To Tool Bar list and click Add. Its name appears in the Current Tool Bar Order list. If you want more items to choose from, turn on the Show More Items check box. The list expands to show at least five times as many items. (Sorry, but I'm too lazy to count them!)

In Quicken 2003, you can include buttons for your saved reports in the toolbar. Click the Select A Saved Report button to display the Select A Saved Report dialog. Choose a report from the drop-down list and click OK. The report name is added to the Current Tool Bar Order list.

You can include as many buttons as you like on the toolbar. If the toolbar includes more buttons than can fit within the Quicken application window, a More button appears on the toolbar. Click this button to display a menu of buttons; choose the name of the button you want.

Removing Buttons

To remove a button, select it in the Current Tool Bar Order list and click Remove. Its name is removed from the Current Tool Bar Order list.

Rearranging Buttons

You can rearrange the order of buttons in the toolbar by changing their order in the Current Tool Bar Order list. Simply select a button that you want to move and click Move Up or Move Down to change its position in the list.

Changing the Appearance of Buttons

There are two Show options that determine how toolbar buttons are displayed:

- **Icons And Text** displays both the toolbar button and its label.
- **Icons Only** displays just the toolbar icon. When you point to an icon, its label appears.

Editing Buttons

You can modify a button to change its label and assign a keyboard shortcut. Click the Edit Icons button to display the Edit Tool Bar Button dialog. Then change the label or shortcut key for the toolbar button's command. Click OK to save your change. The label change does not appear in the Current Tool Bar Order list, but it does appear on the toolbar when you save your customization settings.

Quicken Quick Tip

You can use this feature to assign shortcuts to commands you use most. Just enter a letter key in the Shortcut box and click OK. After saving your customization settings, you will be able to access that Quicken command by pressing ALT-SHIFT and the letter you specified. This is a great way to make the Quicken commands you use most even quicker and easier to access.

Restoring the Default Toolbar

To restore the toolbar back to its "factory settings," click the Restore Default button in the Customize Toolbar dialog. Then click OK in the confirmation dialog that appears. The buttons return to the way they appear throughout this book.

Setting Preferences

The Preferences submenu under the Edit menu gives you access to a number of dialogs for changing Quicken preference settings. In this section, I review all of the options you can change and tell you where you can learn more about the features they control.

Quicken Program Preferences

As the name suggests, Quicken Program preferences control Quicken's general appearance and operations. To access these options, choose Edit | Preferencees | Quicken Program. The General Options dialog appears. It has two tabs of options, each of which are illustrated and discussed next.

General Options

The General tab of the General Options dialog controls a variety of Quicken features, including memorized transactions, sounds, and backup reminders.

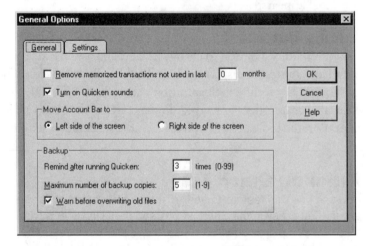

- **Remove Memorized Transactions Not Used In Last ___ Months** tells Quicken to remove memorized transactions that have not been used within the number of months you specify. By default, this feature is turned off; as a result, Quicken remembers the first 2,000 transactions you enter and then stops remembering transactions. By turning on this check box and entering a value of **6** (for example), Quicken memorizes only the transactions you entered in the past six months, thus keeping the memorized transactions list manageable. Using this feature with a lower value (for example, **3**) can weed one-time transactions out of the memorized transaction list. Changing this option does not affect transactions that have already been entered. I discuss memorized transactions in Chapter 7.
- **Turn On Quicken Sounds** enables Quicken sound effects. You may want to turn this check box off if you use Quicken in an environment where its sounds might annoy the people around you.
- **Move Account Bar To** enables you to position the Account bar on either the left (default) or right side of the screen. I tell you more about the Account bar and how to customize it in Chapters 1 and 3.
- **Remind After Running Quicken ___ Times** enables you to specify how often you should be reminded to back up your Quicken data file. The lower the value in this text box, the more often Quicken reminds you to back up. Keep the value low if you don't regularly back up Quicken data with other files. I tell you how to back up your data in Appendix A.
- **Maximum Number Of Backup Copies** is the number of backup copies Quicken should keep. The higher the value in this text box, the more backup copies of your Quicken data are saved. This enables you to go back further if you discover a problem with your current Quicken data file. I tell you more about backing up data in Appendix A.
- **Warn Before Overwriting Old Files** tells Quicken to display a warning before it overwrites old backup files with new ones.

Setting Options

The Settings tab of the General Options dialog controls keyboard mapping, calendar, and multicurrency support.

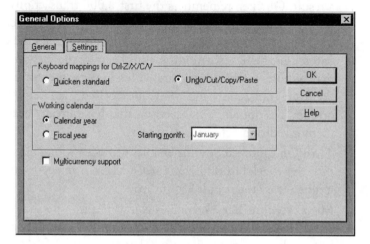

Keyboard Mappings In most Windows programs, the CTRL-Z, CTRL-X, CTRL-C, and CTRL-V shortcut keys perform commands on the Edit menu. Because these commands have limited use within Quicken, you can map several Quicken-specific commands to these keys. Select the option as shown in Table B-1 for the mapping you want.

Working Calendar The folks at Intuit realize that not everyone manages their finances on a calendar year basis. You can use the Working Calendar options to set up your fiscal year.

- **Calendar Year** is a 12-month year beginning with January.
- **Fiscal Year** is a 12-month year beginning with the month you choose in the drop-down list.

Keystroke	Quicken Standard	Undo/Cut/Copy/Paste (Windows Standard)
CTRL-Z	QuickZoom a report amount	Edit I Undo
CTRL-X	Go to Transfer (on Edit pop-up menu for active transaction)	Edit I Cut
CTRL-C	Tools I Category List	Edit I Copy
CTRL-V	Void Transaction (on Edit pop-up menu for active transaction)	Edit I Paste

Table B-1 • Keyboard Mapping Options

Multicurrency Support   If your finances require that you account for transactions and investments in more than one currency, turn on the Multicurrency Support option. This feature assigns a "home" currency to all of your current data, placing a currency symbol beside every amount. You can then enter amounts in other currencies by entering the appropriate currency symbol. You can confirm the default currency in the Windows Regional Settings control panel. It is not necessary to set this option unless you plan to work with multiple currencies in one Quicken data file.

Register Options

The Register Options dialog enables you to fine-tune the way the account register works. I discuss account register windows throughout this book, but provide details for using them in Chapter 5.

To set register options, open the Register Options dialog by choosing Edit | Preferences | Register. There are three categories of options: Display, Miscellaneous, and QuickFill. Each set of options can be found on its own tab in the Register Options dialog.

Display Options

Display options, shown here, affect the way the transactions you enter appear in the account register window. I discuss using the register window in detail in Chapter 5.

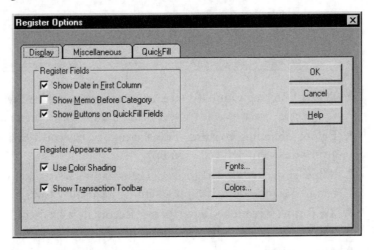

- **Show Date In First Column** displays the transaction date in the first column of the register.
- **Show Memo Before Category** displays the Memo field above the Category field.
- **Show Buttons On QuickFill Fields** displays drop-down list buttons on fields for which you can use QuickFill. I tell you about QuickFill in Chapter 12.

- **Use Color Shading** displays each type of register with a different background color.
- **Show Transaction Toolbar** adds the Enter, Edit, and Split buttons to the currently selected transaction.
- **Fonts** displays a dialog in which you can select the font for register windows.
- **Colors** displays a dialog in which you can select the background colors for the various types of register windows.

Miscellaneous Options

Miscellaneous options, shown next, affect the way you are notified about problems when you enter transactions in the register and the way transactions are entered.

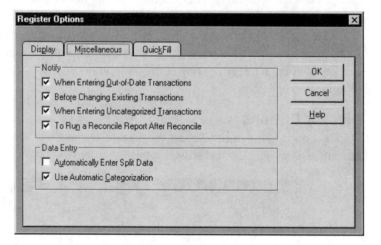

- **When Entering Out-Of-Date Transactions** warns you when you try to record a transaction with a year other than the current year.
- **Before Changing Existing Transactions** warns you when you try to modify a previously entered transaction.
- **When Entering Uncategorized Transactions** warns you when you try to record a transaction without assigning a category to it.
- **To Run A Reconcile Report After Reconcile** asks if you want to display a Reconcile report when you complete an account reconciliation.
- **Automatically Enter Split Data** turns the OK button in the Split Transaction window into an Enter button for entering the transaction.

- **Use Automatic Categorization** uses the Automatic Categorization feature to "guess" which category should be assigned to a transaction based on a database of company names and keywords stored within Quicken.

Setting QuickFill Options

The QuickFill tab's options control the way the QuickFill feature works. I cover QuickFill in Chapter 7.

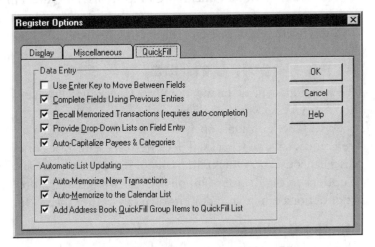

- **Use Enter Key To Move Between Fields** enables you to use both the ENTER and TAB keys to move from field to field when entering data.
- **Complete Fields Using Previous Entries** enters transaction information using the information from previous entries.
- **Recall Memorized Transactions** uses memorized transactions to fill in QuickFill entries. This option is not available if the Complete Fields Using Previous Entries option is disabled.
- **Provide Drop-Down Lists On Field Entry** automatically displays the drop-down list when you advance to a field with a list.
- **Auto-Capitalize Payees & Categories** automatically makes the first letter of each word in a payee name or category uppercase. (It's like having a persistent copy editor built right into Quicken!)
- **Auto-Memorize New Transactions** tells Quicken to automatically enter all transactions for a new payee to the Memorized Transaction List.

- **Auto-Memorize To The Calendar List** tells Quicken to automatically add memorized transactions to the Memorized Transaction List in the Calendar window. This option is turned on by default. The Financial Calendar is covered in Chapter 7; you can display the Memorized Transaction List by choosing Show Memorized Transaction List from the Options menu on the Calendar's button bar.

- **Add Address Book QuickFill Group Items To QuickFill List** tells Quicken to add entries from the Financial Address Book to QuickFill drop-down lists. I discuss the Address Book feature in Chapter 7.

Write Check Options

Check options control the way the Write Checks window looks and works. I discuss the Write Checks window in Chapter 5.

To set Check options, open the Check Options dialog by choosing Edit | Preferences | Write Checks. There are three categories of options: Checks, Miscellaneous, and QuickFill. Many of these options are similar to or the same as options in the Register Options dialog covered in the previous section. Each set of options can be found on its own tab in the Check Options dialog.

Checks Options

Checks options, shown here, affect the way the checks you enter with the Write Checks window appear when printed:

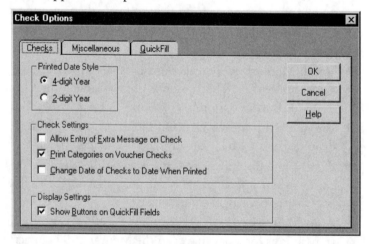

- **Printed Date Style** enables you to select a four-digit or two-digit date style.
- **Allow Entry Of Extra Message On Check** displays an additional text box for a message in the Write Checks window (see the following illustration).

The message you enter is printed on the check in a place where it cannot be seen if the check is mailed in a window envelope.

- **Print Categories On Voucher Checks** prints category information, including splits and classes, on the voucher part of voucher checks. This option only affects voucher-style checks.
- **Change Date Of Checks To Date When Printed** automatically prints the print date, rather than the transaction date, on each check.
- **Show Buttons On QuickFill Fields** displays drop-down list buttons on fields for which you can use QuickFill. I tell you about QuickFill in Chapter 7.

Miscellaneous Options

Miscellaneous options, shown here, affect the way you are notified about problems when you enter transactions in the Write Checks window. All of these options are turned on by default.

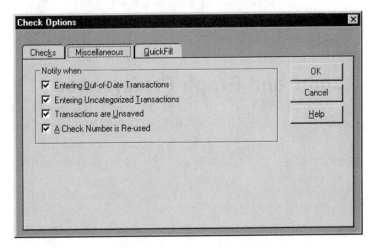

- **Entering Out-Of-Date Transactions** warns you when you try to record a transaction for a year other than the current year.

- **Entering Uncategorized Transactions** warns you when you try to record a transaction without assigning a category to it.
- **Transactions Are Unsaved** warns you when you try to leave a transaction before you have clicked Enter to save it.
- **A Check Number Is Re-used** warns you if you assign a check number that was already assigned in another transaction.

QuickFill Options

As shown next, the QuickFill options in the Check Options dialog are identical to the ones in the Register Options dialog discussed and shown earlier. Only one option is missing: Auto-Capitalize Payees & Categories. I discuss QuickFill in Chapter 7.

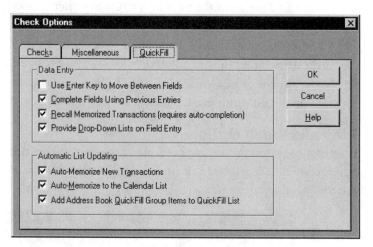

Report and Graph Preferences

The Report and Graph Preferences dialog, which is shown next, enables you to set default options for creating reports and graphs. I tell you about creating reports and graphs in Chapter 9. To display this dialog, choose Edit | Preferences | Reports and Graphs.

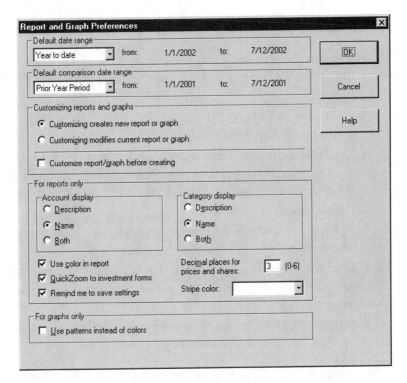

Default Report Date Range and Default Comparison Date Range

These options enable you to specify a default range for regular and comparison reports. Choose an option from each drop-down list. If you choose Custom, you can enter exact dates.

Customizing Reports and Graphs   These options determine how reports and graphs are customized and what happens when they are:

- **Customizing Creates New Report Or Graph**, which is the default setting, creates a sub-report based on the report you customize.
- **Customizing Modifies Current Report Or Graph** changes the report you customize without creating a sub-report. The ability to create sub-reports by customizing a report or graph is new in Quicken 2003.
- **Customize Report/Graph Before Creating** tells Quicken to offer to customize a report or graph when you choose its name from a submenu under the Reports menu.

For Reports Only   This group of options applies only to reports:

- **Account Display** and **Category Display** enable you to set what you want to display for each account or category listed in the report: description, name, or both.
- **Use Color In Report** tells Quicken to use color when displaying report titles and negative numbers.
- **QuickZoom To Investment Forms** tells Quicken to display the investment form for a specific investment when you double-click it in an investment report. With this check box turned off, Quicken displays the investment register transaction entry instead.
- **Remind Me To Save Settings** tells Quicken to ask if you want to save a customized report when you close the report window.
- **Decimal Places For Prices And Shares** enables you to specify the number of decimal places to display for per share security prices and number of shares in investment reports.
- **Stripe Color** enables you to select a color for the horizontal bars that appear on reports when viewed onscreen.

For Graphs Only   There's one option for graphs: Use Patterns Instead Of Colors tells Quicken to fill graph bars or pie slices with patterns rather than colors. You might find this feature useful if you have a black-and-white printer.

Reminder Options

The Reminder Options dialog enables you to set the lead time for calendar notes to appear in Alerts snapshots. I tell you about alerts in Chapter 7. To open the dialog, choose Edit | Preferences | Reminders. Select a lead time period from the drop-down list and click OK to save your settings. This does not affect the lead time for scheduled transactions.

Customize Online Update Options

You can customize One Step Update options in the Connection tab of the Customize Online Updates dialog, as follows. (Other options in this dialog are covered in Chapters 6 and 11.) Choose Edit | Preferences | Customize Online Updates and click the Connection tab.

- **Send Anonymous Product Usage Data During One Step Update** sends information about the way you use Quicken to the product development team at Intuit. This helps them understand how users like you utilize Quicken's features so they can improve Quicken.
- **Run One Step Update When Starting Quicken** automatically starts the One Step Update procedure when you start Quicken. You might find this feature useful if you always run One Step Update as part of a Quicken work session.
- **Remind Me To Run One Step Update When Exiting Quicken** displays a reminder dialog when you exit Quicken if any of the information you maintain on Quicken.com needs to be updated.
- **Change My Quicken.com Member ID And Password The Next Time I Run One Step Update** instructs Quicken to display the Quicken.com login screen when you connect to Quicken.com. With this option turned off, Quicken can automatically enter your saved login information if, when you registered with Quicken.com, you selected the option to save your login information and are connecting with the same computer. This check box is disabled until you set up a Quicken.com login by registering your copy of Quicken online. I tell you about registering Quicken in Chapter 2.

Web Connect Options

The Web Connect Options dialog offers two options, as follows, for customizing the way Quicken's Web Connect feature works. Web Connect, as discussed in Chapter 6, is an alternative method for downloading transaction information from your financial institution into your Quicken data file. To display the Web Connect Options dialog, choose Edit | Preferences | Web Connect.

- **Give Me The Option Of Saving To A File Whenever I Download Web Connect Data** displays a dialog that enables you to save the downloaded Web Connect information to a file on disk. Normally, the data is imported directly into the appropriate account in your Quicken data file.
- **When Quicken Is Launched By My Browser, Don't Close It After Web Connect Completes** tells Quicken to keep running after Web Connect completes a download from the Web if Quicken was launched by your Web browser.

Index

T

U

V